PHILADELPHIA EMPIRE FURNITURE

Allison Boor • Jonathan A. Boor • John William Boor
Peter Boor • Christopher Boor

Distributed by University Press of New England
Hanover and London

For Barbara Marie Boor, *Whose dedication, patience and kindness made everything possible.*

For Kim Forlini, *Whose strength, support and love will never be forgotten.*

For All My Dealers and Friends, *May every hammered lot be right as rain.*

Editorial Staff, *Donald Fennimore, F.J. Carey III, Alexandra Alevizatos Kirtley*

— JOHN WILLIAM BOOR, M.D.

Copyright © 2006 by John William Boor.

Published by Boor Management LLC, West Chester, Pennsylvania

Edited by Andrew Steven Harris
Designed by Verve Marketing & Design, Chadds Ford, PA 19317. www.vervemarketinganddesign.com
Distributed by University Press of New England, One Court Street, Lebanon, NH 03766. www.upne.com

Photography of all furniture in private collections by Allison Boor, Jonathan Boor, Christopher Boor and Peter Boor

ISBN 0-9777816-0-7
Printed in Singapore.

CONTENTS

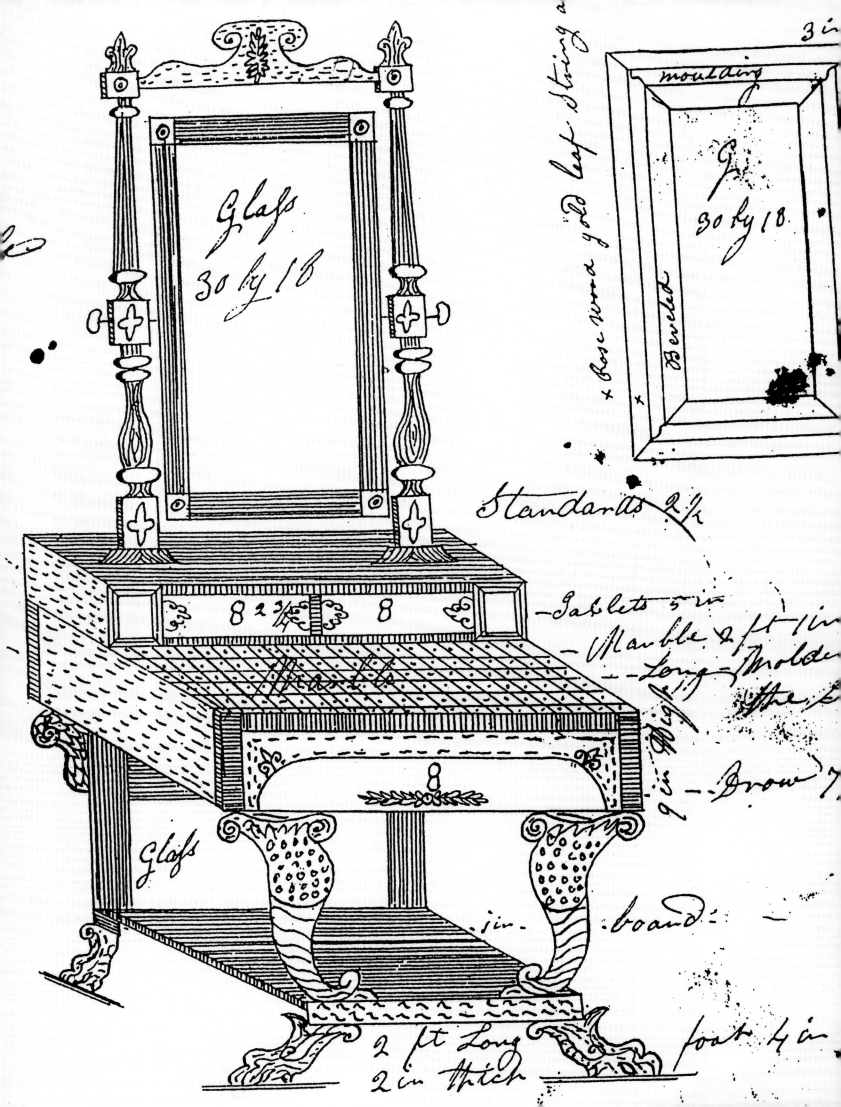

Glass
30 by 18

moulding

30 by 18

Beveled

+ Rose wood gold leaf string a

Standards 2½

Tablets 5 in

Marble 2 ft 1 in

Long Molde

9 in High

Glass

8 2¾ 8

Mantle

board

Drow

2 ft Long
2 in thick

foot 4 in

FOREWORD
Donald L. Fennimore

On October 7, 1811, the assignees of the cabinet joiner, J.M. Evans, placed an auction notice in the Philadelphia newspaper, the *Aurora General Advertiser* that read:

FURNITURE – NEW AND ELEGANT

On Tuesday 8th, instant at No. 16 Chestnut above Front, ten o'clock precisely [will be offered]1 elegant Mahogany sideboard, 1 ditto Bedstead carved, and fashionable various high post camp and low post ditto, Secretaries and book case, Bureaus and Card Tables, Swinging Cradles, Wash Stands and Toilettes, one sett newest order Dining Tables, superior Pembrokes, Work and Play Tables, &c. &c. Worthy the attention of Ladies and gentlemen preparing for the seasonable pleasures of winter.

A related notice appeared in the November 28, 1828 issue of another Philadelphia newspaper, the *American Daily Advertiser*. It was placed by the cabinet and sofa maker, Antoine Gabriel Quervelle and read:

FASHIONABLE FURNITURE

[The subscriber has] so enlarged his Manufactory, as to enable him to keep constantly on hand an extensive supply of CABINET WARE, such as Elegant Fashionable SIDEBOARDS, various Patterns, BUREAUX, various fashions, SOFAS, very elegant, DRESSING TABLES, of all descriptions, WASH STANDS, closed and open, TABLES – Breakfast, Dining and Card, BEDSTEADS – Mahogany, Maple and Cherry, of all sizes...His furniture being manufactured imme-diately under his own direction, will be warranted equal both in material and workmanship to any made in this country.

These announcements are among many such notices found on the advertising pages of all Philadelphia's major English- and German-language newspapers and also in city directories during the early nineteenth century. Individually, they identify the names of many of those in the city active in the furniture trade, as well as the scope and variety of their wares. Collectively, they paint a picture of a large and vital center capable of supplying discriminating householders not only in Philadelphia and its immediate environs but also throughout the United States with good quality furniture of every type in the most fashionable mode.

It comes as no surprise, therefore, to learn that between 1820 and 1840, Philadelphia was home to no fewer than 1,290 cabinetmakers, 299 chairmakers, 265 turners, 99 pianoforte makers, 127 clockmakers, 64 frame makers and 42 chair and ornamental painters.[1] In addition, the city hosted an impressive number of saw mills and mahogany yards (over 250) capable of supplying "the largest assortment, both in quantity and quality, of *Logs, Plank, Boards, Table tops, and Coffin Stuffs,* of Mahogany and Cedar...together with *Veneers* of all kinds...of the best quality...A large quantity of Poplar Plank and half inch boards, very superior and dry. Maple Scantling and Boards, Satin Wood; Rose Wood; together with every other kind of Lumber for Cabinet Makers..."[2]

It might be reasonably presumed that a great deal of the furniture made in Philadelphia (and all American cities, for that matter) between 1800 and 1850 was in response to the everyday needs of householders of moderate means and, therefore, substantial but relatively unremarkable in character. This appears to be amply confirmed between the covers of two pertinent documents of the era, *The Journeymen Cabinet and Chairmakers' Pennsylvania Book of Prices* published in Philadelphia in 1811 (107 pages plus eight plates), and *The Philadelphia Cabinet and Chair Makers' Union Book of Prices for Manufacturing Cabinet Ware* published in 1828 (94 pages plus 12 plates). Both list numerous plain, simple and inexpensive forms, including table bedsteads, counting-house bookcases, chamber tables, candlestands, basin stands and pot cupboards, all of which are modest in price, overwhelmingly functional in purpose and minimally expressive in style.

Though furniture of this type might be thought of as wanting in general interest for most furniture historians, it must necessarily be acknowledged as the backbone of a craft (industry) that contributed substantially to Philadelphia's importance and reputation as a significant urban industrial center. As such, it constitutes a useful record of the city's social, industrial and even artistic history.

At the same time, Philadelphia's cabinet and chairmakers were capable of creating impressive masterpieces for their wealthy clientele that rank equal to or better than counterparts emanating from the shops of their contemporaries in other major East Coast urban centers. Here, too, the price books offer supportive specifics, such as listings that identify serpentine front bureaus with straight wings, cylinder fall writing tables, pedestal sideboards, and library bookcases with wings, all of which are complex constructs, elaborate in appearance, expensive and offered with numerous optional extras, each at additional cost.

Perhaps no better documentation of these artistic creations exists than in the records of the Franklin Institute, organized as "a society of mutual improvement in science and the mechanic arts" in Philadelphia 1824.[3] Annual competitive exhibitions intended to foster innovation and excellence on the part of all craftsmen and manufacturers were a major component of the Institute's fostering role. Attendance at these competitions by thousands of viewers, in conjunction with awards of cash premiums and silver medals for the best offering in each category, encouraged widespread participation.

Fortunately, some of the furniture submitted by Philadelphia's craftsmen to these annual events that won silver medals survives. They offers valuable insight into the vitality of the furniture industry in the city at the time and the exceptional quality of its products, especially in conjunction with the record of the Institute's Committee on Premiums and Exhibitions explaining its reasons for the awards. In 1827, Antoine G. Quervelle submitted a grand mahogany desk and bookcase with carving, veneering and brass mounts for judging (see figure 282). Of it, the judges stated, "They have carefully examined the different articles submitted to their inspection and are of the opinion that the secretary and bookcase deposited by Mr. Anthony Quervelle is the best piece of furniture of that description exhibited for premium."[4]

In 1830, the cabinetmaker Walter Pennery submitted a dressing bureau veneered with highly figured maple further embellished with gilt and verd

antique stenciling (figure 306). In award-
ing it first prize, the Committee noted
that "the manufacture of cabinetware
and house furniture is one in which our
city is deeply interested, from the high
reputation of its mechanics, and the
extensive commerce which it carries
on in this branch of industry... a real
improvement in the mode of attaching
the looking glasses of toilets was mani-
fested in a very beautiful specimen of
maple work, exhibited by John Jamison
of this city and with a view to evince
their anxiety to promote such innovations, the committee has agreed that
a silver medal be presented to him."[5]

Given Philadelphia's importance as
a premiere center for the production of
good quality and stylish furniture as
well as the city's centrality as an entre-
pôt for its dissemination throughout the
United States during the first half of
the nineteenth century, it might be presumed that furniture historians, not to
mention economic, social and industrial
historians, had flocked to the subject
and dealt with it extensively in their
work. This, however, has not been the
case. There has been a comparative
dearth of interpretive and analytical
interest in the subject by historians during the twentieth century. At the same
time New York cabinet and chairmakers,
most notably Duncan Phyfe, Charles
Honoré Lannuier and Michael Allison,
have received ongoing and enthusiastic
attention in surveys of early nineteenth-
century American decorative arts,
regional studies and even monographs.[6]
To a somewhat lesser degree the same
might be said for Boston's early nineteenth-century furniture makers, including Thomas Seymour, Thomas Emmons
and George Archibald, Isaac Vose,
William Fisk and Samuel Gragg, to

name several.[7]

By contrast, the Philadelphia furniture trade between 1800 and 1840 and
its practitioners continue to be little-
known and under-appreciated. Indeed, it
often seems that Quervelle's name is the
only one routinely cited in discussions of
Philadelphia's furniture trade during the
early nineteenth century. That said, it
must be acknowledged that several
scholars have made important inroads
into the matter through research and
publication. Among the most assiduous
of them was Robert C. Smith, who published a series of landmark articles in
the magazine *Antiques* on the city's most
celebrated cabinetmaker of his era.
The first, entitled "Philadelphia Empire
furniture by Antoine Gabriel Quervelle"
appeared in the September 1964 issue
on pages 304-309. It was followed by a
remarkable five-part series entitled "The
furniture of Anthony G. Quervelle".
Part I appeared on pages 984-994 in
the May 1973 issue; part II followed
on pages 90-99 in the July 1973 issue.
After that part III was published on
pages 260-268 of the August 1973 issue
and part IV was on pages 180-193 of
the January 1974 issue. The series closed
with part V on pages 512-621 in the
March 1974 issue.

Complementing Smith's work are
several other articles that appeared
on the magazine's pages sporadically.
The more significant are Francis James
Dallett's article entitled "Michel Bouvier,
Franco-American cabinetmaker" on
pages 198-200 of the February 1962
issue, Anthony A.P. Steumpfig's article
"William Haydon and William H.
Stewart, Fancy-chair makers in
Philadelphia" on pages 452-457 of the
September 1973 issue, Robert T.
Trump's article entitled "Joseph B. Barry,

Philadelphia cabinetmaker" on pages 159-163 of the January 1975 issue, and Peter L.L. Strickland's article entitled "Documented Philadelphia looking glasses" on pages 784-794 of the April 1976 issue. In addition, the author of this foreword published "A labeled card table by Michel Bouvier" on pages 760-763 of the April 1973 issue and co-authored with Robert T. Trump an article entitled "Joseph B. Barry, Cabinetmaker" on pages 1214-1225 of the May 1989 issue.[8] One additional document that adds significantly to the bibliography on Philadelphia furniture of the early nineteenth century is Beatrice B. Garvan's *Federal Philadelphia*, published by the Philadelphia Museum of Art in 1987.[9]

These efforts are undeniably groundbreaking and of immense help to all those interested in early nineteenth-century Philadelphia furniture. Unfortunately, they are scattered, making them somewhat difficult to access after the fact and encompass for research. Similarly, most are narrowly focused essays that, while fascinating, by definition lack the regional and temporal context provided by broader considerations. Without question, additional research and publication of this type on other as yet unknown or little-known Philadelphia craftsmen should be encouraged. At the same time sufficient information has been brought to light by the cited authors and others on early nineteenth-century Philadelphia cabinetmakers and their work to warrant a broadly based pictorial and interpretive survey exemplified by the present work.

All those interested in Philadelphia furniture dating to the first half of the nineteenth century will welcome this book, since it admirably fills a lamentable void on the subject. This survey provides them with a rich and palatable feast of the work of many hands; much of it illustrated and discussed for the first time. Beyond that, this book goes a long way toward identifying the individuality of the Philadelphia school of cabinet and chair making as it came to full flower under the separate and parallel influence of English and French prototypes and counterparts. As a result, the city comes into focus as a major center in its own right, its furniture makers collectively producing chairs, sofas, sideboards, pier, work and dining tables and many other forms that instantly bespeak their place of origin. Furthermore, many prominent features of this furniture, exemplified by carved paw feet with overhanging acanthus leaves, veneered segmented circles or semi-circles and inlaid panels of pictorial brass for instance, contrast vividly in their stylistic character with furniture emanating from other major centers in the United States. These and other features once recognized allow readers to assess the significant influence exported Philadelphia furniture had on the work of furniture makers in many satellite centers, from Baltimore, Maryland, to Pittsburgh, Pennsylvania, to Savannah, Georgia, to New Orleans, Louisiana.

Beyond these considerations, this book opens fruitful avenues of inquiry to numerous other matters, including the extensive variety of forms Philadelphia cabinet and chairmakers were asked to make, identified in chapters 6 through 17. Another is the interesting matter of theme and variation of decorative elements employed by the city's artisans, exemplified by the frontal supports on pier tables pictured in chapter 8. Yet another is the impact of individual craftsmen on their interpretation of the same form, illustrated by the sideboards pictured in figures 248 (Anthony Quervelle), 258 (Michel Bouvier) and 264 (Joseph B. Barry and Lewis Krickbaum). A final point worthy of note addressed by this book involves the stylistic evolution of any given form as it continues to be made through time. This is nicely developed via the folding-top card tables pictured in chapter 7. The insights this book offers into these and many other matters pertaining to the furniture that emanated from Philadelphia's many cabinet and chair making establishments between 1800 and 1850 is invaluable. This book is a welcome addition to the literature on American furniture and will serve its readers well as a rich compendium of information and imagery for a long time to come.

1 Kathleen M. Catalano, *Cabinetmaking in Philadelphia*, 1820-1840, Master's thesis, University of Delaware, 1972, p. 9. Catalano's thesis includes an extensive list of these crafts-men. Another more fully developed list is in Deborah Ducoff-Barone, "Philadelphia furni-ture makers, 1800-1815", *Antiques*, May 1991, pp. 982-995, and Deborah Ducoff-Barone, "Philadelphia furniture makers, 1816-1830", *Antiques*, May 1994, pp. 742-755.

2 Advertisement of the cabinet and chairmaker, Michel Bouvier in the *National Gazette*, July 19, 1833.

3 Bruce Sinclair, *Philadelphia's Philosopher Mechanics*, Baltimore, Md.: The Johns Hopkins University Press, 1974, p. 29.
4*Philadelphia: Three Centuries of American Art*, Philadelphia: Philadelphia Museum of Art, 1976, p. 277, entry 229. This desk and bookcase is owned by the Philadelphia Museum of Art.

5 Object folder 1986.116, Registration Office, Winterthur Museum, Wilmington, Delaware. This dressing bureau is owned by Winterthur Museum and is pictured in Donald L. Fennimore, "Gilding Practices and Processes

in Nineteenth-Century American Furniture", *Gilded Wood*, Madison, Ct.: Sound View Press, 1991, p. 149, fig. 7.

6 A representative survey that emphasizes New York is Berry B. Tracy, *Classical America, 1815-1845*, Newark, NJ: The Newark Museum, 1963. For a regional study of New York furni-ture see John L. Scherer, *New York Furniture At the New York State Museum*, Alexandria, Va.: Highland House Publishers, 1983. One of several monographs on New York furniture makers is Peter M. Kenny, *Honoré Lannuier, Cabinetmaker from Paris*, New York: The Metropolitan Museum of Art, 1998.

7 See Stuart P. Feld, *Boston in the Age of Neo-Classicism, 1810-1840*, New York: Hirschl & Adler Galleries, Inc., 2000.

8 A number of these articles were compiled in a single volume entitled *Philadelphia Furniture & Its Makers*, edited by John J. Snyder, Jr., and published by Main Street/Universe Books in New York in 1975.

9 A few other works should be cited here because of their importance to researchers. One is Charles L. Venable's master's thesis entitled "Philadelphia Biedermeier: Germanic craftsmen and design in Philadelphia, 1820-1850," which he wrote at the University of Delaware in 1986. Venable extracted an article from this thesis entitled "Germanic Craftsmen and Furniture Design in Philadelphia, 1820-1850", which was published in *American Furniture*, Milwaukee, Wisconsin: Chipstone Foundation, 1998, pp. 41-80. Another perti-nent thesis is Morrison H. Heckscher's, "The organization and practice of Philadelphia cabi-netmaking establishments, 1790-1820, written at the University of Delaware in 1964. A doc-toral dissertation written by Elizabeth Page Talbott entitled "The Philadelphia Furniture Industry, 1850 to 1880" at the University of Pennsylvania in 1980, though concerned with the post-1850 era, offers helpful information in the antecedent era.

Fauteuil et Vases éxécutés à Paris dans la Maison du C. D****

3 Pieds

1 Mètre.

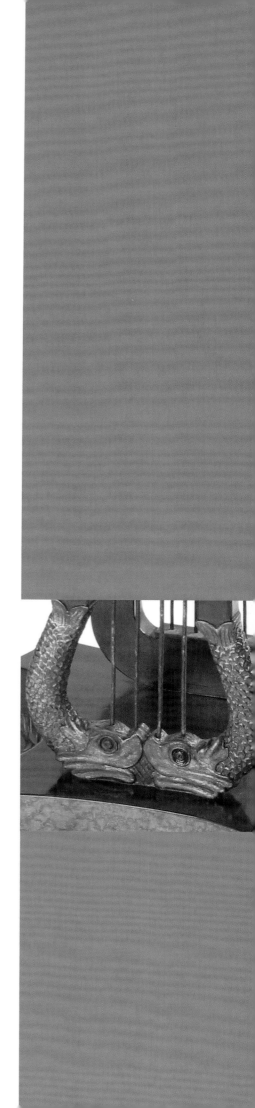

Image 1
Charles Percier Pl. 6:
Fauteuil et Vases (chair and vases),

Recueil de Decorations Interieures,
Paris, 1812
Courtesy, The Winterthur Library:
Printed Book and Periodical Collection

CHAPTER 1
ORIGINS OF NEO-CLASSICISM

Dessus de la Table.

Par Percier et Fontaine.

Table exécutée à Petersbourg pour le C.te S.

Image 2

Charles Percier Pl. 21:
Dessus de la Table (center table),

Recueil de Decorations Interieures, Paris, 1812
Courtesy, The Winterthur Library: Printed Book and Periodical Collection

ORIGINS OF NEO-CLASSICISM

The development of the Neo-Classical style began in Europe as early as 1750, as designers and furniture makers took a renewed interest in classical motifs from ancient cultures. In France, a demand for ornamented and elegant furnishings arose not only among the aristocracy and royalty, but also from the upper and middle classes of society. Publications of antique artifacts became rigidly scholarly in nature and craftsmen adhered to designs that accurately depicted antique furniture of

ancient Rome. French designers sought to produce purely classical furniture, made of richly decorated mahogany or rosewood, and which adhered to the original designs found in antiquity. Although this was the aim of craftsmen, most furniture transcended the boundaries of antique and took on overly ornate tones never before seen in antiquity.

When Napoleon Bonaparte ascended to power in France in 1799, he employed designers Charles Percier (1764-1838) and Pierre Fontaine (1762-1853) to assist him in the redecoration of the royal palaces that had been ravaged during France's period of political unrest.[1] Percier and Fontaine became highly recognized for their work at the palaces, including the Palais Royal and the palaces of Tuileries. Percier was mostly a decorator; Fontaine was more interested in the applications of architecture to other arts.[2] Being great admirers of classical antiquity and the Renaissance, they affirmed that "furniture is too much a part of interior decoration for the architect to remain indifferent to it."[3] Their designs, while affording the indulgence of beautiful colors and materials, also maintained a practicality by which the form of the furniture was dictated by functionality in everyday life.

Together, Percier and Fontaine blended their talents and supplied designs to Napoleon and his courts all over Europe, and their work influenced other designers and furniture makers to produce similar works in the Empire style. Fontaine and Percier saw a parallel between France and ancient Rome and sought to re-create the imperial style, hence this period in French political history became known as Empire.[4] Napoleon was anxious to appear as a great Emperor in the eyes of Europe, and by surrounding himself with royal furniture, he strengthened this image of grandeur. In some cases, Napoleon's initials were even engraved on pieces of furniture.

Percier and Fontaine accompanied Napoleon's armies to Rome and Egypt, where they made drawings of ancient furniture. They documented the massive, heavy and rectangular forms of the furniture in their publication, *Recueil de Decorations Interieures (1801, 1812)*, which established the Empire style all over Europe and America. The influence of their publication outside their own country was powerful; even as far as Russia their designs were being put into effect. Tsar Alexander I (1777-1825) placed an order to France in 1809 for the two architects' manuscript notes of the interior decorations and

[1] William C. Ketchum Jr., *Furniture 2: Neoclassic to the Present* (New York: Cooper-Hewitt Museum, 1981) 18.

[2] Serge Grandjean, *Empire Furniture 1800-1825* (London: Faber and Faber, 1966) 30.

[3] Grandjean 31

[4] Ketchum Jr. 18

Par Percier et Fontaine.

Vue perspective de la Chambre à coucher du Cit.V. à Paris.

Image 3
Charles Percier Pl. 13:
Vue perspective de la Chambre a coucher du Cit.V. a Paris,
Recueil de Decorations Interieurs, Paris, 1812
Courtesy, The Winterthur Library: Printed Book and Periodical Collection

furnishings of the Tuileries, as well as for a series of watercolors.[5] Throughout France patrons of fine furniture were able to find numerous engraved designs in Pierre de la Mesangere's (1761-1831) monthly magazine that published periodicals on fashion between 1802 and 1835.[6] Another source of Empire design was found in the publication, *Voyage dans la Basse et Haute Egypte pendant les campagnes du General Bonaparte,* by Baron Dominique Vivant Denon (1745-1825), who sketched details of Egyptian architecture used by students of decorative arts all over Europe.[7]

The Empire style soon developed into combination of ancient Roman, Egyptian, and Greek classical forms and motifs adopted directly from architectural ruins, fragments of furniture sculpted in stone and pottery. Empire style was defined by severely rectangular shapes, inlaid woods, gilt bronze, lion's paw feet, ancient Greek and Roman military symbols, floral and leaf carving and animal monopodia such as lion's heads, eagles and swans. Napoleon made certain motifs his personal symbols such as the Roman eagle, the bee and the star. The swan was associated with his wife Josephine.[8] Interest in Egyptian motifs rose

[5] Grandjean 32

[6] Oscar P. Fitzgerald, *Three Centuries of American Furniture* (New Jersey: Prentice-Hall Inc., 1982) 110.

[7] Grandjean 33

[8] Fitzgerald 110

from Napoleon's expeditions to the Nile between 1798 and 1801, but it was his companion, Dominique Vivant Denon, who published *Travels in Upper and Lower Egypt* in 1802, and designed furniture in this style for his home and the Tuileries in Paris.[9] Egyptian style can be seen in the massive weight of Empire furniture.

As Napoleon and his armies continued to move across Europe, designers in conquered lands adopted the new Empire style and it became the most fashionable in Europe. To quote Louis Reau it was "the natural consequence of the superiority of the French art."[10] Following the French lead, each of the great monarchies of the time (including those in England, Spain, Italy, Bavaria, Austria, Prussia, Sweden and Russia) set to create its own "Empire" style of decorative art.[11] Napoleon popularized the antique curule, or X-frame stool and chair, which featured crossed sabre legs. Innovations of the X-frame motif were also incorporated into sofas. The X-frame was used for 'archaeological' re-creations; the excavations at Pompeii and Herculaneum introduced variants of the type, including an X-frame stool of which the legs ended in birds' heads.[12] Britain was one of the first countries to adopt the French Empire style.

English furniture designers followed the lead of French designers and were busy trying to interpret the ancient forms of furniture and decoration uncovered during the excavations at the Italian sites of Herculaneum and Pompeii. During the latter eighteenth century, political and economic turmoil between England and France initially resulted in two interpretations of antique furniture forms. The English developed a style based on decorations found on Greek and Roman artifacts. French design adapted the broad flat rectangular shapes of antique Greco Roman and Egyptian objects. The British Isles largely ignored French interpretations until the Prince of Wales encouraged French craftsmen to bring their furniture and designs to renovate his residence, Carlton

House. French style and couture then became highly regarded in England, even though the two countries were often at war. Furniture designers began to incorporate French designs into English interpretations, forming a new style now known as Regency. The term "Regency" was originally derived from the Regency of George IV, the Prince of Wales, who ruled as Prince Regent during the period of 1811-1820.[13]

Today, Regency can be defined as the development of architecture and decorative arts in England from the eighteenth century through to the 1830s. French designers may be credited with being the first to produce the Empire style, but cabinetmakers in England elaborated on it, concentrated heavily on Greek motifs rather than Roman, and documented the style in several important books that American furniture makers would later base much of their work on.

The first English craftsman to be commissioned to refurbish a residence in a French neoclassical style was Henry Holland (1745-1806). He was provided the opportunity by the Prince of Wales in 1783, who was interested in having his estate, the Carlton House, completely remodeled.[14] Although Holland can be credited with the design of the Carlton House, it is questionable whether all the furniture was, in fact, designed by him. Some feel the use of ebony and ormolu in the furniture does not reflect Holland's work, but without proper bills it is difficult to know for sure. Holland's important position as the Prince's architect allowed for his style to become widely popular. He can be credited for introducing the concept of the complete scheme for specific rooms, where the color of architectural features and upholstery are unified.[15] He may have derived these designs from French architects such as Marie-Joseph Peyere, Pierre Patte and Jacques Gondoin, and from his visits to Versailles.[16]

The French had been utilizing this concept for decades, but it did not become

[9] Fitzgerald 110

[10] Grandjean 59

[11] Grandjean 59

[12] John Morley, *The History of Furniture: Twenty-five Centuries of Style and Design in the Western Tradition* (Boston: Bulfinch Press, 1999) 227.

[13] Frances Collard, *Regency Furniture* (England: Antique Collectors' Club Ltd., 1985) 11.

[14] Collard 31

[15] Collard 37

[16] Clifford Musgrave, *Regency Furniture 1800-1830* (London: Faber and Faber, 1961) 31.

popular in England until Holland introduced it at Carlton House. Each room was given a name based on the color scheme or cultural theme, such as the Chinese Drawing Room. Interior design during the Regency era favored treating each room as a separate entity, complete with individual color scheme and matching furniture and wall decoration. The start of the war with France severed Holland's connection with the French craftsmen with whom he had collaborated in the past, and forced him to look elsewhere for a source of inspiration. Unlike many craftsmen who spent their earlier years honing their craft by studying in Rome, Egypt or Greece, Holland never had the chance to study classical remains on site. He decided to send his assistant, Charles Heathcote Tatham (1772-1842), abroad to Rome to copy classical buildings and artifacts, while Holland continued work back in England.

Tatham paved the way for a stricter archaeological approach to furniture and design which Thomas Hope later pursued, and his effect was profound enough that the architect Joseph Gwilt (1784-1863) wrote in 1842 that, "to him perhaps more than any other person, may be attributed the rise of the Anglo-Greek style which still prevails..."[17] Tatham's work in Italy provided Holland with new illustrated designs, mostly of stone artifacts, which were later published as *Etchings of Ancient Ornamental Architecture drawn from the Originals in Rome and Other Parts of Italy during the years 1794, 1795, and 1796.*[18] Based on the excavated ruins of Pompeii and Herculaneum, among others, Tatham introduced many motifs such as the Chimera monopodium, the table of circular form on three monopodia supports, lion's-masks with rings as ornaments for tables, cabinet-supports in the form of figures, and the pedestal of a table or candelabrum rising like a shaft from acanthus leaves.[19] Also illustrated by Tatham is his depiction of a stool, which has led people to believe he was the first in designing its wooden equivalent that simulates marble and copies

his antique original almost exactly.[20] Tatham acknowledged that he was influenced by sculptor John Flaxman (1755-1826), whose line illustrations in the classical design included furniture drawn from antique marbles.[21] Holland fashioned many of his designs based on Tatham's drawings, and published works such as James Stuart and Nicholas Revett's *Antiquities of Athens, 1762.*[22]

It is presumed that Tatham developed many motifs that became the norm in Regency furniture in England, although many images included in his book were already commonplace. Based on illustrations in his publication on the designing of acanthus leaves and gilded dolphins, it is apparent that later designers elaborated on his drawings. Thomas Sheraton (1751-1806) was one furniture designer who recognized the importance of his work and developed more intricate drawings of classical motifs for many different forms.

Sheraton's *Cabinet-Maker and Upholsterer's Drawing Book*, published between 1791-1794, illustrated popular designs and concise instructions for the workmen on how to execute each piece geometrically.[23] This was important because the lack of such instructions in other books made it difficult for workmen to translate drawings into actual objects. Sheraton proposed the idea that furniture makers should learn more about perspective and geometry and advertised himself "as a teacher of Perspective, Architecture and Ornament and seller of drawing books on his trade card".[24] In fact, Sheraton did not manufacture the furniture in his designs although he had previously been a journeyman cabinetmaker for many years. Mention of this was published in *Gentleman's Magazine* in November 1806 which noted that since 1793 he had supported himself and his family "by his exertions as an author."[25]

The *Drawing Book* proved to be an effective, influential source for many cabinetmakers of the period, and continued to gratify the French designers' neo-

[17] Musgrave 35

[18] Collard 53

[19] Musgrave 36

[20] Morley 220

[21] Morley 220

[22] Collard 51

[23] Collard 62

[24] Collard 64

[25] Musgrave 38

classic style. Sheraton is credited with producing French inspired designs for many forms, including beds, chairs, couches (Chaise Longues), drawing rooms and upholstery. His subscribers in the first edition included cabinet makers, carvers, gilders, engravers, upholsterers and chair makers.[26] Sheraton made painted decoration in the Italian style popular, as well as the use of inlaid, contrasting woods often in the shape of a shell or fan and square, tapered legs. Other important elements introduced were reeding for the legs of tables and chairs, and for the shelves and uprights, and the use of splayed "claw feet" for tripod and table-supports, in all the three forms of a concave, convex or double curve.[27] Sheraton named some of his chairs that possessed arms ending in small scrolls on concave supports sweeping down in a strong curve to the forelegs "Herculaniums."[28]

These motifs, among many others that Sheraton popularized such as lyre form on splayed feet, flattened scroll and clawed feet, provided a guideline for future furniture makers throughout the world, especially the United States. When America began to recognize the different types of ornamentation and architectural design in the latter eighteenth century as increasingly fashionable, Sheraton's book served as an important source of inspiration for French émigré and American cabinetmakers alike. He advocated the use of mahogany, which at the time was not the most popular wood in England or France and was to become the chief primary wood for almost all pieces of Empire furniture found in America. He recommended mahogany for dining rooms, libraries and more masculine pieces, while satinwood is better used for drawing rooms and ladies writing tables.[29] American Empire furniture transcends the boundaries set by Sheraton, incorporating mahogany into every sort of form, from cellarettes to beds to lady's worktables.

In 1803, Sheraton introduced the Greek style in his second book, *Cabinet*

Dictionary, which illustrated lion's heads and paws, and the first piece of a true Regency couch with a scroll-end and lion's paw feet.[30] The rise of animal monopodia would mark the beginning of the Regency period in England, and antique designs with dolphin and eagle motifs were produced with gracefulness and precision. Sheraton advocated the use of brass borders and beading for decoration on dark woods, but felt the English were incapable of producing decoration of high quality; "In the brass work adapted for cabinet-work, the French far exceed this country; as well as in their manner of gilding, stiled, or molu."[31]

Carving, gilding, painting and stained wood inlay were a few more techniques heavily employed in England, and which became extremely popular in America in the early nineteenth century. Sheraton's last book, *The Cabinet-Maker, Upholsterer and General Artist's Encyclopedia*, published 1804-1807, illustrates designs in the Egyptian taste, including sphinxes' heads appearing on beds, bases for cabinets, bookcases or sideboards.[32] Sheraton was one of the earlier designers to publish designs in the Egyptian taste in England. He delved into Gothic design as well, but will be most remembered for his originality in interpreting what was fashionably to become known as early Regency. His final designs were fantastical, and his critics believed they stemmed from an insane mind, while others conclude although the designs were wild in nature, they should not be dubbed irrational.

Classical taste in furniture continued to be cultivated in England by Thomas Hope (1769-1831), a banker and collector of classical objects, who published *Household Furniture and Interior Decoration* in 1807.[33] Hope was born of a wealthy family from Amsterdam and had the opportunity to study the archaeological remains of classical reminants in Greece, Turkey, Asia Minor, Syria and Egypt.[34] The combination of the experience he gained from his travels and his close friendship

[26] Collard 69

[27] Musgrave 39

[28] Musgrave 42

[29] Collard 77

[30] Collard 79

[31] Collard 80

[32] Collard 82

[33] Collard 86

[34] Collard 86

with the pioneers of Empire design, Percier and Fontaine, enabled him to become an authority on classical antiquities. There are marked differences between the work of Percier and Fontaine and Hope, one being that Hope concentrated mainly upon Greek and Roman motifs. Percier and Fontaine preferred to create designs that incorporated grotesque, while Hope tended to employ ornament from stone originals in places where grotesque might have been used earlier.[35]

Hope was able to exhibit his ideas on Neo-Classical interiors by using his London home on Duchess Street, which he remodeled to encase his many acquisitions with the appropriate decorative elements to match. His house was open to the public, where they could enjoy numerous paintings, sculpture and designs that were Egyptian, Moorish and Greek in nature. There were rooms dedicated to each individual style, such as the Egyptian Room, which was decorated with a frieze based on papyrus rolls and antiquities of Egyptian gods, goddesses, and scorpions.[36] The Indian Room exhibited equally impressive paintings of Moorish temples and mosques. The furniture was in the classical style, with a combination of Greek and Roman motifs, including winged lions forming the arms of ottomans.[37]

The attention to detail and meticulous designs in matching furniture with pieces of artistic ornament, and even the arranging of all the objects, was meant to exude an air of complete harmony. One of the difficulties of creating such a high standard of design work was finding the craftsmen who were qualified enough to execute detailed furniture. Hope complained that, "Throughout this vast metropolis (London), teeming as it does with artificers and tradesmen of every description, I have, after the most laborious search, only been able to find two men, to whose industry and talent I could in some measure confide the execution of the more complicated and more enriched portion of my designs..."[38] Sheraton had foreseen this

problem, acknowledging that craftsmen were not properly trained in geometry or perspective, one of the reasons Hope's designs are produced in such elaborate detail in his book.

Hope enjoyed using classical ornament such as anthemion, palmette, acanthus, lion monopodia, lyres and swans, all of which appeared in the past, but not in such a contemporary fashion. The purpose of Hope's book was to provide a guide for everyday furniture, however many felt the designs were unsuitable for the contemporary home. He was criticized by Sydney Smith in the Edinburgh Review, who thought he was too preoccupied with "fantastical luxuries" during a period of national emergency, and although "unquestionably beautiful", the designs were too bulky and massive to be convenient.[39] Despite being perceived as extravagant and impractical, Hope's designs were more restrained than Percier and Fontaine's, which were obviously only meant for the regal courts and the very wealthy.

Pieces of furniture modeled after marble structures created a difficulty in mobility and Hope's ideas on symbolic decoration were also criticized for being inconsistent. The interpretation of classical designs became questionable as "Light-hearted decoration that came largely from ancient painted sources, such as the 'Pompeian' scrolls and dancing maidens, was turned into rigidly sculpted bas-reliefs, in gilt or patinated bronze in France and carved wood in England."[40] Designs taken from Greek sculpture and antique stone structures were perceived as too massive and heavy, so they were transformed into wood, only later to regain their true identity when they were converted back to stone.

Overall, Hope's designs and illustrations personified the classical style and inspired many cabinetmakers and upholsterers to take more account of stylistic principles in ornamentation and decoration. Hope had attempted in his work to create great furniture that possessed comfort and beauty and that could provide

[35] Morley 216

[36] Collard 86

[37] Collard 87

[38] Morley 212

[39] Collard 96

[40] Morley 219

that "breadth and repose of surface, that distinction and contrast of outline, that opposition of plain and enriched parts, that harmony and significance of accessories... which are calculated to afford to the eye and mind the most lively, most permanent, and most unfailing enjoyment."[41]

His work was further popularized by George Smith's (1782-1869) *A Collection of Designs for Household Furniture and Interior Design*, published in 1808, that extended the notion that "the beauty and elegance displayed in the fittings-up of modern houses may not be confined to the stately mansions of our Nobility in the metropolis, but be published for use of the country at large, as a guide to foreign nations, and as an evidence of the superior taste and skill exhibited in the manufactures of this country."[42] Smith provided a large range of designs for both rich and ordinary households, setting his work apart from Hope's, which can only be interpreted as meant for wealthier patrons of society. He also included designs in the Gothic and Chinese manner that Hope did not favor.

Smith elaborated on Hope's idea to provide patterns of design for manufacturing furniture and continued the use of animal ornamentation in several forms of furniture, including sideboards and sofa tables. Smith's chairs did not follow the same Greek klismos form that Hope advocated with sabre legs, brass inlay of stars, and anthemia on the crest, but were more rigid in outline. Smith favored the use of the lion's paw for the feet of table, chair, sofa and cabinet furniture legs, and arranged them in a number of ways, including pointing them forwards, pointing them sideways and depicting more natural looking paws.[43] Smith's lion's paw designs have a more realistic appearance than those by French Empire designers, which were more abstract. Smith seems to have popularized the claw foot with wings used for the foot of a table or cabinet, which had first appeared in a design for a "Chinese Light" in Sheraton's *Cabinet Encyclopedia*.[44]

Smith impacted the fashion of Regency furniture by providing a guide that people from many social spheres could utilize and exhibited all the standard designs put forth by past designers such as Hope, Sheraton, Holland, and the French. He embedded the motifs into popular culture, and although his designs did not have the same exactness to antiquity or refinement, they embodied the main principles of Regency by remaining fantastical and daring in design.

Smith's ideas were later acknowledged by Rudolph Ackermann (1764-1834) to have provided a base of study for developing furniture in the classical taste. Ackermann's widely popular and widely distributed *Repository of Arts, Literature, Commerce, Manufactures, Fashions, and Politics* featured Greek and Egyptian designs that differed from Smith's in that he tried to create a harmony that came not only from matching the ornaments and the colors of the furniture, but by creating a well proportioned balance of designs in both. Smith's designs were seen by many to be more realistic depictions of household furniture than Hope's, but still the problem of finding manufacturers who could produce forms of elegance without receiving higher training existed. Although these technicalities made producing certain forms difficult, the patterns of Greek and Egyptian design were firmly planted in the minds of many English cabinetmakers who later refined the massiveness of character and over-ornamentation into a more chaste style in the future.

English designers often did not consider the expensive and time-consuming tasks of marquetry work and carving practical, and in their wartime economy there were few craftsmen available to perform such work.[45] In addition, brass was often substituted for gilt bronze and inlay confined to narrow bands of contrasting wood called stringing, while paint might be used to hide the presumed defects of native woods.[46] Regency furniture types such as Grecian couches, sewing tables, circular

[41] Musgrave 50

[42] Collard 104

[43] Collard 112

[44] Musgrave 55

[45] Ketchum Jr. 24

tables and the Trafalgar chair were popular and purchased by the upper and middle class. George Smith's designs were easier to produce in large quantities, even though they were less sophisticated than earlier designs. Regency furniture eventually became less popular, as revivals of Gothic and Rococo furniture prevailed in creating new styles.

The decline of the Empire style began around 1830, when cabinetmakers replaced the classical designs for the Pillar and Scroll style and in later years, the Victorian style that combined Gothic, Rococo and classical elements. The Pillar and Scroll, also known as Restoration (*Restauration*), was introduced in France as early as 1815. Furniture forms were simplified, carving and ornamentation were dropped and C and S curves were cut into pillars and scrolls. The Restauration style was geometrically simple and was more economical, since without the ornamentation it could be produced at a quicker rate. This allowed for a wide range of households to afford sofas and other furniture that before were considered luxuries only available to the wealthy.

With the introduction of the steam driven band saw, manufacturers could mass-produce pillars and scrolls. Furniture making depended less on the skill of a highly specialized cabinetmaker and became more of a mechanized process.[47] The Industrial Revolution ended the tradition of patrons communicating with their cabinetmaker, and furniture buying became just another impersonal consumer buying process. Furniture-makers, needing to adhere to the changing trends in order to survive, soon began producing designs that incorporated the more modern styles of both Rococo and Gothic motifs, later known as Victorian .

The rococo, Old French, or "florid Italian characterized by curved lines and excess of curvilinear ornaments," reflected the Louis XIV forms with metal mounts in pieces with console supports replacing animal or human monopodia.[48] The persist-

ence of French themes continued to pervade the furniture trade in England, and large quantities of French furniture and decorative arts in the style of Louis XIV continued to be imported. Designs that were revived by Sheraton included the French sofa-bed with its Louis Quatorze bun-feet and dolphins as supports for chairs and tables. Many patrons admired the furniture for its authenticity, and its reminder of the elaborate, ostentatious style that once surrounded French royalty. Most furniture designers saw the style as over ornamented and rather tawdry, and criticized designs that tried to reinvent the style by combining the overdone, grotesque ornament with a more restrained English form.

When the designs were correctly executed they could appear quite beautiful, and as *The Architectural Magazine* pointed out in 1834, "when confined to proper limits, as applied to various articles of furniture, it is at once characteristic and elegant."[49] The Empire style was considered purer in that it strictly adhered to classical forms and motifs and did not combine adaptations of old French stylistic elements, which would make the final result of solely French design, as the Rococo Revival style did.

The Gothic Revival incorporated medieval designs onto furniture, and enjoyed a short span of popularity in the early- to mid-nineteenth century. The Gothic Revival centered on medieval antiquities, objects such as armor and swords would surround a room in the Gothic design, accompanied by oak woodwork and sometimes stonework meant to appear in the medieval design. The Gothic designs brought the style of the church into one's home, which was not only expensive, but also difficult for furniture makers to translate the designs into household furniture because they did not have previous experience in producing furniture of this caliber. John Claudius Loudon (1783-1843) exemplifies this point in his comment, "What passes for Gothic furniture among cabinet makers and upholsterers is, generally, a

[46] Ketchum Jr. 24

[47] Patricia Petraglia, *American Antique Furniture 1640-1840* (New York: Friedman/Fairfax Publishers, 1995) 138.

[48] Collard 132

[49] Collard 162

very different thing from the correct Gothic designs supplied by Architects who have imbued their minds with this style of art."[50] In describing a Gothic sofa, table, chair and footstool in the *Repository* for June 1810, the commentator gave warning that, "no person of a genuine taste will introduce articles in this style into his apartments, unless there is a general correspondence in the appearance of his house..."[51]

Gothic designs appeared in cabinet making books as early as 1788, but George Smith was the first to show a large range of fashionable designs in *A Collection of Designs for Household Furniture of 1808.*[52] Other published sources of Gothic design include *The Cabinet Makers' London Book of Prices* (1788) and Sheraton's *Cabinet Dictionary and Encyclopedia.* Smith's most successful Gothic compositions were those for furnishing halls and libraries, which Ackermann expanded on in his *Repository* by publishing plates of Gothic furniture in 1810 with a sofa, table, chair and footstool for a library.[53] Oak was the primary wood used in Gothic design, which proved to be a suitable wood that gave the overall appearance of the carving and panel's true beauty.

In 1827, Ackermann published *Gothic Furniture*, but it is now believed that designs in his book were produced by Augustus Welby Northmore Pugin (1812-1852), who produced designs for Windsor Castle in which he specified different woods and decoration for the different rooms.[54] Pugin selected carved oak with burr walnut panels for the Beaufette Room and Gallery, rosewood with some gilding and gilt bronze mounts for the Dining Room and oak with some gilding for the Coffee Room.[55] Pugin is believed to have commented in the March 1827 Repository that, "No style can be better adapted for [the library's] decoration than that of the Middle Ages, which possesses a sedate and grave character, that invites the mind to study and reflection. The rays passing through its variegated casements cast a religious light upon the valuable tomes on either side, the beautiful arrangement of its parts combining to produce an impressive grandeur in the whole design."[56]

Gothic furniture was in part popular because of the horrific Gothic novels of the day, the romances of Walter Scott and the interest in medieval castles such as the Lowther Castle and Eastnor Castle.[57] The Gothic designs embodied Gothic fantasies and were incorporated into domestic furniture quite easily after 1827, when makers were more skilled in producing items and the prices were more moderate. Although known for its gaiety in appearance and richness of detail, the run of Gothic design proved to be short lived in popularity. Today, occasional elements of Gothic can be recognized on American Empire furniture, such as bookcases with Gothic features.

American Empire furniture can be defined in the time period between 1800 and 1840, when the designs of French Empire and English Regency grew in popularity in the cities including Philadelphia, New York, Baltimore, Boston and Savannah. Admirers of French culture imported French furnishings but when tariffs rose on imported goods, the need to have locally produced furniture increased. The Empire style could not have been popularized in America without the numerous French and English immigrants who were highly skilled at producing this type of furniture and decorative details. The French had introduced the style to the English, who introduced it to the Americans through various pattern books; however it was not until immigrant craftsmen arrived in America that the Empire style reached its height. The Neo-Classical movement was a continuum that had no specific beginning or end, but which had three phases: neoclassicism, c. 1785-1810; archaeological classicism, c. 1810-1830; and debased classicism, c. 1830-1850.[58] The period of the most outstanding work was during archaeological classicism, the focus of this book.

French cabinetmakers left their coun-

[50] Collard 180

[51] Musgrave 75

[52] Collard 181

[53] Collard 182

[54] Collard 183

[55] Collard 183

[56] Musgrave 86

[57] Musgrave 87

[58] Joseph T. Butler, *American Furniture From the first Colonies to World War I* (London: Triune Books, 1973) 129.

try to work in America, where it was less troubled, the economy was improving, and the demand for Empire furniture was on the rise. French émigrés and their American craftsmen counterparts created designs that combined French Empire and English Regency styles into the new design of American Empire. American craftsmen selected pillars, brass paw feet, casters, reeding, waterleaf carving and dolphins from the English Regency style and gilt mounts, swags and Egyptian details from the French Empire style.[59] American furniture unintentionally was less imperial than French or English designs; craftsmen often substituted gold leaf decoration for brass mounts and painting for marble or ebony. It is not known to this day how much of American Empire design was cultivated from English or French design sources, since it is difficult to locate what sources were owned by what maker. It is believed that designs taken from both countries were incorporated in a number of ways and that imported items of furniture may have served as models for the early designers.

American Empire furniture is constructed of mahogany with inlaid geometric designs of crotch veneer, fine ormolu mounts and front legs in the form of lion's paws carved with wings or acanthus.[60] It is heavy in form with well-articulated carving that appears three-dimensional. Exclusively American features include the imitation of use of Greek-curved legs with a definite projection on the knee, a multiplication of sections in pillars and posts, and painted or stenciled imitation of metal ornament.[61] Wooden bands of inlay were replaced by stenciled gilt borders simulating ormolu.[62] The klismos or "Grecian" chair was a popular form, executed in many variations that were derived from antique Greek models.

Painted or stenciled decoration was adopted because trade embargoes restricted cabinet-makers from exporting large amounts of brass ornament from London and Paris, as they had done in the past. Marble was a material that was readily available and was incorporated into many forms, including center tables by Anthony Quervelle, where he used inlaid marble in a circular design. The furniture industry grew, especially with the invention of the machine saw in 1820, making it easier to obtain sheets of veneer and implement vertical crotch veneer.

The top competing firms in America during the period were located in Philadelphia, New York, Boston and Baltimore; furniture was exported from each of these urban centers. Regional differences in the furniture provide a way to decipher where they originated from. In Baltimore, for example, light wood icicle inlays (teardrops in reverse) are sometimes seen on the legs on sideboards.[63] Plain stringing (thin lines of inlay in lighter or darker woods) is common on New York furniture, whereas different patterns of stringing are found on pieces from Baltimore.[64] Characteristic features of Philadelphia furniture are shell, eagle, floral and leaf motifs. New York and Philadelphia share some of the same motifs, but their execution of the form is often different. In the search of American Empire furniture, Philadelphia is often unfairly overshadowed by the work of New York's Duncan Phyfe (1768-1854), Michael Allison (1773-1855) and Charles Honoré Lannuier (1779-1819). There is no doubt these were among the top furniture makers of the period, however Philadelphia had competent, if not equally talented makers such as Anthony Quervelle (1787-1856), Joseph Barry (1759-1838) and Henry Connelly (1770-1826). While Phyfe is credited with introducing the sabre leg Greek klismos chair and curule base (Grecian cross), Quervelle can be credited with introducing numerous stylistic elements to Philadelphia. Although no absolute proof exists, it appears that Quervelle was the first cabinetmaker in Philadelphia to produce center tables with pedestals incorporating vase and leaf forms.[65]

The eventual decline in the popularity of Empire furniture in America came at the same time as it ended in Europe, in the

[59] Petraglia 124

[60] Celia Jackson Otto, *American Furniture of the Nineteenth Century* (New York: The Viking Press, 1965) 45.

[61] Otto 45

[62] Petraglia 124

[63] Doreen Beck, *Book of American Furniture* (England: The Hamlyn Publishing Group Limited, 1973) 66.

[64] Beck 66

[65] Robert Smith, "Part II: The Pedestal Tables," *The Magazine Antiques* July 1973: 95.

1840s. Already by 1830, there was no time lag between styles in America and Europe, and the rate of the change in styles was much in synch. The pillar and scroll style that was fashionable in Europe had reached America and the carved lion's paws, eagles and other Empire motifs had disappeared, replaced by simple classical lines. Brass ormolu mounts, gilding and stenciling no longer resided on mahogany veneers. Only the occasional wooden rosette, beading, lotus leaf or anthemion was found on objects in the pillar and scroll style.[66]

As the pillar and scroll style spread across America, even the highly popular New York firms of Joseph Meeks & Sons and Duncan Phyfe offered a variety of furniture in this style. In 1833, Joseph Meeks & Sons illustrated over forty pieces in the pillar and scroll style, including sofas, chairs and tables. Anthony Quervelle, a French émigré who worked in Philadelphia and was known for his impressive Empire forms, even he changed his style in the mid to late 1830s to conform to the newly popular pillar and scroll forms. Several comparisons of Quervelle's early and later works have shown that they share the same structural principles, but rich carving was replaced by plain scrolls that have a stylistically disappointing effect compared to the intricate carving and ornamentation of the Empire era.

The Restoration style was the equivalent of modern contemporary avant-garde, while Empire was what remained as "antique" and classical. Classical forms were debased, made into crude forms hardly recognizable as Empire, and mass-produced in factories; the designs now the property of the inventors of patented folding beds, extension tables, and dentist's chairs.[67] Often blamed on the effects of industrialization, the Pillar & Scroll style did not exhibit the same graceful movement or animation in carving of the preceding period of Empire furniture. Some antiquarians regard it as disgraceful, as Duncan Phyfe did in 1847, referring to it as "butcher furniture."[68]

Empire designs managed to stay alive even in the 1850s, which is evident in Andrew Jackson Downing's (1815-1852) statement in his *Architecture of Country Houses* that "the furniture most generally used in private houses is some modification of the classical style," which he found, "has the merit of being simple, easily made and very moderate in cost." [69] The Empire period is not forgotten, with traces of Empire designs still evident in modern, factory produced furniture forms. Unfortunately, none of these mechanically produced forms have anywhere near the same grandeur and impressive detail as original American Empire furniture.

[66] Fitzgerald 129

[67] Robert Smith, "Late classical furniture in the United States, 1820-1850

[68] Fitzgerald 131

[69] Smith, Late Classical 523

CHAPTER 2
PHILADELPHIA IN THE
CLASSICAL PERIOD
(1800-1840)

Front portico of the Samuel Painter House (built 1757)

This impressive Greek revival portico was added when the house was
enlarged circa 1825. The home is located a short distance from
Philadelphia in West Chester, Pennsylvania.

PHILADELPHIA IN THE CLASSICAL PERIOD (1800-1840)

The change in the design of furniture making leading to the Empire period in America reflected the political situation of the early nineteenth century. As the country was emerging as an independent nation, Americans were striving to create a style that would represent strength, beauty and culture. Since America was a new nation with a limited cultural heritage, people were anxious to find a way to integrate the styles of foreign decorative arts within their homes in the hope of educating themselves and others in the taste of fine art. Following the lead of many nations that adhered to the Napoleonic virtues of French Empire furniture, America modeled their furniture from classical Roman, Greek and Egyptian sources, many of which were derived from French and English design and pattern books.

The Empire style is not purely French, as even the authority of French Empire design, Percier & Fontaine, point out in their Recueil de Decorations Interieures:

> Those of our works in the nature of furniture, which, by the importance of the places they were destined for, or the rank of those who ordered them, may be regarded as appropriate to attest the correct way of seeing things, composing them and ornamenting them at the present period. This style does not belong to us; it is entirely the property of the ancients and as our only merit is to have understood how to conform our inventions to it, our true aim in giving these to the public is to do all that is within our power to prevent innovations to corrupt and destroy the principles which others will doubtless use better than we.[1]

In the quest to produce furniture based on designs found in antiquity, there have been numerous adaptations combining modern forms with ancient motifs, many of which look nothing like classical remnants, but which are created in the spirit of fashion and the good taste of the period.[1]

Percier and Fontaine further elaborate on this point:

> The decoration and furnishing of houses are to houses what clothes are to people: everything of this nature becomes old, and in a very few years seems to be superannuated and ridiculous...To do everything according to reason in such a way that the reason may be perceived and justifies the means used- this is the first principle of architecture. However, the first principle of fashion is to do everything without reason and never to do otherwise. The form and needs of the body give no reason for the forms of clothes; because people do not dress to cover themselves, but to adorn themselves. Furniture does not make a virtue of necessity with regard to forms.[2]

Indeed, designs by Percier and Fontaine were elaborately ornamented, but were fantastical and could not be used in American

[1] Esther Singleton, *French and English Furniture* (New York: McClure, Philips & Co., 1903) 371.

[2] Singleton 371

homes because their forms were often impractical. In Philadelphia furniture of the early nineteenth century, the same principles apply in that not all the new forms created were practical (often they were massive and bulky), but were meant to convey a sense of style in the homes of patrons seeking fine taste. In furnishing their homes, some people were searching for a way to convey the beauty of classicism and to showcase their knowledge of fine and decorative arts.

The outcome of combining different aspects of French, Roman, Greek and Egyptian architecture and design with American forms resulted in a new mode of Empire furniture which was unlike forms produced in European nations. The period from 1800-1840 marks the height of success for the furniture trade; there was much opportunity and demand for fine furniture, not only among wealthy elements of society, but also in ordinary American homes. The authors of this book will be concentrating chiefly on Philadelphia Empire furniture, which has historically been given little consideration in the world of American antiques and which deserves much attention due to the numerous examples of finely executed pieces of furniture in every form imaginable. The time frame for American Empire Furniture has changed throughout the years, as different periods have a way of overlapping and intertwining with each other. The authors will be defining American Empire from 1800-1840, although clearly there are examples of Empire furniture dating as late as 1845. As with furniture of any era, it is first important to have a historical background to gain context and perspective on the period. In the first four decades of the nineteenth century, Philadelphia experienced a period of rapid growth and prosperity that accounted in part for the type of furniture that was produced.

[3] Edgar P. Richardson, "The Athens of America 1800-1825," *Philadelphia: A 300-Year History*, Ed.Russell F. Weigly (New York: W.W. Norton & Company, 1982) 202.

[4] Richardson 212

[5] Richardson 212

I. PHILADELPHIA: 1800-1840

In the beginning of the nineteenth century, Philadelphia as the former capital was a large, thriving city not yet immersed in industry, but which maintained a sense of beauty unsurpassed in other American cities. Levels of both domestic and foreign trade increased, and the prosperity of the city was highly dependant on the commerce of the seas.

Since much of the wealth of the city came mainly from commerce, it is not surprising that the city was dominated by merchants, ship owners, shipbuilders and seamen.[3] Philadelphia played an important role in the trade with China and the city was filled with imports such as tea, porcelains, silk and cotton. Philadelphia's largest manufactured product was flour, and it exported vast quantities of it each year. The development of trade had moved the city to create better means of transportation during the first half of the nineteenth century. Paved turnpikes and water canals better connected Philadelphia with her neighboring areas.[4]

The trade with China helped stimulate the economy and increased the profitability in trade, while at the same time providing a direct link with the ancient culture of China, which many people found fascinating. China was no longer unimaginably far away; now one could decorate his or her home with Chinese amenities and traditional Chinese Art, provided they had the money to spend. Andreas Everardus van Braam Houckgeest, a Dutch merchant who had spent years in China in the service of the Dutch East India Company, settled in Philadelphia and bought a farm on the Delaware near Bristol. Here he built a fifteen-room home called "China's Retreat," where he lived surrounded by Chinese servants and curiosities he had brought back with him.[5] There was a re-awakening of a thirst for antiquity, history and customs, which was illustrated by the extent to which people wanted to decorate their homes in the newest, most fashionable style that was developing. A combination of Egyptian, French, Italian and Greek ancient designs permeated the development of a style that was to become known later as American Empire.

In 1800, Philadelphia was the largest city in the United States and houses were expanding and taking over farmlands, forests and marshes. Even with an enormous amount of growth, the city remained medieval in the respect that craftsmen still lived over their shops and citizens from all walks of life lived side by side; the establishment of rich and poor neighborhoods had not yet begun. The city was heterogeneous, and it was common for affluent families to live next door to peasants. There were areas where certain groups tended to form small communities, for example the Germans lived mainly in the northwest and African Americans on the southeast edge of town, near where the Mother Bethel African Methodist Episcopal Church stands on Sixth Street below Pine.[6] However, divisions of rich and poor areas did not become strictly stratified until much later. Philadelphia maintained a quaint, charming appearance with cobble stone paved streets and tree-lined blocks.

Fountains and statues sprang up around the city. Philadelphia's street plan, with decorative public squares, became a model for other American cities that were built in accordance with the same rectangular design. In the eye of some European travelers it may have seemed unimaginative and much like a grid when compared to ancient cities such as Rome or Athens, but it did set a standard for the classic American city. Philadelphia residents were proud of their city, which was clean and continued to be filled with new symbols of American pride. The city's first fountain that was built in 1809 and was called *The Nymph of the Schuylkill*, carved all in wood by William Rush (1756-1833), and placed in the Centre Square.[7] Philadelphia was

[6] Richardson 222

[7] Richardson 218

[8] Richardson 218

filled with exceptional hotels, theaters, restaurants and museums, which made it very cosmopolitan and caused it to draw a large amount of tourism.

The city hosted many distinguished visitors including state legislators and federal officials. Albert H. Smyth, the editor of Benjamin Franklin's writings, described it as such: "At the beginning of this century, Philadelphia was the most attractive city in America to a young man of brains and ambition".[8] Politically, the city was exciting since the diverging views of the two emerging parties were in constant conflict. The struggle of the small farmer and the poor against the old ruling class of merchants and landowners was eventually settled peacefully through voting.

The most important civic improvement during the time period was the waterworks system on the Schuylkill River. The system for providing fresh water was devised by Benjamin Henry Latrobe and put into place in 1801, when Nicholas Roosevelt was hired to build the steam engines capable of supplying the water. This was a vast improvement over using water from wells and cisterns, which were easily contaminated by surface drainage from the streets and outhouses (it is believed this is what spread various diseases such as yellow fever around the city). The Waterworks and its neighboring buildings were popular tourist spots at the time period, as it was such an intricate part of society.

These improvements, especially the new forms of transportation later in the period such as bridges, turnpikes, canals and steamboats, helped to modernize Philadelphia. Highways connected Philadelphia to nearby cities such as New York, Harrisburg, Baltimore, and Trenton. One important problem that was solved was the building of a bridge to cross the Schuylkill. There had been two floating bridges that were often swept away during storms, so a stronger bridge was built in its place - the Permanent Bridge. The building of this bridge began a series of bridges built in many other states. The most

popular bridge builder was Lewis Wernwag (1770-1843), who designed a bridge across the Schuylkill known as the Upper Ferry Bridge, furnished in wood.[9]

The free enterprising spirit of the time period was dampened slightly with the war against Great Britain in 1812, which interrupted ocean trade for a time. After the war, the port of Philadelphia had a difficult time regaining its former position of strength and a depression set in. New York was developing at a rapid rate and began to outshine Philadelphia in the trade business because it had several natural advantages. One of them was that their harbor was ice-free and was more accessible than Philadelphia's harbor.[10] British manufacturers chose New York over Philadelphia as the port to bring large amounts of textiles and buyers came from all around the country.

Philadelphia no longer controlled the trade market but this was not a huge loss since other trades, which became more important later, were developing in the beginning of the technological revolution. Philadelphia remained the center of shipbuilding and a major port for the South Atlantic and Gulf trade, but by 1824 its foreign commerce had declined to a poor third or fourth place in the nation.[11] This resulted in a city no longer dependant on trade, and free of the burden, businessmen had found more profitable ways to obtain and keep capital.

In the 1820s, Philadelphia was well on its way to becoming an industrial city; its geographic location provided abundant water power and easy access to coal and iron. The cities proximity to the hinterlands and its agricultural products was also important. Philadelphia was home to a great number of intellectuals and inventors and did not have to resort to slavery to accomplish many feats; numerous skilled workers were employed.[12] Within the realm of cabinetmaking, guilds were created with masters and journeymen to meet the demands of the public with high degree of quality. Later, industrialization would replace the system with factories that

[9] Richardson 223

[10] Richardson 214

[11] Richardson 218

[12] Richardson 218

[13] Richardson 245

were completely mechanized for the highest output.

Philadelphia was home to many lawyers, scientists, doctors, clergymen and publishers. A scientific community had been created, along with the American Philosophical Society, various religious associations and the American Medical Association. Intellectual organizations such as the Franklin Institute held design competitions for furniture. Clubs for neighborhoods and different political views sprang up, uniting people in a way that had not been possible before. As the population increased, the city became less heterogeneous and people had to find a way back into smaller communities using different societal clubs.

Improvements in all fields were being made, and two fields in particular gained the highest recognition—the physicians and the lawyers. Physicians created medical journals and developed improved teaching techniques that would set a standard for many other states, including pharmacy and psychiatry programs. Leaders of the local bar set a tone of increased learning and responsibility, which produced highly educated philosophical thinkers.

Another area that flourished was the arts, as several new museums opened that depicted classical arts such as paintings and sculpture. Painters, sculptors and engravers often used themes of nature, such as Pennsylvania landscapes, city views and the Schuylkill River. Portrait painting was popular and the most important artists of the time were Thomas Sully, Bass Otis and Rembrandt Peale. When the Pennsylvania Academy of Fine Arts was established in 1805, the building used to house the Italian art collection donated by Mr. Joseph Allen Smith of Carolina was developed in a classical style.[13] Seibert described the Academy of Fine Arts, still in existence as both a museum and a school, as "the oldest museum and school in America and among the oldest in the world."[14] The Academy of Fine Arts sustained art activity and held numerous exhibitions, which the public flocked to in great numbers.

The first American structure built in the classical form was the Virginia State capitol in Richmond, completed in 1789.[15] Thomas Jefferson designed the building after the Maison Carrée, a first century Roman temple he had seen when visiting France. Shortly thereafter in 1795, the First Bank of the United States became the earliest classical structure of Philadelphia. An English critic in 1803 described the building: "It excels in elegance and equals in utility, the edifice, not only the Bank of England but of any banking house in the world."[16] Other buildings that were erected in the classical style included playhouses and banks. The Chestnut Street Theatre, for example, was a Palladian building modeled after a theater in Bath (Image 4). This was destroyed by fire in 1820 and was rebuilt in the classical Greek manner in 1822 (Image 5). Playhouses were a popular form of entertainment and were frequented by everyone except the Quakers, who were extremely conservative and disapproved of the plays. There was obvious English influence in the theater, many producers were English and Philadelphia hosted many theater groups from London. Performing arts became a highly respected form, and the skill of the performers brought the plays and musicals to life. Music was also a popular source of entertainment, and concerts were given regularly in concert halls and auditoriums.

The Bank of Pennsylvania, built from 1799-1801, utilized white marble and had a Greek Ionic temple portico facing Second Street and a similar portico in the rear.[17] The exterior of the building was built with classical ornament in the columns and molding, which gave it the appearance of it being a Greek structure. A movement in architecture, known by some as the American Greek Revival, had begun and was shaped from Greek designs combined with American to make a unique style. The second Bank of the United States was an even more impressive Greek style struc-

[14] Richardson 245

[15] Fitzgerald 111

[16] Richardson 253

[17] Richardson 252

[18] Richardson 256

Image 4

The late Theater in Chestnut Street Philadelphia, Destroyed by Fire in 1820

Drawn and Published by William Birch, 1804
The Historical Society of Pennsylvania (HSP)

ture with large, white marble columns and an overall massive appearance. Nicholas Biddle (1786-1844), the director of the bank at the time, was known to have been an admirer of Greek temple architecture and it was probable that he influenced the construction of the building in such a style.

The War of 1812 and depression in 1819 affected every part of life in the city, and the disorganization of commercial and investment banking certainly didn't help matters. This was a time period where banks could not be trusted and panics

were a common occurrence. One Philadelphia merchant described the situation, "The whole country was involved in one universal scene of distress and ruin."[18] One person who attempted to rectify the situation was Mr. Nicholas Biddle, who became the president of the second Bank of the United States in 1823.

The city would survive crises and reach a heightened sense of popularity for its artistic design and intellectual society later in the period. Many exiles from the Napoleonic Wars brought culture

[19] Nicholas Wainwright, "The Age of Nicholas Biddle 1825-1841", *Philadelphia: A 300-Year History*, Ed. Russell F. Weigly (New York: W. W. Norton & Co, 1982) 258-306.

to America with them. Joseph Bonaparte filled his estate in Point Breeze, New Jersey, with many great works of art that eventually became the country's first major art collection. A taste for refined European art was cropping up in and around Philadelphia and the most impressive example of bringing this style to America was by Nicholas Biddle.

Biddle traveled in Italy and Greece and was especially impressed by Greek architecture. When he returned to America years later he decided to refashion his estate, Andalusia, with Greek style structures. The interior of the estate provides numerous examples of the type of decorative arts that were in fashion, while the exterior resurrects an edifice of ancient Greece. Biddle

not only succeeded in bringing classically inspired artistic styles, but also made improvements in agriculture and was called upon numerous times to help develop an effective banking system for America. The state of the Bank of the United States was terrible. It was difficult to obtain a loan and money was scarce, making economic growth very difficult. When Biddle took over control of the bank, he re-opened lines of credit for legitimate business needs and restored faith and stability in the Bank.

Stephen Girard (1750-1831), a French born banker during the Empire period, greatly admired the Greek architecture and left a large amount of money for the building of a university in this style, which was constructed after his death. Girard's many

[20] Jonathan Fairbanks and Elizabeth Bidwell Bates, *American Furniture 1620 to Present* (New York: Richard Marek Publishers, 1981) 252.

[21] Fairbanks and Bates 252

Image 5
The new Theater in Chestnut Street Philadelphia, Built in 1822
Published by William Birch, 1823
The Historical Society of Pennsylvania (HSP)

marble structures transformed public buildings into true works of art. One New York editor wrote, "The best architectural taste in the country is found at Philadelphia, as her public buildings make manifest. It is not to be wondered at, therefore, that we are indebted to the American Athens, instead of our own."[19] The legacy of the buildings will always be a reminder of the time in history when architecture took on a new tone, one of artistic simplicity and beauty. Domestic architecture was also changing, as prominent architects such as John Haviland (1792-1852) and Thomas Walter (1804-1887), who built Girard College, were commissioned to build impressive homes in the Greek and sometimes Egyptian styles.

The architectural revival of ancient past in Philadelphia was also introduced by Benjamin Henry Latrobe (1764-1820), the first fully trained architect-engineer to make a career of designing buildings, furniture and the waterworks system on the Schuylkill River. In 1808, Latrobe designed the furniture and setting for the Oval Room in the White House for President James Madison, which burned in the 1814 fire during the War of 1812. Fortunately the drawings and correspondence survive as a testament to the stunning effect of the room.[20] The drawings of antique classical furniture that Latrobe made for the White House were influenced by Thomas Hope's Household Furniture and Interior Decoration, published in London in 1807.[21]

[22] Wainright 269

The city once again would rise from depression to prosperity, with moderate increases in trade and more exports to South America and Mexico. Private and public parties were common, and Biddle was well known for hosting social events at his home in Andalusia. Quality of living seemed to have improved, but this period of prosperity would not last long because in comparison to other states, Philadelphia was falling behind. As the first quarter of the nineteenth century ended, a decline in trade led Philadelphia to be surpassed in both population and trade figures by New York. It continued, however, to be the main source of capital for America and the Chesapeake and Delaware Canals were built to facilitate more trade by providing quicker routes. The city struggled to make internal improvements, one of which was the introduction of coal to replace burning wood. From having an ample coal supply, steam power was used in mills to provide power for such enterprises as carpet weaving, breweries, flour mills and iron manufacturers.[22] By the mid-nineteenth century, even furniture making was moving towards mass production in factories over the handcrafted pieces made by skillful craftsmen of the past.

The rise of industrialization in Philadelphia ended the period of classical revival in both furniture and architecture. The height of fashion for the classical forms in furniture was from the beginning of the nineteenth century until around 1840, and is known as American Empire. American Empire replaced the Federal era of decorative arts at the end of the eighteenth century with a more robust, fashionable taste that was meant to showcase the majesty of ancient works of art. The markings of early Empire were apparent in decorative arts and the architecture of public and private buildings at the end of the eighteenth century and especially at the beginning of the nineteenth century. Changes in architecture from 1800 to 1840 were reflected in the decorative arts. Philadelphia evolved into the American city of classical influence, fashioned from ancient Greek, Roman and Egyptian motifs and architecture. The influence of ancient classical forms permeated the decorative arts of Philadelphia and dictated the classical forms of Philadelphia Empire Furniture, which will be depicted in this volume. As before mentioned in the changing architecture of theaters and banks, other buildings sprang up in a similar style all across the city. As a way to give the city history and culture, buildings of monumental stature were constructed in a style that was based on that of the ancient Greek Roman culture. Philadelphia would not have been able to develop such a rich cultural identity without this period in history, and for that the craftsmen, architects, supporters and patrons of the neoclassical movement during the period are owed a great debt.

CHAPTER 3

ARCHITECTURE

Image 6
Benjamin Asher, Plate 30: Portico, Practice of Architecture, Boston, 1847

Courtesy, The Winterthur Library: Printed Book and Periodical Collection
This design of a portico by Asher Benjamin incorporates several classical motifs, including scrolls, shells, foliage and columns.

ARCHITECTURE

I. ORIGINS OF PHILADELPHIA ARCHITECTURAL DESIGN

When foreign archetics came to Philadelphia, up until around 1798, they found that "Architecture was at a low standing and Master carpenters directed the taste of city edifices."[1] Regarding the profession of architects, Americans could not understand how architects differed from builders; carpenters and bricklayers were often hired to design buildings using English pattern books. The result was often poorly designed domestic architecture based on British pattern books.

The situation improved somewhat when more pattern books started appearing, led by both American and British architects. Asher Benjamin (1773-1845) is known as the American leader of pattern books (see image 6). He published seven handbooks in forty-seven editions between 1797 and 1856; Minard Lafever (1798-1854) later published five handbooks (1829-56), which had great influence in the Greek revival.[2]

English publications including James Elmes's *Metropolitan Improvements* (1827) and James Stuart and Nicholas Revett's *Antiquities of Athens* (1762-1830) were important sources for American architects. John Haviland (1792-1852), an English architect who immigrated to Philadelphia, is credited with publishing the first American pattern book on Greek revival architecture, *The Builder's Assistant* (1818).[3] This publication was a guide that gave detailed illustrations and instructions to builders on how to create Greek revival structures. Haviland designed the St. Andrews Episcopal Church and Franklin Institute in Philadelphia in the 1820s.

Following the publication of Stuart and Revett's *Antiquities of Athens*, Greek architecture became increasingly popular in England and then spread to America. The approaches to interpreting architecture became more scientific and learned. Theorists emphasized the preeminence of Greek architecture of the fifth century B.C. as the first flowering of classicism, purer and more austerely beautiful than the corruptions introduced later by the Romans.[4] Often architects of the Greek revival claimed their work to be "purely Grecian," which was often incorrect because it was many times a combination of Greek, English, French and Roman elements. An example of this is when Robert Mills (1781-1855) described Latrobe's House of Representatives as "purely Grecian in design and decorations", yet the semi-domed ceiling was not Greek in the least, but was derived from English and French design.[5]

The transition of Greek-inspired architecture from government buildings to domestic homes may be explained by the desire for innovation at a time when people began to have the means, through the improving economy, to cultivate taste in their homes. Grecian forms began to appear

[1] W. Barksdale Maynard, *Architecture in the United States 1800-1850* (New Haven; London: Yale University Press, 2002) 25.

[2] Maynard 26

[3] Robert K. Sutton, *Americans Interpret the Parthenon* (Colorado: U P of Colorado, 1992) 18.

[4] Maynard 221

[5] Maynard 221

in towns all over America and the enduring cultural image of the white temple gleaming in solitary splendor in the Arcadian landscape perfectly summarized the American effort to domesticate and civilize a continent.[6] The addition of Greek details to plain, square, white-painted wood frame buildings made homes appear more stylish and less primitive. As modern architectural historian Talbot Hamlin points out in his book *Greek Revival Architecture in America* (1944), the Greek revival movement never really revived ancient architecture but instead adapted classical forms to modern conditions.[7] The interpretation of Greek and Roman forms by nineteenth century architects was subjective, and in no way were buildings in Philadelphia duplicates of the Greek buildings of the past which they were partly modeled after. The movement can be better described as the reinvention of Greek principles as applied to modern American architecture to suit contemporary purposes. The use of the word "Greek" was questionable later. It became known to imply classicism in general, as Grecian architecture was consonant with antiquity and was the product of "countries' and "nations" in plural, not merely of Greece.[8]

Twentieth-century historians sought to demonstrate that the "Greek Revival" was a purely American phenomenon, independent from European influences. In the nineteenth century when American art and antiques were not recognized as being very valuable, the "Revival" was clearly seen as having certain outside influences. Many of the top architects and cabinetmakers had emigrated from Europe to begin introducing classicism to America. In the twentieth century when American arts and antiques had become valuable, the "Revival" was known simply as American. In 1926, Howard Major called the revival, "An American Style for Americans...It is the only thoroughly American architecture" and was our "national style, our independent of contemporaneous European influence."[9] Many proclaimed the Greek styled architecture as the first national American style, when in fact it was an international phenomenon. The need of the Americans to separate themselves from Europe and the rest of the world in the twentieth century was great, as it was a time of intense patriotism. Yet, the fact remained that many of the greatest American monuments were inspired from British and French examples and to discredit European influence would be ridiculous. For example, upon examination of the Treasury Department, which has been called "distinctly American," it is apparent that it has a close likeness to English designer John Nash's redevelopment of the western districts of London, particularly that of the Carlton House Terrace.[10] A closer look at many of America's top architectural achievements, it is evident several aspects can be traced back to British and French design origins. Clearly, this segment of history is one of the greatest periods of American architecture, but it is necessary to understand how and why this distinct style prevailed over all others.

The explanation of the popularity of this type of architecture in America during 1800-1840 is that every effort was made by both foreign and domestic architects to develop buildings of the classical design to inspire beauty and pride, and to follow in the fashionable taste of the time period. Classicism, or Neo-Classicism, as it was known, was not restricted to Greek, but included Greek, Roman, Egyptian and Gothic elements. The neo-classical taste was internationally popular and Americans were desperate to be considered tasteful, explaining the immense popularity of classicism from the beginning. America was still in its developing stages and did not have a definitive style of architecture, and the point had come where there was vested interest from foreign and domestic architects to seek fame and make their mark by creating bold buildings in the new style of the period.

[6] Maynard 221

[7] Maynard 221

[8] Maynard 222

[9] Maynard 244

[10] Maynard 246

Architect William H. Ranlett wrote in the 1840s:

> It has often been made a reproach to our national character that we imitate all other people in our architecture, while we have nothing that we can claim as our own. But so far from this being a reproach, it is rather a credit, that having a knowledge of the old world's experience we have the intelligence to avail ourselves of the wisdom of our ancestors.[11]

In terms of architecture Americans did not have to re-invent the wheel. Grecian architecture was widely accepted by most civilized countries as being superior in art and taste, which is one of the reasons it was chosen. American architects were obsessed with keeping the correct Greek standard of excellence. They also used innovative arrangements of different classical motifs and applied them to the buildings, which made them unique to America. Essentially, America employed the greatest architectural achievements in history to suit the needs of the developing modern life, which required a higher degree of sophistication. The monumental Greek style buildings were to people of the early- to mid-nineteenth century what skyscrapers are for the twenty-first century.

Greek-inspired architecture coincided with the development of fine classical furniture in Philadelphia from 1800-1840. A need developed for appropriate furnishing for the new monumental residences of classical design. By this time cabinetmakers in England and America (as well as all over the world—France being one of the leaders of this style) had begun to produce furniture that was considered to be classical, designed from antiquities of Greece, Italy and Egypt. In his commissions for private houses, Benjamin Henry Latrobe recommended that the interior of houses be furnished appropriately with classical furniture unique to the theme of every room. Latrobe often designed suites of furniture himself. The architects that came after Latrobe, William Strickland (1788-1854),

John Haviland and Robert Mills (1781-1855), did not have experience with this new concept (as it was practiced in London) and may or may not have advocated it to clients, though this was not considered of utmost importance. To be considered in good taste during the time period, many homes simply had to contain various pieces of furniture in the classical style.

II. ARCHITECTURE IN PHILADELPHIA 1800-1840

The end of the eighteenth century and beginning of the nineteenth century marked the inauguration of classical Greek architecturally structured buildings in the city of Philadelphia. Until the end of the eighteenth century, buildings in Philadelphia were furnished in brick. From a European perspective, the city somewhat paled in comparison to cities well established for their architectural development and beauty such as Rome and London. Sensing the need to cultivate the image of Philadelphia as an intellectual, stimulating and artistic city, architects were commissioned to erect buildings reminiscent of Greek style structures. The decision to employ Greek designs was made for several important reasons. Greek buildings have always embodied a sense of virtue and simplicity, which, when applied to government and bank buildings, illustrates the connection between the arts and political power.

The Parthenon and other Greek and Roman buildings inspired awe by their immense size and fluted marble columns. They stood as symbols of civic and national achievement. In many early European cities the connection between the arts and political power was recognized and utilized by creating impressively designed structures to instill pride and to inspire awe in the people. The political system of the United States shared the ideals of democracy with that of the Greeks. At the time, Greece was trying to establish its independence from Turkey just as America

[11] Maynard 249

Image 7

Historical view of the First Bank of the United States

Drawn, Engraved & Published by W. Birch & Son, Philadelphia 1804.
The Historical Society of Pennsylvania (HSP)

was freeing itself from the control of the British. Since Philadelphia was still a developing city, it seemed necessary to create images of strength, beauty and security using Greek structures. Such buildings would instill pride in Americans and entice people from all over the world to come and marvel at the accomplishment of re-establishing classical remnants of Greek culture in America.

There are several reasons that Greek architecture became fashionable in Philadelphia, including the presence of the Franklin Institute (housed after 1826 in John Haviland's takeoff on the Choragic Monument of Thrasyllus); the drawing school that it ran, where leading architects taught the beauties of the Greek orders; the Grecian culture advocacy of Biddle and the journal he briefly edited (1812-14), the *Port Folio*, and the public response that stimulated tourism.[12] Architectural landmarks of the city, such as the Bank of Pennsylvania, Girard College and the Waterworks fast became popular tourist attractions, which is evidence of the high esteem people held in regard to the Greek revival buildings. Marble and stone structures erected over the first half of the nineteenth century changed Philadelphia from a primitive brick, stone and wood city into a more sophisticated city with a European air.

The first Philadelphia building to be constructed based on Greek designs was the First Bank of the United States (1795-1797), which incorporated Corinthian order columns carved in white marble (see images 7 and 8). The Irish-educated draftsman, Christopher Myers, is credited with the original design prototype.[13] Samuel Blodget Jr., a New Hampshire architect, was in charge of construction. Secretary of the Treasury Alexander Hamilton, was the

[12] Maynard 232

[13] Beatrice Garvan, *Federal Philadelphia 1785-1825, The Athens of the Western World* (Philadelphia Museum of Art, 1987) 38.

[14] Richard G. Miller, "The Federal City," *Philadelphia: A 300-Year History*, Ed Russell F. Weigly (New York: W.W. Norton & Co., 1982) 175-176.

Image 8
First Bank of the United States, later Girard Bank Building, Third Street Philadelphia
The Historical Society of Pennsylvania (HSP)

GIRARD BANK BUILDING, Third Street near Walnut Street.

1893

driving force that created this institution to stabilize American finance and encourage commerce.[14]

The Bank of Pennsylvania, designed by Benjamin Henry Latrobe from 1799-1801, was considered the model of Grecian architecture[15] (See Image 9). Latrobe came from London to America in 1796 and introduced a new standard for design excellence with his buildings and engineering projects.[16] Latrobe is recognized as adding distinguishing elements of French classicism to his buildings, which were sometimes perceived as solely "Greek" in nature. Upon Latrobe's arrival in Philadelphia in 1798, the design and construction of the Bank of Pennsylvania on Second Street commenced. The basic form was derived from the Greek Ionic temple on the Illyssus near Athens, with additions of Latrobe's own innovations such as the low central dome, broad wall surfaces, arched windows and central skylit vaulted banking hall, which were inspired from antiquity.[17] Latrobe did not reproduce exact replicas of Greek designs, but instead interpreted them with a modern view; he had to take into account that the building he designed had to be used for public purpose. Latrobe argued, "the forms, and the distribution of the Roman and Greek buildings which remain, are in general inapplicable to the objects and uses of our public buildings."[18] Converting Greek temples to modern banks was a challenge in and of itself, since there were space constrictions and the interior had to be furnished with offices. Critics claim that Latrobe's Bank of Pennsylvania was incorrect in its design as a Greek prototype; considering

[15] Garvan 38-39
[16] Sutton 18
[17] Sutton 18
[18] Maynard 223

Image 9
Bank of Pennsylvania on South Second Street, Philadelphia

Engraved by William Birch, 1804. The bank was remarkable for a vaulted dome interior that was new to American Architecture. The building was demolished shortly after the Civil War. Photo courtesy of Independence National Historic Park

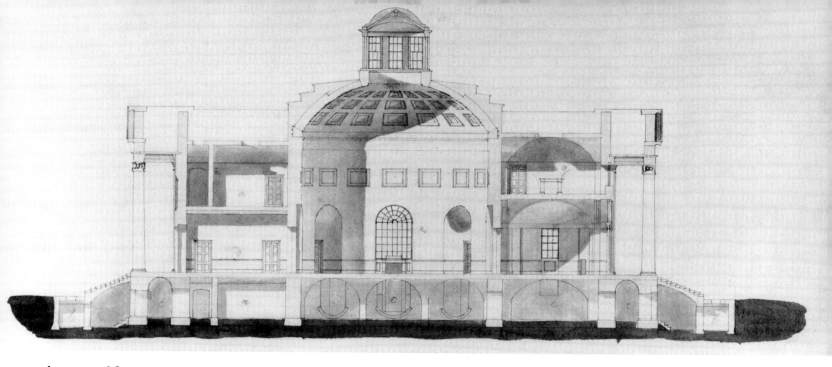

Image 10
Design by Benjamin Latrobe of the Interior of the Schuylkill Engine House.
Circa 1800
The vaulted central dome was an architectural feature favored by Latrobe. The Historical Society of Pennsylvania (HSP)

further the restrictions of modern living, it was an excellent example of the new evolving Greek and American architectural style.

After the Bank of Pennsylvania was completed, Latrobe designed the Philadelphia Water Works and a classical structure to mask the offices. These consisted of a cubical base with Greek Doric columns at the entrance and a vaulted dome[19] (see Images 10 and 11). Latrobe's knowledge of vaulting proved to be one of his major contributions, since vaulted ceilings were rarely used in America before 1800. In 1811, Latrobe addressed the Society of Artists of the United States. He noted that the ideals represented by the ancient world would continue and that "the days of Greece may be revived in the woods of America, and Philadelphia become the Athens of the Western world."[20] Latrobe later designed the nation's capital buildings after the War of 1812. One of his English contemporaries, George Hadfield (1763-1826), supervised the construction of the new Capitol.[21] Latrobe had a profound effect on many American cities including Virginia (where he first settled), Philadelphia, Baltimore,

[19] Sutton 19

[20] Garvan 39

[21] Sutton 20

[22] Sutton 19

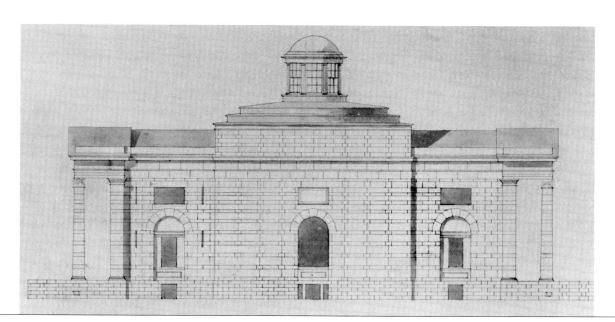

Image 11
Design by Benjamin Latrobe of the Exterior of the Schuylkill Engine House

Circa 1800
The Historical Society of Pennsylvania (HSP)

Image 12

Second Bank of the United States, 420 Chestnut Street (1819-1824)

Designed by William Strickland
The dramatic façade with Doric columns is modeled directly from the Parthenon in Athens.
William Bartlett, © 1836 Photo Courtesy of Independence National Historical Park

and finally New Orleans, where he died of yellow fever before finishing a water system for the city in 1820.[22]

Of Latrobe's students, Robert Mills and William Strickland became the prominent leaders of Greek Revival architecture. The Second Bank of the United States (1819-1824), designed by William Strickland, was modeled after the Parthenon in Athens (Image 12). Strickland attempted to preserve the characteristics of the Grecian temple, while at the same time incorporating modern necessities for the interior. The Greek Doric order for the porticoes on the front and rear facades and large columns were perceived as a great achievement in American architecture. The appearance helped strengthen the banking system, by making it seem more secure in a time when banking was regarded with appre-

hension. Strickland was instantly famous: "The most faultless monument of its size in the United States and of the purist Doric, classic in its proportions and severely chaste and simple."[23] Soon, under the encouragement of the bank president, Nicholas Biddle, other branches of the bank were established in the Grecian style. Strickland's last major project was the Merchant's Exchange (1834), which he designed with a rounded Corinthian portico and tower, copied from the Choragic Monument of Lysicrates (image 13).[24] The replica of the Choragic Monument of Lysicrates was copied right out of Stuart's and Revett's *Antiquities of Athens*. The capitals of the columns, able to seen from the windows, were carved by Peter and Philip Bardi from Carrara, Italy and were praised by Strickland, "The excellence of

[23] Maynard 226
[24] Sutton 29
[25] Maynard 230

their art will be a lasting model for our American chisels."[25]

Robert Mills began his career working with Irish architect James Hoban (1762-1831) on the White House in Washington. He then moved to Philadelphia where he worked for Latrobe for several years, eventually graduating to designing churches; the first was the Sansom Street Baptist Church.[26] Mills designed residential and commercial structures and supervised the reconstruction of office wings on Independence Hall in 1811. Later he designed Monumental Church in Richmond, Virginia. This octagonal-shaped building, with a ceremonial entrance on the front, was similar to the Athenian treasury building in Delphi.[27] Mills was chosen as the chief engineer and architect by President Andrew Jackson in the 1830s. Jackson himself had his estate, the Hermitage, remodeled by adding a two-story front portico supported by ten slender Doric columns.[28] Mills was also renowned for designing fireproof buildings.

An apprentice to Strickland,

[26] Sutton 22

[27] Sutton 22

[28] Sutton 23

Image 13

Merchants Exchange and First Bank of the United States

Engraved by William Strickland, © 1834
Photo Courtesy of Independence National Historical Park

Image 14
Panoramic view of Girard College

Circa 1840
The "classroom building" in the foreground closely resembles the Roman design temple of Zeus in Athens.

Philadelphia-born Thomas U. Walter (1804-1887) went into business in 1829 and by 1833 was selected by Stephen Girard to design Girard College with an almost unlimited budget (Image 14).[29] Girard required Walter to meet many specifications when designing the building, which included fireproofing the inside and outside and only using wood for the doors, windows and shutters.[30] The interior of the school was divided into four different rooms, which were accessed by magnificent stairways and Ionic-columned hallways.[31] It is interesting to note that as a classroom building, Girard College was an instant failure — its thirty-eight thousand square feet of shiny marble floor-tile with vaulted ceilings above shimmered with echoes. It survives today as an extraordinary monument of antebellum American architecture."[32] Hellenophile trustee Nicholas Biddle, who had visited Greece in 1806, saw that the final design was properly chaste. It still resembled the Roman Temple of Zeus at Athens more than any Greek building and surely rivaled what Latrobe once praised as, "the immense size, the bold plans and arrangements of the buildings of the Romans."[33]

[29] Sutton 30

[30] Maynard 38

[31] Sutton 30

[32] Maynard 231

[33] Maynard 231

Image 15
Delaware River View of Andalusia

The monumental proportions of the ionic columns and triangular pediments are remarkable.
Courtesy of the Andalusia Foundation, Pennsylvania

Image 16
Carriage Entrance of Andalusia

While Walter was busy working on Girard College, Nicholas Biddle hired him to remodel his home on the Delaware River. Walter designed a large portico with Doric columns at the back of the house, facing the river. Biddle named his country seat Andalusia. Also built on the property was a "little temple" housing a billiard room. Biddle once said "that there were two great truths in the world, one was the Bible, and Greek architecture the other."[34] Andalusia has been preserved as a historic site and is one of the finest examples of domestic Greek inspired architecture around Philadelphia. In 1840, Walter designed the National Bank of West Chester, PA in a similar version to the Philadelphia Second Bank. Walter was later the fourth architect of the Washington, D.C. Capitol.

[34] Maynard 262

Another example of Greek Revival architecture are the row homes on Summer Street in Philadelphia, which were designed in the 1830s by Thomas U. Walter (Image 17). The fourteen row home development utilizes multiple balanced Greek revival elements including columns, triangular pediments, anthemion decoration and elaborate Greek-inspired entrances accessed by rising marble steps. This type of housing had been developed earlier in Great Britain and examples still exist in towns such as Bath, England. Each house had a decorative garden in front of

Image 18

Second Floor Front Sitting Room of Joseph Sorger's Residence at 1624 Summer Street

Note the Octagonal table, attributed to Cook and Parkin. The Grecian couch behind this, attributed to Quervelle, has open Anthemion pedals above the lion claw feet. Photo and Historical Information Courtesy of Mr. Joseph Sorger

it and six-foot-wide ascending marble steps with elaborate iron work, including railings. The interior of 1624 Summer Street is illustrated in this chapter (Images 18 and 19), as well as the period furnishings of Joseph Sorger, owner of the property. The 1624 home is also of interest due to a middle-aged female apparition which appeared periodically over many years in the second floor hallway. Joseph Sorger struggled for years to preserve this historically significant row of classical homes, but the city of Philadelphia ultimately approved their demolition to make way for a modern development that was never completed.

Another public building important in establishing classical architecture in Philadelphia was the Odd Fellows Hall

Image 19
First Floor Front Parlor of Joseph Sorger's Residence at 1624 Summer Street

In the foreground is a monumental Quervelle bookcase.
Photo and Historical Information Courtesy of Mr. Joseph Sorger

Image 20
Odd Fellows Hall, Dedicated September 17, 1846, The Historical Society of Pennsylvania (HSP)

at Third and Brown Street. This was built in a combination of Greek and Egyptian motifs, wich included multiple anthemion carved circular Etruscan ornaments to the roof, rectangular columns with complex Greek and Egyptian inspired Capitals and elaborate cornice trim to the windows of the second floor. The first floor had a twelve foot ceiling, while the meeting hall above featured grand twenty-foot ceiling heights. The basement was finished with Egyptian columns and arches and was used as a speakeasy during the Prohibition (Image 20).

Philadelphians who lived in eighteenth century homes updated their interior furnishings during the classical period. An example of this is the Waynesboro homestead in Paoli, near Philadelphia. This building was originally constructed for Revolutionary War General "Mad" Anthony Wayne and was updated with classical furnishings in the 1820s. The photograph below was taken in the 1930s and shows both a Philadelphia classical dining room table and a Philadelphia sideboard. Cook and Parkin sold the sideboard to the Wayne family in August 1823. A copy of the Cook and Parkin invoice is still in the possession of the Waynesboro

Historical Society.

Outside of Philadelphia there are examples of American/Greek design. One of these is the Capitol Building in Washington, D.C., which was built over a period of forty years. Over six architects worked on the project, including Benjamin Latrobe, who was hired by President Thomas Jefferson in 1802. Jefferson saw the Capitol as the "first temple dedicated to the sovereignty of the people, embellishing with Athenian taste the cause of a nation looking far beyond the range of Athenian destinies."[35] For the Senate rotunda, Latrobe created delicate tobacco-leaf capitals for the Corinthian columns in the place of traditional Greek acanthus leaves and, with Jefferson, convinced Congress to appropriate funds to bring in talented stone masons from Italy.[36] The result is one of the most impressive structures in the country and an architectural prototype for many public buildings.

The White House in Washington, D.C. was originally designed on a plan based on Irish manor houses by the Irish-American architect James Hoban. The preliminary structure was modified by Benjamin Latrobe, who added classical elements, including porticos and pavilions. The White House had been extensively furnished in the Greek revival taste prior to its destruction by the British during the War of 1812. The British set fire and destroyed most of the original classical furniture. Andrew Jackson was among the presidents who re-introduced classical forms. He placed an order to Anthony Quervelle for a number of items, several of which are still in use at the White House (figures 6 and 107).

Image 21
Dining Room of Waynesboro

Photograph Circa 1930
A classical dining table is in the foreground. Beyond this is a Cook and Parkin Philadelphia Sideboard made in 1823.

[35] Sutton 33

[36] Sutton 33

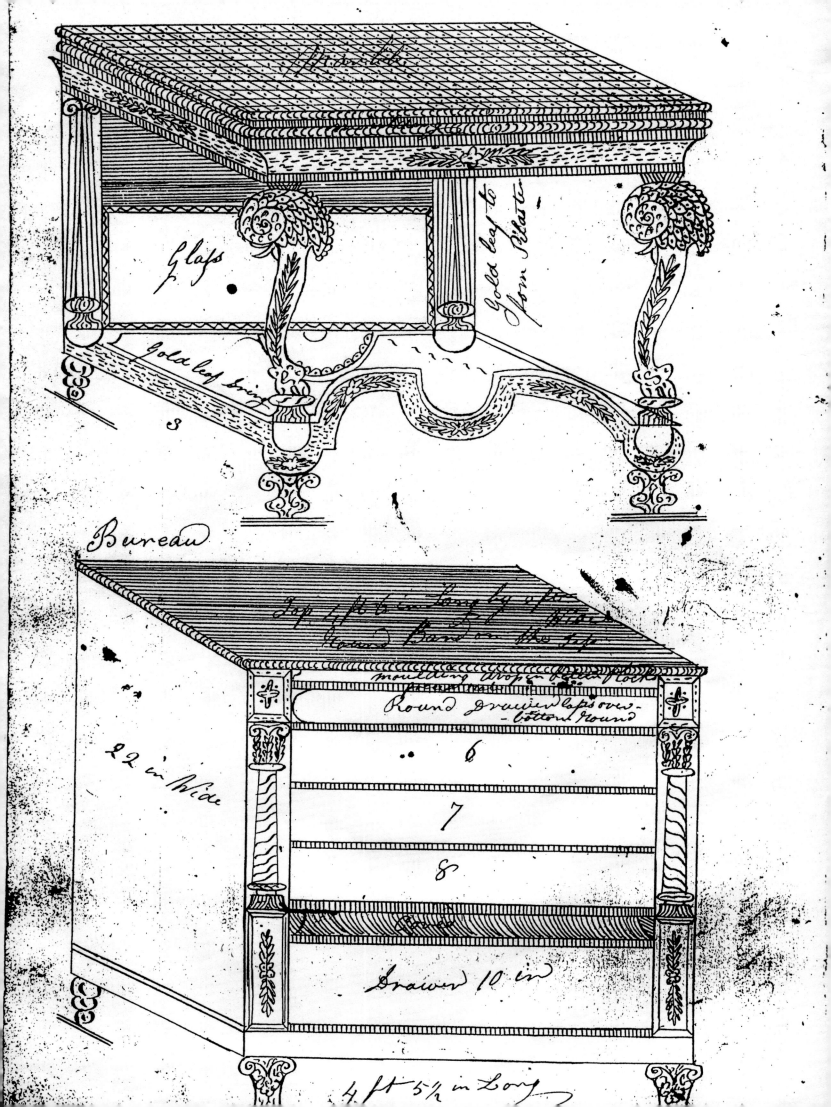

Marble

Glass

Gold leaf to form Pilaster

Gold leaf front

8

Bureau

Top 4 ft 6 in Long by 1 ft thick
round band on the top

moulding drop in gold flock

Round drawer laps over bottom round

22 in Wide

6

7

8

Drawer 10 in

4 ft 5½ in Long

CHAPTER 4
FURNITURE MAKERS

FURNITURE MAKERS

I. UNDERSTANDING PHILADELPHIA EMPIRE FURNITURE

The concepts of distinct periods in American furniture (i.e. Chippendale, Hepplewhite, Sheraton and

Empire) was somewhat arbitrary and created for convenience in cataloging and for identification.

Although the Chippendale period utilizes many Rococo elements that are not classical, the beginnings

of classicism (including elements such as the use of fluted quarter columns and urns with flame finials)

began to emerge during this time. The Hepplewhite period illustrated a further movement into

classicism with the elimination of Rococo elements and the movement to clean, linear forms derived from classical sculpture and monumental architecture. The Sheraton period further introduced elements from antiquity including reeding, brass hardware and the use of acanthus and other foliage carving. The so-called American Empire period followed and is actually the culmination of all these prior periods with the final introduction of fully expressive classical forms muted or only partially expressed in earlier eras. In this sense, the Empire period represents the culmination of the prior 100 years of American decorative arts style and represents the fullest expression of the emerging classical movement of decorative arts in America. In keeping with this definition, Empire or American classical furniture is the ultimate achievement of American decorative design and marks the high water mark in American decorative achievement prior to the onset of the machine age, changing the manufacture and regional expression of furniture forever. It is surprising that given these facts there is so little understanding or recognition of Empire furniture, especially that of Philadelphia. It is clearly recognized that

in the Chippendale period the finest furniture in the colonies was designed and manufactured in Philadelphia and this tradition continued during the classical age, despite challenges from New York and Boston.

In the classical period the contributions of New York makers, especially Duncan Phyfe and Charles Honoré Lannier, have overshadowed Philadelphia Empire furniture. Other than the articles in *The Magazine Antiques* by Robert Smith on Anthony Quervelle, and by Donald Fennimore and Robert Trump on Joseph Barry, little has been written to illustrate or illuminate this era of Philadelphia furniture making history. Much of the misunderstanding regarding Philadelphia Empire furniture stemmed from the work of pioneer authors of American decorative arts who did not focus on or understand Empire furniture and tended to criticize it on that basis. For example, Wallace Nutting notes:

> We are, of course, ready to admit that we do not regard the late Empire style as the highest type, nor even as a high type. This, however, can be said of it: the workmanship of the cabinetmakers was faithful, and the pieces held together. We should, perhaps, comfort ourselves that the decline of taste was not confined to America.[1]

This was the typical attitude of the early and mid-twentieth century collectors toward Empire furniture. Many older antique reference volumes contain photographs of ungainly, over-carved or even out-of-period Empire furniture pieces, which are particularly large, poorly proportioned or otherwise of little redeeming quality. These are labeled as typical examples of craftsmanship during the Empire period. It must be remembered that equally ugly, ungainly, poorly executed examples of baroque, rococo, and early Neo-Classical furniture also exist, which could as easily be put forth as examples of the poor overall decorative arts skills of those periods. This attitude towards Empire period reached its climax in the 1950s and 1960s, when many antique dealers were chopping up all sorts of American Empire furniture so that they could obtain the veneers for repairs of Chippendale and Hepplewhite pieces or to modify the pieces so that they then had the appearance of being earlier. Undoubtedly, many fine pieces of Philadelphia and other American Empire furniture met that fate based on a total lack of understanding of the intrinsic qualities or the importance of the forms. It is openly recognized that the quality of the mahogany and mahogany veneers is always the best in the American Empire period. A simple examination of the forms that are to be presented in this volume should also allow the reader to make their own judgment regarding the quality of the overall proportions and success of the design. In many ways Philadelphia Empire furniture is the apex of American furniture, with monumental forms which are a unique interpretation of antique classical prototypes. Various carving styles, including the plastic carving of the Quervelle School, as well as those of yet unidentified Philadelphia craftsmen illustrated herein, attest to work that rivals the best of the Philadelphia Chippendale period. The use of multiple techniques, including veneering, inlay, brass work, contrasting woods, gesso, paint decoration and carving are combined to create objects of timeless beauty that are at once both classical and Philadelphia/American. These objects are in fact the final achievement of a group of Philadelphia craftsmen which began in the Queen Anne period and that culminated in the Empire period and were then lost forever at the onset of the machine age with the loss of regional individualization of furniture forms in America. The authors are confident that the items illustrated in this volume will stand the test of time against other regional furniture of this period, not only in terms of form, but in terms of quality of materials, quality of carving, execution and of the overall success of the presentation of the piece. This volume is partially written to dispel the erroneous concepts based on earlier misinformation, lack of information or simple prejudice, which has led to a misunderstanding in certain circles regarding the true value of Philadelphia Empire furniture. Philadelphia Empire furniture is the ultimate expression of classicism in American furniture that will be apprectated with a better and more complete understanding of its development and expression.

II. IDENTIFICATION AND ATTRIBUTION OF PHILADELPHIA FURNITURE

The attribution of Philadelphia furniture to certain makers, especially Anthony Quervelle, is often made with no real basis or foundation in fact. This is especially true of pieces being sold at auctions or by private dealers who find the Quervelle attribution to be helpful in encouraging buyers to bid on mediocre pieces of late Empire furniture which otherwise would have little to lend themselves to the potential buyer. Any piece of furniture, Philadelphia or otherwise, that has an Empire appearance and a degree of carving, is labeled Anthony Quervelle or school of Anthony Quervelle, with no foundation for this other than the aspiration of the

[1] Wallace Nutting, *Furniture Treasury* (New York: Macmillan Publishing Co Inc., 1928) 997.

seller that this will increase the sale or auction price. Numerous dealers and museum curators have asked our staff to avoid the gratuitous attribution of particular pieces to particular makers, especially Quervelle, without any concrete foundation. An attempt has been made within this volume to comply with these requests.

In the case of case of Anthony Quervelle, special attention and effort has been placed on avoiding attributions to his shop unless certain specific criteria exist. Utilized to make attributions to Quervelle are the following: pieces known to be nearly identical to labeled Quervelle pieces may be considered to be attributed to Quervelle if multiple structural similarities exist to labeled Quervelle furniture. This similarity is not just in general stylistic form (i.e. the form of pedestals, etc, such as with acanthus carving, gadrooning, etc.), but must also include less variable details of construction, including details of interior drawer arrangements, or interior drawer dividers, or unique structural elements that have appeared consistently in labeled Quervelle pieces and that are unusual enough that they can be identified as relating to his shop. For example, the general appearance of a pedestal, a foot or other structural element as being in a Philadelphia or Quervelle manner is not criterion for attribution but is specifically excluded from criterion because these features are seen on many pieces of fine furniture made by a number of competent Philadelphia craftsmen. Many of these makers are currently unknown, but it is obvious that they also were capable of excellent work and in some cases produced forms that were of the same or even better caliber than Quervelle himself. The attributions of furniture to Joseph Barry follow the criterion set down by Donald Fennimore and Robert Trump in their pioneering articles regarding this maker; they identify forms with certain unusual characteristics that are attributed to Joseph Barry and Sons. In some cases this attribution may be less than totally accurate, as it is

obvious that other makers including William Camp in Baltimore and many unknown makers competed with and imitated Barry's work and in some cases were certainly talented enough to have duplicated or even exceeded the skills of that workshop.

This volume will introduce certain previously little known makers such as Charles White and Cook & Parkin, who also contributed materially to the production of high quality Philadelphia furniture in this period. Labeled examples of these makers, as well as other makers, will be introduced and hopefully serve as models for future attribution of pieces yet to be found. Certain stylistic features of these makers will emerge that appear characteristic of their workshops. The box sofas of Cook & Parkin, for example, utilize a complex, highly carved Chippendale shell at the top of the arms that is very similar to highly carved Chippendale shells on the finest Philadelphia highboys. In contrast to that, the shells noted on signed Joseph Barry and Charles White sofas have entirely different appearances. Other construction details also appear to have varied from shop to shop, making attribution to certain shops more accurate. Similar subtle distinctions in the turnings of the Roman type leg utilized on certain box sofas can also can help distinguish the makers, and this is discussed on the section on box sofas.

III. PHILADELPHIA FURNITURE MAKERS 1800-1835

The development of the classical style in America during the first several decades of the nineteenth century was based on popular French Empire and English Regency styles that combined ancient Greek, Egyptian, Etruscan and Roman motifs with forms designed to showcase the majestic style of the era. The war between these two countries brought many French cabinetmakers seeking asylum

Philadelphia, ready to facilitate the classical style in an undeveloped market. The Empire, or "style antique" as it was called, maintained greater historical accuracy to ancient classical designs and maintained a three-dimensional nature, rather than the two-dimensional quality of the Federal style. Often the carving of Empire furniture is described as having a certain plasticity, relating to the three-dimensional quality. By studying the remains of classical ruins, furniture makers were able to re-create ancient classical motifs and stimulate a new trade of fashionable furniture. The most prominent makers who contributed in introducing and popularizing the Empire style in Philadelphia were Joseph B. Barry, Joseph Beale, Michel Bouvier, Henry Connelly, Thomas Cook, David Fleetwood, Ephraim Haines, Isaac Jones, Richard Parkin, Walter Pennery, Isaac Pippit, Anthony Quervelle, Charles White and Thomas Whitecar. Many additional furniture makers worked in Philadelphia during the empire period. A detailed list of Philadelphia makers is available in the article "Philadelphia Furniture Makers 1816-1830" by Deborah Ducoff-Barone, *The Magazine Antiques*, May 1994, pages 742-755.

William Alexander

William Alexander is listed in Pittsburgh business directories from 1837 through 1844, although his shop was actually located in the suburb of Sharpsburg, Pennsylvania. He is known for a heavily carved Empire sideboard in mahogany, which is stamped in several places **Wm ALEXANDER**, Ref: Antiques, May 1983.[2] William Alexander, although he worked outside of Philadelphia, produced work that clearly was inspired by the heavily carved style of Anthony Quervelle's shop, demonstrating that cabinetmakers were influenced by and imitated each other's work. A pier table by William Alexander is illustrated as figure 112. William Alexander's stamp is illustrated in Image 22.

Joseph B. Barry (1759 or 1760-1838)

Joseph B. Barry, a native of Dublin, Ireland, trained in London before moving to Philadelphia in the 1790s. Barry first appears in the Philadelphia Directory in 1794, in partnership with cabinetmaker Alexander Calder at 75 Dock Street. The following year he is said to have joined one of Calder's competitor's, Lewis G. Affleck.[3] He continually moved shops until he was able to found his own at 134 South Second Street, where his son also worked.[4] After maintaining a successful business in Philadelphia, Barry decided to export his products to Savannah and Baltimore. He may have left for Savannah to escape the yellow fever epidemic of 1793. He advertised in a Savannah newspaper: "A most complex assortment of elegant and warranted well finished mahogany furniture."[5] Unfortunately, both his new shops were closed within a few months of opening. His Philadelphia shop remained his only furniture warehouse.

[2] William C. Ketchum Jr., *American Cabinetmakers Marked American Furniture 1640-1940* (New York: Crown Publishers Inc., 1995) 8.

[3] Donald Fennimore and Robert Trump, "Joseph B. Barry, Philadelphia Cabinetmaker," *The Magazine Antiques* May 1989: 1212.

[4] Fennimore and Trump 1213

[5] Ethel Hall Bjerkoe, *The Cabinetmakers of America*, (New York: Bonanza Books, 1957) 38.

Image 22

In 1811, he traveled to Europe to study and obtain materials for his stockroom. Upon his return on January 12 1812, he advertised in the Aurora General Advertiser that "during his stay in London and Paris, he made some selections of the Most Fashionable and Elegant Articles...which are well worth the attention of the respectable citizens of Philadelphia."[6] Barry was one of the earliest cabinetmakers of the time who advertised exotic styles of furniture and he declared he had in his "ware-rooms a variety of the newest and most fashionable Cabinet Furniture, superbly finished in the rich Egyptian and Gothic style, which he would dispose of on the most reasonable terms."[7]

His trip to Europe proved to be time well spent; he enjoyed a successful business for several years, producing high-quality beds, knife cases, chests of drawers, dining tables, secretaries, clocks and desks. It is believed that Barry maintained a partnership with carver William Rush, since some of Barry's pieces are ornamented with carved eagles, a feature of Rush's work.

Despite his success, Barry advertised in 1815 that he was retiring from cabinetmaking and selling his remaining furniture at discounted prices. Barry perhaps felt an inclination towards other business ventures, or simply wanted a break from his busy furniture trade. Whatever the reason, he later resumed his work and remained in the city Directories until 1833, five years before his death on February 22, 1838.[8]

Several distinct elements characterize work from Barry's shop, such as the carved motifs of acanthus leaves, fleur de lys, palmetto leaves, horizontal beehive reeding, eagles, dogs, lion's paw feet, female heads and serpents. Barry liked to use brass medallions, highlights and inlay, but the severe restraints on trade from 1807 to 1812 would have made it difficult for him to obtain brass articles from London and Paris and forced him to alter his style slightly and to incorporate carved decoration. Some forms can be traced from Thomas Sheraton's *The Cabinet-Maker*

and Upholsterer and General Artist's Encyclopedia, while others are a combination of English and American elements. A sideboard (figure 243) and a box sofa (figure 233), both signed, are illustrated in this volume. Joseph Barry was in partnership with Lewis Krickbaum shortly before his death in 1838. A sideboard by Barry and Krickbaum is illustrated in figure 264.

Joseph Beale

Joseph Beale was active as a cabinetmaker at 261 High Street from 1797-1807. He is known for at least two signed pieces of furniture, a mahogany and satinwood secretary desk pencil-signed on a drawer bottom "J. Beale", and a lyre-based worktable upon which the same name is branded.[9] The lyre-based worktable stamped by Beale is pictured as figure 123 in this volume.

Michel Bouvier

Michel Bouvier was born was born in March 1792 at Pont Saint Esprit, an old town in the Languedoc country on the Rhone River. He trained in France and came to work in Philadelphia as a cabinetmaker in 1815. Bouvier was one of the few craftsmen able to successfully make the transition from small-scale furniture shop to a large factory producing warehouse without having the standard of his furniture go down in quality.[10] After having served an apprenticeship in France, as well as having served in the army of Napoleon, Bouvier sailed from Bordeaux and landed in New York on August 6, 1815, at the age of twenty-three.[11] He traveled to Philadelphia, where he began to establish himself as a cabinetmaker. The location where he initially began his work is unknown.

It is apparent that Bouvier maintained excellent craftsmanship; Joseph Bonaparte chose him to furnish his estate at Point Breeze, New Jersey from 1818-1820. To have received a furniture order by a man of such high social stature, Bouvier

[6] Fennimore and Trump 1214

[7] Fennimore and Trump 1214

[8] Fennimore and Trump 1213

[9] William C. Ketchum Jr. 30

[10] Francis J. Dallett, "Michel Bouvier, Franco-American cabinetmaker," *The Magazine Antiques* Feb. 1962: 198.

[11] Dallett 198

Image 23
M. Bouvier stencil label
This is from the sideboard illustrated in figure 258.

must have been well on his way to owning and maintaining a successful business. This was supported by the Philadelphia Directories, which lists him in 1819 as a cabinetmaker who kept shop at the southeast corner of Fifth and Walnut Streets, diagonally across from Independence Square.[12] It is likely then that most of the furniture that Bouvier supplied to Joseph Bonaparte was produced in this shop. He remained at this address until 1823, when he married Sarah Ann Pearson, stepdaughter of William Goodfellow, a Scots-born clockmaker for whom Bouvier may have made clock cases.[13]

After furnishing Joseph Bonaparte's Point Breeze estate, Bouvier apparently went on to do some work for Stephen Girard, the Philadelphia shipping merchant financier. Only minor repair work has been documented as being done by Bouvier for Girard. Given that Girard died in 1831, Bouvier may only have been commissioned for small items, since no record exists to prove otherwise.

In 1825, Bouvier had opened his own steam mill, where imported Italian marble was cut to make bureau and table tops for the mahogany furniture produced in his shop.[14] His wholesale marble and mahogany importing business became the largest supplier in the city and Bouvier became quite

wealthy from both this and cabinetmaking. His new warehouse, which advertised mainly sofas and chairs, was located at 91 South Second Street. It was here that Bouvier produced most of his furniture ware including tables, bureaus, knife boxes, sofas and lounges. Despite his apparent production of furniture types, labeled pieces of Bouvier are rare today. It is unclear whether the Frenchman chose not to mark much of his furniture or whether his actual output of finished pieces was much lower than historical references might suggest.

There is no doubt that Bouvier took much of his inspiration from French design sources, but there has also been some speculation that he may have also used English designs, as Don Fennimore points out in his article in *Antiques Magazine* in 1973. The Bouvier card table illustrated in that article appears to be closely related to Plate 72 of Peter and Michael Angelo Nicholson's *The Practical Cabinet Maker, Upholsterer and Complete Decorator*, which illustrates a similar card table except for its extensive use of light-color figured-maple veneers and ebonized feet, which were favored by French cabinetmakers during the first two decades of the nineteenth century.[15]

One of the traits that Bouvier is famous for is the extensive use of veneers in the making of furniture. Bouvier handled veneer with special care and often would use one single piece of veneer for a form, which would be joined so that the grains perfectly connected, making the entire piece stand out for its composition.[16] Even with the amount of time invested for the attention to detail in his work, it is clear from reading Bouvier's advertisements in 1832 that furniture producing was not his main enterprise anymore. Although he continued to produce furniture, he was concentrating more on wholesale selling and buying of mahogany logs, boards and veneers. After 1839, Bouvier only advertises mahogany and marble.

[12] Dallett 199

[13] Dallett 199

[14] Dallett 199

[15] Donald L. Fennimore, "A labeled card table by Michel Bouvier," *The Magazine Antiques* Apr. 1973: 760, 761.

[16] Fennimore 760-761

Although pieces of furniture have been identified as being made by Bouvier in the 1840s, they may have been the last pieces ordered, perhaps by special favor of Bouvier. By 1844 his firm was M. Bouvier & Co., and it remained as such until its dissolution about 1861.[17]

In 1848, Bouvier took on another investment and purchased the Mansion House Hotel Site on Third Street, which had been a very impressive building until it was ravaged by fire in 1823 and 1847. Bouvier had the building demolished and in its place three brownstone houses were built, the middle one used as his own residence for four years, at 260 South Third Street.[18] These houses still exist in Philadelphia today.

Up until his death on June 9, 1874, Bouvier devoted his time to his family, the French Benevolent Society (of which he was the president at the time of his death), and to numerous Catholic churches and charities.[19] Always the businessman, he died a wealthy man and left behind a legacy of real estate and furniture, which his descendants have been able to enjoy over the years. One of his more famous descendants was Mrs. John F. Kennedy, the former Jacqueline Bouvier. She was the great-great-granddaughter of Michel Bouvier.[20] A stenciled Bouvier card table (figure 87) and sideboard (figure 258) are illustrated in this volume. This stencil is illustrated as image 23.

Henry Connelly

Henry Connelly began his career as a cabinet and chair maker in Newville, Pennsylvania, located 127 miles from Philadelphia, a mere village in 1790 with only forty-one houses and a population around three hundred.[21] Born of humble beginnings, Connelly became one of the most prosperous cabinetmakers in the business. By the time he opened up his shop at 16 Chestnut Street in 1801 in Philadelphia, his list of clientele included Stephen Girard, the Quaker banker, Henry Hollingsworth, and Captain John Carson, commander of the ship *Pennsylvania Packet*.[22]

His rise to the top was not easy and he had much competition to overcome in Newville, including his once-partner, John Peebles. Connelly and Peebles may have known each other growing up, since the town of Newville is close to both of their relatives' homes. It is not documented when their partnership began, but Peebles announced in the March 23rd, 1796 issue of *Kline's Carlisle Weekly Gazette* that "Whereas the partnership of John Peebles and Henry Connelly, Cabinetmakers, is this day, by mutual consent, dissolved."[23] After the partnership was terminated, Connelly immediately went into business with John Bratton of Newville and the notice appeared in the same issue of the newspaper, directly under Peebles's, stating: "Henry Connelly, late a partner of Mr. John Peebles, informs his friends and the public in general, that he has entered into a partnership with John Bratton of Newville, where they intend to carry on Cabinet and Chair Making Business in all its various branches, and hopes by a steady attention and the excellence of their work to merit the patronage of a generous public."[24]

Shortly after the dissolution of the two partners, Peebles's cabinetmaking shop was set on fire and Peebles's claimed during a deposition that "he has reason to suspect, and does suspect, Henry Connelly and John Fox (or some persons actually employed by aforesaid Connelly or Fox) of setting it on fire."[25] The case was dropped and Peebles moved to Shippensburg, where he opened a shop. Connelly may not have felt comfortable in the town after the incident and left as well, around 1797. Connelly disappeared to an unknown location (perhaps Delaware where his wife was from). In 1801, he had opened up his own shop at 16 Chestnut Street in Philadelphia.[26]

Connelly's early work in Philadelphia

[17] Dallett 200

[18] Dallett 200

[19] Dallett 200

[20] Dallett 200

[21] Dallett 200

[22] Scribner Schaumann, Merri Lou, "Henry Connelly, Cabinetmaker…," *Cumberland Co. Historical Society Journal*, (1996).

[23] Sribner Schaumann 93

[24] Sribner Schaumann 94

[25] Sribner Schaumann 94

was in the Sheraton style, with chairs and sofas that featured acanthus carvings and "delicately tapered and reeded" legs that ended with a spade foot.[27] Connelly's style evolved over the years to include classical elements. Some of his pieces can be traced back to published designs by Thomas Sheraton. Connelly's most famous clients include Stephen Girard, Henry Hollingsworth, and Captain John Carson.

In 1806, Connelly made a sideboard in the Sheraton style for the Hollingsworth family that is now in the Philadelphia Museum of Art, an example of his work early in the period. Connelly produced a variety of furniture in the Sheraton style including worktables, dressing tables and washstands in the latest designs of the time. It is apparent that Connelly was influenced by English designers. As he approached retirement in 1824, his furniture had become remarkably classical and refined in design.

In 1818, Connelly made a pair of card tables for Stephen Girard with lyre-shaped pedestals formed by dolphins, with four curved fluted legs ending in brass paw feet, and a cross band of light wood surrounding the mahogany base.[28] This table is important because it shows Connelly's use of inlay and brass paw-footed furniture.[29] One of this pair is illustrated in figure 67.

Connelly's work is similar to that of his contemporary, Ephraim Haines, who also made furniture for Stephen Girard and Henry Hollingsworth. In 1811, Haines declined Girard's business in order to run his successful mahogany yard and Connelly took over producing furniture for him.[30] Haines and Connelly both worked from English patterns, each with slight alterations that made their work original. One distinction of Connelly's work is the round spade foot, whereas Haines preferred to use a bulb above a long turned terminal.[31] Other elements typical of Connelly include the bulbous knee and the tapered or reeded leg.

It is difficult to attribute pieces without labels to either maker, since their work seemed to be of equal craftsmanship with several similarities in appearance and form. Any cabinetmaker in Philadelphia at the time would have access to the same designs and materials and it is always possible that any unlabeled piece could have been made by one of the hundreds of cabinetmakers that had established shops in Philadelphia at this time.

Thomas Cook & Richard Parkin

Cook & Parkin were chair and cabinetmakers registered at 58 Walnut Street in Philadelphia, between Park and Third Streets on the South Side, and listed as working together from 1820-1825.[32]

Information about their careers is limited and few documented or marked examples exist. In 1811, Richard Parkin was one of the three cabinetmakers responsible for and listed in the front of the *Philadelphia Book of Prices* indicating that he was well established as a cabinetmaker by that time. The earliest known piece by the firm is an important sideboard in the collection of the Baltimore Museum of Art bearing the firm's label and dating, presumably, to 1820-1825. Inspired by a design in Thomas Hope's 1807 *Household Furniture*, it is pictured in Wendy A. Cooper's *Classical Taste in America 1800-1840* (Baltimore Museum of Art, 1993), page 56. A "plain style" labeled linen press, in a private collection in Natchez, dating from 1825-1830, indicates that the cabinetmakers worked together into the early 1830s.[33] Support for this theory is provided by documentation that the firm retailed a sofa table made by the Baltimore cabinetmaker David Bodensick (w. 1833-1860) to clients in Natchez, Mississippi about 1833. Several labeled pieces of Cook & Parkin furniture are illustrated in this volume including two marble top center tables (figures 10 and 11) and a box sofa (figure 234).

"Plain style", inspired by the flat architectural surfaces of Greek antiquity and the styling of the French Restoration (*French Restauration*), became prevalent in

[26] Sribner Schaumann 94

[27] Sribner Schaumann 94

[28] Marian S. Carson, "Sheraton's Influence in Philadelphia," *Philadelphia Furniture and its Makers*, Ed. John J. Snyder (New York: Main Street Universe Books, 1975) 87.

[29] Marian S. Carson 87

[30] Marian S. Carson 87

[31] Bjerkoe 69

[32] William C. Ketchum Jr. 83

[33] Jason T. Busch, "Furniture Patronage in Antebellum Natchez," *The Magazine Antiques* May 2000: 804-813.

the United States about 1830. The firm of Cook & Parkin was an early proponent of it and evidently was involved in its spread to other American cities through consignments to retailers and auction houses located particularly in the South. An example of this is the Thomas Cook table illustrated as figure 43 in this text. Cook and Parkin continued in the cabinetmaking business separately and together until 1840. From 1831-1835 Parkin worked alone at 94 South Third Street. From 1835-1840, he was located at Egyptian Hall, 134 South Second Street, a building he appears to have leased from cabinetmaker Joseph Barry.[34] A set of very high style side chairs inspired by chairs by Georges Jacob and published in Pierre de la Mesangere's *Collection de Muebles et Objets de Gout*, bearing the paper label of Richard Parkin at the Egyptian Hall address is in the collection of the Landis Valley Farm Museum. A set of eight identical chairs to these, probably part of the Landis Valley Museum set, are in a private collection in Texas.[35] A pair of these chairs are seen as figure 166 in this volume. A rectangular black marble "Egyptian" center table bearing a blue calling card of Richard Parkin is pictured as figure 27 and 27a.

John Davey & John Davey Jr.

John Davey is listed in the Philadelphia Directories throughout the period 1797-1822 (primarily at 12 Christian Street); the cabinetmaker is known for only a single secretary bookcase, illustrated in figure 271, in mahogany, inlaid with satinwood and oval mirrors, and which has several penciled inscriptions:

John Davey, three times: John Davey, Philadelphia, three times: John Davey, Maker, and John Davey Jr., and John Davey, Jr. Philadelphia.[36] John Davey Jr. was likely an apprentice to his father, who assisted him with work on this secretary.

David Fleetwood

David Fleetwood worked in Philadelphia as a cabinetmaker from 1830-1840. He is known to have produced a number of finely crafted dressing tables in the Empire taste during the period. There is a labeled box sofa by David Fleetwood, illustrated in figure 238, as well as a labeled card table illustrated in figure 90. David Fleetwood's calling card, found on the box sofa in figure 238, is illustrated below as image 24.

[34] Wendy A. Cooper, *Classical Taste in America* 1800-1840 (Baltimore Museum of Art, 1993) 270.

[35] Description of Cook & Parkin courtesy of Mr. Carswell Rush Berlin.

[36] William C. Ketchum Jr. 90

Image 24
David Fleetwood, Calling Card

Ephraim Haines
(1775-1837)

Ephraim Haines began his career in 1791, as an apprentice to Daniel Trotter of Philadelphia, and by 1799 he had become his partner and son-in-law, after marrying Trotter's twenty-one year old daughter Elizabeth.[37] After Trotter's death, Haines informed the public through an advertisement that he would continue the business on his own. In 1804, he was listed in the Philadelphia directories as the proprietor of a lumberyard, and from 1806-1813 as the owner of a cabinet warehouse.[38]

Haines made "pretzel back" chairs that resemble a ladder-back type. One identifiably unique feature of Haines is the swelled bulb foot, which came after his earlier work in a Chippendale style with a claw-and-ball foot.[39] In 1806 and 1807, he supplied Stephen Girard with a field bedstead and a set of black ebony furniture including a chair-back settee, ten matching chairs and two armchairs at a cost of $500.[40] He was listed again in the Philadelphia directories in 1813 at a new home and shop address and was described as a lumber merchant until 1833. Whether or not he gave up cabinetmaking to become a lumber merchant is unclear, it is peculiar that the inventory of his estate in 1837 gives no indication of his occupation as a cabinetmaker.[41]

The Ephraim Haines ebony settee (figure 150) and ebony chair (figure 148) purchased by Stephen Girard on November 27, 1807 are illustrated of this volume.

Isaac Jones

Isaac Jones was a cabinetmaker listed in the Philadelphia Directories from 1818-1840: 1818, 4 Perkinpine Ct.; 1819, 25 Brewer's Alley; 1820, 77 N. Front Street; 1825, 77 N. Front St., h. Smith's Ct.; 1828, 77 N. Front St., h.Smith's Ct.; 1829, 59 and 77 N. Front Street, h.3 Elfreth's Alley; 1830, 75 and 77 N. Front Street.[42] A sideboard Jones made is illustrated in figure 257, as is a bed attributed to him in figure

330. A bedroom set (figure 330) that includes a secretary desk (figure 284) from his shop is illustrated in this volume. From these pieces it can be inferred that Isaac Jones was a master craftsman with detailed knowledge of form, carving and gilding.

John Mitchell

Chair maker from 1816-1819 listed at 76 South Fourth Street, Philadelphia. A painted chair Mitchell made for Steven Girard is pictured as figure 195 in this text.

Walter Pennery

Pennery is believed to have been an apprentice or journeyman cabinetmaker working, c. 1820-1830, for the Philadelphia cabinetmaker John Jamison. Ref: *Antiques*, May 1994.[43] A dressing bureau by Walter Pennery is illustrated in figure 306.

Isaac Pippit

Isaac Pippit is listed in the Philadelphia directories as a cabinetmaker, 1820-1833. The locations of his shop are listed below.

1820, 71 Walnut Street; 1823 [and chairmaker] 71 Walnut Steet; 1825, 71 Walnut Street; 82 Dock Street 1826-27, 71 Walnut St.; 1828, 148 Spruce Street; 1829, 148 Spruce St., h. cor. Catharine and S. Fourth sts.; 1830, cor. Spruce and S. Third sts. Employment for 4-5 journeymen cabinetmakers (RPG, April 21, 1820). Furniture stock sold cheap (FJ, Feb. 17 and March 2, 1825). Notice of insolvency (FJ, Aug. 4, 1825). Employment for 4 journeymen cabinetmakers, will pay Pennsylvania Society of Journeymen Cabinetmakers prices (FJ, April 26, 1826). Freeman auction notice, list of furniture stock (NG, July 2, 1827).[44]

A classical carved mahogany card table, offered at Sotheby's, January 28-31, 1994, is labeled

ISAAC PIPPITT/CABINET & CHAIR MAKER/ No. 71 Walnut St. below 3d.St./On the Nth Side—All Orders Thankfully/Received and Punctually Attended To[45]

[37] Ethel Hall Bjerkoe 119

[38] Milo M. Naeve, "Daniel Trotter and his ladder-back chairs," *Philadelphia Furniture and its Makers*, Ed. John Snyder (New York: Main Street Universe Books, 1975) 81.

[39] Bjerkoe 119

[40] Bjerkoe 119

[41] Naeve 81

[42] Deborah Ducoff-Barone, "Philadelphia Furniture Makers 1816-1830," *The Magazine Antiques* May 1994: 742-755.

[43] William C. Ketchum Jr. 258

[44] Deborah Ducoff-Barone 751 (All information on Pippit)

[45] William C. Ketchum Jr. 262

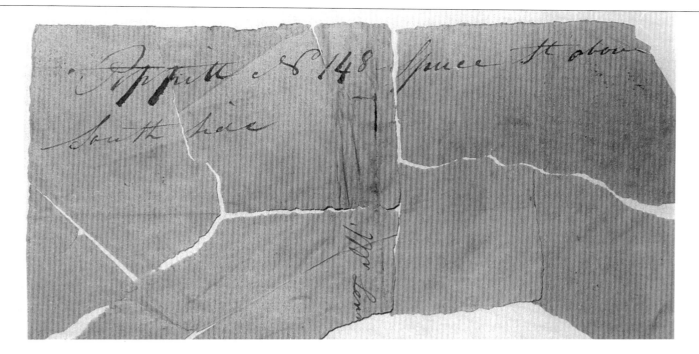

The Isaac Pippitt cornucopia sofa with accompanying Pippitt invoice is illustrated in the sofa chapter of this volume (figure 220 and image 25).

Anthony Quervelle

Anthony Quervelle is renowned as one of the most brilliant and influential cabinetmakers of the Empire period in Philadelphia. In accordance with his gravestone in Old St. Mary's Catholic cemetery in Philadelphia, Quervelle was born in Paris in 1789.[46] It is possible he was from a family of cabinetmakers, since there was a Jean-Claude Quervelle who worked at Versailles, but this is only speculation. The reasons for his coming to Philadelphia are unknown, but it is possible that Quervelle was disillusioned with his country after the fall of Napoleon. Quervelle was known to own several portraits of Napoleon and was clearly an admirer of his, thus he may have been distraught over the collapse of his Napoleon's empire.

The earliest legal documentation proving he lived in Philadelphia was his wedding certificate recorded by Old St. Joseph's Roman Catholic Church, on January 30, 1817, when he married Louise Genevieve Monet.[47]

He was first listed as a cabinetmaker in 1820, and quickly moved to legitimize his status from émigré to citizen of the United States in 1823. His furniture warehouse was opened at 126 South Second Street and was called the *United States Fashionable Cabinet Ware House or Cabinet and Sofa Manufactory.* Like many artisans of the time period in Philadelphia, Quervelle lived at his shop until 1849, when he apparently moved to 71 Lombard Street.

Proof of Quervelle's popularity and role in developing the taste of the period can be shown by the annual reports of the Franklin Institute, where, in the exhibition of 1825, he displayed two pier tables that won him an honorable mention.[48] Quervelle went on to receive many awards for various forms, including a "sideboard with a marble top" that was awarded a bronze metal in 1826. The year after that he earned the silver metal for the best "cabinet book case and secretary" that was judged a "splendid piece of furniture from the establishment of this excellent workman."[49] Quervelle made quite a reputation for himself and produced many forms of expertly carved furniture including ladies' worktables, sofas and sideboards, with the help of several assistants.

When President Andrew Jackson began furnishing the East Room of the White House in 1829, he employed Quervelle to design tables for it. The center and pier tables that Quervelle provided were in perfect harmony with the ornamental

Image 25
Isaac Pippit invoice

[46] Robert Smith, "Philadelphia Empire furniture by Antoine Gabriel Quervelle," *The Magazine Antiques* Sept. 1964: 304.

[47] Smith, Phil. Empire 305

[48] Smith, Phil. Empire 305

[49] Smith, Phil. Empire 305

decor supplied by Louis Veron's firm (one Quervelle pier table, illustrated in figure 107, is still at the White House, as is a marble top center table illustrated as figure 6 in this text). Veron, another French émigré, was believed to have recommended Quervelle for the job, but by then President Jackson may have already known him by reputation. After completing the set of tables, Quervelle advertised in 1830 that "he had been employed as well by some of the first individuals of the city as by the general government" and he thanked "his friends and the public, for the liberal patronage they have extended to his establishment," urging them to come inspect his "complete assortment of plain and elegantly ornamented Mantel and Cabinet Furniture."[50] His shop sold everything from bureaus, sofas, sideboards and washstands to breakfast, dining and center tables. He received orders from outside Philadelphia as well, advertising in 1830 that "orders from any part of the Union will be promptly executed on the most reasonable of terms and gratefully received."[51]

Quervelle maintained a busy patronage with citizens of Philadelphia and around the country. Today, a number of labeled pieces of his work can be found. Throughout the years, several labeled pieces have been located. From examining these, attributions to others can be made, but with a great deal of apprehension since most of the makers listed here influenced each other in one way or another.

The labeled and documented Quervelle furniture is made chiefly of mahogany and is expertly and authoritatively carved. His style can be identified in several characteristic elements of his work, which include the following: the use of gadrooning to decorate prominent moldings in several places on each piece, a variety of vase and urn forms that are often enriched with reeding and gadrooning, the use of a fan-shape panel on the front of a desk or top of a table, and the combination of scrolls, acanthus leaves and grapevines into a single opulent decorative manner.[52] Quervelle is known to have identified his work in four different ways.

1. CALLING CARD LABEL, EARLY 1820s

A calling card of Anthony Quervelle has been found on several card tables which exhibit saber legs and gadrooned foliage decorated urns. The style of these tables suggests that they were early products of Quervelle's shop, and this calling card may represent his earliest period of work in Philadelphia during the early 1820s. This calling card is illustrated as image 26 and reads:

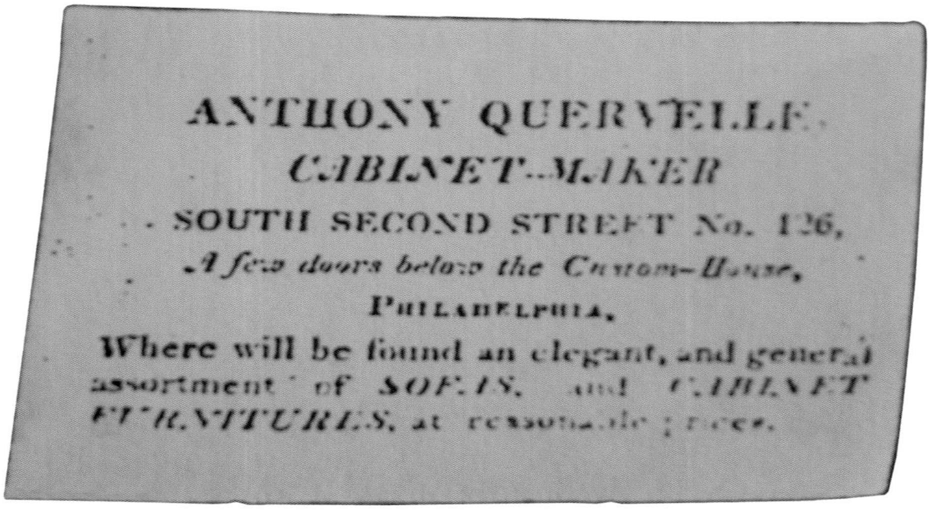

ANTHONY QUERVELLE
Cabinet-Maker
SOUTH SECOND STREET NO. 126
A few doors below the Custom-House,
Philadelphia
Where will be found an elegant, and general assortment of SOFAS, and CABINET FURNITURES, at reasonable prices.

2. DRESSING GLASS LABEL,

Image 26

[50] Smith, Phil. Empire 306
[51] Smith, Phil. Empire 306
[52] Smith, Phil. Empire 307

APPROXIMATELY 1825-1829

This label, which shows a large dressing glass with the number 126 reflected in the mirror, appears to be in use in the latter 1820s. The labeled Quervelle desk bookcase (figure 282) at the Philadelphia Museum of Art, exhibited at the Franklin Institute in 1826 and the closely related desk bookcase (figure 281) from the Munson-Williams-Proctor Institute both utilize this type of label. A breakfast table with the Quervelle dressing glass label is illustrated in this volume as figure 57. This stylistically appears to relate to the 1825-1829 period. See image 27.

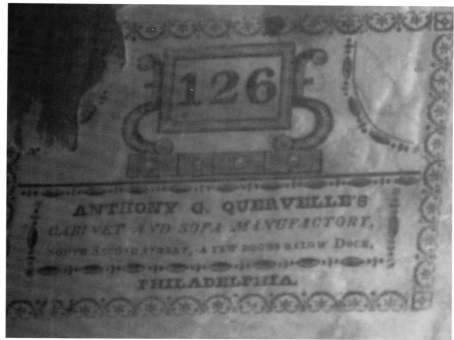

Image 27

126
ANTHONY G. QUERVELLE'S
CABINET AND SOFA MANUFACTORY,
South Second street, a few doors below Dock
PHILADELPHIA

3. DELMES LABEL, APPROXIMATELY 1830-1835

This elaborate dolphin-decorated dressing table label is signed at the base of the table by the engraver, Delmes. This label is found on multiple pieces of Quervelle furniture at Rosedown Plantation, St. Francisville, Louisiana (lounge figure 230, secretary bookcase figure 283, and wardrobe figure 317). The invoice for those pieces of furniture is dated August 1835. The Delmes-labeled worktable illustrated in this volume (figure 129) was exhibited at the Franklin Institute in 1831. These dates form a rough basis for creating a timeline for this label. See image 28.

Image 28

A.G. QUERVELLE./United States/Fashionable/CABINET WARE HOUSE./No. 126./South Second Street/Below Dock./PHILADELPHIA

4. STENCIL OF ANTHONY QUERVELLE, APPROXIMATELY 1835-1845

This stencil label has been identified as being Quervelle's last from the period of 1835-1845.[53] A worktable with this stencil is illustrated in figure 138. See image 29.

ANTHONY G. QUERVELLE'S/CABINET
& SOFA /Manufactory/126 So.2d
Street/PHILADA/

It is apparent Quervelle's shop produced an extremely attractive and much sought-after style of the period. Most of the furniture was based on fashionable English forms that by 1825-1830 were current in America and which in Philadelphia, according to the Journal of the Franklin Institute for 1830, varied little from year to year.[54] Quervelle's designs are similar to those published in George Smith's *Cabinet Maker and Upholsterer's Guide*, but with definite stylistic differences, the most important being the heaviness that each piece exuded. English Regency pieces were more chaste in design and did not have the same heaviness, as it was thought of as impractical for everyday life. Quervelle apparently disagreed because his interpretation of the style included massive, heavy forms that were often complemented with

two or three of his above characteristic elements.

Smith illustrated many plates that Quervelle made use of, such as the designs for pier tables involving grape carving (plate LXIV), the constant use of gadrooning (plates X, XLII, LV, LXXI, LXXIV and CXIX), the use of frilled shells and dolphins (plate CXV), and the outspreading acanthus carving (plate XVIII).[55] Quervelle often interpreted these plates into new designs such as combined bases with plinths and columnar shafts, geometric ornament and grandiose fanlike forms of convex veneering, and lion's paw feet that seem to come to life with expert carving and attention to detail.[56]

Much of Quervelle's work has both English Regency and French Empire features, the combination of which accounts for a unique style that is present in the work of other Philadelphia makers of the period. The elements of French, English and American workmanship were deftly incorporated into each piece of furniture, making them distinctly Philadelphia. It is not surprising from the quality of the furniture he produced, as well as other business ventures he was involved with, that he died a wealthy man.

[53] William C. Ketchum Jr. 272

[54] Smith, Phil. Empire 309

[55] Smith, Phil. Empire 309

[56] Smith, Phil. Empire 309

MICRO-CARVING

In the course of evaluating Quervelle attributed furniture, a certain unusual feature has become evident. There is a consistent use of very small decorative carving at central points on certain furniture forms. This carving will be referred to as "micro-carving" because the carving is of such small size that one must be very close to the piece to recognize and appreciate it. Sketches 4 and 7 of the Quervelle sketch book (chapter 5 of this volume) illustrate a worktable which exhibits a micro-carved shell between the front legs and a sideboard with a micro-carved fan at the base of the pilaster. It is therefore proven that Quervelle employed this design motif, which in itself is somewhat unusual. This does not mean that other makers did not use micro-carving, but all four of the identified pieces in this volume have multiple other characteristics which strongly connect them to a carver associated with Quervelle's shop. This strengthens the theory that micro-carving appears to have been a feature of workmanship from Philadelphia and especially his establishment. The size of micro-carved elements varies from one to two-and-a-half inches. These micro-carved elements are illustrated below along with the figure numbers for the furniture forms on which they were found (See images 30, 31, 32 and 33). The presence of micro-carving on an otherwise unidentified piece of furniture may be suggestive of a Philadelphia origin. This decorative device is most closely associated with Quervelle's shop, but was also occasionally utilized by other Philadelphia cabinetmakers as well.

Lawrence Sink

Philadelphia cabinetmaker 1816-1823. Located at 186 South Second Street. His usual label illustrates a sideboard with his name and address below. A library table attributed to Lawrence Sink is illustrated as figure 73 in this text.

Image 30
Detail of Figure 134
Size 1"

Image 31
Detail of Figure 251
Size 1 3/4"

Image 32
Detail of Figure 249
Size 2 1/2"

Image 33
Detail of Figure 360
Size 1 7/8"

Charles White

From labeled pieces of furniture dating from 1824-1830, it is known that Charles White operated in a cabinetmaking shop at 109 Walnut Street in Philadelphia.[57] During the years 1828-1851, he maintained a partnership with his brother, John Ferris White. The label of their furniture read: C.H. & J.F. White/ Cabinet Warehouse, No. 107 & 109 Walnut Street, Philadelphia.[58] Charles White worked alone again at No. 250 Chestnut Street from 1850-1860, and a Victorian Rococo Revival carved rosewood armchair in the Ebenezer Maxwell Mansion in Philadelphia bears this label.[59] His calling card is illustrated as image 34.

Image 34
Calling card of Charles and John White from worktable, figure 139.

[57] William C. Ketchum Jr. 364

[58] William C. Ketchum Jr. 364

[59] William C. Ketchum Jr. 364

Image 35
Stencil of Charles and John White from box sofa, figure 236.

Thomas Whitecar

Thomas Whitecar was a chairmaker in Philadelphia, 1823-1824. In 1823 he worked at 209 S. Front Street; 1824 at 106 Lombard Street.[60] Whitecar is believed to have produced side chairs of excellent quality with a unique amebic central oval design on the splats. Whitecar made this type of chair for exportation and sets have been found in Virginia and Rhode Island.[61] Examples of the Whitecar pattern can be seen in the chairs section, figures 157 through 161. In 1809, Thomas Whitecar supplied Lydia Poultney, of Philadelphia, with a large suite of furniture for which the invoice still exists. A card table (figure 75), a side chair (figure 157), a sofa (figure 209), and a wash stand (figure 363) from the suite are pictured in this text. His stencil is illustrated in image 35.

[60] Deborah Ducoff-Barone 755

[61] Garvin 71

IV. The European Basis for Philadelphia Decorative Design

Cabinetmakers in Philadelphia and other American cities were inspired by reference design books published in England and on the continent. Examples of these include Ackermann's *Regency Furniture and Interiors*, Thomas Sheraton's *Cabinet-Maker and Upholsterer's Drawing Book*, London 1802, William Smee & Sons' *Designs of furniture* and George Smith's *Collection of Designs for Household Furniture*, London 1808. These and other European drawing books served as references for American cabinetmakers eager to adapt the latest in European fashion. The Philadelphia cabinet shops then used these patterns as a basis for their own creative adaptations which were to become uniquely regional and Philadelphia in character. As is clear from the Quervelle sketches presented in the next chapter, Philadelphia makers created entirely new forms which at times had little resemblance to their European prototypes. In many cases the Philadelphia forms were as good, or better, than the original English and continental designs. This continued a trend in independent thinking among Philadelphia cabinetmakers that had been in place since the founding of Philadelphia. Earlier makers of Chippendale furniture such as Thomas Affleck had extensively modified English prototypes to the point that their American counterparts were distinctive furniture design forms that differed significantly from that of the English originals. This same Philadelphia creative genius was at work in the shops of the Philadelphia Empire period. Many of the pieces seen in this volume appear uniquely different from their English predecessors. This modification of English furniture design is not always extensive. Other examples of Philadelphia Empire furniture closely follow English design prototypes. Illustrated examples that follow should clarify this further.

DRESSING CHESTS

The elliptical fronted bureau from Thomas Sheraton's *Cabinet-Maker and Upholsterer's Drawing Book* (above) and Philadelphia elliptical bureau, School of Joseph Barry (figure 292)(below).

Image 36

Thomas Sheraton, *Appendix to the cabinet-maker and upholsterer's drawing book,* London, 1802, partial plate 15. Courtesy, Winterthur Library: Printed Book and Periodical Collection

Image 37

CELLARETTES

The upper cellarette in the English print is compared here to the attributed Quervelle cellarette with fan, image 39 next page (see figure 360). The lower cellarette in the print is compared with the attributed Barry cellarette on lions, image 40 next page (see figure 358).

Image 38
Charles F. Montgomery and Benno M. Forman, ed., *George Smith's Collection of Designs,* London 1806 (republished New York: Praeger, 1970) plate 98.
Courtesy, The Winterthur Library: Printed Book and Periodical Collection

Image 39
Cellarette attributed to
Anthony G. Quervelle
(See figure 360)

Image 40
Cellarette attributed to Joseph
B. Barry (see figure 358)
Philadelphia Museum of Art:
Given in memory of Caroline S.
Gratz, by Simon Gratz, 1925

LOO OR CARD TABLE

The English prototype and Philadelphia version of the same, image 42 below, (see figure 19) are extremely close in character, the Philadelphia using leafage carving at the base of the pedestal.

Rosewood or mahogany Loo Table french polishd	4 ft 6 in.	S	III V	V
	4 ft 3 in.	S	V	V
	4 ft	I	III V	V
Ditto superior	extra	II	V	V
Ditto with moulding edge	extra	II	V	V

Image 41

William Smee & Sons,
Designs of furniture,

London, plate 52.
Courtesy, The Winterthur Library: Printed Book and Periodical Collection

Image 42

Philadelphia Loo Table
(figure 19)

The center chair of plates 66 and 67 (Ackermann's) is extremely similar to the Biddle family crest chair made in Philadelphia for Andalusia seen in image 44 below (see figure 197).

Image 43

Pauline Agius, Ackermann's Regency Furniture and Interiors, London: 1809-1828 (The Crowood Press, 1984) P.94, plate 67- Hall chairs/ pl. 66-bed room chairs Courtesy, The Winterthur Library: Printed Book and Periodical Collection

Image 44

Biddle chair from Andalusia (see figure 197).

SIDEBOARDS

Egyptian-influenced English design prototype (image 45 top) with its American interpretation in image 46 bottom.

Image 45
P. 142: pl. 127- Sideboard & cellaret
Pauline Agius, Ackermann's Regency
Furniture and Interiors, London: 1809-
1828 (The Crowood Press, 1984)
Courtesy, The Winterthur Library: Printed
Book and Periodical Collection

Image 46
Sideboard; Philadelphia or Baltimore (see
figure 261)
The Saint Louis Art Museum, Decorative
Arts Society Funds and Eliza McMillan
Fund

IMAGE 47

The prototype English design for a box sofa (image 47 top) and the Philadelphia interpretation of the same design (image 48 bottom). Generally speaking, Philadelphia box sofas tend to be monumental in size. Philadelphia makers decorated the front of the armrests with distinctive patterns that sometimes can be related to specific shops. This shop-related variation in carving is discussed in chapter 11 of this volume.

Image 47

P.132: pl.116- A dress sofa Pauline Agius, Ackermann's Regency Furniture and Interiors. London: 1809-1828 (The Crowood Press, 1984) Courtesy, The Winterthur Library: Printed Book and Periodical Collection

Image 48

Philadelphia Interpretation of English Box sofa design (see figure 233)

The chair in Ackermann's Pl. 11 (image 49 top) is similar to the American klismos chair pictured below as image 50.

Image 49
P. 49: pl.11-
Cabinet writing table and chair
Pauline Agius, Ackermann's Regency
Furniture and Interiors. London: 1809-
1828 (The Crowood Press, 1984)
Courtesy, The Winterthur Library: Printed
Book and Periodical Collection

Image 50
Philadelphia Interpretation of
Klismos Chair
(see figure 182)

The English-design "parlor chair" with saber legs (image 51 left) and Philadelphia or New York equivalent, image 52 right (see figure 173).

Image 51

Partial Plate
Pauline Agius, Ackermann's Regency Furniture and Interiors. London: 1809-1828 (The Crowood Press, 1984)
P. 41: Pl. 2- Secretaire and parlor chair
Courtesy, The Winterthur Library: Printed Book and Periodical Collection

Image 52

Philadelphia or New York sidechair
(see figure 173)

The prototype English-design dolphin pedestal center table and the Philadelphia interpretation of this from Andalusia (image 54).

Image 53
Pauline Agius, Ackermann's Regency Furniture and Interiors. London: 1809-1828 (The Crowood Press, 1984) P. 41: Pl. 141-Table, Chair and Window-Seat Courtesy, The Winterthur Library: Printed Book and Periodical Collection

Image 54
Philadelphia Dolphin Center Table from Andalusia (see figure 17)

V. Furniture Hardware During The Empire Era

With the onset of the nineteenth century, the earlier brass bat-wing hardware was replaced by oval or circular brass hardware that was derived from classical sources. The circular and oval brass plates were adorned by various decorative designs. Motifs included floral, with classical and portrait patterns. Brass pulls in the form of lion's heads were also popular.

By the 1820s the brass hardware began to be replaced by fashionable pressed-glass knobs in a variety of shapes. These created luster and visual appeal to the fronts of desks, chests of drawers, tables and other furniture forms. The frequent breakage of glass knobs accounts for the relative scarcity of original glass knobs on Philadelphia furniture forms of this era. A second drawback of glass was the potential for sharp edges. It was rumored that the Philadelphia City Council had considered a ban on certain types of pressed-glass knobs due to citizen complaints of lacerations from the pointed edges. Despite these limitations, glass hardware set the standard during the latter empire era and is one of the distinguishing features of fine Empire furniture.

Wooden knobs are one of the most ancient forms of furniture hardware. The use of wooden hardware on formal furniture became fashionable during the Empire period. These utilitarian wood knobs were popular after 1815 and many exceptionally fine examples of Philadelphia

Image 55

Various pressed-glass knobs found on Empire furniture. The knob on the far left of the bottom row is cut glass. This type of knob has been found on several pieces of Quervelle-attributed furniture.

Empire furniture are adorned with mahogany wood knobs (see figure 280). Occasionally these knobs were carved into shapes to simulate glass hardware. See figure 139 in the text for an example of this.

Image 56
Examples of wood and brass Empire knobs. The bottom three on the left are bed bolt covers.

VI. CLASSICAL UPHOLSTERY
By Alexandra Alevizatos Kirtley

In 1834, in the introduction to his prescriptive manual for upholsterers, London upholsterer John Saville Crofton wrote that the young student or apprentice in the trade of upholstery should study "fashions that have gone by, as which prevail today, and to make himself perfectly acquainted with the practical part."[i] A self-described "fashionable upholsterer," Crofton's manual proceeds to elucidate two points that illustrate the crossroads of the upholsterer's craft at the end of the classical or Empire period. First, upholstery craft had evolved by the late nineteenth century from related traditions of several craftsmen (mainly the upholder, the cofferer, and the saddler[ii]) into a specialized craft. The late eighteenth and early nineteenth century upholsterer produced the support, cut (and sometimes acquired) the material, attached it to the furniture, and, if requested, produced loose-fitting covers for furniture and for windows and beds. In addition, this same craftsman acquired designs, procured the fabrics and *passementerie* (trimmings) and fabricated the materials to produce the grand effects that upholstery undoubtedly bestowed upon furniture. Secondly, Crofton's manual forecasts the further evolution of the upholsterer in the late nineteenth century—into one of an interior decorator who rather than fulfilling orders for fashionable furniture upholstery actually dictates taste and completes interior decoration for room and furniture arrangement.[iii]

The display of classical, or Grecian, taste in America and specifically in Philadelphia depended a great deal upon the upholstery chosen to dress the furniture. Furniture that required upholstery included not only the most obvious—chairs and sofas—but also windows, beds, bookcases, work tables, screens and dressing tables. The styles of upholstery were transmitted from the fashion centers of Paris and London to Philadelphia through recently immigrated craftsmen, design books and prescriptive manuals, furniture being imported into the port of Philadelphia. In addition, some wealthy merchants maintained agents in London and Paris and ordered their furniture directly from them, requesting "the most fashionable" furniture and upholstery and even designs for windows and room arrangements.

The modern study of classical upholstery is based on physical evidence left behind on furniture; surviving furniture covers, window or bed curtains; descriptions and orders for upholstery; and furniture, windows or interiors illustrated in paintings, prints and drawings.

In the mid-eighteenth century baroque and rococo period (commonly associated with the work and styles of Thomas Chippendale), upholstery had achieved new dimensions. Fabrics of different colors and materials were combined with lavish trimmings, and the interiors and furniture of American colonists were no exception. With heightened interest in silk and wool woven with damasks or stamped, calendered or printed for the primary surfaces of upholstery, upholsterers and designers also experimented with the comfort of the under-upholstery of seating and sleeping furniture. Ideas seemingly as modern as air mattresses and waterbeds (suggested to have been made from filling pigs bladders with water or air[iv]) and certainly spring cushioning was already in its infancy in 1793 when Thomas Sheraton published a design for a sprung seat.[v] For seating furniture, the straight or Marlborough leg and trapezoidal seat was greatly preferred in England (and America) during the mid-18th century, and so her upholsterers excelled at forming squared under upholstery forms. Pillows were generously stuffed with down and, based on their depiction in paintings and prints, provided luxurious comfort. Brass nails disguised nails and added decorative effect; Chippendale even suggested that they perhaps imitated fret. In America, the use of brass nails extended well beyond the time that they were fashionable in France and even England. Any discussion of American mid-eighteenth century upholstery is incomplete without mentioning portraits by John Singleton Copley (1738-1815) that often include provide a context for the sitter with upholstered furniture such as a back stool or the camelback sofa in the portrait of an unknown lady.[vi] While the sitter remains unknown and the perspective treatment of the sofa is actually completely artificial, the painting validly illustrates the stiff, squared seating covered in generously stuffed pillows.

While the squared edges of the English upholstery complemented the squared edges of the seats, the French preferred rounded edges for their seating furniture, such as the *fauteuil*, and their eighteenth century upholsterers excelled at it. French rococo upholstery consists of rounded seats, corners and chair elbows.

With the advent of Neo-Classicism, the French abandoned their rounded edges and adopted the English method of squaring seat edges, but indeed perfected the squared seat to such an extent that squared seating was described as "French stuffing" even in England by the close of the eighteenth century.[vii] And with the rounded French rococo upholstery, went the rounded chairs—the French *fauteuil* of the classical period has squared seats, seat backs and arms.[viii] *Squareness* is the single term to best describe the upholstery of classical seating furniture (including the squared edges of bolster pillows) and such square seats are most associated with the most popular seating form of the period—

the klismos or Greek chair with incurved front legs and rear stiles. One example is a set of chairs made in Philadelphia possibly by Joseph Burden and painted by John P. Fondé in 1818.[ix] The faux maple graining consists of a light brown stripe and a dark brown stripe; the original upholstery color matches the color of the light brown stripe and is a watered silk twill. The seat and tablet back are both tufted, a method of securing the stuffing of the seat that was more commonly employed by English upholsters than French during the early nineteenth century. The tufts themselves were handmade from silk strings dyed to match the silk.

Other known Philadelphia seating furniture in the Grecian style with evidence of original upholstery is the furniture designed by English-born, American architect B. Henry Latrobe (1764-1820) for the drawing room of Philadelphia merchant William Waln.[x] The famous suite of furniture was made in 1807 and bears incredibly ornate red, yellow and gilt japanned decoration on a black ground. The archaeological correctness of the klismos form of the suite of chairs, benches and sofa is remarkable for being the earliest example of the klismos chair in America. The decoration is an amazing survival, but truly, compared to their upholstery, the painted scenes were the inexpensive way to introduce color into the Waln drawing room. Fairly large patches of yellow silk surviving under the applied gesso and plaster decorated rail suggests that, in classic European design book style, yellow silk swags adorned the spaces between the front legs and the front and rear legs on the sides. Furthermore, on the pier table in the suite, yellow silk remains behind the carved rosettes located above the columns. This yellow would have helped highlight the yellow painted decoration, which today is obscured by browning varnishes and is all but indistinguishable from the gilt decoration. When the suite was made in 1807, the yellow and gilt would have contrasted and the yellow silk swags would have com-

plemented the yellow paint. The caned seats were also painted and a large, poofy squab most likely ornamented with tassels or other passementerie would have covered the seats.

Loose covers to protect the primary surfaces of seating furniture, a tradition developed in the eighteenth century to cover expensive upholstery, remained in fashion during the Grecian period. Such covers were not seasonal, but rather protective, and their owners were neither ashamed of them nor ashamed to have them depicted; they can be seen in numerable American portraits and paintings and prints of interiors. And it is noted that American upholsterers employed decorative brass nails (to disguise purely functional nails) for longer than their European counterparts, but that Americans preferred fringe on their seats and covers long after such "baroque" styles had waned in Europe.[xi] Hepplewhite's *Repository of Designs* noted that coverings may be various and include squabs on round-stuffed seating furniture, "with a duplicate linen to cover the whole"[xii] and for the most part eighteenth century covers were checked or striped linen, while more elaborate prints and toiles were fashioned as loose covers on classically styles furniture.[xiii]

Another innovation during the classical period was the upholstery of the outbacks of chairs. In earlier periods, furniture was arranged against the walls. Upholsterers and furniture designers did not focus on the backs of chairs and other seating furniture, though French upholsterers of the mid-eighteenth century were careful to web their seat backs neatly because they were not to be covered with any sort of elegant fabric but were dragged to the middles of rooms when in use. In contrast, new styles for room arrangements called for furniture to be seen, enjoyed, and displayed in the center of rooms and the designs for furniture and upholstery, painted and carved decoration for the outbacks of chairs adjusted to this new style. Even design books focus more on the look of the backs of chairs. A Frenchman visiting Osterey Park in London (redecorated by Adam in the 1760s and 1770s) commented:

> Such is the modern fashion of placing furniture carried to an extreme, as fashions always are, but the apartments of a fashionable house [now] look like an Upholsterer's or cabinet-maker's shop...tables, sofas, and chairs were studiously deranges about the fireplaces and middle of the rooms, as if the family had just left them, although the house had not been inhabited for several years.[xiv]

Square seating for Neo-Classical and classical chairs and sofas were often delineated or emphasized with applied tapes or ribbons. For instance, Sheraton wrote "the sofas are bordered off in three compartments, and covered with figured silk or satin" (*Drawing Book*, 1793, plate LXI). Textile historian Mary Schoeser is currently researching and producing a large database of evidence and examples of this practice on Neo-Classical and classical seating furniture and bed furniture.[xv]

Where squareness best defines the classical or Grecian upholstery for seating furniture, the swag best defines the Grecian style for window and bed furnishings. Cornice boxes survive that bear evidence of swags and tassels[xvi] and a French beds survive that would have been simply armatures of profusions of rich fabrics with extraordinary passementerie. Window draper hung in multiple layers; an overhang design (directly inspired from classical vocabulary) such as a palmette, lancet or harlequin with a tassel hanging off of each of them or simple swags hung over top of transparent curtains or Venetian blinds. Another window drapery device that developed during the classical period was the French rod. Excess amounts of drapery were hung off of these rods, which terminated in ormulu mounts in the shape of spears heads or other classical ornaments and often spanned two windows. Drapery material sometimes hung to the floor and settled in literal heaps. The drapes were tethered to the walls, creating

a soft half-swag, with U-shaped brackets or round tie-backs made of glass, silvered glass, silver, porcelain, brass or ormolu with rosette or paterae designs pressed or painted on them. The 1818 *Paxton's Philadelphia Annual Advertiser* illustrates an advertisement by Philadelphia upholstery trimming supplier Henry B. Korn, whose shop was located at 82 North Second Street. To promote his shop and services, Korn chose a sophisticated swag and drapery window cornice design with seemingly little concern for conserving the amount of fabric used and literally dripping in trimmings. Of course, the advertisement is in black and white, but one can only imagine the contrasts produced by numerous colors on the fabrics, the window covering (usually somewhat sheer) and all of the trimmings. The colors of the window upholstery in American interiors are well documented in paintings and even show how the left and right sides were sometimes in different colors.[xvii] The measurement and cutting of fabric for draperies and swags was considered a wholly other specialty for an upholsterer. One can imagine that as an upholsterer gained stature and business, he would perfect the art of measuring and cutting drapery.

Although chairs, beds and windows are most commonly considered as upholstered, other furniture forms received upholstery. Bookcase doors—either glazed or open (unglazed)—were always covered with fabric. Rods were often hung on the upper and lower rails to receive the materials. Vertical box pleating was also used, for instance on the Anthony G. Quervelle secretary bookcase at the Philadelphia Museum of Art, but the sunburst pattern was also seen. The sunburst pattern was also common on pianos. The advertisement for Loud and Brothers of Philadelphia in Joshua Shaw's *United States Directory* (1822) illustrates three variations of the sunburst pattern for his upright pianos. The writing surfaces of desks and secretaries also was upholstered, with a fringed piece of wool[xviii] or inset with leather or, as

Sheraton remarked in the *Drawing Book*, "lined with green cloth".

Philip D. Zimmerman's article "New York City Federal Furniture" in *The Magazine Antiques* (May, 1997, 716-723) illustrates a remarkable survival of not only a suite of tapestry upholstered furniture now known to have been made in New York in 1819 for the Beekman family, but also of evidence of the upholstery of a New York dressing table, circa 1800. Designs for the upholstery of ladies' dressing tables of this style abound in popular design books of the early nineteenth century such as by George Smith and Thomas Sheraton who described his lady's cabinet dressing-table: "Behind the drapery, which is tacked to a rabbet, and fringed or gimped, to cover the nails, is a shelf... Behind the center glass is drapery; it may be real to suit that below, or it may only be painted in imitation of it."[xix] Indeed on the New-York Historical Society example that retains its padding, the swag was almost definitely the overwhelming design in the upholstering of the table, which was a predominantly feminine form. The padding on the bottom of the rails reminds us of the craft of the saddler in that of the early nineteenth century American upholsterer. Examples similar to the design of the New York City-made dressing table were made in Philadelphia and Baltimore, but the evidence on New-York Historical Society's example is singular.

Philadelphia work tables deserve more significant consideration than can be given here. The box or bag was a palette for the upholsterer. Each work table design had a myriad of possibilities—swags, pleats, sunbursts, passementerie. Octagons, ovals, ellipses and astragals are only a few of the forms of the tables that were sent to the upholsterer to be outfitted with a special, and certainly colorful, box or bag. Sheraton described the manner by which the upholstery is attached to the table (see his 1793 *Drawing Book* appendix) and Smith noted that the top should be "covered with morocco leather, under which is a drawer for writing apparatus...The Work-bag in Plate 76 may be lustring or satin, round which is suspended a silk fringe."[xx] Illustrations of work table and fire screen designs are both replete with a variety of possibilities for the upholsterer to outfit the table. The screens in the drawing room, counter-balanced with weights, were dictated to be upholstered with "satin, lustring, or velvet" by Smith in 1808 and "green silk, needle-work, &c at pleasure" by Hepplewhite in the 1780s.

Carpets are an item of the classical interior that should not be omitted from any discussion of upholstery. The use of a carpet had become less exclusive in America by the early nineteenth century and several domestic weavers produced fine floor coverings. Ingrain carpets were widely produced in nineteenth century America. Still, carpets from the European style centers were the most sophisticated. Brussels (a looped pile) competed with Wilton carpets, a cut-pile carpet. Other factories produced large woven carpets, such as at Aubusson and Savonnerie in France and Axminster and Moorfields in England. It is Morrfields from which Philadelphian William Bingham purchased his stylish carpet so famously described in the late 1790s. William Sprague's Philadelphia manufacture produced hand-piled carpets in strips that were sewn together. The designs of these carpets were large scaled classical, Adam-esque and Pompeian-inspired compositions often made to suit the plaster designs of the same pattern on the ceilings. Evidence for American's use of carpets (and green cloth covers) survive well in numerous interiors paintings and portraits.

Inventories and advertisements reveal that most cabinetmakers and upholsterers worked as undertakers. They performed a complete service that included embalming the body, laying it out in the family's home, and hiring the carriage to transport the body outside the city to the graveyard. As mourning and funereal traditions became more and more complex into the 1840s, this profession became more of a dedicated one.

Upholsterers probably serviced the funeral directors. Needless to say, we cannot study *surviving* coffin upholstery evidence.

Upholsterers, especially in America from the eighteenth and into the first half of the nineteenth century, supplied wallpapers or fabrics for the walls (stretched on battens nailed to the walls). In the classical period in America, scenic views were all the rage along with columns and arches that created trompe l'oeil interiors. Gilt fillets were sometimes used to disguise the manner in which the paper or fabric was attached to the wall. Painted decoration could also be used to ornament the walls of a fashionable classical drawing room in America.

Upholsterers depended upon the skills of many others in their communities for supplies to complete their work. Specialists provided the trimmings and fringes by Henry Korn in Philadelphia. Hair curlers and feather makers provided the stuffings. The upholsterers often sold floor cloths, but he acquired them from specialists. Specialist makers supplied transparent and Venetian blinds and springs and cornices. If those were painted, they too required special painters. Sacking and webbing and all of the tools for performing the upholstery work were also supplied by specialists. As the upholsterer evolved throughout the nineteenth century into something more akin to the modern interior decorator, he became more and more dependent upon the skill and quality of his suppliers. He knew his work was vital to the cabinetmaker's and chairmaker's crafts: descriptive terms for furniture often depended upon the type of upholstery on it—i.e., a hall chair was distinguished from a drawing room, gothic, dining, easy, and any other kind of chair because of its lack of upholstery.

In the classical period in Philadelphia, the firms of Laforgue, McCauley's, Wevill & Nicholas, Lawrence, Oilphant & Wilson, Anthony, and John Rea, famous for supplying upholstery to Latrobe for the Madison White House[xxi], predominated the scene. Wevill was a second generation upholsterer: his father Richard Wevill emigrated from England in 1799 and immediately too over the trade of recently deceased upholsterer Samuel Benge.[xxii] Wevill outsourced work or had working for him Lewis Nicholas, with whom his son partnered.

As late nineteenth century tastes for interiors diverged to include not simply one unified design or style such as Grecian, but rather encompassing and layering many, the work of the upholsterer moved from fashioning furniture to scheming about creating the look for an entire interior. Their influence could be seen in furniture characterized by overstuffed seats and backs with high, sprung seating and deep buttoned tufting. Design moralists reacted against it and pined for the days when one style based on authentic antique or Grecian design prevailed. Gone were the sleek lines and ordered arrangements of the classical period and in favor was the discord and raucous extravagance of materials with, what was to some, a lack of taste and certainly no truth to nature or the natural furniture form, inciting moralist John Ruskin (1891-1900) to write that a critic's work was "to distinguish the artist's work from the upholsterer's." In contrast, the upholstery of Grecian or classical furniture was indeed the most salient feature of much of the furniture fashioned in that style, and it is regrettable that little of it survives. With the significant evidence that survives today, it is the duty of collectors and museums to honor the furniture, the art of the early nineteenth century upholsterer, and indeed the tenets of the Grecian style by upholstering classical furniture appropriately.

[i] John Saville Crofton, *The London Upholsterer's Companion* (London: John Williams, Library of the Fine Arts, 1834): preface, page 5.

[ii] Information gleaned from a lecture given by furniture upholsterer and scholar Robert F. Trent, March 4, 2004.

[iii] This short article does not consider the extent and range of materials or upholstery of carriages, though this was an important and lucrative aspect of the upholsterer's work.

[iv] Most upholsterers relied and still rely on curled hair for stuffing. Crofton amusingly refers to hay as "French hair."

[v] Carriage seats were the main impetus for the advancement of better seating support that lead to the perfection of spring seating.

[vi] *Mrs. Isaac Smith*, by John Singleton Copley (American, 1738-1815), 1769, Yale University Art Gallery and *Unidentified woman* (once thought to be Mrs. Thrale), by John Singleton Copley (American, 1738-1815) New York, 1771, Los Angeles County Museum of Art.

[vii] In short, the English sewed their edges (side to top) once to produce a square cake, while the French cakes were produced by being sewn three times. Crofton even said that it is best to seek out a French upholsterer to sew your seat square as they are better at it than any London born upholsterer.

[viii] See Shippen-Burd suite of American furniture in the collections of the Philadelphia Museum of Art and a portrait by Gilbert Stuart of the Marchioness of Casa Rijo on loan to the Philadelphia Museum of Art.

[ix] Chairs from this set were donated by James Biddle to the Philadelphia Museum of Art, Winterthur Museum. The Metropolitan Museum of Art, the Baltimore Museum of Art, and the Art Institute of Chicago. The one at the Baltimore Museum of Art retains its original upholstery and the one at the Philadelphia Museum of Art is signed by Fondé.

[x] Furniture from this suite is at the Philadelphia Museum of Art, the Metropolitan Museum of Art, the Museum of Fine Arts-Houston-Bayou Bend, and in a private collection.

[xi] Peter Thornton, *Authentic Décor: The Domestic Interior, 1620-1920* (New York: Sterling, 1984): 156.

[xii] Hepplewhite, plate 28.

[xiii] See Figure 253 in Richard C. Nylander, "Upholstery Documents in the Collections of the Society for the Preservation of New England Antiquities" in Edward S. Cooke, Jr., *Upholstery in America and Europe from the 17th century to World War I* (New York: Norton & Co, 1987) 251 to 260.

[xiv] As quoted in Thornton, 1984, page 147.

[xv] From a lecture she delivered at Winterthur, November, 2003.

[xvi] See Alexandra Alevizatos Kirtley, "New Discoveries in Baltimore Painted Furniture" in *Catalogue of Antiques and Fine Art*, Spring, 2002 and 2003.

[xvii] Without a doubt, the best compendium of paint and print evidence documenting American interiors, including window treatments, is Elisabeth Donaghy Garrett, *At Home: The American Family, 1750-1870* (New York: Harry N. Abrams, 1990).

[xviii] See Ralph Earle, *The Angus Nickelson Family*, 1791, Museum of Fine Arts, Springfield, Massachusetts as illustrated in Garrett, 1990, page 66.

[xix] Thomas Sheraton, *Drawing Book* (London, 1793), plate XLIX.

[xx] George Smith, *Collection of Designs* (London, 1808), plates 75 and 76.

[xxi] Information abounds on this commission. See Latrobe Papers, Maryland Historical Society, Baltimore, and numerous secondary sources. The Baltimore painted furniture manufacturers the Finlays who supplied and Madison suite and John Rea were both painted

[xxii] See Patricia Chapin O'Donnell, "Richard Wevill, upholsterer" in Cooke, 1987, pages 114-119.

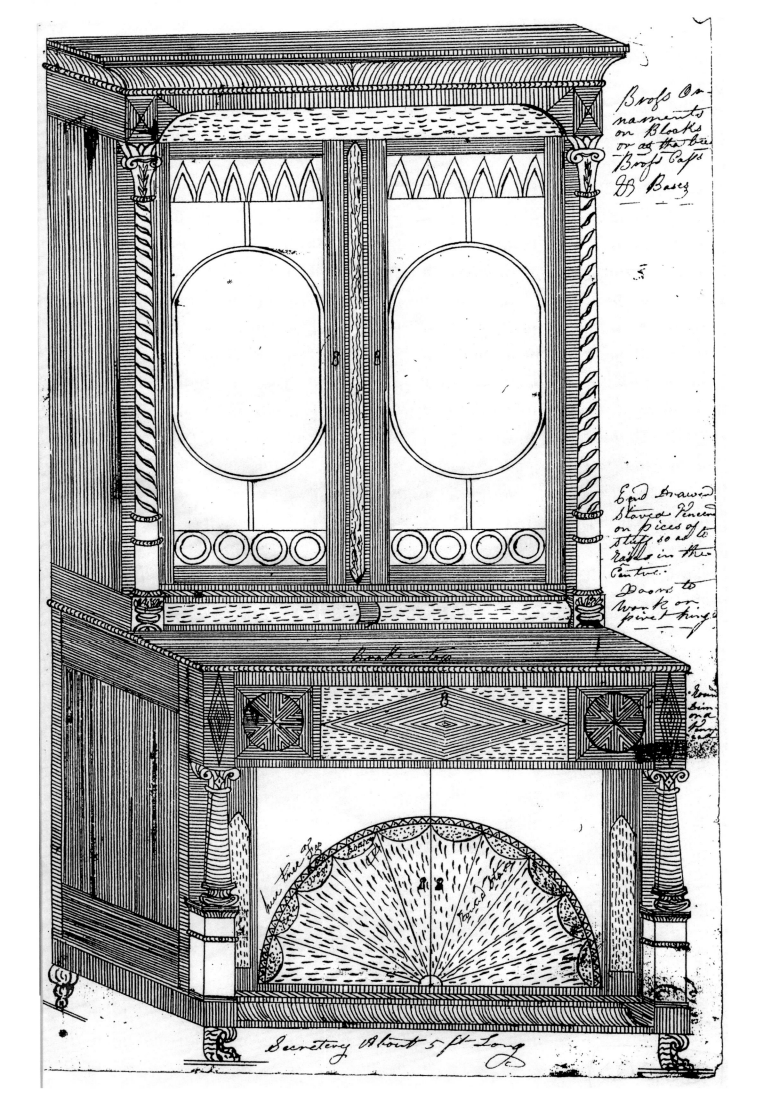

Brass Or
naments
on Blocks
or at the
Brass Case
off Bases

End Drawers
Staved Veneered
on pieces of
stuff so as to
raise in the
Centre
Doors to
Work on
pivet hinges

Brakt in top

Knee tree off top

Figud Stuf

Secretary About 5 ft Long

CHAPTER 5
THE ANTHONY QUERVELLE SKETCHBOOK

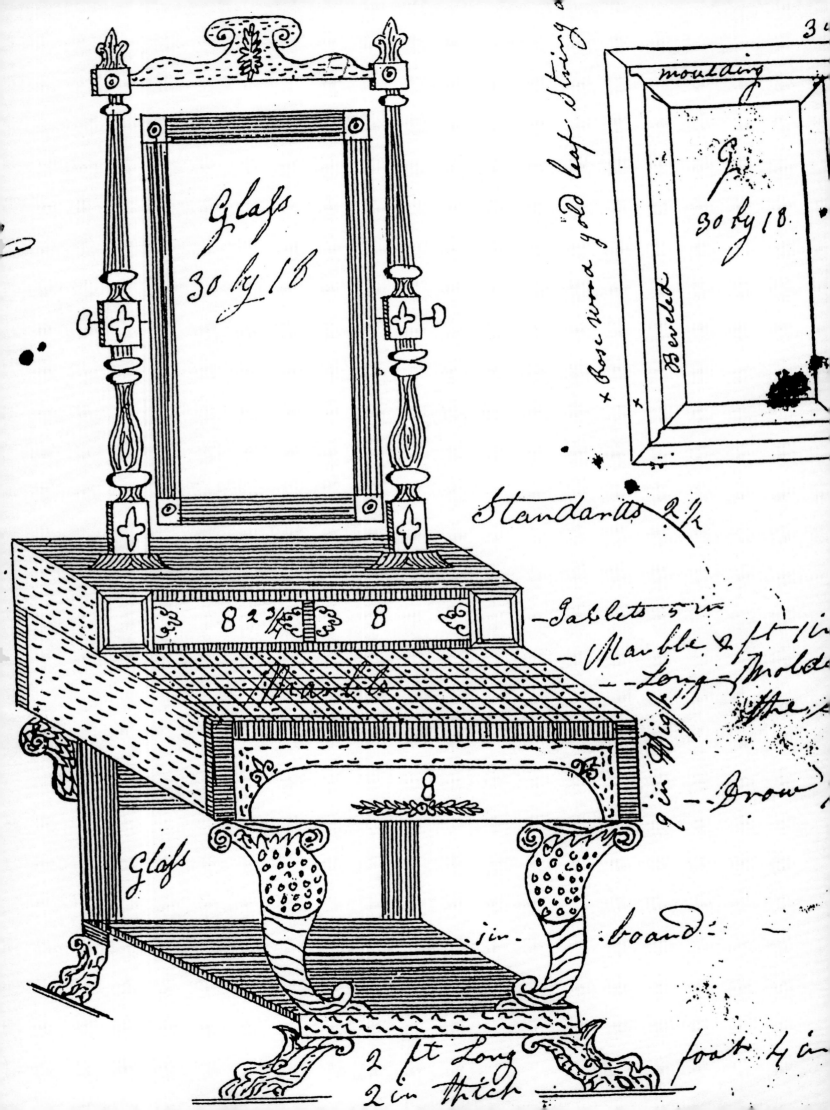

Glass
30 by 18

Glass

moulding

30 by 18

Bevelld

+ Rose wood gold leaf string

Standards 2½

Tablets 5 in

Marble 2 ft 1 in

Long Molde

9 in High the

Drow

in board

2 ft Long
2 in thick

foot 4 in

THE ANTHONY QUERVELLE SKETCHBOOK

Regarding the work of Anthony Quervelle, an unpublished sketchbook of his is owned by the

Philadelphia Museum of Art. The authors obtained copies of these drawings many years ago, shortly

after they were discovered inside a chest at auction. These sketches are now presented in this chapter.

This cabinetmaker's sketchbook illustrates a number of different items, including bureaus, sofas and

desks, some of which follow English precedence and others which appear to be clear independent

modifications by Quervelle of English and French designs. Some of these forms do not appear to have any close equivalents in the English pattern book references. These include certain desks and work tables, illustrated in the unpublished manuscripts, and now presented in this volume.

Of special interest are the desks which are illustrated in Quervelle's drawings. Desks drawn by Quervelle have marked similarities to a small group of Philadelphia empire desks, all of which show certain features including a sunburst base, the use of diamond lozenges, and other elements known to be favored by Quervelle.

Of equal interest in the Quervelle sketches are the interior details of certain desks, which show the use of a convex, concave molding above the drawer spaces, which appears to be uniquely his design. The molding above the interior drawer spaces can be found on the secretaire a abattant illustrated in this volume (see figure 286). This same secretaire a abattant was also identified by Robert C. Smith in the 1970s as being virtually identical to a labeled Quervelle secretaire a abattant, which that author had seen but was unable to publish in his original Quervelle articles in the Magazine Antiques. The

same interior molding is also seen used in one of the otherwise typical monumental Quervelle desks, illustrated in the original Smith articles, "The furniture of Anthony G. Quervelle, part IV", *The Magazine Antiques*, January 1974, page 185.

A second form, the cornucopia fronted worktable which, based on the Quervelle drawings at the Philadelphia Museum of Art, also appears to be a unique Quervelle creation. This table utilizes a pair of cornucopias supporting the front of the worktable and a lyre form supporting the back of the worktable. It is strikingly similar to worktable in figure 130 of this volume. In addition the interior compartmentalization of the top section, worktable 130 appears identical to that of a labeled worktable in the Smith articles, "The Furniture of Anthony G. Quervelle, part III", *The Magazine Antiques*, August 12, 1973, page 267. This further supports the strong attribution that this form is a creation of Quervelle's shop and that pieces conforming to this form have Quervelle attributions. Again it cannot be stated categorically that these are only by Quervelle, as imitation is the sincerest form of flattery and it is impossible to exclude that other makers may have appreciated this form and mimicked it.

Sketch 1

This sketch demonstrates multiple Quervelle design motifs including the use of the sunburst with lunate edges, diamond lozengers, and circular raised panels. Compare to figures 280, 281, and 282 in this volume.

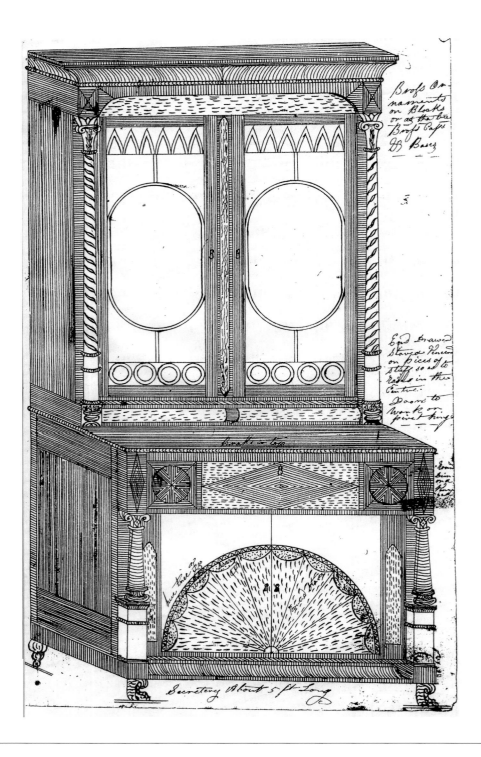

Sketch 2

The decorative molding above the pigeon holes is identical to that of the Quervelle attributed "French secretary" illustrated as figure 286a in this volume.

Sketch 3 and 4

The worktable sketched on the right closely relates to the Quervelle attributed worktable illustrated as figure 130 in this volume. Notice the micro-carved fan motif between the front legs.

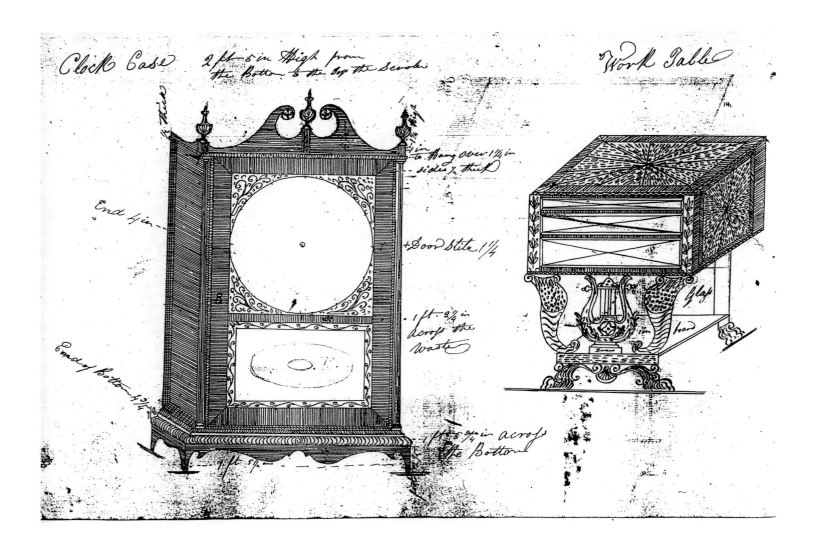

Sketch 5 (pier table) and 6 (bureau)

Regarding the upper sketch of a pier table the following can be noted: the front scroll column supports with urns below support an in-cut shelf with a central semi-circle. These are identical to the Quervelle-attributed pier table that is figure 102 in this text.

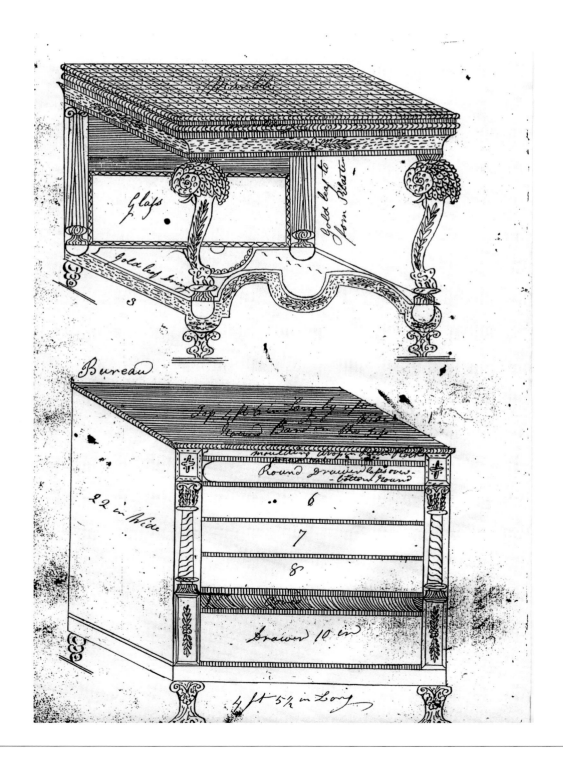

Sketch 7, Pedestal End Sideboard

Note that the base of the left front pilaster exhibits a micro-carved fan.

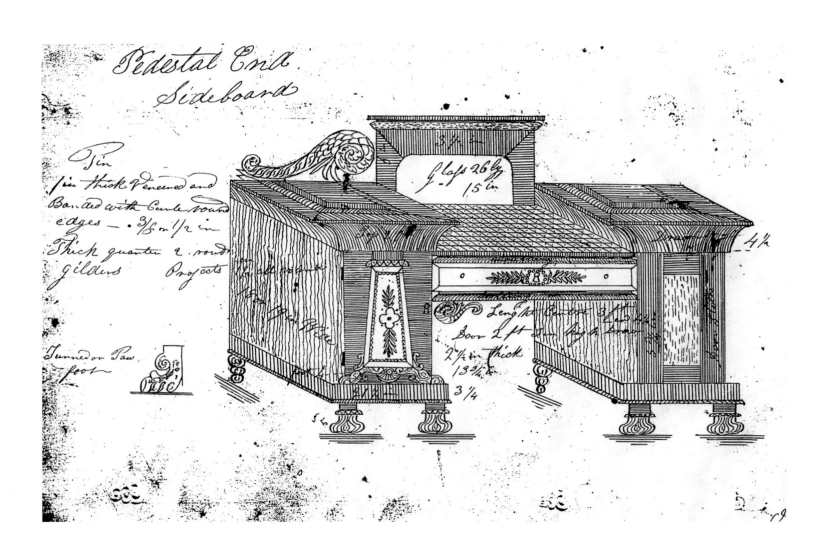

Sketch 8, Brake Center Sideboard

The center cupboard doors contain diamond lozengers that appear identical to figures 247 and 249. The star motif on the outer cupboard doors relates to the stars on the Quervelle-attributed wardrobe illustrated as figure 316 in this text.

Sketch 9, Brake Center Sideboard

The cornucopia side supports are typically seen in Philadelphia,
but also were used in other regions.

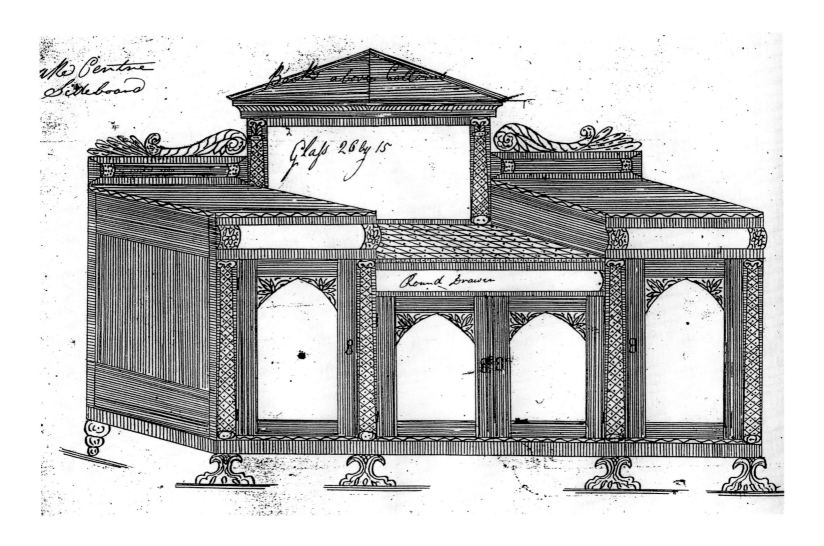

Sketch 10

This sideboard is designed with an open center section decorated with glass.

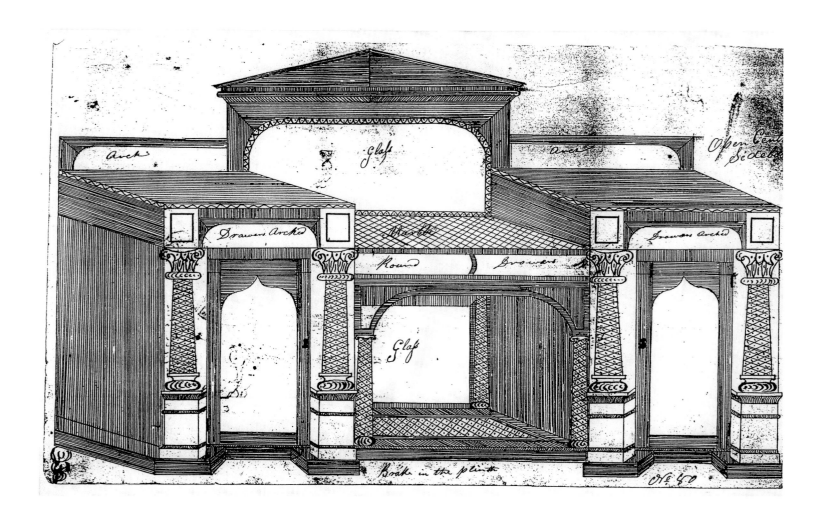

Sketch 11

This sketch shows a typical Philadelphia drop-center section sideboard with cornucopia supports and central marble slab.

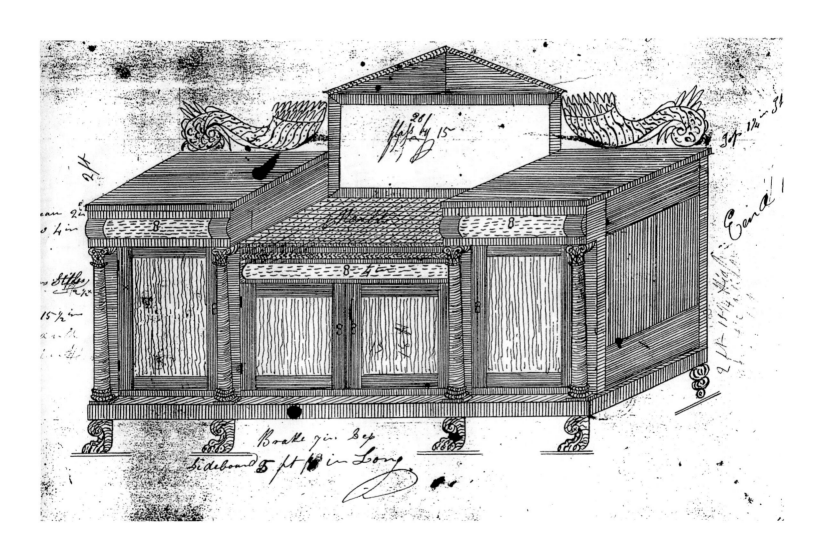

Sketch 12, Flat Topped Sideboard

Note the central cylinder cupboard drawers in this sketch relate to doors on Quervelle-attributed sideboards in figures 249, 250 and 251.

Sketch 13, Basile End Sideboard

This unusual form has certain aspects of a much enlarged pier table. The design relates closely to president Andrew Jackson's sideboard at the Hermitage, illustrated in figure 255, which Jackson's wife may have ordered from Quervelle.

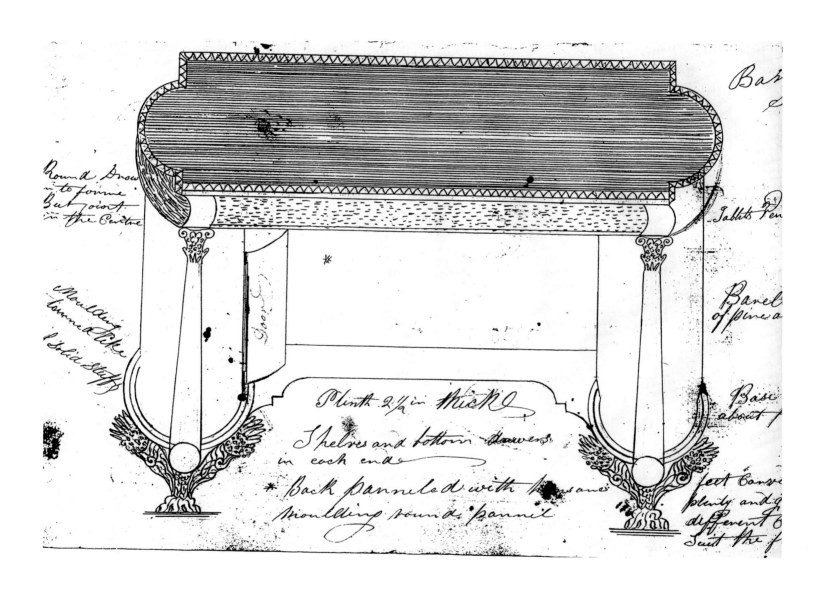

Sketch 14 (Loo Table) and 15 (Card Table)

The Loo table exhibits a star motif in the center of a sunburst-radiating top with lunate edges, which is typical of Quervelle. Note that he specifies that the pedestal is to be double-through tendoned, which is the case with the labeled Quervelle Breakfast table illustrated in figure 57.

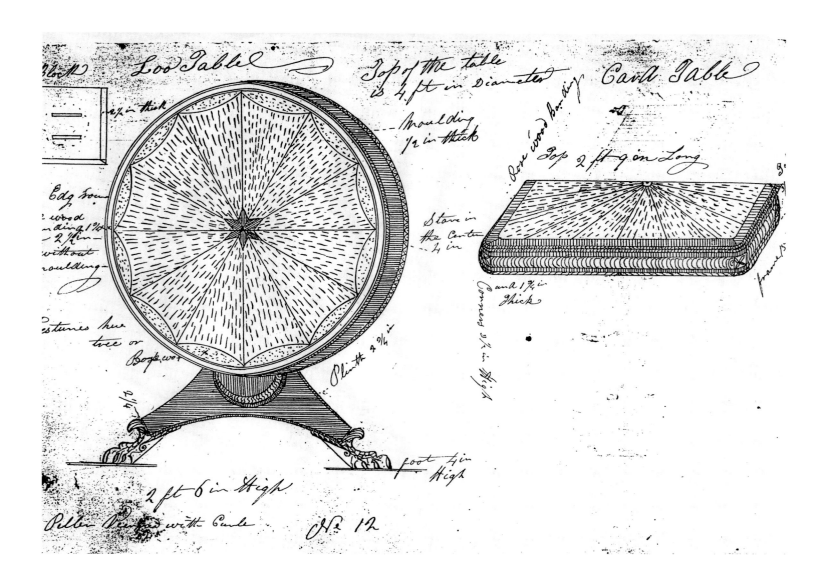

Sketch 16

This dressing table with mirror has contrasting maple drawer fronts, which Quervelle favored.

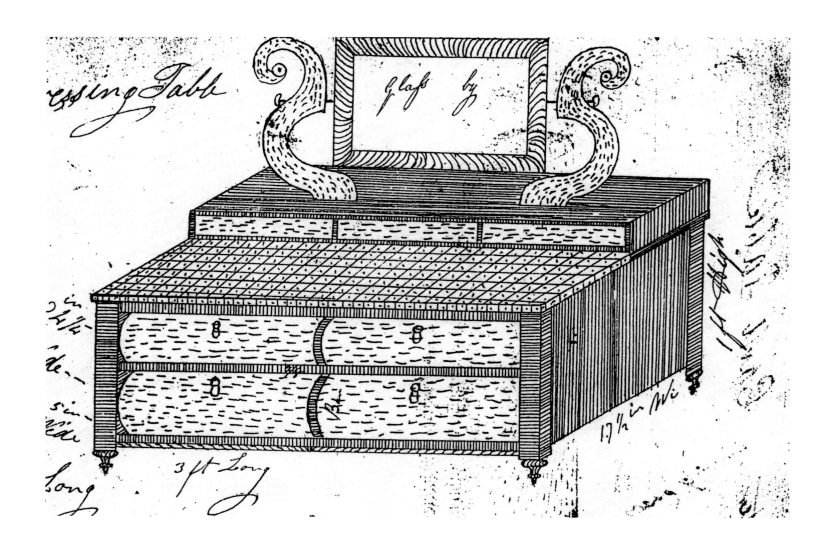

Sketch 17, Sofa

This sofa is a typical Philadelphia sofa design of the 1820s. The feet exhibit lion claws with wings above.

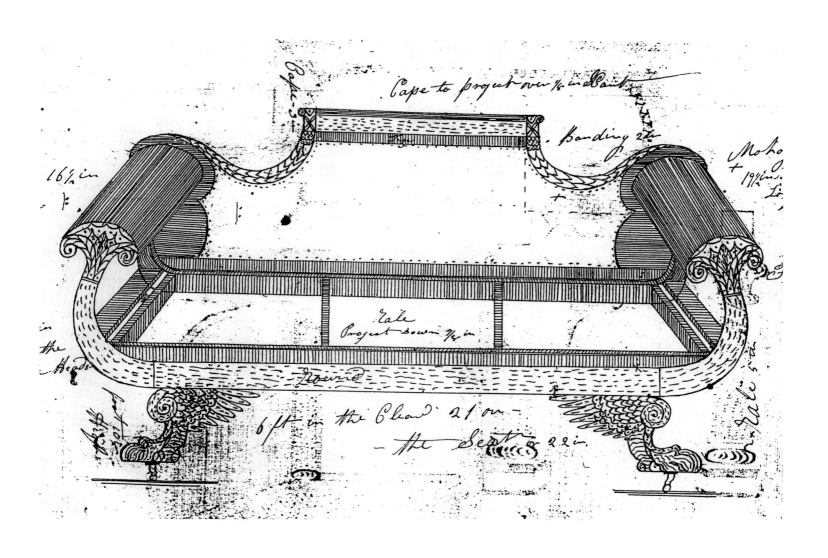

Sketch 18

This sofa sketch features arms decorated with open curling anthemion pedals. Quervelle later utilized this design motif for the upper portion of the front feet of his sofas (see figure 215).

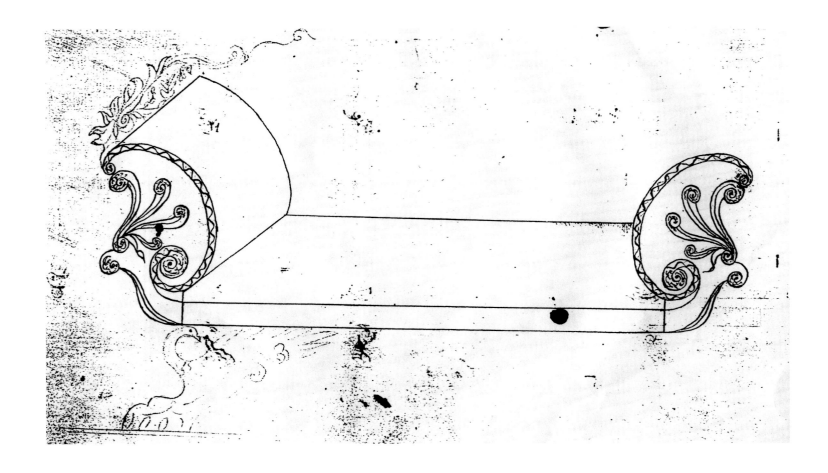

Sketch 19

This wardrobe drawing exhibits a host of design motifs favored by Quervelle including carving, star and stencil decoration. The base of this wardrobe is supported by an unusual double dolphin foot that relates to the feet of the Andrew Jackson Quervelle-attributed sideboard illustrated in figure 255. The star motif is often utilized by Quervelle. Please see figure 316 for the Quervelle-attributed wardrobe that appears to have been directly constructed from this design sketch.

Sketch 20, Clock Case

A typical empire form with gothic arch door and turned feet.

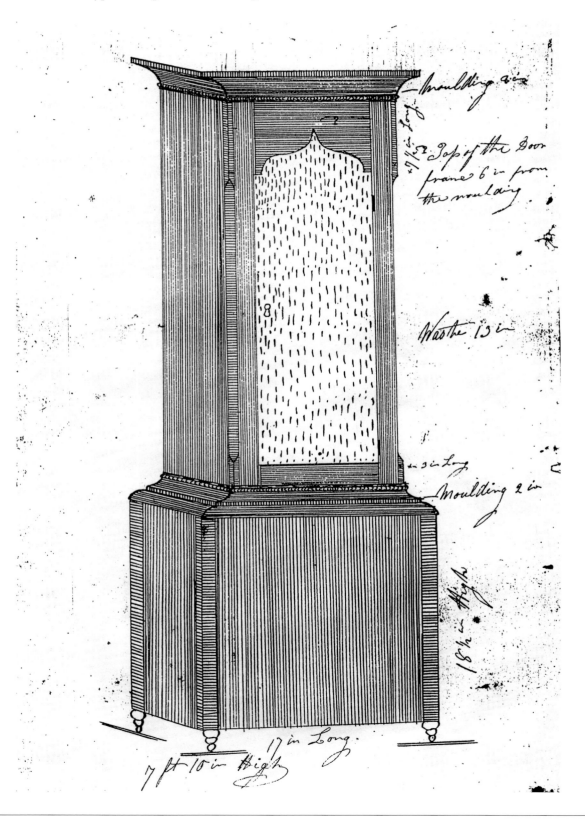

Sketch 21, Clock Case

This sketch exhibits an unusual form with a typical Quervelle star.

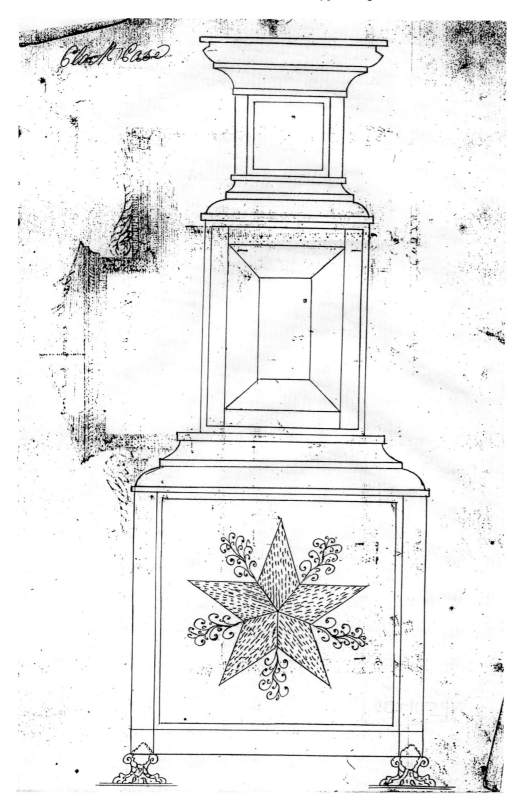

Sketch 22, Box Sofa

The carving of the arm rests appears detailed as is typical of Philadelphia box sofas illustrated in this volume.

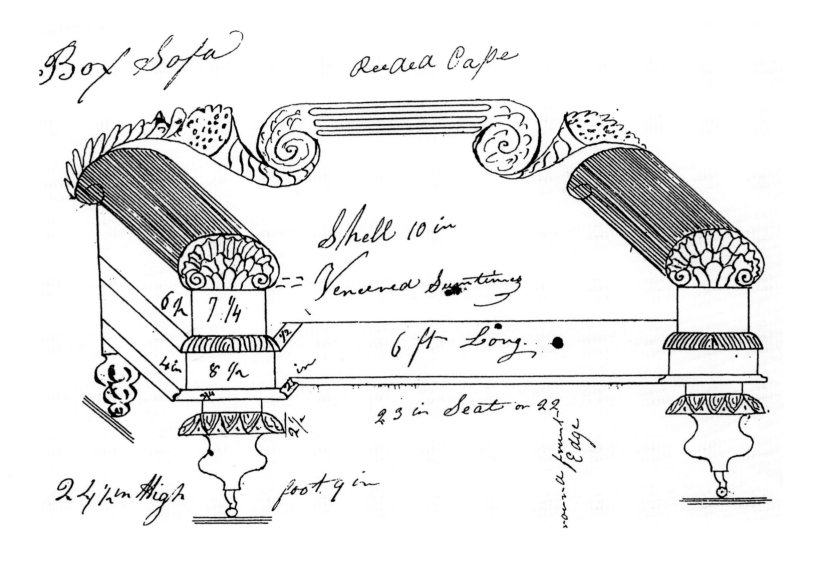

Sketch 23, Dressing Table

Dressing tables of similar form, but lacking the front cornucopia design, have been found with Philadelphia attributions.

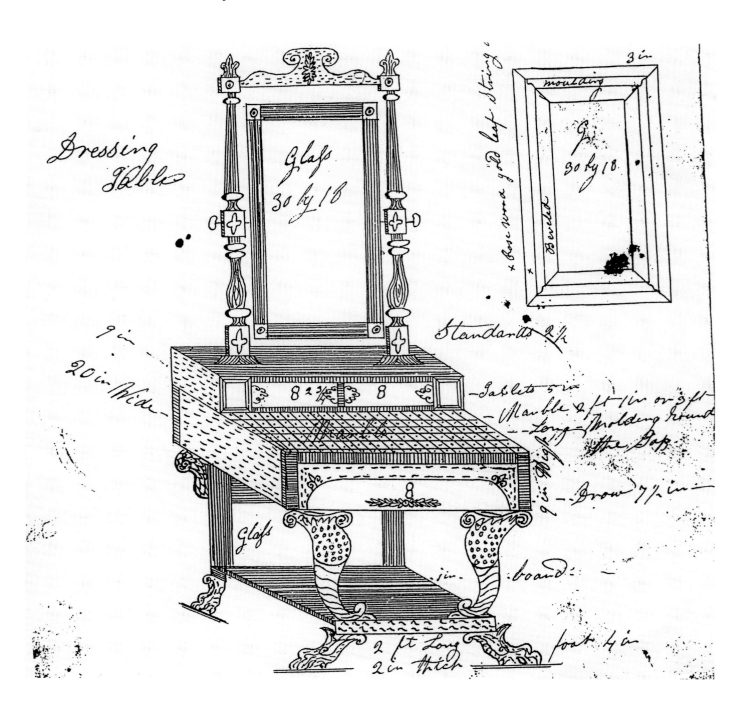

CHAPTER 6
PLATFORM
PEDESTAL TABLES

PLATFORM PEDESTAL TABLES
(CENTER TABLES, DINING TABLES)

Pedestal tables are often regarded as a purely Empire piece of furniture and were one of the most popular forms of the time. In this chapter pedestal tables will refer to two types of tables, round-topped center tables and rectangular dining tables. Empire designed tables replaced the straight legged tables of the past with platform bases composed of a square boxed section with concave sides, chamfered corners over four legs and four colonettes on its corners as supports to the table.[1]

This type of support is found especially on dining tables but is also seen on other tables, such as worktables. A variation of this is the square or triangular platform with claw feet below at the corners and a single central carved pedestal above supporting the top. The richly carved pedestals that arose from the platform bases became the staple for all Empire tables of this type, as did lion's paw feet combined with acanthus carving. Mahogany and rosewood were popular types of wood that were used. On more expensive pieces marble tops, ebonized and gilded wood, and brass inlay were often applied.

One source of design for pedestal tables for Philadelphia makers may have included George Smith's Household Furniture of 1808, which published a table (Plate 69) with a vase form, a belt of gadrooning and a coating of tightly overlaid leaves.[2] Plate 69 shows a simple design for a "Pillar & Claw Table" that may have been elaborated upon with more detail and carving to arrive at the impressive pieces that makers were turning out in the period. While it is impossible to know exactly who used what design prototypes, it is safe to say that Philadelphia makers were inspired by English and French designs and furniture.

The round-topped center table utilized a rectangular or triangular platform base with claw feet below the corners and a central carved pedestal supporting the top.

The platform base distinguishes this table structurally from earlier Philadelphia tea tables, in which the legs are affixed directly to the pedestal with no platform base. An example of a tea table was advertised in the Philadelphia Price list of 1828 as "Three feet diameter; Turned pillar, 3 claws, Greek."[3] Center tables often had a tilt-top that enabled it to be folded up and pushed away if not in use. Often used in libraries and parlors, they were usually made with a great deal of attention to detail since they were highly displayed pieces of the household.

In any household, the one essential piece that was used in many aspects of everyday living was the dining table. The dining table was massive in size and had both official and domestic uses, including entertaining large groups for card games, business meetings and dinner parties. The drop leaves made the tables easier to store when they were not needed. The pedestals tended to be carved with acanthus leaves and the platforms often rested on four distinct lions paw feet. Dining tables with four splayed, or sabre, legs also existed. While a stylish and well-ornamented dining table was a necessity for more wealthy patrons, plainer versions also displayed a massive quality that was still quite impressive. Both round-topped and dining tables exude a sense of weight that is characteristic of almost every form of Empire furniture.

[1] Otto 76

[2] Smith, Pedestal Tables 94

[3] Otto 84

Figure 1
Candle Stand, mahogany
Philadelphia, Circa 1815-1825

Height 29",
Width 17 1/2",
Depth 22"

Collection of
Mr. F.J. Carey III

Candle stands were apparently a fairly common piece of furniture to find in a household, yet few examples of Empire candle stands survive today. These types of tables were also referred to as "occasional" tables, for their light and small appearance made them perfect for serving multiple needs. It is most likely that sofa, card, and work tables also served the same purpose as candle stands when not in use, making this piece of furniture less useful and therefore less popular as the years passed. Being the type of furniture that was often in use gave this form more of a chance to be damaged, which could also explain why so many have not survived. On this candle stand there is cross-banding around the top, horizontal, and spiral reeded turnings and brass lion's paw casters for the feet.

Figure 2

*Center Table with Clouded
Limestone Top, curly maple,
maple veneer*

Philadelphia, Circa 1825-1835

Secondary woods:
oak and white pine

Height 28",
Diameter 43"

Collection of the
Andalusia Foundation

This table exhibits a pedestal carved with tight leafage. The saber legs have acanthus carved knees that end abruptly in a Philadelphia manner. The clouded limestone (King of Prussia marble) top is discussed by R. Curt Chinnici in *American Furniture*, 2002, Figure 42, pg. 120. This uncommon form of limestone, which can be polished to resemble blue-gray streaked marble, came from local quarries in the three counties immediately surrounding Philadelphia. The use of this limestone declined during the Victorian Era. By the turn of the century, competition from imported marbles combined with depletion of limestone from the local quarries resulted in the decorative demise of this unusual limestone.

The mahogany top has a curly maple veneered edge. Curly maple veneered panels decorate the apron. The maple pedestal is decorated with leafage. A triangular maple platform below has an edge decorated with a variant of egg and dart carving. The feet are stylized lion's claw with scroll carving above. This table is part of the original furnishings of the Telfair house, Savannah (see figures 192 and 229 for chair and couch from this suite).

Figure 3
Center Table, Curly Maple
Philadelphia, Circa 1820-1830
Secondary woods: pine, poplar, and oak
Height 29", Depth 48 1/8"
Courtesy of Telfair Museum of Art, Savannah, Georgia.

Figure 4

Center Table, mahogany

Once owned by Cooper-Wister Morris
and Elizabeth Giles Morris
Philadelphia, Circa 1815

Secondary wood: ash

Height 29 1/2"
Diameter 49"

Collection of Mr. F.J. Carey III

The legs of this table are affixed directly to the pedestal with no platform base. They are extensively carved with foliage that extends to the base of the pedestal, which is also richly carved. A white marble slab adorns the central portion of the table top. The rim is surrounded by gadrooning, below which is mahogany veneer. The combination of the marble and superb carving make this a more impressive and expensive piece.

This center table is nearly identical to the center tables made by Quervelle for the White House in 1829, although the present table incorporates a white marble inset top while the White House tables have black and gold marble inset slabs. The gadrooning, carving, design of the pedestal and acanthus and lion's paw feet of the present table are similar to those on the White House tables (see Figure 6).

Figure 5

Center Table, mahogany

Anthony Quervelle
Philadelphia, Circa 1825-1830

Height 30",
Diameter 36"

Private Collection

Photo Courtesy of Joan Bogart
Antiques, Rockville Centre,
New York

Figure 6

Center Table, mahogany with black and gold marble slab insets into the top (1 of 3 tables).

Made by Anthony G. Quervelle
Philadelphia, 1829

Height 29 1/2",
Diameter 40 1/2"

Currently in the Lincoln Bedroom
of the White House

Photo by Bruce White
for the White House Historical
Association

This center table is one of three made by Quervelle in 1829 for President Jackson and was originally placed in the East Room of the White House. Characteristics of Philadelphia design, especially Quervelle's shop, are the gadrooned edges, scrolls, lion's paw feet, and pedestal carved in a vase and leaf form. Each of the three supports of the pedestal exhibit a droopy flower emerging from a volute which is a Quervelle design also seen on the Quervelle attributed sideboard in figure 251a. The design of the three center tables are similar to those found in George Smith's *Collection of Designs for Household Furniture* (London 1808).

"An American Classical carved mahogany marble top center table, the circular top uniquely inset with a mosaic of gray, red, blue, black and white marbles having an outer band of gray and a band of clovers in various colors on white ground; the center inlaid with a geometric design of spades, hearts, clubs and diamonds. The pilaster with carved and gilded foliate design on shaft, on tripartite base, supported by carved, ebonized and gilded paw feet, on casters." According to oral tradition, General Lafayette visited Destrahan Plantation during his last visit to the United States in 1824 and played cards on this table. The inlaid marble playing cards are unique on an American gaming table. The pedestal design is nearly identical to the labeled marble top center table by Quervelle at the Metropolitan Museum of Art in New York (see figure 15).

Figure 7
Marble Top Gaming Table

Strong attribution to
Anthony G. Quervelle
Philadelphia, Circa 1824

Height 29 1/2",
Diameter 42"

Photo and description courtesy of Destrahan Plantation, Destrahan, Louisiana

Figure 8

Tea Table, mahogany

Attributed to Anthony G. Quervelle
Philadelphia, Circa 1820-1830

Secondary woods:
poplar and maple

Height 29",
Diameter 30 1/2"

Private Collection

The top of this table is held in place with a spring-loaded brass catch, which when released allows the top to rotate ninety degrees to a vertical position exactly like circular pedestal tea tables made in Philadelphia during the eighteenth century. It has always been with a card table labeled by Anthony G. Quervelle, both of which were original-ly owned by John (1777-1861) and Rebecca (Horner)(1782-1863) Ruckman of Bucks County, Pennsylvania, and remained in the possession of the family until 1965. It is pictured in Robert C. Smith, "The furniture of Anthony G. Quervelle Part II," *The Magazine Antiques*, July 1973, page 92, figure 6.

Figure 9
Center Table, mahogany

Philadelphia, Circa 1825-1830

Secondary wood: poplar

Height 29",
Diameter 29 3/4"

Collection of
Mr. F.J. Carey III

This tilt-top table features a unique combination of foliage on the vase pedestal, with acanthus leaves curling outwards at the middle, and a fairly large band of foliage on the platform. The carved lion's paw feet have leaves that curl outwards, which almost appear to look like shells.

Figure 10

Classical Paint and Gilt Decorated Carved Mahogany Marble Top Center Table

Thomas Cook & Richard Parkin
Philadelphia, Circa 1820-1825

Height 29",
Diameter 38"

Photo and description
courtesy of
Mr. Carswell Rush Berlin,
New York, New York

"The circular white marble top above a conforming apron raised on a turned standard bracketed by three carved gilt and *vert-antique* paint decorated paw footed scrolled elements resting on a tripartite plinth raised on lotus carved melon-ribbed feet on casters. The ash cross-brace under the marble top bears two stencils:

COOK & PARKIN/
Cabinetware/Mahogany (?) seating/
No. 36 Walnut St./Philadelphia.

The stencil incorporates what appears to be a sofa. *Repaired cracks to marble.* Cook and Parkin are listed in partnership in Philadelphia directories between 1820 and 1825."

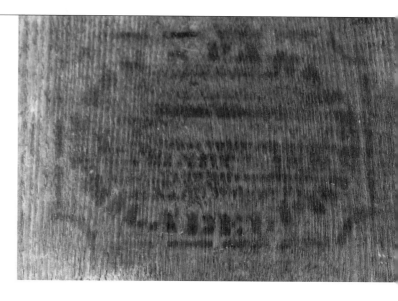

A white marble top is supported by three carved vert-antique and gilt decorated scroll elements resting on a tripartite plinth. The three scrolls resemble fantastical animals, possibly dolphins. Reeded, melon-like feet support the triangular platform.

Figures 11 and 11a
Marble-Topped Center Table, mahogany
Stencil of Cook & Parkin

Philadelphia, Circa 1820-1825

Dimensions unrecorded

Photo Courtesy of Doyle Auction Galleries, New York

Photo by Wit McKay

Figure 12a
Detail of tilted top

A sunburst of radiating wedges of mahogany veneer adorns the top. The pedestal is decorated with foliate carving at the top and bottom portions and a fruit basket-like motif between these. A band of carved leafage surrounds the triangular platform.

Figure 12 and 12a
Round Tilt-Top Breakfast, or Library, Table, mahogany with rosewood and amboyna

Philadelphia, Circa 1830

Secondary woods: oak, mahogany, and pine, with brass castors and hardware

Height 29 3/4",
Diameter 47 1/2"

Private Collection

Photo Courtesy of Hirschl & Adler Galleries, New York

"This handsome round table, which may have been intended as a center table, or possibly as a breakfast or gaming table, partakes of the vocabulary popularized by Quervelle and others working in Philadelphia in the years around 1825. This table bears a strong resemblance to one of the designs in the Quervelle sketchbook, the pie-shaped veneers of one kind of wood, the lunettes of another kind of wood, and the star-shaped motif in the center of yet another wood, all suggested in the fairly primitive technique and perspective of a design for a "Loo Table." Elsewhere among Quervelle's drawings, in his designs for sideboards, sofas, card tables, and a dressing table, appear the turned feet, the boldly gadrooned borders, the simple pedestal, and other elements that are part of a Quervelle vocabulary that apparently became synonymous with a Philadelphia style for at least a generation."

Figure 13

Center Table, mahogany, satinwood and rosewood

Attributed to Anthony G. Quervelle Philadelphia, Circa 1825-1830

Secondary woods: pine and mahogany, with brass hardware and gilt-brass castors

Height 29 1/2", Diameter 44 1/4"

Private Collection

Photo & Description Courtesy of Hirschl & Adler Galleries, New York.

Figure 14

Small Center Table, mahogany

Attributed to Anthony G. Quervelle
Philadelphia, Circa 1825-1830

Secondary woods: pine and poplar,
with inset scagliola top, and with
gilt-brass and iron casters

Height 29 3/8",
Diameter 31 1/8"

Private Collection

Photo and Description Courtesy of
Hirschl & Adler Galleries,
New York

This small center table (opposite page) partakes of the vocabulary popularized by Quervelle around 1825-30. For example, the bold gadrooning seen around the upper edge of the table top and above the feet, as well as a smaller-scale gadrooned border on the lower edge of the skirt of the table, the acanthus-carved lion-paw feet, the uniquely configured composite pedestal, and the modified triangular platform are all characteristic elements found on much of Quervelle's documented oeuvre.

This table features a combination of a square pedestal block surmounted by carved prince-of-wales feathers on an octagonal shaft. The present table is most closely related to a slightly larger, twice-labeled center table with an inset specimen marble top in the collection of The Metropolitan Museum of Art (see Figure 15 in this volume). In contrast, the Metropolitan Museum's table has a shaft composed of an acanthus-carved urn surmounted by gadrooned, turned, and carved elements.

Figure 15
Marble Inlaid Center Table, mahogany, intarsia marble, brass

Label of Anthony G. Quervelle Philadelphia, Circa 1830

Height 29 13/16",
Diameter 34 1/2"

The Metropolitan Museum of Art, Purchase, Edgar J. Kauffman Foundation Gift, 1968 (68.96)

This table (above) was discussed in Robert Smith's article, "The Furniture of Anthony G. Quervelle Part II: The pedestal tables," *The Magazine Antiques*, July 1973, pp. 90-99 (illus. Plate III, p.99).

The impressive depressed mosaic of colored marble, gadrooning, and band of gilt-brass encircling the base of the top and verde antique lion's paw feet make this one of the finest labeled examples of Quervelle's furniture.

Figure 16

Center Table, mahogany

Philadelphia, Circa 1825-1830

Height 30 1/4",
Diameter 47"

Private Collection

The edge of the top has egg and dart carving, below which is a veneered skirt. Underneath is a richly carved pedestal with acanthus leafage, gadrooned at the base. A triangular concave platform below is decorated with egg and dart molding. The lion paw feet are well carved with leafage above.

Figure 17a
close up of dolphin pedestal supports

The scrolled feet support a double platform from which four verde painted and gilded dolphins rise up to bear the circular mahogany top. Most stylistic elements of this table are directly derived from *Ackermann's Regency Furniture and Interiors*, as discussed in Chapter 4, image 53 and 54.

Figure 17 and 17a
Dolphin Support Center Table, mahogany

Philadelphia, Circa 1825-1835

Secondary wood: white pine

Height 28 1/2",
Diameter 32"

Collection of the
Andalusia Foundation

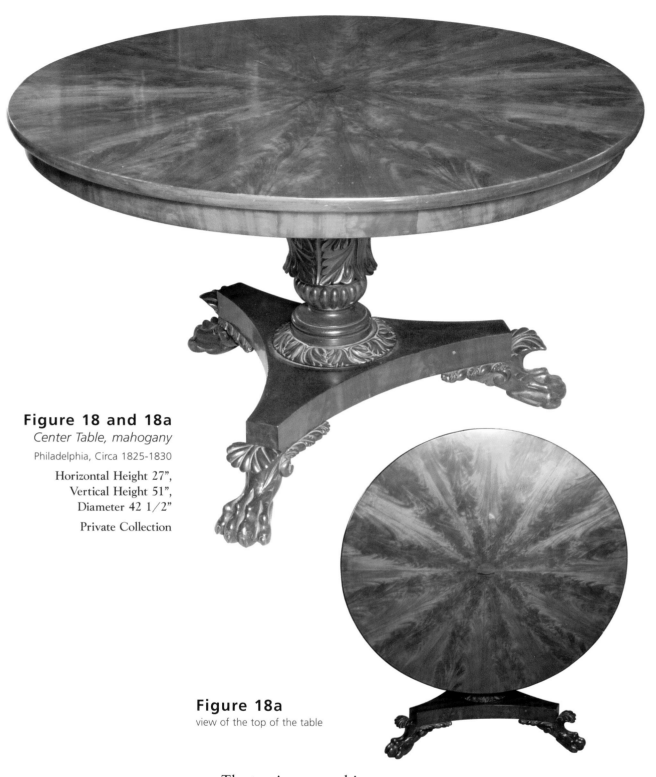

Figure 18 and 18a

Center Table, mahogany

Philadelphia, Circa 1825-1830

Horizontal Height 27",
Vertical Height 51",
Diameter 42 1/2"

Private Collection

Figure 18a

view of the top of the table

The top is veneered in rays radiating from a central rosewood disc. A leafage covered urn pedestal with gadrooning below is typical of Philadelphia. The concave triangular platform below supports three lion claw feet, which have typical leafage radiating outward above.

The mahogany veneered top is set in radiating rays from a central yellow insert. A one inch rosewood band is inset one and three quarter inches from the table edge. The octagonal mahogany veneered pedestal has a leafage carved base. A concave platform below is supported by lions paw feet with cornucopia decoration to the crests of the feet. The English prototype for this table is discussed in Chapter 4, Images 41 and 42.

Figure 19
Loo Center Table
Philadelphia, Circa 1825-1835

Height 28",
Diameter 49"

Private Collection

Figure 20 and 20a
Center Table, tilt-top gilded and painted

Philadelphia, Circa 1825-1830

Height 28 1/2",
Diameter 37"

Private Collection

Figure 20a
View of the table with the top down, illustrated cornucopia and eagle motifs.

This impressive center table features a top with gilded and painted designs of cornucopias filled with fruits, including grapes, pears and apples. The cornucopia was a popular motif seen on many forms of Empire furniture. Four cornucopia are equally proportioned, with a circle of foliage in the center. The cornucopia symbolizes prosperity. A design of gilded leaves is painted on the sides and the top of the tripartite base. The band of gilt foliage on the apron adds to the overall beauty of this well executed piece. Painted tables of this type were often placed against the wall when not in use, which allowed them to be easily viewed and admired.

A variety of motifs decorate the top, pedestal platform, and legs. The table top has four cornucopia ending in eagles heads surrounded by stars. A central circular portion of the top is decorated with a formal Chinese landscape scene. The pedestal foliage is gilded and the platform decorated with gilt designs as well.[4]

[4] A further discussion is available in Charles L. Venable, *American Furniture in the Bybee Collection*, (Auston: U of T Press, 1989) 115.

Figure 21
Tilt Top Table

Philadelphia, Circa 1820-1830

Woods: most exterior surfaces are eastern white pine; feet and pedestal are poplar; cleats are cherry.

Horizontal Height 27 7/8", Diameter 36 1/2"

Photo Courtesy of the Dallas Museum of Art, The Faith P. and Charles L. Bybee Collection, General Acquisitions Fund

Figure 22

Center Table, gilding, mahogany, rosewood, bird's eye maple

Philadelphia, Circa 1820-1830

Height 29",
Diameter 46"

Collection of the
Andalusia Foundation

This masterpiece of design incorporates decorative elements such as gesso, gilt, inlay, and veneering. The top has radiating rosewood veneers with an inlaid floral motif on the perimeter; beyond this there is a band of carved gilt leaves. Gilt foliage adorns the dramatic urn pedestal. The platform is surmounted with three gilt scrolls. At the lower edges of the platform there is gilt gadrooning. Gilt leafage carved scrolls decorate the feet.

"This remarkable and very large center table relates to two very similar tables by Anthony Quervelle, one long at Montgomery Place, Annandale-on-Hudson, New York, and now in a private collection (see Anita Delafield, "Living with Antiques-Montgomery Place, the home of Major and Mrs. John White Delafield," in *Antiques* LXXXXI [Feb.1967], p. 236 illus. center hall showing table at center), and a second table, bearing three of the familiar Quervelle stenciled labels, which was acquired by the Baltimore Museum of Art, Maryland, and featured in the exhibition *Classical Taste in America, 1800-1840* (see Wendy A. Cooper, *Classical Taste in America, 1800-1840*, exhib.cat. [The Baltimore Museum of Art/Abbeville Press Publishers, New York], p. 60 fig.36. Although the three tables vary in size (the one formerly at Montgomery Place measures 51 3/8" in diameter, the Baltimore Museum example 46 3/4" in diameter and Hirschl & Adler table 53 1/2" in diameter), all three tables are essentially the same in form- a large round drum, or skirt, being supported by five volutes carved with acanthus leaves and grapevines, each resting on boldly carved monopodia, which in turn stand on a platform centered by a raised five-pointed star. The top of this table is ornamented with a series of pie-shaped sections of mahogany "matchbook" veneers all cut from the same flitch, centered by a burled ash rondel, and bordered by bands of ebony inlay and mahogany. This represents a purely native solution to the creation of a dramatic and decorative top for an unusually large table, in contrast to the imported Italian "specimen" marble tops of the Montgomery Place and Baltimore examples. Similarly, this table rests on five boldly carved and reeded "bun" feet, which shelter concealed brass castors, whereas the other two tables have gilt-brass bun feet made and marked by Yates and Hamper, "Cabinet brass-founders, coffin furniture manufacturers, and wholesale ironmongers and factors" at 75 Long Acre, Birmingham, England (again, with concealed castors), surmounted by carved mahogany gadrooned borders."

Figure 23
Center Table, mahogany

Made by Anthony G. Quervelle
Philadelphia, Circa 1827-1830

Secondary woods: mahogany, white pine, and poplar with ebony and burled ash inlay, concealed brass castors

Height 29 1/4",
Diameter 53 1/2"

Private Collection

Photo and Description Courtesy of Hirschl & Adler Galleries, Inc.,

New York

Figure 24

Center Table, mahogany, inlaid marble and brass

Attributed to Anthony Quervelle
Philadelphia, Circa 1825-1830

Height 31",
Diameter 39"

Private Collection

Figure 24a

Detail of Micro-Mosaic Marble Top

The inset mosaic marble top has a floral and circular design with a central cross. Stenciling and gadrooning adorn the mahogany rim of the top. The mahogany veneered apron contains a gilt brass band at its base. Three scroll-lion claw columns are decorated with acanthus and grape carving. The triangular concave platform is stenciled on the edges and the platform rests on brass ball feet.

The inlaid marble top is surrounded by a wide band of gadrooning. Each leg is carved with an acanthus leaf, vines of grapes and leaves on the sides and lion's paw feet at the bottom. The five intricately carved legs rest on a star-shaped platform. This type of platform with a star motif is characteristic of Quervelle. The star is a design motif found in the Quervelle Sketchbook, discussed in Chapter 5 of this text. The feet are of oval brass forms topped by gadrooning, commonly seen on Quervelle's pier and center tables.

Figure 25

Center Table, mahogany, mahogany veneer, cast bronze feet, and various inlaid ancient marbles

Stencil of Anthony Quervelle (1789-1856)
Philadelphia, Circa 1826-1835

Height 30 1/8",
Diameter 46 3/4"

The Baltimore
Museum of Art:

Friends of the American Wing Fund; Decorative Arts Fund; and Purchase with funds provided by eighteen donors.

BMA 1990.73

Figure 26

Center Table, mahogany, gilt, ebony, bronze, brass and marble

Philadelphia, Circa 1825-1835

Length 30",
Diameter 43"

Courtesy, Winterthur Museum

The frame of the top is encircled by bands of mahogany, ebony and gilt. A black marble slab with gold and white veins decorates the top. The four scrolled legs have carved gilt acanthus leaves at the top. These are followed with descending carved grape vines and clusters that terminate at the feet. All feet are carved lions paw which are verde antique painted and rest on a concave rectangular platform. The platform rests on brass casters under each round corner. This table is believed to have originally been owned by Charles Jared Ingersoll (1782-1862) of Philadelphia.

Figure 27
Center Table with Egyptian Marble Top, mahogany

Label of Richard Parkin
Philadelphia, Circa 1830-1835

Secondary wood: poplar

Height 29 1/2",
Width 44",
Depth 22"

Photo and Description
Courtesy of Aileen Minor

Figure 27a
The blue Richard Parkin "Egyptian Hall" calling card is affixed to the bottom of the center table.

"This rare labeled carved center table with an 'Egyptian' marble top has end supports with classical anthemion motifs and a marble plinth below designed for a vase or piece of sculpture. The design for this table was taken from a design by Thomas Hope's 'Household Furniture and Interior Decoration' published in London, 1807, Plate XII. The blue paper label is tacked to the medial support of the top and reads:

RICHARD PARKIN
EGYPTIAN HALL
—SOUTH SECOND STREET"

Figure 28

Library Table, bird's eye maple, rosewood, painted slate top

Delmes label of Anthony Quervelle
Philadelphia, Circa 1828-1835

Secondary wood: poplar

Height 29",
Width 54 1/2",
Depth 30",

Collection of the
Andalusia Foundation

This masterpiece features a painted inset slate top bordered by lyres, trumpets and griffins, with a spectacular waterfall scene at the center. The form has a trestle base with scroll feet. A turned and carved stretcher connects the pedestals. The underside of the table contains a Quervelle Delmes label.

Figure 28a

Detail of the Painted Slate Top

The rays of tiger maple veneer on the top surface of the octagonal table are in the shape of a flower with a circle of ebonized wood at the center. Crescent shaped veneers edge each side of the top surface as well. The apron features a rectangular design made by attaching pieces of veneer to the flat surface of the wood. An octagonal bulbous pedestal blends well with the eight sided top above. The scroll feet suggest the date of this piece is at the beginning of the "Pillar & Scroll" era. This type of table is sometimes referred to as a "rent" table due to the revolving top of the table and the multiple drawers, which was used by the proprietors or the head of the household to collect bills. This was done by placing a bill in the drawer, turning the drawer toward the person on the other side, who would in turn place his/her money in the drawer and turn it back around so the payment would be received. Interior

Figure 29

Center Table (Rent Table), maple, tiger maple, and walnut

Philadelphia or Chester County, Circa 1830-1835

Secondary woods: poplar and white pine

Height 26 1/4", Width and Depth of Top 25"

Private Collection

Figure 29a

Detail of the underside of the table, illustrating the screw mechanism which allows the table to be rotated.

construction of this piece can be seen by the view of the disconnected top, which shows how the table screws into the pedestal, thus having the ability to rotate. A similar type of table is illustrated in Charles Montgomery's *American Furniture The Federal Period*, 1978, Figure 377, pg. 387, which is labeled as a center table. The description of this table reads, "This table is patterned on the so-called rent table made in England with numerous small drawers in the apron lettered alphabetically for the rent gatherer's convenience."[5] English design sources influenced this rent table. The use of walnut rather than mahogany may reflect the preference of Quaker abolitionists, who condemned the use of imported wood.

[5] Charles F. Montgomery, *American Furniture The Federal Period*, (New York: Bonanza Books, 1978) 388.

This table is a simply decorated Empire center table. The absence of carving and ornamentation reflects Restoration design which favors flat, un-carved veneered surfaces for visual effect. This was made at the end of the classical period, in the early Restoration style that eventually replaced Empire.

Figure 30
Tilt-Top Center Table, mahogany
Philadelphia, Circa 1830-1840

Height 27 1/8",
Diameter 31 5/8"

Private Collection

Figure 31
Carved and Veneered Mahogany Marble Top Center Table
Philadelphia, Circa 1835-1850

Height 28 3/4",
Diameter 40 1/2"

Photo and Description Courtesy of Christie's Auction Gallery, New York
© Christie's Images Limited 2006

"The circular dished marble top above a conforming frame with beaded edge over a tripartite pedestal with clustered columns above a conforming base with beading and gadrooning centering carved shells, on scrolled feet with carved shell embellishment, fitted with castors. The unusual scrolled feet recall foot designs of the mid-18th century, and suggest that this table was perhaps made at the beginning of the Rococo Revival period. Further evidence of an 1840's date for the table is the pedestal, which is suggestive of the Gothic Revival style, and which was not popular in America until the 1840's." This table illustrates the transition from classicism to Gothic Revival and Victorian Rococo Revival that occurred in America between 1835-1850.

Multiple extension pieces are available with the table, which can be expanded. The apron is decorated with reeded urns on the corners. Scrolls are supported by saber feet that are acanthus decorated. The feet end in large brass caps decorated with eagles. This table was originally owned by physician and planter James Proctor Screven (1799-1887) of Savannah, Georgia.

Figure 32

Accordion Action Extension Dining Table, mahogany

Philadelphia, Circa 1810-1820

Secondary Wood:
pine and maple

Height 28 7/8",
Width 51 1/2",
Depth 50" (folded)

Photo courtesy of the Telfair Museum of Art, Savannah, Georgia

Figure 33
Accordion Dining Table, mahogany

Possibly School of Joseph Barry
Philadelphia, Circa 1810-1825

Secondary wood: oak

Height 29 1/2",
Width 47",
Depth 48"

Storage rack with seven leaves,
Width 14 3/4"

Collection of the
Andalusia Foundation

The mahogany dining table has a type of caster composed of a lion's head with protruding front paws. This design of the brass caster is found on furniture associated with Joseph Barry of Philadelphia and William Camp of Baltimore. Joseph Barry may have had some relationship with William Camp of Baltimore for a time and it is not surprising that their work could have similarities (see Figure 77 of this text for further discussion). The sets of saber legs expand away from each other to increase the top dining surface.

"In three sections: the two outer sections with D-shape tops and hinged leaves flanking a central station with square top, all above three bulbous waterleaf-carved pedestals over flaring and tapering ring-turnings and spreading carved base above a square box-base with carved down swept legs and brass animal paw feet castors."

Figure 34
*Carved Mahogany
Three-Pedestal Dining Table*
Philadelphia, Circa 1820-1830

Height 28 1/2",
Width 132",
Depth 53 3/4"

Photo and Description Courtesy of
Christie's Auction Gallery,
New York City
© Christie's Images Limited 2006

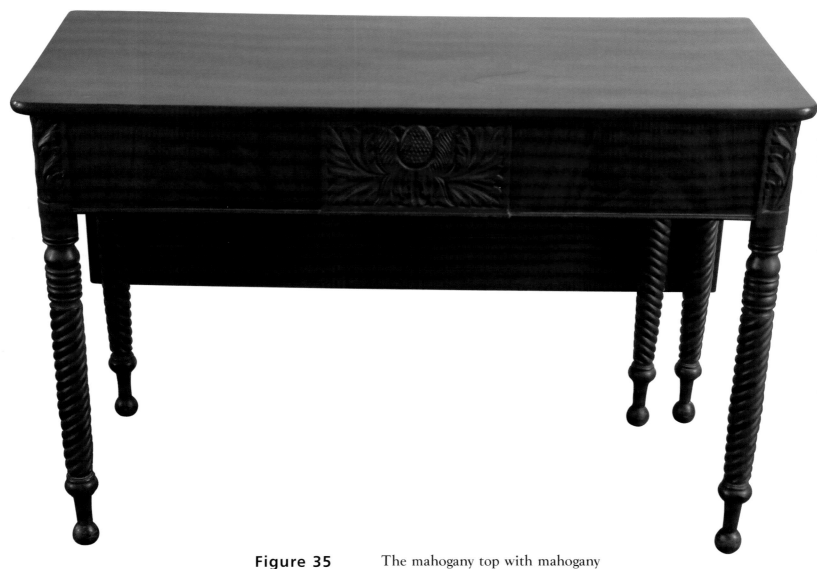

Figure 35
*Dining Table, mahogany,
mahogany veneer*
Philadelphia, Circa 1820-1825

Height 29",
Diameter 42",
Depth 20"

Private Collection

The mahogany top with mahogany veneered apron has a central carved tablet of leafage and pineapple. Spiral turned legs have disc turnings below foliage carved corners. The feet are ball and spire terminating in a ball.

This table exhibits spiral turned legs with unusual conical feet. The carving of the apron is crisp. An enclosed original Charles White bill of sale (see figure 36a on next page) to David Newbold notes the table was shipped to New Jersey via the steam boat Pennsylvania on March 29, 1827. This letter gives instructions for assembly of the multiple sections of the table.

Figure 36
Dining Table, mahogany, mahogany veneer

Made by Charles White
Philadelphia, March 1827

Secondary wood: pine

Height 28",
Width 46",
Depth 22 1/8"
(exclusive of leaf)

Courtesy, The Winterthur Library: Decorative Arts Photographic Collection

Phila'd March 29. 1827

David Newbold will find
all the artickles on Board of
Steam Boat Pennsylvania
Put on Board with Small Slips
of Paper on them
2 Beaurous one Sofa 2 Diny
Tables one wash Stand one candle
Do. one high Post Bedstea
one work Table — the Zug ter
one Shut. Two carpets one couclid
2 Blankets 1 Bag & 1 Piece of Bag
the will please to return as Soon
as a chance may offer as I was
obligd to Lend Some Such things
with Mr Job Sricks thing it makes
us in want of them a little Sooner
when you go to put up the Bedstea
take out a Screw of the side Piece
and put through the Post the
Backward way and punch off the
caps that are over the Screw hole

The Dining Tables when you go to
open them to Set them together
Just Raise the leaf up Level and
Turn the whole Top Round on the
frame and when Leting the leaf
Down again be Carefull to Bring
the Top entirely Back again
befor the Leaf goes Down or the
corner may catch on the frame
there is a Bundle under the work
Table Tied in that has the note
and Keys & 2 Brass fasteners for
the Diny Tables ———
My family are all well as usuale
Rebecca & my Self was at Trenton last
Sunday Samuel family was as
wall as usual Except their child
it had a Bad cold, please to accept
this from thy friend & Brother in law
Chs White ———

This table was originally owned by John (1777-1861) and Rebecca (Horner) (1782-1863) Ruckman of Bucks County, Pennsylvania, and remained in the possession of the family until 1965. It has always been with a card table labeled by Quervelle that is pictured in "Queries and Opinions," *The Magazine Antiques*, May 1935, page 199. A card table labeled by Anthony G. Quervelle with identical features is pictured in *The Magazine Antiques*, June 1977, 1061 (See also figure 86 in this text).

Figure 37

Two-Pedestal Dining Table, mahogany

Attributed to Anthony Q. Quervelle
Philadelphia, Circa 1825-1835

Secondary woods: poplar, ash, and white pine

Height 28",
Width 48",
Depth 22 1/4"

Private Collection

Figure 38

Dining Table, Mahogany

Philadelphia, Circa 1810-1825

Height 28 1/2",
Width 54",
Depth (to leaf) 24 1/2"

Photo Courtesy of
Mr. F.J. Carey III

This illustrated section is one of two identical parts that fit together to form the assembled table. The mahogany top has a veneered mahogany skirt decorated with a central medallion of leafage. A pedestal below has a foliage carved urn finished above with vertical reeding. Four saber legs support the pedestal. These curve upward and outward above the knee and are decorated with reeding, foliage carving, and circular disks. The feet are reeded brass caps.

This dining table features a pedestal base composed of four carved, scrolled supports which surround a carved pineapple at the center of the base. The outer surface of each support is intricately carved with fruit and foliage. A single drop leaf is hinged to a rotating top supported by a plain, rectangular frame which rests on the scrolls. The platform rests on four carved lion's paw feet with overhanging acanthus leaves on the top of each, terminating in castors. Please see Figure 91 for a card table with a similar lyre and scroll arrangement.

Figure 39
Dining Table (one of a pair), mahogany

Related to the shop of Anthony G. Quervelle Philadelphia, Circa 1820-1840

Secondary woods: pine

Height 30",
Width 52",
Depth 51 1/4"

Courtesy, Winterthur Museum

Gift of the Aetna Life and Casualty Insurance Company

Figure 40

*Dining Table, mahogany
(one of a pair)*

Philadelphia or Baltimore,
Circa 1820-1840

Secondary woods:
poplar, white pine,
basswood, and cherry

Height 29 3/4",
Width 36 5/8",
Depth 18 3/4"
(Drop-leaf down)

Height 25 5/8",
Width 36 5/8",
Depth 78 1/2"
(two tables joined)

Collection of Munson-Williams-
Proctor Arts Institute, Museum of
Art, Utica, New York.

Museum Purchase 60.20.a-b

Photo by John Bigelow Taylor,
N.Y.C.

The apron of the mahogany top is carved with foliage. An intricately carved basket of fruit makes up the pedestal. This rests on a veneered platform supported by four lion claw feet which rise up to become eagles' heads. The use of fruit baskets as a decorative motif is often associated with Baltimore furniture. Opposed eagle heads are often seen in the empire period on chair backs made by Charles Honoré Lannuier. Additional information about this table is in Anna Tobin D'Ambrosio, *Masterpieces of American Furniture* from the Munson-Williams-Procter Institute, Albany, New York, 1999, pages 58 and 59.

The pedestal supports have bulbous turnings ending in saber feet. Reeding adorns the top of the saber legs. The central extension section of the top lacks the apron on the ends.

Figure 41
Dining Table, mahogany
Philadelphia, Circa 1810-1820

Height 29 1/2",
Width 101 1/2",
Depth 53 3/4"

Private Collection

Figure 42

Dining Table, mahogany

Philadelphia, Circa 1830-1840

Height 29 1/2"
Width 47"
Depth 48"
Leaves: 14 1/4"W, 14 5/8"W,
14 3/4"W, 14 7/8" W

Collection of the
Andalusia Foundation

This table has circular ends expanded with leaves, conforming to a mahogany veneered skirt. The pedestal bases are finished with a variant scroll foot which suggests the influence of the later restoration style which was to become the vogue by 1840.

This table is one of the few documented pieces by Thomas Cook after his business separation from Richard Parkin. The table was made toward the end of the Empire period, which is evident by the large scroll supports and scrolled feet. Margaret Telfair, of the prominent Savannah family, ordered this table from Thomas Cook in 1836 during the annual trip north. It was common for southern planters to visit and shop in Philadelphia on an annual basis.

Figure 43
*Circular Dining Table
(with leaves), bird's-eye maple*

Made by Thomas Cook
Philadelphia, 1825-1830

Secondary woods:
oak and pine

Height 28 5/16",
Width 52 1/2",
Diameter with
small leaves 72 1/2",
Diameter with
large leaves 85 1/2"

Telfair Museum of Art,
Savannah, Georgia (1875.57)

Bequest of Mary Telfair, 1875

Peter Harholdt, 2003

Platform Pedestal Tables Outside Philadelphia

Figure 44a
Detail of foliage carved pedestal

Figure 44
Center Table, mahogany
Baltimore or Possibly Philadelphia,
Circa 1820-1830

Secondary wood: white pine,
pedestal double through tendoned
into platform

Height 30",
Diameter 37"

Private Collection

This table has a foliated vase pedestal on which acanthus leaves curve outwards towards the top. The form of this table may have derived from Plate 69 in George Smith's *Collection of Designs for Household Furniture*, published in 1808, which illustrates a "Pillar and Claw Table" with a rectangular platform and a pedestal with a foliage design. Leafage at the top of the lion claw feet does not curve upward and outward as with Philadelphia feet of the period, but lies flat against the crest of the foot. This is typical of Baltimore style. The leafage carving of the pedestal has a very Philadelphia like appearance, which illustrates the stylistic interplay between these closely geographically related centers.

Concentric reeding decorates the outer edge of the white marble top. The mahogany veneered apron below is divided into two horizontal elements. An urn shaped pedestal is sharply incised with vertical reeding. This type of vertically reeded urn pedestal has been commonly found on proven Baltimore furniture of this period. Below the urn and between the legs is additional applied vertical reeding. All three legs are decorated with leafage to the knees and end in upturned scroll feet (Please see Figures 70 and 71 for similar upturned scroll feet on Connelly attributed Philadelphia tables of the same period).

The use of vertical and horizontal reeding to create a unified flowing form makes this an exceptionally fine example of Baltimore craftsmanship. Marble top center tables of Baltimore origin are relatively rare.

Figure 45 and 45a

Marble Top Mahogany Center Table

Baltimore, Maryland, Circa 1815-1825

Secondary Wood (by micro analysis): Apron frame is white pine, cross support of top is white oak.

Height 27 3/4", Diameter 39 3/4"

Figure 45a
Detail of the Reeded Marble Top

The shape of the pedestal and feet reflect a linear simplification of classical elements typical of the Pillar and Scroll Restoration period combined with early Victorian Rococo features.

Figure 46

Center Table, mahogany

American, Circa 1840-1850

Dimensions unrecorded

Flomaton Antique Auction

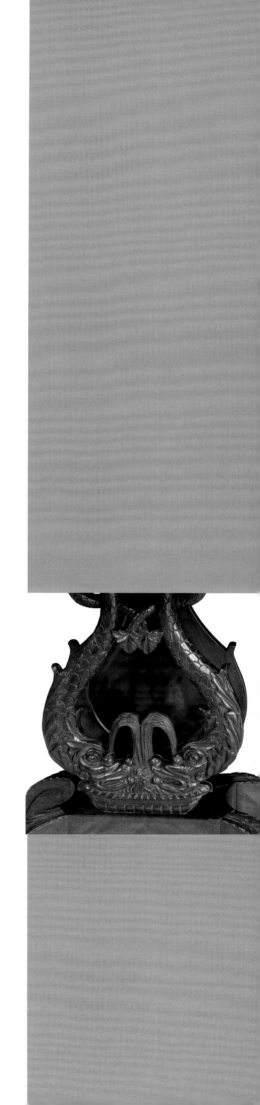

CHAPTER 7
CARD, BREAKFAST, SOFA, CONSOLE AND OCCASIONAL TABLES

Card, Breakfast, Sofa, Console and Occasional Tables

Card tables made in the beginning of the nineteenth century were noticeably different from Federal and earlier tables. The tables were heavier in form and elegantly carved and ornamented. The plain, straight-legged card tables of the past disappeared, replaced by a variety of styles, including lyre-based supports, foliage-carved pedestals, carved dolphin supports and lion's paw feet, which were either carved or ended in brass casters. Frequently made in pairs, card tables (along with worktables) have

survived in greater abundance than many other furniture forms. This can be credited to the fact that card tables, when not in use, were often treated like pier tables and placed against the wall, thus saving them from the becoming scratched or damaged.

American card tables were often made of mahogany veneered on pine, poplar or ash. The carving of the pedestals and other elements of Philadelphia tables was more intricate and lavish compared to New York or Boston examples. There were two types of pedestals that were popular; the first was a Doric column set on a square or rectangular plinth and the second type was a vase form combined with a Doric column. The second type of pedestal found on card tables was similar to pedestals found on center tables, which often incorporated a vase form with tightly overhanging leaves, bands of gadrooning or rings of concentric disks. The origin of the overhanging leaf design has often been attributed to London cabinetmakers, namely Rudolph Ackermann, who illustrated the front legs of an upholstered chair with this leaf design in the *Repository of Arts* in 1817, and George Smith, who illustrated a "Pillar & Claw Table", (plate 69), published in *The Cabinet-Maker and Upholsterer's Guide of 1826*.[1]

Plain or reeded saber legs with brass paw feet are seen on early Empire card tables, although this design became less fashionable in the 1820s. Four carved lion's paw feet with overhanging leaves, which rested below the rectangular or square platform, are more commonly associated with Empire card tables. Another distinguishing feature includes the frame of the top, which had plain, rounded or canted front corners, and often have a combination of convex and concave planes that contrasted with the flat surface of the central tablet, which remained plain, reeded or carved. Elements that increased the price of card tables and made them fancier in appearance included using other veneered woods such bird's eye maple instead of mahogany, extensive carving on the central tablet, pedestal and/or supports and feet, and the use of the above-mentioned dolphin and lyre motifs.

The breakfast or Pembroke table was a rectangular form with a drawer at one of the narrow ends with a leaf on each of the broad sides, which could be lifted and fixed to expand the top surface. Classical breakfast tables are identical in basic design to earlier Pembroke tables, but are larger in size than earlier examples so that they can seat four. The supports and feet of this type of table vary and are illustrated in this section.

[1] Smith, Pedestal Tables 94

Sofa tables are considered by some to be the rarest of all American drop leaf tables. The sofa table was a popular form in England and became a fairly fashionable form in America, although they were only produced for a brief period (about 1810-mid-1830s).[2] Several fine examples were made in New York, Philadelphia and Boston. Thomas Sheraton published a sofa table in his *Cabinet Dictionary* of 1803 and described its function to be "used before a sofa", and that "the ladies chiefly occupy them to draw, write and read."[3] The sofa table may have served the same purpose as a modern day coffee table and was meant to be viewed from all sides. The tops of sofa tables often employed similar ornamentation used on other table forms at the time such as veneers, inlay, brass mounts and pulls, molding, banded borders and sometimes canted corners.[4] The form itself was in the newest taste and was associated with convenience, ease and mobility. Sofa tables feature rectangular tops with two long drawers in the front skirt, with short end leaves that provide little additional surface when raised.

Sofa tables differ from other tables in their dimensions; the sofa table is longer and the breakfast table is wider. Both types of tables incorporate drawers; Pembroke and breakfast table drawers are usually narrower than those of sofa tables, which tend to have two drawers placed side by side on both facades (since the tables were meant to be seen from both sides, although one side is likely to have false drawers). In 1808, after Sheraton's *Cabinet Dictionary* was published, George Smith suggested, in his *Collection of Designs for Household Furniture and Interior Decoration*, that sofa tables could be used "for the Drawing Room, Breakfast Parlor, or Library".[5] The designs of sofa tables varied. The most common was the table supported by two standards which would each rest on two feet. Several other designs were also popular. One of these was a pedestal base with four feet that supported the table frame. Another was the lyre-based support. A third design was a support consisting of a straight stretcher and four claws. The pedestal bases were often carved and/or turned with saber legs. A table sharing the same form as the sofa table but without the end leaves that elevate was known as the occasional table. The occasional table might be placed in front of or behind a sofa, or in any part of the room where it would be useful. Another type of table that is illustrated in this chapter is the console table, which is similar in form to a card table except that the top does not open (see figure 53 in this chapter, which has a fixed white marble top, reminiscent of the type of top used on a pier table) and it is meant to be placed against the wall.

[2] Philip D. Zimmerman, "The American sofa table," *The Magazine Antiques* May 1999: 750.

[3] Zimmerman 746

[4] Zimmerman 748

[5] Zimmerman 747

Figure 47

Specimen Table, satinwood, mahogany, rosewood, poplar, white pine

School of Joseph Barry
Philadelphia, Circa 1810-1820

Secondary woods:
white pine and poplar

Height 39",
Width 49",
Depth 27"

Photograph and Description
Courtesy of the Winterthur
Museum

"This remarkable and singular table was probably fashioned exclusively for the display of marine shells. Its hinged lid is mirrored on the underside and opens to reveal multiple removable compartmented trays in layers. The carcass is entirely veneered with panels of satinwood that are arranged as a fan of pie-shaped wedges emanating from a semi-circle on the top. Those on the front and sides are rectangular and outlined with rosewood crossbanding. All four legs in the form of tapered reeded columns with hairy paw feet and acanthus leaf capitals relate closely to those on the fronts of sideboards signed by or attributed to Joseph B. Barry. They and the spread eagles sitting atop the front two are entirely verde antiqued."

"The table displays Barry's characteristic torus molding (at the top and bottom of the apron), combination of flat palmetto leaves (on the pedestal), crisp acanthus leaves (on the knees), brass highlights and a top veneered in rays."[6]

Author's note: The skull motif at the base is a bacranium, the skull of a sacrificial ox, around the neck of which garlands were hung during ancient rituals.[7] The motif as it is used here derives from ancient Greek architecture where it was carved into metopes, part of the frieze on temples of the Doric order in Greece and Rome.

Figure 48
Card Table, mahogany

School of Joseph Barry
Philadelphia, Circa 1812

Secondary wood:
poplar and white pine

Height 30",
Width 36 1/2",
Depth 18"

Private Collection

[6] Fennimore and Trump 1212-1225

[7] Morley 40

Figure 49

Mechanical Card Table, mahogany

Philadelphia, Circa 1810-1820

Secondary wood:
oak, poplar, and Atlantic
white cedar

Height 30",
Width 39",
Depth 22 1/4"

Photo Courtesy of The Biggs
Museum of American Art,
Dover, DE

The top has serpentine corners with an elliptic front; below the skirt are beehive-shaped drops. An urn-shaped pedestal rests on three long legs, all of which feature acanthus carving at the tops and a carved shell, or fan, motif cut into the sides. When the table is pulled forward, the two rear legs swing backward. These are connected by an iron mechanical mechanism through the pedestal to two butterfly supports through the back of the skirt. The butterfly leaves simultaneously extend outward to support the opened top. This "trick" mechanism is occasionally seen on New York card tables and is very rare on Philadelphia examples.

The top is elliptical with serpentine corners with conforming apron. Four reeded and carved colonnettes support the top. The platform is carved with a panel of acanthus leaves at the front. The saber legs are topped with abruptly ending foliage in a Philadelphia manner. There are inset panels on the sides of the legs; this is a common technique of Philadelphia craftsmen.

Figure 50
Pedestal Base Card Table,
mahogany and brass

School of Henry Connelly
Philadelphia, Circa 1810-1820

Height 29",
Width 36",
Depth 19 1/4"

Courtesy, Winterthur Museum

Bequest of Henry Francis Du Pont

Figure 51
*Card Table (one of a pair),
mahogany, mahogany veneers*
School of Henry Connelly
Philadelphia, Circa 1810-1820

Secondary wood:
white pine and poplar

Height 30 3/4",
Width 36 3/8",
Depth 19 5/8"

Published: Sweeney, "Furniture in
the Biggs Collection," p. 903, fig. 3

Photo Courtesy of The Biggs
Museum of American Art,
Dover, DE

The top rests on four colonnettes,
each with reeding on the swelled portion of the column and carved acanthus
leaves on the bottom section. Acanthus
leaves are again seen on the tops of
each of the legs and on all sides of the
platform base. The feet are capped with
brass lion's paws. "The association of
this table with Ephraim Haines and
Henry Connelly is based on its similarity to a pair of card tables with dolphin
standards that Connelly made for
Stephen Girard in 1817, a similar table
is published in Montgomery, American
Furniture, pages 337 & 339, no. 316."

[8] Philip D. Zimmerman and Jennifer Faulds
Goldsborough, *The Sewell C. Biggs Collection of
American Art, A Catalogue*, Vol. 1 (Iceland: Oddi
Printing, 2002) 50.

Figure 52
Card Table, mahogany

School of Henry Connelly
Philadelphia, Circa 1810-1820

Secondary wood of frame:
front and sides, white pine; back,
poplar; support brace, poplar; the
apron is constructed with stack
lamination.

Secondary wood of base platform:
oak and white pine

Height 31",
Width 36",
Depth 17"

Private Collection

The top and conforming apron are elliptical with serpentine sides. Reeding decorates the edge of the tops. Finials are placed below the apron of the top and are attached to square blocks fitted into the sides of the table in a manner favored by Connelly. Four colonnettes that rise from the platform are reeded and swell with carved leafage towards the base. A flame-topped urn is placed between the columns. The saber legs have inset carved panels on the sides that are typical of Philadelphia, as is the reeding on the top of the legs which ends abruptly. The shape of the top, molded legs and combination of reeding and leaf carving on the columns relates to work by Henry Connelly.

Figure 52a
Detail of the unusual x brace support constructed into the bottom of the platform.

Figure 53

Console Table, mahogany, marble and brass

Philadelphia, Circa 1810

Height 33 13/16",
Width 36 11/16",
Depth 18 3/4"

The Saint Louis Art Museum. Acquired in honor of the 50th anniversary of Mr. G. S. Rosborough with the Measuregraph Company of St. Louis. Given by The Measuregraph Company through Mr. and Mrs. George S. Rosborough Jr.

The marble top and conforming mahogany apron are of elliptical shape. Four colonnettes that arise from the platform are reeded and surround a flame urn that has concentric discs at its base. Toward the base of the columns is leaf carving. Each column terminates in a turned and horizontally reeded design, known also as a beehive design, which is sometimes seen (as feet) on sideboards (see figure 266).

The length of the pedestal portion is slightly longer than usual, but the saber legs with acanthus carving at the tops, brass lion's paw casters and white marble top give the table an overall sophisticated and balanced appearance.

Author's Note: This closely relates to the Philadelphia card table illustrated in figure 52, and is from the Connelly-Haines School.

Each pair of saber legs is connected to a pedestal support, which is then joined by turned stretchers. The side leaves of the table are elliptical; the knees have leafage carving that ends abruptly in a Philadelphia manner. This table and similar forms have been attributed to Henry Connelly, although the foundation for this is conjectural.[9]

[9] Garvan 52

Figure 54
Breakfast Table, mahogany

Attributed to Henry Connelly
Philadelphia, Circa 1800-1820

Height 29",
Width 23",
Depth 42"

Photo Courtesy of
Mr. F.J. Carey III

Figure 55

Breakfast Table, mahogany

Philadelphia, Circa 1815

Secondary wood: poplar

Height 29",
Width 24",
Depth 42"

Collection of
Mr. F.J. Carey III

This small-scale breakfast table has a neatly carved foliage pedestal with a brass lion's face drawer knob and brass lion's paw casters. There is acanthus carving at the top of the legs, below which is reeding.

The mahogany top has two rectangular leaves with rounded corners. Both ends of the apron contain an inlay of brass. Profuse leafage carving decorates the urn pedestal. The platform below is X-shaped with four saber legs projecting from the four elements of the cross. The ends of the saber legs are finished with lion claw feet that exhibit typical Philadelphia upturned leafage carving above. The sides of the saber legs are paneled, which is also a common decorative device of Philadelphia cabinets makers of this period.

Figure 56
Breakfast Table, mahogany
Philadelphia, Circa 1810-1820

Secondary wood (transverse case support board above pedestal): chestnut

Height 29",
Width 40",
Depth 24 1/2"

Private Collection

Figure 57

Pembroke or Breakfast Table, mahogany

Philadelphia, Circa 1820-1825
126 Dressing Glass Label by Anthony Quervelle

Secondary wood: pine and poplar

Height 30", Width 24", Depth 42"

Private Collection

This well-balanced and well-carved mahogany table employs a platform base supporting a gadrooned vase and acanthus-carved pedestal, a form often favored by Quervelle and other Philadelphia makers. At a distance the downward-flowing leafage of the urn pedestal resembles a "spouting fountain." A drawer contains a partial 126 dressing glass Quervelle label. The original lion's head brass hardware on the drawer relates to that of the attributed Quervelle secretaire a abattant illustrated in figure 286a. This design closely relates to a breakfast table, figure 13, in Robert C. Smith's article, "Part II: The pedestal tables," *The Magazine Antiques*, July 1973, page 96.

Lion paw feet support a concave curved rectangular platform, above which the pedestal is initially hexagonal and then circular. The top includes an apron containing a drawer. An original glass knob decorates the drawer.

Figure 58
Breakfast Table, mahogany
Philadelphia, Circa 1825

Height 30 1/2",
Width 23 1/2",
Depth 40 1/2"

Private Collection

Figure 59

Breakfast Table, mahogany

Philadelphia, Circa 1825

Secondary wood: poplar

Height 29",
Width 23",
Depth 34"

Collection of the
Andalusia Foundation

The four round column supports are unusual. They rest on two platforms joined by two turned horizontal braces. This trestle design imparts strength, but is less decorative.

Tables of this type served as occasional tables in a parlor and were used
for cards, reading or serving small
meals. The long saber legs and urn shaft
are similar to Charles Montgomery's
Federal Furniture, page 332, except this
table has three legs, while the table in
Federal Furnitures has four.

Figure 60
Pembroke Table, mahogany
Philadelphia, Circa 1800-1820

Height 28 1/2",
Width 26 1/2" (Leaves up),
       13 1/2" (Leaves down),
Depth 20 1/2"

Private Collection

Figure 61

Pair of Game Tables with Lyre Bases, mahogany

Philadelphia, Circa 1810

Secondary woods: poplar, pine, and cherry, with gilt-brass lyre strings and paw toe caps and castors

Height 28 1/16",
Width 18 5/8"

Open 36 x 37 5/16",
Open Width 37 5/16"

Private Collection

Photo & Description Courtesy of Hirschl & Adler Galleries, New York

"This pair of games, or card, tables fits neatly into one of several groups of lyre-based card tables produced in Philadelphia in the years surrounding 1810. One group of tables, of which there are examples in the collections of the Los Angeles County Museum, CA, Cleveland Museum of Art, Ohio, the house museum Cliveden, Philadelphia, and the collection of Linda and George Kaufman, Norfolk, VA (see J. Michael Flanigan, *American Furniture from the Kaufman Collection* [Harry N. Abrams, New York, 1986], p. 184-5), has been documented by Henry Hawley in a study called "Philadelphia Tables with Lyre Supports," published in The Cleveland Museum of Art Bulletin [January 1988], vol. 75, pp.3-27. A second group of Philadelphia card tables with lyre bases, to which the present pair belongs, lacks the exotic veneers that are the signature characteristic of the first group, but typically display a carved lyre support of excellent proportion and scale and occasionally other bits of carving, as seen in a similar table published in *American Antiques from Israel Sack Collection* [Highland House Publishers, Inc., Alexandria, VA, 1989], IX, p. 2535 no. P6022 illus., where it is given to Philadelphia and broadly assigned to the years 1810-25. Other than slight decorative differences, notably the addition of carved rosettes, flanking the bowed front and on the plinth, and ormolu rosettes, on the sides of each of the tops of the four saber legs and at the top of the lyre, the Sack table and the present example are identical, with classically bowed fronts, acanthus-carved open lyre supports with brass strings, and molded splayed legs terminated by gilt-brass paw foot toe-caps and castors."

The rectangular top with canted corners has a conforming skirt veneered in mahogany. Lyre supports are carved with acanthus leaves. "Unlike most card tables that are ornamented on the front aspects only, the acanthus carving of the front lyre also appears on the back one."[10] The legs, in the form of scrolls, have acanthus carving at the tops, terminating with brass lion's paw casters at the feet. "Both leaves of the top, decorated with highly figured mahogany veneers, rotate on a swivel set off center so that the frame supports the hinged leaf. This innovation avoids the need for a swinging leg or a hinged support, called a "fly".[11]

Author's Note: The table features a "square-edge top", which is more frequently associated with New York than Philadelphia.[12]

[10] Zimmermann and Jennifer Faulds Goldsborough 54
[11] Zimmermann and Jennifer Faulds Goldsborough 54
[12] Montgomery 340

Figure 62
Card Table with Lyre Support, mahogany
Philadelphia, Circa 1810-1830

Secondary woods: yellow pine, poplar, and maple

Height 31",
Width 36 7/8",
Depth 18 1/8"

Photo Courtesy of The Biggs Museum of American Art, Dover, DE

Figure 63

Card Table, mahogany,
mahogany veneer,
ebony, brass inlay

Philadelphia, Circa 1810-1830
Attributed to Joseph Barry

Secondary wood: white pine

Height 28 3/8",
Width 36 3/8",
Depth 18 1/8"

Photo Courtesy of The Biggs
Museum of American Art,
Dover, DE

On the top there is a band of ebony with foliated brass inlays and rounded edges. The apron of the top has a panel of ebony with brass inlay of a bow-and-arrow motif. Crossed lyres align with the corners of the base to make up the pedestal. The lion legs combine acanthus leaves on the tops and gentle scrolls on the sides, known as scrolled palmettes. Unusual brass caps decorate the base of the feet. These caps consist of a lion's head with protruding front paws (see figures 33, 77 and 78 for other items in this text decorated with identical brass caps).

The rectangular top and apron have swelled fronts. Satinwood veneer decorates the top edges, below which are two whirling rosette and spike brass mounts on either side. The lyre-based pedestal is ornamented with whirling rosette and spike brass mounts; mounts of this design have been found on a number of lyre-based pedestal worktables. On the front of the platform is a large brass mount that features a wreath design flanked on either side by cornucopias. The saber legs terminate in brass lion's paw casters.

Figure 64

Card Table, mahogany, satinwood and maple veneers

Philadelphia, Circa 1815-1820

Secondary wood: ash

Height 29 1/4",
Width 34 15/16",
Depth 17 7/16"

The Baltimore
Museum of Art

Gift of Mr. and Mrs. Bernard Trupp

BMA 1964.51.1

Figure 65 and 65a

*Lyre-based Card Table,
mahogany*

Possibly School of Joseph Barry
Philadelphia, Circa 1818

Height 30",
Width 37",
Depth 19"

Private Collection

The use of brass ornamentation on the front of the top, lyre and feet are suggestive of Barry's work. For a full discussion, see "Joseph B. Barry, Philadelphia Cabinetmaker," by Donald L. Fennimore & Robert T. Trump, *The Magazine Antiques*, Volume 135, 1989 pages 1212-1225.

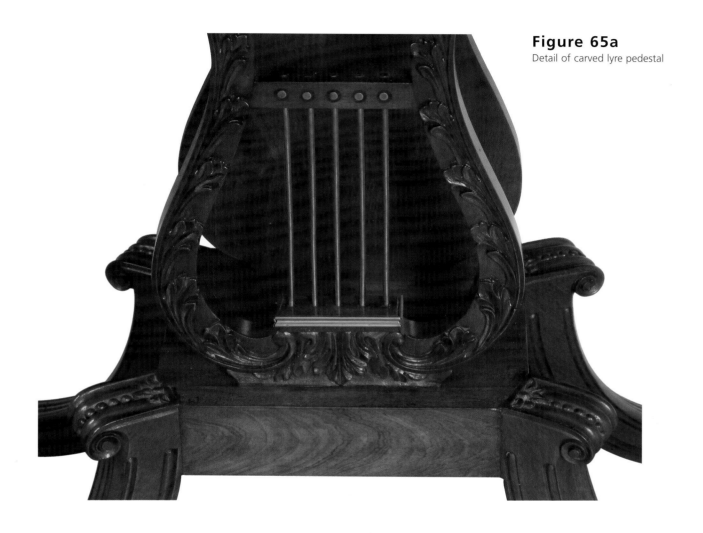

Figure 65a
Detail of carved lyre pedestal

Figure 66

Card Table with Lyre Base,
mahogany, brass, brass casters

Philadelphia, Circa 1815

Secondary woods: white pine

Height 29 1/2",
Width 35 1/4",
Depth 17 3/4"

Courtesy, Winterthur Museum

Bequest of Henry Francis du Pont

Canted corners are used to decorate the front of the top. The veneered apron below rests on a lyre support pedestal. Brass leaves and rosettes adorn the lyre. Acanthus brass foliage decorates the saber legs. This brass foliage of the knees ends in an abrupt Philadelphia manner. The square-cornered top and apron are more frequently seen in New York than Philadelphia.

Two opposed dolphins that spout water support the double elliptical top and apron. The platform below is joined to four saber legs decorated with foliage and reeding. This table serves as a standard for defining the best quality of workmanship. The superb use of matched mahogany veneers, unique design of carved dolphins in a lyre-formed pedestal and reeded saber legs capped in brass lion's paws are indicative of Connelly's skill as a cabinetmaker.

Figure 67

Card Table (one of a pair), mahogany (Swietenia sp.)

Made by Henry Connelly
Bill of Sale, Philadelphia October 27, 1817: one pair Card Tables…$90

Secondary wood: white pine

Height 30",
Width 36 3/8",
Depth 19 1/2"

Courtesy of the Stephen Girard Collection, Girard College, Philadelphia, PA

Figure 68

Card Table, mahogany

Attributed to Henry Connelly
Philadelphia, Circa 1800-1820

Height 28",
Width 35 3/4",
Depth 18"

Private Collection

The elliptical top exhibits a double curve in the front with a conforming apron. A band of rosewood veneer decorates the base of the apron. The pedestal is in the form of two dolphins that spout water. Saber legs with acanthus-carved knees are joined to the platform above. This piece is very similar in form to the Stephen Girard card table pictured in this volume (figure 67).

This superbly carved card table features a lyre-based pedestal formed by dolphins and acanthus carving on the tops of all four legs and small lion's paw feet (brass casters). The side pilasters of the apron terminate into acorn finials on either end. This table is very similar to a carved dolphin base card table made in 1817 by Connelly for Stephen Girard (figure 67), except Girard's table does not feature the acorn finials. The carved spouts of water above the dolphins' heads and intertwined dolphins' tails that terminate in a leaf design are nearly identical on these two pieces.

Figure 69
Card Table, mahogany

Henry Connelly (1770-1826)
Philadelphia, Circa 1815-1820

Secondary woods: maple and pine

Height 28 3/4",
Width 36 3/8",
Depth 35 7/8"

The Metropolitan Museum of Art,
Gift of Fred F. Rogers, Jr., 1965
(65.142)

Figure 70

Game Table, mahogany,
mahogany veneer

Attributed to Henry Connelly
Philadelphia, Circa 1810-1820

Secondary woods:
pine, poplar, and oak

Height 29 3/4",
Width 36",
Depth 18 1/2"

Private Collection

Photo and Description Courtesy of
Didier, Inc., New Orleans

"The revolving, fold-over straight-fronted top with half-serpentine ends is rayed at the back, having segmented mahogany veneered panels extending toward the front. The apron is veneered in matched crotch mahogany. It rests on a vigorously carved lyre dolphin base, silhouetted in the back by a mahogany and mahogany-veneered lyre support, all resting on a veneered, shaped platform over a straight-fronted veneered apron surrounded by banded veneer, which continues on the concave sides. The whole rests on four mahogany sabre legs, "hollowed out" on each side, terminating into an upturned scroll, having carved bosses on either end resting on ball feet. The legs are tapered and the knees are carved in acanthus panel."

Figure 70a

Detail of opposed dolphins

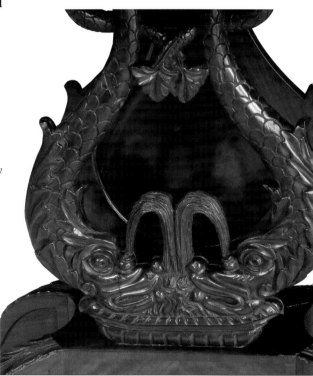

"The stylized pedestal lyre-end drop-leaf table by Connelly is very similar to the dolphin base card table in form and is characteristic of Connelly. The mahogany drop-leaf ended top is shaped in a serpentine form, which rests on a working and false drawer retaining their original-period round glass pulls and brass backs. The side pilasters terminate into acorn finials on either end. The whole rests on a pair of stylized mahogany lyre supports having carved bosses on each side and connects the pair of delicately turned, internecking baluster-shaped stretchers connecting a graduating ring turning. The whole rests on four tapering sabre legs in mahogany, "hollowed out" on each side terminating into an up-turned scroll, having carved bosses on either end resting on ball feet."

Figure 71
Game Table, mahogany

Attributed to Henry Connelly
Philadelphia, Circa 1805-1820

Secondary woods:
pine and oak

Height 28 1/2",
Width 19",
Depth 36"

Private Collection

Photo and Description Courtesy of Didier, Inc., New Orleans

Figure 72

Sofa Table, mahogany, mahogany veneer, brass mounts

Philadelphia, Circa 1810-1825

Secondary woods: white pine, poplar, and maple

Height 28 5/8", Width 45 1/4", Depth 24 7/8"

Photo Courtesy of The Biggs Museum of American Art, Dover, DE

As described by Thomas Sheraton in 1803, sofa tables were generally made between five and six feet long and from 22 inches to two feet broad; the frame is divided into two drawers...[13] The sofa table was used for reading and writing, but the form was not overly poplar in America and few examples exist. This sofa table has typical short leaves at each end, two drawers with lion's head handles and a lyre support pedestal. The absence of carving on this table is supplemented by the many brass ornaments, including brass rods on the lyre, a brass mount on the front platform base and the brass lion's paw casters.

[13] Montgomery 352

The top case with drawer and side leaves is supported at each end by a lyre pedestal surmounted on two saber legs. Double turned stretchers connect the two ends. An identical table bearing the printed paper label of Lawrence Sink is pictured in Antiques Magazine, December 1995, page 730. Another closely related example is in Newton Elwell, *The Architecture, Furniture and Interiors of Maryland and Virginia during the Eighteenth Century*, plate VI.

Figure 73
Mahogany Table
Attributed to Lawrence Sink
Philadelphia, Circa 1800-1823

Secondary woods:
poplar and white pine

Height 29 1/2",
Width 24 1/2",
Depth 42"

Private Collection

Figure 74

Pair of Classical Carved Mahogany Dolphin Base Game Tables

Philadelphia, Circa 1825-1835

Height 29 1/2",
Width 38",
Depth 19"

Photo and Description Courtesy of
Mr. Carswell Rush Berlin,
New York City

"Each with an oblong hinged, swivel top with conforming frieze of highly figured mahogany with ebonized molding and burl maple trim supported by a pair of forward-facing carved dolphins resting on a trestle base with an elaborately carved stretcher, raised on carved animal paw feet on brass castors." Secondary wood: Cherry. Minor veneer replacement and restoration to cracks in two dolphins. Descending in the family of Moses Levy and Charles Ridgely Carroll, these tables were published in Edgar G. Miller, Jr. American Antique Furniture (New York: M. Barrows & Company, 1937) Volume Two, page 803. Miller says, "a monstrosity in the Empire style...the time and skill spent on carving on [these] card tables was worthy of a better style, especially on the carving of the scales, of the shells under the skirt, and on the leaves over the feet..." Miller's quaint and parochial perspective belies the power and fancifulness of these great tables.

The use of dolphins as a decorative motif in Rococo furniture seems to appear first in a dolphin-footed chair in William de la Cour's *First Book of*

Ornaments, 1741, published in London. This concept was adopted by Thomas Chippendale and published as a "French Chair" in *The Gentleman and Cabinet-Maker's Director*, (London 1754) in Plate 20 (PL. 21 in the 1762 edition). In fact, Chippendale made liberal use of the downward-facing dolphin motif, incorporating it in designs for a cistern (Pl. 151), a pedestal (Pl. 150) and a candle stand (Pl. 145). The use of dolphins in this period in American furniture appear first in a Masonic Master's chair made by Benjamin Bucktrout in the years 1766-1777, now in the collection at Colonial Williamsburg, Virginia. The base and dolphin-carved legs of this chair are inspired by the previously mentioned Chippendale "French Chair" (see: Ronald Hurst and Jonathan Prown, Southern Furniture 1680-1830,

The Colonial Williamsburg Collection, (Virginia, 1997), Plate 54). As the Neo-Classical style spread across Europe following the discovery of Pompeii and Herculaneum in Italy in the second quarter of the eighteenth century, zoomorphic details became popular on furniture of all forms. Lion, goat and dogs legs and feet were used repeatedly, as were griffins and swans. Dolphins seem to appear first in the Consulate period in France and can be seen on a suite of chairs and sofas made by Jacob Freres about 1802. See Yvonne Brunhammer and Monique de Fayet, *Meubles ET Ensembles Époque Directoire et Empire* (Paris: Editions Charles Massin, 1965) p. 25."

Figure 75

Card Table, Mahogany

Made by Thomas Whitecar
Philadelphia, 1809

Height 29 1/2",
Width 36 1/4"

Photo Courtesy of the Philadelphia
Museum of Art

This swing-leg card table with a fold-over top with reeded edges has a conforming serpentine skirt inlayed along the base and central panel. The feet below are horizontally and vertically reeded. This form was extremely popular in early nineteenth century Philadelphia and many similar surviving examples still exist. This table was part of the Lydia Poultney suite for which the Whitecar invoice still exists at the Philadelphia Museum of Art.

The top is veneered in rays and has a multi-plane frame with canted front corners. Spiral foliage decorates the pedestal, at the base of which is a carved wreath. A spiral leafage column is also seen on the Joseph Barry pier table illustrated as figure 99. Brass lion's paws cap the reeded saber feet. The donut-shaped wreath was placed over the pedestal before the top was set and is mobile.

Figure 76
Card Table, mahogany

Philadelphia, Circa 1810-1820
School of Joseph Barry

Secondary wood of the apron: white pine

Interior of the base: poplar

Secondary wood of base: white pine; cherry support brace dovetailed into the front and back of apron. The apron is stack laminated.

Height 30",
Width 35 1/4",
Depth 17 3/4"

Private Collection

Figure 77
Card Table, mahogany
Philadelphia, Circa 1810-1820
School of Joseph Barry

Secondary wood of apron:
white pine, poplar, with hard
pine support brace

Height 29 1/4",
Width 36",
Depth 18"

Private Collection

The top is a thick mahogany veneer with a conforming apron with rounded front corners.

Spiral-carved foliage decorates the pedestal, larger than the foliage in figure 76, but sharing the same wreath where the pedestal and platform meet. The reeded saber legs are bulbous above and terminate below in brass caps. These consist of a lion's head with protruding front paw feet. This type of lion's head and paw brass has also been seen on Baltimore furniture usually associated with William Camp, who may have had some interaction with Joseph Barry. Camp may have worked briefly in Philadelphia as this name is listed in the 1801 Philadelphia directory as being in the same ward as Joseph Barry. Barry also was known to have established a warehouse in Baltimore in 1803. The same feet are noted on the accordion action dining room table from Andalusia, illustrated in figure 33. This same form of brass foot has been seen in association with other furniture of the school of Joseph Barry (see figures 63 and 78). The donut-shaped mobile wreath at the base of the pedestal was carved separately and was placed over the rest of the column before the top was set.

Angular front corners and a concave apron decorate the top, which is also veneered in rays. The pedestal decoration begins with a narrow ring of rectangles with star-punched centers. Below this is a second narrow band of foliage. At the pedestal base is a wide rotating leafage decoration crowned below with a wreath (see figures 76 and 77 for identical pedestal decoration). The rectangular platform below is decorated with a gilt brass medallion. The saber legs end in lion's head and paw brasses identical to figures 63 and 77.

Figure 78
Mahogany Card Table

Philadelphia, Circa 1810-1820
School of Joseph Barry

Height 29",
Width 36",
Diameter 18 1/2"

Figure 79
Breakfast Table, mahogany
Philadelphia, Circa 1815-1825

Height 18 5/8",
Width 41 5/8",
Depth 52 1/4"

Photo Courtesy of
Freeman's, Philadelphia

This table has distinctive carving that is seen on a small number of Philadelphia tables of the period. The carver is yet to be identified. Acanthus carving of the knees ends abruptly in a manner seen on other Philadelphia made furniture. The unusual spiral foliage carving of the pedestal and the floral medallion of the platform below both closely relate to the illustrated card table in figure 80. Both are almost certainly the work of the same exceptional, currently unidentified Philadelphia shop. This table was part of the original furnishings of General Anthony Wayne. The table now resides in Wayne's Mansion "Waynesborough", outside of Philadelphia (open to the public).

Rays of mahogany veneer decorate the top. The apron has a multi-plane frame with canted front corners. An urn-shaped pedestal is decorated with deeply incised tight rotating leafage carving of the highest quality, which is repeated on the concentric discs below. The front and two sides of the platform are carved with anthemion and leaves. Acanthus carving decorates the knees of the saber legs which end in lion's claw brass caps. Inset veneered panels adorn the sides of the legs. The proportions of the form, skill of carving, veneering and detail of execution make this one of the masterpieces of Philadelphia classicism. A small number of closely related forms are known, including a breakfast table illustrated in this volume (figure 79), which all appear to be the work of one shop. The carver is currently unidentified.

Figure 80
Card Table, mahogany
Philadelphia, Circa 1810-1820

Secondary wood: poplar

Height 30",
Width 35 1/2",
Depth 18"

Private Collection

Figure 81
Card Table, mahogany and maple veneer
Philadelphia, Circa 1820-1825

Height 29 3/4",
Width 36 1/2",
Depth 18"

Philadelphia Museum of Art:
Bequest of R. Wistar Harvey, 1940

Photo by Graydon Wood, 1990

The rectangular top with rounded front corners with conforming apron is supported by a foliage-carved pedestal that, at a distance, has a spouting fountain-like appearance. These saber legs have more vertical angle than many Philadelphia forms. This vertical lift to the upper portion of the saber legs is a feature of English and Boston empire tables, occasionally seen in Philadelphia.

The top has an inset of rosewood veneer. A "spouting fountain" effect is created by the down-flowing foliage of the heavily carved urn pedestal. Upturned and spiral-carved foliage typical of other labeled Quervelle pieces decorate the feet. The maker's printed label is located in the well under the top. This table is pictured and discussed in "Queries and Opinions,"

The Magazine Antiques, May 1935, page 199, and in Robert C. Smith, "The furniture of Anthony G. Quervelle Part II," The Magazine Antiques, July 1973, page 95, figure 11. It was originally owned by John (1777-1861) and Rebecca Hornor, (1782-1863) Ruckman of Bucks County, Pennsylvania, and remained in the possession of the family until 1965.

Figure 82
Card Table, mahogany, rosewood

Label of Anthony G. Quervelle Philadelphia, Circa 1820-1830

Secondary woods: white pine, poplar, and ash

Height 29 1/2",
Width 36 1/2",
Depth 18 1/2"

Collection of
Mr. Charles V. Swain

Figure 83

Card Table, mahogany

Philadelphia, Circa 1820-1830

Secondary woods: the apron sides and back are white pine, support brace is white pine, platform is poplar, construction of the feet is mahogany with lamination.

Height 29 3/4",
Width 35 1/2",
Depth 17 3/4"

Private Collection

The skirt below the folding top has two carved blocks with a leaf design on either side. An arrangement of ring compressed foliage, gadrooning and concentric discs adorn the pedestal. The feet are a combination of foliage, scrolls and lion's paw. The overall form is one loosely associated with Quervelle, although other Philadelphia shops undoubtedly produced this form as well.

The carving of the pedestal and lion's paw feet is three-dimensionally detailed and represents what Robert C. Smith was referring to in his article, "The furniture of Anthony G. Quervelle Part II: The pedestal tables," The Magazine Antiques, July 1973, page 96, as "plastic carving". This type of carving is very often seen on pedestals made by Quervelle and exhibits a life-like quality. Smith speculates that the use of this "plastic" style of carving in Philadelphia may have been started by Quervelle, although there is no definitive proof that other makers of the time period were not already employing it.[14] At a distance, the pedestal gives a "spouting fountain" effect. The horizontal leafage above the feet is also seen on work table figure 135. This worktable has other features not attributed to Quervelle's shop which illustrates the caution one must exercise with attributions. The leafage above the lion paw foot on Quervelle labeled furniture is often spiral as illustrated with figures 57, 82, 134 and 136.

[14] Smith, Pedestal Tables 94

Figure 84
Card Table, mahogany
Philadelphia, Circa 1820-1830

Height 29",
Width 35 1/2",
Depth 18 1/2"

Photo Courtesy of
Mr. Joseph Sorger

Figure 85

Card Table, mahogany

Philadelphia, Circa 1820-1830

Secondary wood: poplar

Height 29 3/4",
Width 36 1/2",
Depth 18"

Collection of
Mr. F. J. Carey III

The rectangular top with rounded front corners has a conforming concave apron. In the center of the apron is a flat tablet carved with curving leafage. A full discussion of this card table is published in *The Magazine Antiques*, "The furniture of Anthony G. Quervelle Part II: The pedestal tables," by Robert C. Smith, July 1973, 90-99 (Figure 12). Well carved, downward drooping leafage flows from the urn pedestal. The appearance of the urn at a distance is that of a "spouting fountain" effect.

This card table features a pedestal consisting of a Roman Doric column set on a square plinth with a gadrooned base, below which is a concave rectangular platform. The design of the card table is very similar to a dining table illustrated in *The Magazine Antiques*, (July, 1973), pg. 92, figure 7. Both tables share the same type of pedestal; gadrooned edges, leaf carving at the top corners and lion's paw feet with overhanging leaves. A closely related Quervelle attributed dining table is pictured as figure 37 in this text.

Figure 86
Card Table, mahogany

Labeled by Anthony Quervelle
Philadelphia, Circa 1825-1830

Dimensions unrecorded

Private Collection

Courtesy of *The Magazine Antiques*

Figure 87

Card Table, maple, mahogany, and rosewood

Stencil of Michel Bouvier
Philadelphia, 1830

Secondary woods: white pine, poplar, and chestnut

Height 30",
Width 36",
Depth 18 1/2"

Private Collection

The entire top, pedestal and platform are veneered with figured maple. Ebonized lion claw feet support the platform. The maker placed his ink stamp in the well under the top. This table was given to Thomas Henry (1809-1883) and Susan Ross (Glasgow) (1811-1881) Larkin when they married in Philadelphia in 1830, as recorded via an ink inscription in the card well. That inscription also notes that the table passed through four generations from mother to daughter. See Donald L. Fennimore, "A labeled card table by Michel Bouvier," *The Magazine Antiques*, April 1973, pages 760-763.

Label: Under top, two stenciled labels; beneath stretcher, single stenciled label; each base support, single stenciled label (five total):

ANTHY G. QUERVELLE'S CABINET & SOFA/ MANUFACTORY/ 126 So. 2d Street/ PHILADA

(The final Y in ANTHY, the d in 2d Street, and the final A in PHILADA are all raised, with two dots underneath)

"Inlaid buff, brown, white and gray marble top set within rounded-corner frame on narrow skirt. Each side of trestle base consists of paired scrolls flanking central pilasters on round cor-

nered plinths atop two compressed-ball feet. Crossing stretcher has paired scrolls below. Stenciled or freehand applied gold-leaf linear striping and foliate ornament with scrape shading."

Author's note: The lack of carving and extensive use of scrolls dates this toward the end of the Empire era. This opinion is supported by the stencil of Quervelle label. Stenciling of the label is believed to be Quervelles final identification form (please see chapter 4, image 29 for further discussion).

Figure 88

Occasional Table, rosewood, marble and gilding

Made by Anthony G. Quervelle
Philadelphia, Circa 1827-1835

Secondary woods:
poplar and white pine

Height 28 3/44",
Width 42 1/4",
Depth 26 7/16"

Photo and Description Courtesy of
The Saint Louis Art Museum

Figure 89

Card Table (one of a pair), mahogany & rosewood

Made by Anthony G. Quervelle
Philadelphia, Circa 1830-1835

Height 28 1/4",
Width 35 5/8"

The Metropolitan Museum of Art,
Rogers Fund, 1943 (43.132.2)

This card table is a rather unique labeled piece by Quervelle. An unusual apron features opposing stenciled scrolls. The more common central pedestal has been replaced by four columns that end in carved scrolls. A concave rectangular platform below is decorated with stenciled foliage. The feet are scrolls with gadrooning above. The extensive use of scrolls, especially on the feet, is evidence that this card table was made at the end of the Empire period.

Retailer David Fleetwood nailed his printed paper label as the vendor on the underside of the card well. It notes that he had chair, sofa and cabinet ware rooms on 95 Walnut Street in Philadelphia. Thomas Roberts carved his name as a possible worker of this table on the underside of one of the feet. Such arrangements between worker and retailer were not uncommon in Philadelphia during the nineteenth century, as discussed in Deborah Ducoff-Barone's, two-part article "Philadelphia furniture makers 1800-1830," *The Magazine Antiques*, May 1991, pages 982-995, and May 1994, pages 742-755.

The foliage of the pedestal radiates upward, which is opposite of the downward "water spout" effect most commonly employed by makers such as Quervelle. This pedestal arrangement is nearly identical to the labeled Charles White worktable illustrated in figure 139 in this volume. It is of interest that David Fleetwood's shop was at 95 Walnut Street and that Charles White's address was 109 Walnut Street. With the proximity of the two shops, it is not surprising that designs (such as for pedestals) might have been shared or copied by the two cabinetmakers.

Figure 90
Card Table, mahogany

Label of David Fleetwood
Philadelphia, Circa 1833-1837

Secondary wood: white pine

Height 30 1/2",
Width 36 1/4",
Depth 18"

Private Collection

Figure 91

Lyre with Scroll Card Table

Philadelphia, Circa 1820-1830

Secondary wood:
white pine and poplar

Height 30 3/4",
Width 40 1/2",
Depth 19 3/4"

Private Collection

A closely related two-part dining table using the same unusual carved lyre support is pictured in Robert C. Smith, "The furniture of Anthony G. Quervelle Part III," The Magazine Antiques, August 1973, page 264. This type of support in the form of a lyre with deep and vigorously carved fruit and foliage sides is specifically identified as an option for purchases of tables in The Philadelphia Cabinet and Chair Makers' Union Book of Prices 1828. See Donald L. Fennimore, "American Neoclassical Furniture and its European Antecedents," The American Art Journal, Autumn 1981, page 57, figure 13. A dining table with a similar lyre and scroll arrangement is illustrated as figure 39 of this text.

The rectangular top with conforming apron has short finials placed below vertical blocks. A complex pedestal consisting of swans arising from the sides of a skillfully carved fruit basket supports the top. The platform below is supported by four profusely carved lion claw feet with foliage, set with casters.

The use of the fruit basket motif is also popular in Baltimore and Philadelphia. The heavy carved feet with profuse foliage to the knees as well as the shape of the drop finials are all more typical of New York. See figure 98 of this text for a New York breakfast table with a similarly carved foot and knee.

Figure 92
Card Table, mahogany and mahogany veneer with brass inlay

Probably New York, Possibly Philadelphia or Baltimore, Circa 1820

Height 30 7/8",
Width 36",
Depth 18"

Philadelphia Museum of Art: Gift of the Friends of the Philadelphia Museum of Art, 1976. Photo by Graydon Wood, 2003

Figure 93

Card Table with Snake Motif,
mahogany

Philadelphia, Circa 1820-1830

Height 29 1/2",
Width 33",
Depth 16"

Photo Courtesy of Joseph Sorger

The table displays a concave apron with reeding to the edges of the top. A double lyre central support is decorated with two opposing snakes. The saber legs have cornucopias at the knees. This card table presents a very unusual and interesting form. The use of snake motifs appears occasionally in Philadelphia work of this period.

The top has semicircular satinwood inset from which radiate alternatively bands of light and dark mahogany. An uncarved circular mahogany column comprises the pedestal. The saber legs are decorated with leafage carving to the knees, which have a vertical tilt reminiscent of English or Boston card tables of this period.

Figure 94

Card table, mahogany

Descended in Wister Randolph Family
Philadelphia, Circa 1820-1835

Secondary wood: white pine

Height 29",
Width 36",
Depth 17 3/4"

Collection of the
Andalusia Foundation

Figure 95
Card Table, mahogany
Probably Philadelphia, Circa 1830-1840

Dimensions unrecorded

Photo Courtesy of Joseph Sorger

This card table was produced in the transitional stage from late Empire to the "Pillar & Scroll" period. The pedestal is a tapering rectangle, but in the middle there is carved scroll motif. The feet are scrolls above which is overhanging leafage.

The simplistic design of this table, absent of any carving, is illustrated to show a later example of a card table that would be considered in the "Pillar & Scroll" fashion of the 1830s-1840s. The column (pedestal) resembles a debased lyre form and the feet are plain scrolls. As the Empire period grew to a close in 1830s-1840s, this style of table became increasingly popular. Even the most distinguished Empire cabinetmakers such as Meeks & Sons of New York and John Hall of Baltimore advertised furniture made in this fashion. As mass production developed, regional stylistic characteristics began to fade. This identical style table was also made in Boston, New York, and other major manufacturing centers. In this manner the individual regional characteristics of American furniture began to be lost. This is a trend that has continued into the present.

Figure 96

Card Table, mahogany
Philadelphia, Circa 1830-1840

Secondary woods: white pine

Height 29",
Width 35 1/2",
Depth 19 1/2",
Leaf 19 1/2"

Private Collection

Tables Outside Philadelphia

Figure 97

Card Table with Stencil Decoration, mahogany

New York, Circa 1820-1835

Height 30",
Width 35 1/2",
Depth 19 1/2"

Photo Courtesy of Joseph Sorger

This table exhibits a cylindrical pedestal with a circular platform below with saber legs with lion claw feet. There is no carving, though stencil decorations are found on the apron, pedestal and knees. The form of the decoration and the use of black outlining of the stencil is typically New York. The oval platform support is also seen frequently in New York.

The mahogany top has two rectangular leaves with curved corners. A copiously leafage-carved urn-shaped pedestal supports the top. Lion claw feet are mortised directly into the base of the pedestal. The feet are all profusely carved with fur covered in leafage. At the base of the pedestal between the feet is a carved slash bud motif. This breakfast table demonstrates the tendency of some New York cabinet makers to use massive amounts of carving on virtually every surface that could be decorated. Despite this extensive carving, the form lacks the overall balance and grace of Philadelphia examples from the same period. The Philadelphia forms, at times, placed more emphasis on overall design and balance and less on secondary elements such as carving.

Figure 98
Breakfast Table, mahogany
New York, Circa 1820-1830

Height 28 1/2",
Width 39 1/2",
Depth 24 1/8"

Private Collection

CHAPTER 8
PIER TABLES

PIER TABLES

The pier table was known as a console table in France and is one of the most characteristic forms of the Empire period. Often placed between parlor windows or in hallways, it served as a prominent part of the decorative effects of any room. Sheraton defined pier as, "that part of a wall which is between the windows, hence the term pier table, in cabinet work, which are made to fit in between the architraves of the windows, and rise above the surbase."[1] Although they were not in constant use like the

card table, the pier table was a highly ornamental and elegant piece. Anthony Quervelle and other Philadelphia cabinetmakers made ornamentation with gilded stencil painting, which was applied on the front of the shelves, between the legs, and sometimes on the front of the base. This was a popular trend of the time period. Quervelle applied gilded stencil painting in the form of anthemia, acanthus, scrolls and other classical motifs that appeared flat compared with New York pieces, which had a more three-dimensional quality, or Baltimore pieces that utilized more subtle modeling.[2]

Severe and rectangular in form, the pier table was supported by columns on either side, often with pilasters in the back with a shelf uniting the legs and a solid or shaped plinth below. The shafts of the columns were sometimes combined with various vase forms having plain or gadrooned surfaces, and sometimes a band of acanthus carving.[3] The pier table was a solid piece of furniture often with a mirror back between the two back legs used to reflect the front pair, to create the illusion the table was twice as large. The table varied in design, although mahogany was the wood of choice. Exquisite carving and mounts of gilded bronze might be employed and the top was often made of marble. Motifs such as eagles' heads, dolphins, painted scrolls, anthemia and lion's paw

feet were often used on Philadelphia pier tables.

The types of feet for pier tables varied from ball vase turned to lion's paws. In some cases, the columns or scrolls in the front supports would terminate in either a lion's paw or vase form at the base, below which the feet of the table would incorporate another set of lion's paw or a vase form. Sometimes a lion's paw foot would be used at the bottom of a column and then a vase form for the feet, or vice versa, or other times lion's paws were used for both. The combination of these elements allowed the makers to exhibit their own individual personal style and at times differentiated their work from other makers.

Cabinetmakers in Philadelphia may have derived their designs from multiple sources, such as George Smith's *Cabinet-Maker and Upholsterer's Guide*, published in London 1826, which illustrated several patterns for front supports. Rudolph Ackermann also illustrated several designs that may have been a source of inspiration for many makers in his *Repository of the Arts*, a journal published over a number of years in the early nineteenth century. The commonly seen motif of petals emerging from a scroll may be traced back to Thomas Sheraton and the designer Giovanni Battista Piranesi, who is credited with being one of the principle innovators of Neo-Classical ornament.[4]

[1] Montgomery 358

[2] Robert C. Smith, "The Furniture of Anthony G. Quervelle: Part I: The Pier Tables," *The Magazine Antiques* May 1973: 985.

[3] Smith, Pier Tables 986

[4] Smith, Pier Tables 987

This pier table is the same one that was illustrated in Robert Trump's article, "Joseph B. Barry, Philadelphia cabinetmaker," *The Magazine Antiques*, Jan. 1975, p. 160, figure 3, and was listed as being made by Barry & Son for Louis Clapier of Philadelphia. The top of the pier table is veneered in rays from a central circle. The front and sides of the top are veneered with both mahogany and satinwood. Extensive ornamentation includes gilt-brass mounts and spiral-leaf carving on all four columns. The carved design of the back includes a lyre in the center from which leaves branch outward in either direction. Below is a horizontal panel decorated with Gothic crosses. Underneath the panel is a pair of carved winged griffins with additional star and figural

brass mounts. The gilt-brass swans, set in the center of the front top, are motifs popular in the classical period and favored by Josephine Bonaparte.

Figure 99

Pier Table, mahogany, satinwood, amboyna, gilt-bronze mounts

Made by Joseph B. Barry & Son
Philadelphia, Circa 1815

Height 38 5/8",
Width 54",
Depth 23 3/4"

Photograph ©1979
The Metropolitan Museum of Art, Purchase, Friends of the American Wing Fund, Anonymous Gift, George M. Kaufman Gift, Sansbury-Mills Fund; Gifts of the Members of the Committee of the Bertha King Benkard Memorial Fund, Mrs. Russell Sage, Mrs. Frederick Wildman, F. Ethel Wickham, Edgar William and Bernice Chrysler Garbisch, and Mrs. F. M. Townsend, by exchange; and John Stewart Kennedy Fund and Bequests of Martha S. Tiedeman and W. Gedney Beatty, by exchange, 1976. (1975.324)

Figure 100
*Pier Table, mahogany, metal,
glass, white marble top*

Possibly Joseph Barry & Sons
Philadelphia, Circa 1810-1825

Secondary wood: pine

Height 37 7/8",
Width 38 1/2",
Depth 19 1/2"

Photo Courtesy of the White House
Historical Association

This pier table once belonged to
Louis Clapier of Philadelphia (1764-
1837). Later it was moved to the Statue
of Liberty Monument, National Park
Service.[5] Currently, this pier table is
located in The White House. Although
in the past this table has been attributed to Barry, it is entirely possible it
may have been made by one of Barry's
skilled Philadelphia contemporaries.
The compressed lion claw feet have
been seen with other pier tables
attributed to Barry.

[5] Information about this piece was found at Winterthur
DAPC, Accession # 72.337

This table was originally owned by William (1779-1865) and Matilda (Dallas) (1798-1881) Wilkins of Pittsburgh, Pennsylvania, and remained with their descendants until 2001. A closely related pier table labeled by Quervelle is pictured in Robert C. Smith, "Philadelphia Empire furniture by Antoine Gabriel Quervelle,"

The Magazine Antiques, September 1964, pages 304 and 306. The front columns are scrolled with leafage carving to the knees and terminate in lion claw feet. Both sides of the scrolls are decorated with grape leafage. The bottom shelf below contains a marble insert for the placement of objects. Below this, the table rests on lion paw feet.

Figure 101
Pier Table, mahogany

Attributed to Anthony G. Quervelle
Philadelphia, Circa 1820-1830

Secondary woods:
poplar and white pine

Height 41 1/4",
Width 39 1/2",
Depth 19"

Private Collection

Figure 102

Pier Table, mahogany

Attributed to Anthony G. Quervelle
Philadelphia, Circa 1825-1830

Height 41",
Width, 44",
Depth 20"

Collection of
Mr. Joseph Sorger

This pier table features supports of the paw-scroll type surmounted by eagles. Glued to the frame of this table is a Quervelle advertisement from an unidentified newspaper that reads "respectfully invites all persons who may be in the want of Cabinet Furniture to call and view the largest and most fashionable assortment of furniture ever yet offered for sale in this city, From the well known character of this establishment the public may depend upon every article being made of the best materials and workmanship which will be sold on very reasonable terms for cash or acceptance." The eagles, gadrooning, and many other details are gilded or bronzed, while the marquetry semicircle of the shelf is composed of inlaid woods which are reflected in the mirror to form a full circle."[6]

[6] Smith, Pier Tables

"The top of the table is rectangular white marble with square edges, the skirt is molded where it joins the top and then curves down to half concave molding. Below the top, at the corners and center, there is a gilt painted palm and scroll design, with a shell motif at the corners. The top is supported at the front by tapering columns with Doric capitals. There are bands of metal at the top and base, while the back pilasters with Ionic capitals are ring turned at the top and base. The back mirror extends most of the way up. The columns and pilasters rest on a shaped plinth with scroll-cut front edge. The plinth is painted in the center with a double-gilt semi-circle, which is reflected in the mirror. The front feet are gilt-painted lion's paws, the back are turned."

Figure 103
Pier Table, mahogany

Possibly by Anthony Quervelle
Philadelphia, Circa 1817-1830

Height 38 1/4",
Width 38 3/16",
Depth 20"

Photo and Description Courtesy of
The James Buchanan Foundation,
Lancaster, PA

Figure 104

Pier Table, mahogany

Philadelphia, Circa 1825-1830

Height 40",
Width 51 1/4",
Depth 25"

Collection of
Mr. F.J. Carey III

This pier table exhibits the type of gilded stenciling favored by Quervelle. The stencil on the apron is nearly identical to the stenciling on the top front of figure 103. Below the marble front columns are carved vases under which is a cylindrical portion of the shelf that ends in a gadrooned ball foot. This same top to bottom arrangement at the base of the front columns of carved vase to cylinder to gadrooned-topped ball foot is seen on figure 102. The white marble columns and top lend an architectural feel to the piece.

"The rectangular marble top above a conforming coved and veneered frame with gilt scroll and anthemion-stenciled corners centering similar decoration over a gilt-stenciled apron above scrolled molded supports headed by water-leaf carving and with grape and oak-leaf carved sides over animal paw feet, all backed by ionic pilasters centering a rectangular mirror, above a veneered and gilt-stenciled shaped shelf, on acanthus-leaf-carved ball feet. Indicative of Quervelle's work are the stenciled designs on the cavetto molding under the top and on the edge of the shelf. The distinctive grape and vine carving on the side of the scroll supports is seen on several pier tables including the pair of pier tables made for the White House (Smith, "The Furniture of Anthony G. Quervelle, Part I: The pier tables, *Antiques* (May 1973) Figures 4 & 5, pp. 985-987)."

Author's Note: The central apron stencil appears identical to several other Quervelle-attributed pier tables in this chapter.

Figure 105

Classical Stenciled Mahogany Marble-Top Pier Table

Possible Attribution to Anthony G. Quervelle Philadelphia, Circa 1825-1835

Height 38 1/2",
Width 44 1/2",
Depth 20 1/2"

Photo and Description Courtesy of Christie's Auction Gallery, New York City
© Christie's Images Limited 2006

Figure 106

Painted and Gilt Ormolu-Mounted Marble-Top Pier Table

Philadelphia, Circa 1815-1825

Height 36",
Width 48",
Depth 22"

Photo and Description Courtesy of Christie's Auction Gallery, New York City
© Christie's Images Limited 2006

"The rectangular marble top above a conforming frame with brass-mounted foliage and scrolling embellishments, over scrolled volute supports with similar brass embellishments, on brass paw feet backed by a rectangular mirror plate above a rectangular base (top replaced; repainted). As seen on many examples of American-made classical furniture, the bronze mounts on the pier table appear to be imported. One of the large, acanthus leaf scrolls is marked "CA" and "2314" on the reverse. These initials conform to the initials on the back mount that adorns one of a pair of card tables by Charles Honoré Lannuier. The initials refer to a French or English bronze founder who has yet to be identified and the numbers undoubtedly refer to numbers in a trade catalog from which such mounts could be ordered. The maker CA and the use of such mounts by Lannuier and other American cabinetmakers are discussed in Peter Kenny, *Honoré Lannuier: Cabinetmaker from Paris* (New York, 1998), pp. 168-172. Despite the New York associations of its mounts, the overall design and carved work indicate this pier table's Philadelphia origins. Several examples of Philadelphia-made furniture bear mounts that were also used by Lannuier and Duncan Phyfe. Rather unusual on this table are its architectural aspects provided by the lack of feet under the molded base and the unframed mirror."

This pier table is the only one of four originally ordered by President Andrew Jackson that survived in the White House collection. Carved eagles heads rest at the top of scrolled leg supports, whose sides are decorated with grape leafage. The table is decorated with gilt stenciled scrolls and anthemia around the mirror and front of the bottom shelf. Carved eagle decorative motifs were poplar on American furniture made in the Empire period. Eagles became one of the symbols of national pride and liberty, and were often employed on girandole mirrors and sometimes the back rail of sofas. The length of this pier table indicates its intended use in the expansive state rooms and halls of the White House.

Figure 107

Pier Table, mahogany with gilt stencil and carving

Made by Anthony G. Quervelle
Philadelphia, Circa 1829

Height 43 1/2",
Width 66",
Depth 25 15/16"

Photo by Bruce White for the White House Historical Association

Photo Courtesy of the White House Historical Association

Figure 108

Pier Table, mahogany, marble, glass and gilt brass mounts

126 Dressing Glass Label of
Anthony Quervelle
Philadelphia, Circa 1825-1829

Height 37 3/4",
Width 48",
Depth 22"

Photo Courtesy of the
Athenaeum of Philadelphia

A white vein marble is used for the top of this piece. The center and corners of the skirt are decorated with gilt brass mounts. Acanthus leaves decorate the upper section of the front paw-scroll supports. The back columns are designed as reeded cylinders above which are reeded urns. This is nearly identical to the back columns of the White House Quervelle pier table illustrated as figure 107. The straight-edged shelf has a line of gadrooning on the front edge. Both front feet are a combination of a melon foot surmounted by gadrooning.

The marble top has a conforming mahogany apron decorated with stenciling and floral carving and is supported by scroll lion claw feet in front. Both front feet are decorated with stencil carving and verde decoration. The shelf below has a concave front and is supported by stenciled gilt and verde bulbous feet. Carved foliage decorates the back pilasters.

Figure 109

Pier Table

Philadelphia, Circa 1825-1830

Height 38 1/2",
Width 47 1/2",
Diameter 22"

Photo courtesy of Carswell Rush Berlin, New York City

Figure 110

Pier Table, mahogany, gilt stencil

School of Anthony Quervelle
Philadelphia, Circa 1825-1830

Height 38 1/8",
Width 36 5/8",
Depth 19 3/4"

Photo Courtesy of Joan Bogart
Antiques, Rockville Centre,
New York

The rectangular white marble top has a conforming mahogany veneered and gadrooned apron with brass armoire mounts of figures in the corners and a floral medallion in the center. Both Doric columns have brass capitals. A lower shelf has a gadrooned upper edge with stenciling below. The front lion paw feet are ebonized and gadrooned at the top.

The white marble top and apron are supported in front by two dolphin-shaped supports. Below the apron are two cornucopia corner brackets. The carved dolphins are standing on their chins with their tails curved in a backward scroll. Partially free standing acanthus decorated vertical scrolls comprise the rear supports. The front edge of the veneered shelf below is shaped in serpentine curves that flank a central lunette. Behind the lunette is a looking glass set into a wood panel. The use of gilt and vert-antique finish intensifies the decorative effects of the carving. This pier table is one of a pair that also originally had a matching center table.

Figure 111
Pier Table, mahogany, stencil, gilt, glass, bronze, marble
Philadelphia, Circa 1825-1840

Height 43 9/10",
Width 50 1/10",
Depth 23 9/10"

Courtesy,
Winterthur Museum

Museum purchase with partial funds provided by the Claneil Foundation

Pier Tables Outside of Philadelphia

Figure 112

Pier Table, mahogany veneer with marble and stenciling

Made by William Alexander, Sharpsburg (A suburb of Pittsburgh), Pennsylvania
Circa 1837-1844

Height 37 1/2",
Width 41 3/4",
Depth 21 1/2"

Photo Courtesy of Pook and Pook Auctions, Downingtown, PA

The rectangular marble top has a conforming ogee mahogany veneered apron decorated with floral and medallion stenciling in a Philadelphia manner. Ebonized front columns with Corinthian capitals support the top. The shelf below exhibits a central semicircle decorated with gilt foliage, which is also typical of Philadelphia. The bulbous feet are gadrooned with floral leafage. William Alexander worked at the very end of the classical period, the late 1830s, and yet his forms are stylistically related to Philadelphia furniture of the latter 1820s. This illustrates the lag time in fashion from urban areas, such as Philadelphia, to frontier areas such as Pittsburgh at that time.

Please see Image 22, page 60 of chapter 4 for the stamped signature found on this pier table.

The front supports consist of lion-headed monopodia, also called trapezophorons, which were initially seen in Thomas Hope's *Household Furniture and Interior Decoration*. Hope derived the form from a doorway on fourth-century B.C. Erechtheum in Athens.[7] Baltimore examples often have cast lead lion-headed monopodias, whereas this example has mahogany carved monopodia. The brass mounting on the base of the apron and the brass inlay of the drawers enhance the overall effect.

[7] William Elder, *American Furniture 1680-1880* (Baltimore Museum of Art, 1987) 166.

Figure 113
Pier Table, mahogany
Philadelphia or Baltimore, Circa 1825

Height 35 5/8",
Width 43 3/4",
Depth 19 3/4"

Photo Courtesy of
Andalusia Foundation

Figure 114

Pier Table, Mahogany

New York, Circa 1825

Height 52 1/2",
Width 37 3/4"

Photo Courtesy of Musuem
of Arts and Sciences,
Daytona Beach Florida

The white marble top has a con-forming rectangular skirt decorated with a central medallion with two fruit basket medallions flanking. Typical of New York design are the large leafage stencils applied to the front Doric columns. Below the columns is a concave shelf supported by two lion's claw feet. The acanthus leafage above is connected medially with cornucopia. This arrangement of lion claw feet with attached cornucopia is frequently found on New York pier tables of this period.

The white marble, rectangular top with conforming mahogany apron is supported by marble Corinthian columns in the front and marble pilasters in the rear. A concave shelf below is raised on four lion-claw feet. The central apron medallion has some geometric elements as seen with Philadelphia stenciled decoration, but also incorporates cornucopia elements not typical of Philadelphia. More typical of New York design are the stenciled lyres in the corners of the apron. New York makers of this era use stencils as a method to create the appearance of gilt brass mounts. In contrast, Philadelphia stencils are more abstract and please on the basis of their artistic merit rather than their similarity to brass mounts.

Figure 115
Pier Table, Mahogany and Marble

Probably New York City, Possibly Philadelphia, Circa 1820-1830

Height 38",
Width 50"

Photo Courtesy of the Owens Thomas House of the Telfair Museum, Savannah, Georgia

Figure 116
Pier Table, mahogany
New York, Circa 1820-1830

Height 38 1/2",
Width 44 1/2",
Depth 18 1/2"

Collection of
Mr. Joseph Sorger

The two front columns are made of marble with gilt bronze composite capitals. The feet are lion claw with gilded cornucopias above, medially extended to decorate the front of the lower shelf. This "lion claw-foot-cornucopia" form of front feet is especially common on New York pier tables, but is rare in Philadelphia pier tables. Please see figure 114 for a similar New York foot design.

The "Egyptian" black marble top
rests on a deeply concave mahogany
skirt. The front columns are rectangular, tapered pylons. The base of the
pylon is decorated with foliage. A concave shelf below has a central semi-circle that is topped with flowing leafage
carving. The compressed ball feet below
are reeded. This type is Egyptian in
style, as seen at temples in Luxor.

Figure 117
Pier Table, mahogany
Boston, Circa 1825

Height 36",
Width 48",
Depth 24"

Photo Courtesy of
Mr. Joseph Sorger

CHAPTER 9
LADIES' WORKTABLES

LADIES' WORKTABLES

Ladies' worktables first developed in the Federal period and further grew in popularity and distinction during the Empire period. Empire worktables differ from Federal tables in the shape, style and decoration; Empire tables were heavy pieces that were often intricately carved, rectangular in shape and did not usually incorporate the silk pouches that were an unmistakable feature on Federal tables. A ladies' worktable was used for organizing and holding sewing or work material. It distinguished the lady of the

house and was often on display in the family parlor. Sometimes given as a wedding gift, the worktable was both a useful and valuable piece of furniture for any woman to have in the period. Worktables were placed in parlors, bedrooms and sitting rooms, frequently against the wall when not in use. Empire worktables have survived in greater quantity than many other furniture forms. This may be credited to women developing other interests in the mid- to late-nineteenth century and eventually abandoning the worktable for its original purpose, instead using it as a lamp or sofa table.

Philadelphia worktables were primarily made from mahogany and mahogany veneer on a base of pine and tulip poplar. Bands of rosewood, curly maple or burl ash veneer were not uncommon on more heavily decorated tables and lent an impressive feel to the piece. The height of the tables varied from twenty-nine to thirty-four inches and the shape is very architectural in design. Pedestals of worktables are a single or multi-pedestal support, or a trestle type of support.[1] The first type, the single pedestal support, could remain a plain column or a column with a vase form sometimes covered in an acanthus leaf design. The single pedestal support was often intricately carved and the design very similar to pedestals found on center tables. The single pedestal on this type of worktable would

often rest on a plain mahogany veneered base, below which usually were carved lion's paw feet.

The second type, a multi-pedestal support, usually incorporated four supports rising from the base, which often were richly carved dolphins, serpents, cornucopias, scrolls or floral and leaf carved motifs. It was also common for multi-pedestal supports to rest on a rectangular base, below which were the carved lion's paw feet. Another popular design for a multi-pedestal support incorporated the lyre form. This used two lyre supports; the front one often ornamented with brass and the back lyre in the same shape but unadorned. The use of bird's eye maple veneer, or other light wood veneer, was sometimes applied to the front of the two drawers, sides, top, or even the front of the base. It was fairly common for worktables of this type to be adorned with applied brass ornament in the form of swirling rosettes, lion's faces or paws, dolphins or fruit baskets. Brass ornaments were sometimes placed on the lyre itself, the drawer handles and the feet or on the sides of the top, opposite each drawer. It is highly probable that some Philadelphia makers obtained the brass from London, perhaps by importing or bringing a supply with them, if they were newly emigrating cabinetmakers. The feet of the lyre pedestal tables were either saber-like, almost like the legs of some Empire

[1] Robert Smith, "The Furniture of Anthony G. Quervelle, Part III: The Worktables," *The Magazine Antiques* Aug. 1973: 260.

chairs, or carved lion's paws.

The third type is the trestle type, which employed two solid vertical supports, and was illustrated by George Smith's *Collection of Designs for Household Furniture* as a design for sofa tables.[2] The two supports on either side were joined by stretchers, which were often turned. Sometimes the two supports were in the shape of carved bottle-nosed dolphins, cornucopias or lyres, which would rest on plain or acanthus carved bases. There was much emphasis placed on geometry and bands of veneer were often placed on the top of the cases. The front of the cases were fitted with drawers, either plain or recessed, beneath an overhanging arch that was often cross-banded in veneer. The feet on trestle-supported worktables were positioned below each support on either side and resemble saber legs on chairs, but are turned downward instead of being splayed outward.

[2] Smith, Worktables 275

Figure 118
Oval Inlaid Worktable, mahogany with rosewood inserts, holly and sycamore banding, ivory pulls
Philadelphia, Circa 1785-1800

Secondary woods: sides and back of drawers are mahogany, bottom is white pine, inside of sewing compartment is white pine, center support rail is white pine, bottom of sewing compartment is poplar, sides are stack laminated.

Height 30 5/8",
Width 24",
Depth 17"

Private Collection

This table, with clean tapering geometric lines and inlay, reflects the Neo-Classical movement in America away from the earlier rococo and marlborough forms to those derived from classical architecture as expounded by Hepplewhite and others. This represents the beginning of Philadelphia classicism that within a few decades would blossom into full Philadelphia Empire. The table is an unusually well proportioned version of a type made both in Philadelphia and Baltimore. High tapered legs give the form grace and a sense of vertical lift. The table descended in the Sharpless family.

Figure 119
Worktable, astragal mahogany
Philadelphia, Circa 1810-1815

Secondary woods:
poplar and white pine

Height 30",
Width 23 1/2",
Depth 13"

Photo Courtesy of
Owens Thomas House of
the Telfair Museum,
Savannah, Georgia

The case, with astragal ends, has two drawers that are flanked with reeding. An urn pedestal below is supported by four reeded saber legs which have leafage carving to the knees. This carving ends abruptly in a manner typical of Philadelphia. The lion-head brass hardware is a twentieth century replacement.

This Sheraton style worktable features the lyre-based pedestal. A lyre is carved on either side with an acanthus leaf design and two carved rosettes in the center. The front drawer knobs are brass lion's heads and the legs are carved with acanthus leaves, reeded on the sides and capped in brass lion's paws. The design of the legs of the table relates to designs for the legs on chairs by Thomas Sheraton.

Figure 120
Worktable, mahogany
Philadelphia, Circa 1810-1820

Secondary woods: white pine

Height 29 3/4",
Width 24 1/2",
Depth 18 1/2"

Private Collection

Figure 121

Worktable, mahogany

Philadelphia, Circa 1810-1820

Secondary woods: white pine

Height 33 1/4",
Width 24 3/4",
Depth 13 1/2"

Private Collection

Similar to figure 120, except the proportions are much different; the top section on this worktable is larger, heavier and contains two drawers. The hardware of the drawers, as well as the carrying handles on the sides, are lions-head brasses. A lyre pedestal below is decorated with leafage carving and brass strings. The base platform is supported by saber legs with brass lion paw feet.

"Two-drawer worktable with Sheraton-style double lyre base, four splayed legs with claw feet and wheels, and ormolu mounts. Turned columns at corners of table with finials underneath. The top drawer has small compartments and a removable work surface with green padding that can be set up in the drawer, resting on ridges along the sides; this piece used to be attached to hinges in the front of the drawer; the screws have been removed and placed in one of the small compartments.

The original owner is believed to be Ann Ross Hopkins (1774-1816), a grand-daughter of George Ross, and wife of James Clemson Hopkins (1762-1834), a wealthy attorney." This lyre-based pedestal worktable is similar to figures 123 and 124. All three share the same lyre-based pedestal design, use of veneers on the top drawers, ring turned columns at the corners with finials below and saber legs. The applied brass ornament is another distinctive feature of this type of worktable.

Figure 122

Worktable, mahogany with bird's eye maple veneer

Philadelphia, Circa 1810-1820

Height 29",
Width 20 1/4",
Depth 15"

Photo and Description
(in quotes)
Courtesy of Collections of the
Heritage Center Museum of
Lancaster County

Gift of the James Hale
Steinman Foundation

Figure 123
*Lyre Based Worktable,
bird's eye maple*

Made by Joseph Beale
Philadelphia, Circa 1797-1807

Height 28 1/2",
Width 15"

Collection of the
Andalusia Foundation

The exterior of this table is entirely bird's eye maple with cedar drawers, brass inlay, and four tenons through the base platform. This worktable closely relates to a small group of Philadelphia tables with rectangular turret cornered tops and double through tenoned lyre pedestals with platform bases supporting sabre legs. The use of brass inlay on the top and bottom edges of the case, as well as the brass hardware and circular mounts, all enhance the effect and contrast well with the bird's eye maple. This table is stamped with the makers name "Joseph Beale."

The rectangular work area has turret corners decorated with ring turnings. Curly maple veneer decorates the drawer fronts, sides, and top of the case. The top of the turrets are highlighted with small, round ivory inserts. A pedestal support is in the form of a double-lyre with brass stringing. The platform below supports four saber legs with lion claw feet. Gilt brass mounts decorate the base of the front lyre and front surface of the platform. This worktable has been attributed to Michel Bouvier; the evidence for this is the partial label on a nearly identical worktable in the Halpin Collection, which has the word "Philadelphie" on the label.[3]

3 Further discussion of this Philadelphia worktable form can be found in *The Bulletin of the Cleveland Museum of Art*, Volume 75, page 22.

Figure 124
Work Table, mahogany, curly maple and gilded brass

Possible Attribution to Michel Bouvier
Philadelphia, Circa 1815-1820

Secondary woods: pine

Height 29 3/4",
Width 20 1/2",
Depth 15 1/4"

Philadelphia Museum of Art:
Bequest of Caroline D. Bache, 1958

Photo by Will Brown, 1986

Figure 125

Worktable with Lyre Dolphin Supports, mahogany, curly maple

Philadelphia, Circa 1815-1825

Secondary woods: drawer bottoms are pine, sides of drawers are poplar, inside framing of upper compartment is white pine, turrets are white pine that is gilded and gessoed.

Height 29 1/4",
Width 19",
Depth 16"

Private Collection

Turret corners of the table are pine that is gessoed and gilded with a leaf design with finials below. Both drawers and front portion of the platform are veneered with bird's eye maple. The pedestal supports are in the shape of lyres. The front lyre has two gessoed and gilded dolphins. Both lyres are double through tenoned into the platform below. The use of the lyre in worktables, pedestal tables and chairs throughout the Empire period was derived from antiquity, and was a favorite motif of Napoleon's. He had his top designers, Percier & Fontaine create many forms of furniture using this motif, as well as those of swans, eagles and lion's heads. Bird's eye maple veneer combined with various gilt gesso motifs gives this piece an even more impressive appearance.

The design of this worktable may have been derived from Thomas Sheraton, who illustrated many designs for tables using the double lyre base. This table relates to a small group of Philadelphia worktables that exhibit rectangular turret corners with bird's eye maple drawer fronts and lyre supports that are double-through tenoned to the base. This table has several variations including lion's paw feet (instead of saber feet), the use of gessoed and gilded dolphins on the front lyre and the use of gessoed and gilded leafage decoration to the turrets. The gessoed gilt ornamentation of the turrets and lyre is unique for a table of this form. Stamped images of Benjamin Franklin adorn the brass pulls.

Figure 126
*Worktable, mahogany,
mahogany veneer*
Philadelphia, Circa 1810-1825

Secondary woods:
poplar, maple, and
Atlantic white cedar

Height 28 1/2",
Width 22",
Depth 15 3/4"

Photo Courtesy of The Biggs
Museum of American Art,
Dover, DE

The design of the four turret turned corners of the case is found on worktables labeled by Joseph Beale and Michel Bouvier, as well as other Philadelphia, Baltimore, and Boston cabinetmakers. The pedestal of this worktable combines carved acanthus leaves above a series of concentric disks. On the front panel of the platform there is acanthus carving. Carved acanthus leaves also appear on the tops of the scrolled legs. Scroll feet terminate in lion's paw casters.

Figure 127
*Worktable, mahogany,
mahogany & rosewood veneers,
brass inlay*

Philadelphia, Circa 1815-1825

Secondary woods: oak, red cedar,
white pine, and ash

Height 31",
Width 20",
Depth 14 7/8"

Photo Courtesy of The Biggs
Museum of American Art,
Dover, DE

Although similar in form to figure 126, there are many distinctive design elements on this table. Acanthus-carved colonnettes are recessed into the corners of the case. The pedestal has acanthus carving on and below the urn. Acanthus carving is continued on the platform below and on the sides of the legs. The creativity and design elements, such as swelled drawers, scrolled feet and the recessed side panels with carved colonnettes, bestowed on this table are explicative of Empire furniture in its height of fashion. The feet are capped with brass lion's paw casters.

The top has inset leafage-carved columns on the corners. A supporting pedestal is sharply carved with outward and downward flowing leafage creating a "spouting fountain" effect when viewed from a distance. The platform and sides of the scroll legs are decorated with foliage carving. Brass lion claw casters decorate the ends of the feet.

Figure 128

Worktable, mahogany

Philadelphia, Circa 1810-1825

Secondary woods: Case and drawers are white pine, backboard and other elements are poplar.

Height 30 5/8",
Width 22",
Depth 15"

Photo Courtesy of the Dallas Museum of Art, The Faith P. and Charles L. Bybee Collection, gift of Mr. and Mrs. C. Thomas May, Mr. and Mrs. S. Roger Horchow, Mr. and Mrs. Claude C. Albritton, III, and an anonymous donor.

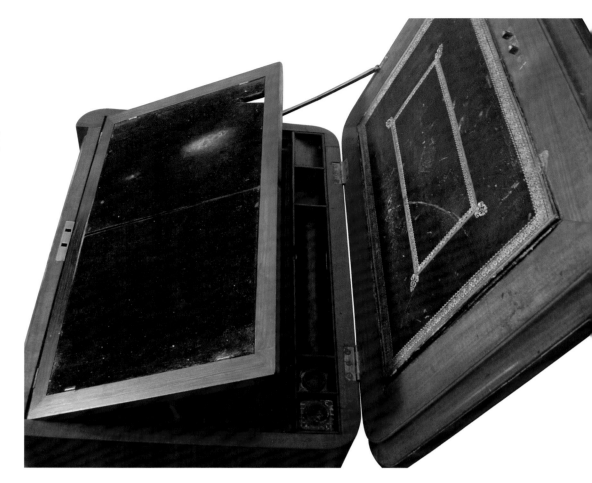

Figure 129a
Open top view of writing surface and green leather tooled storage area

Figure 129 (opposite page)

Multi-Pedestal Worktable, mahogany

Label of Anthony Quervelle, inscribed Delmes (Sculp) Philadelphia, Circa 1828-1832

Secondary wood: drawer, sides, back, and bottoms are mahogany. Inside of work compartment is yellow pine. The cut glass knobs are of a type found on some Quervelle furniture.

Height 30",
Width 21 1/2",
Depth 16 3/4"

Private Collection

Multi-pedestal worktable with four supports rising from the platform is carved with a combination of rosettes and acanthus leaves, all in the shape of gentle rolling scrolls. The scrolls end at the top in disks with concentric circles. Below the bottom drawer is a strip of gadrooning. The corners of the case are rounded. An oval panel of mahogany rays edged in rose wood decorates the top of the case. This labeled Quervelle worktable was illustrated and discussed as figure 4 in Robert Smith's article, *"The Furniture of Anthony G. Quervelle, Part III: The worktables,"* The Magazine Antiques, August 1973, page 263. Robert C. Smith notes in the article:

> Typical of Quervelle's finest carving are the crisp and sensitively modeled layered foliage of the lower half of the scroll supports." "This piece may have been exhibited at the Franklin Institute in 1831. The inside of the

top is of green leather tooled in gold. Work of this sort was produced by William Tail of 225 Arch Street.[4]

The judge of this exhibition was Joseph Barry himself, who praised the "Ladies' Work Table." This worktable, along with the Quervelle Secretary now at the Philadelphia Museum of Art (figure 282), was originally purchased from Quervelle by Robert E. Griffith of Philadelphia.

Provenance: Robert Englefield Griffith; son, Dr. Robert Griffith; daughter, Mrs. Edward Coleman; nephew, Robert Englefield Griffith; daughter, Elizabeth (Griffith) Page (Mrs. Edward C. Page).

4 This worktable was illustrated in *The Magazine Antiques*, "Philadelphia Empire Furniture by Antoine Gabriel Quervelle," Sept. 1964, vol. 86: 305 and "The furniture of Anthony G. Quervelle, Part III: The Worktables," Aug. 1973: 62.

Figure 130

*Cornucopia Support
Worktable, mahogany*

Strong Attribution to Anthony Quervelle
Philadelphia, Circa 1825

Secondary woods: the drawer
sides are mahogany, the drawer
bottom is poplar, and the drawer
back is poplar, compartment is
white pine. The upper sewing
compartments are lined with a
deep red floor cloth or paper,
which is original. The top has a
5/16" rosewood band. Mirror is
attached to inside of lift-top.

Height 30 5/16",
Width 22",
Depth 17"

Private Collection

The top of the case has a 5/8" band
of rosewood. A concave semi-circular
arch design with gadrooned base decorates the large front drawer. The front
supports consist of opposed cornucopia,
while the back support is in the shape of
a lyre. Below the cornucopia and lyre
pedestals each rest on their own platform. These platforms are then connected with turned stretchers. The platforms
are supported by lion claw feet which
face to the sides. The ends of the cor31-
copia and top of the front platform are
decorated with concentric disks. This
disk motif was often used by Quervelle,
but also by others including H. Lannier,
of New York City.

This form is of Quervelle's design, as
proven by the Quervelle sketches, which
illustrate a very similar worktable (see
sketch 4, chapter 5). This is further
supported by the configuration of the
interior dividers in the upper lift top
section, which match those of a labeled
Quervelle worktable illustrated by
Robert C. Smith as figure 12 in his
pioneering article (The Furniture of
Anthony G. Quervelle, Part III, The
Worktables, *The Magazine Antiques*,
August 1973). This is one of Quervelle's
most successful and creative worktable
forms, which unfortunately is rare.

Figure 130b
Detail of cornucopia supports

Figure 131

*Trestle Dolphin Worktable,
mahogany*

Attributed to Anthony Quervelle
Philadelphia, Circa 1825

Secondary woods: sides of drawers
are mahogany, back is poplar, bottom is white pine. Interior of work
compartment is white pine. The
sewing compartments are finished
in orange red paper or cloth, which
is original. The bottom of the lift-top contains a mirror. The top has
1" wide band of rosewood.

Height 31 1/4",
Width 24 3/8",
Depth 19 1/4"

Private Collection

The top opens to reveal several
compartments and a mirror. The design
of this worktable is similar to figure 12,
a labeled Quervelle worktable, illustrated in Robert C. Smith's article, "*Part
III: The worktables,*" *The Magazine
Antiques*, August 1973, page 267. On
the trestle supports are carved bottle-nosed dolphins, above which is a shell
design. The case has rounded corners
and a strip of gadrooning across the
lower front edge, which are both features found on the labeled worktable.
Vertical supports are joined by a pair
of turned stretchers, the design of
which is actually closer to figure 13 of
Smith's article since the size and design
is nearly identical. The heaviness the
table exudes is typical of Philadelphia
Empire worktables. A mirror is
attached to the inside of the lift-top.
This worktable descended in the
Hempwell family of Philadelphia.
It is believed to have been among the
original furnishings for "Strawberry
Mansion", a home that is still open
to the public in Fairmount Park,
Philadelphia.

Figure 131a
detail of interior compartments
and mirror with top opened

Figure 131b
Detail of dolphin supports

Figure 132

*Worktable, mahogany
with oval inlay on top*

Attributed to Anthony Quervelle
Philadelphia, Circa 1825-1830

Height 31",
Width 24",
Depth 18"

Collection of
Mr. F.J. Carey III

The design of this worktable is similar to figure 13 in Robert C. Smith's article, "The furniture of Anthony G. Quervelle, Part III: the worktables," *The Magazine Antiques*, August 1973, page 267. The combination of a recessed semi-circular arch with stained ash lunate ends, strip of gadrooning, rounded case corners, and design of the supports with a shell motif at the top and bottom of the lyres are all elements that Quervelle favored in his worktables. A pair of turned stretchers joins the scroll bases of the supports. The curved bases are overlaid with acanthus leaves, followed by reeding that terminates at the end of each foot.

The top has a two-inch band of mahogany veneer with two central book match panels. All four corners of the case are decorated with a tight convex reeding of a type seen on the Philadelphia suite of furniture purchased by the Telfair family in the 1820s (see figures 192 and 229). The lower case drawer is decorated with two concave arches in a manner favored by Quervelle. A typical Philadelphia foliage-carved urn pedestal supports the concave rectangular platform below. The lion's paw feet have well-carved spiral foliage above. This worktable has several features including the corner reeding, dropped fineals and flat drawer fronts, which suggest that this was made during the earlier empire period.

Figure 133
Reeded Cornered Worktable, Mahogany

Philadelphia, Circa 1815-1825
School of Anthony Quervelle

Secondary woods:
drawer sides are mahogany, drawer backs are poplar, drawer bottoms and case are white pine.

Height 30",
Width 21 1/2",
Depth 18 1/4"

Private Collection

Figure 134a

detail of gadrooning with micro carved shell and scrolling of leafage above the feet.

Figure 134 (opposite page)

Acanthus Cornered Worktable, mahogany and white pine

Attributed to Anthony Quervelle
Philadelphia, Circa 1825-1830

Secondary woods: sides of drawers are mahogany, bottom and back of drawers are poplar. The upper compartment is lined with a blue green paper or cloth. The pedestal is double-through tenoned into the platform. Interior wood is white pine. The top has a 2" edge of veneered mahogany.

Height 29 1/2",
Width 21 1/2",
Depth 15 1/4"

Private collection

The top is banded with rosewood and lifts to a mirrored storage compartment lined with blue paper. Inside the two drawers is a work area. The upper drawer is fitted with a lift-up writing surface. All four corners are decorated with acanthus leafage that rises up and outward, giving the form vertical lift and balance. This table exhibits a gadrooned, acanthus carved "spouting fountain" vase pedestal typical of Quervelle, which is double-through tenoned to the concave arched platform base with typical Philadelphia spiral foliage and feet. The proportions, carving quality, and detail of execution are all superlative, leading to an overall form which exceeds the sum of its parts. Note the small seashell carved at the center of the base of the gadrooning; this relates to shells noted on the attributed Quervelle cellarette (figure 360) and sideboard (figure 251). Inside the case, the word "front" is written in a handwriting which appears very similar to that of Quervelle's found in the Quervelle sketchbook.

Figure 135a

Note that the leafage above the foot is not scrolled as typically seen on Quervelle feet, but rather it is raked back in a horizontal manner. Compare to labeled Quervelle Worktable shown in Figure 136.

Figure 135
(opposite page)

Worktable with Arched Drawer, mahogany

Philadelphia, Circa 1825

Secondary wood: upper compartment sides and bottom are white pine, drawer is poplar, pedestal connects to the platform with a single circular tenon. The lift-top sewing compartment contains a green felt writing surface below which the work area is finished with paper, which may be painted red. The top is decorated with a 5/16" band of rosewood. Mirror is attached to inside of lift-top.

Height 29 1/4",
Width 22 3/4",
Depth 16 1/2"

Private Collection

The worktable exhibits motifs favored by Quervelle, such as the gadrooned vase pedestal support and concave arched drawer. This worktable shows several construction details including lack of double through tenoning of the pedestal to the base and atypical horizontal leafage carving at the crest of the feet, which suggest this is the work of a competing Philadelphia cabinetmaker who apparently admired Quervelle's work. This confirms that imitation was a sincere form of flattery among nineteenth century Philadelphia cabinetmakers and underscores the need to avoid labeling all Philadelphia empire furniture as that of Quervelle, as certain auctioneers and dealers are inclined to do (often for secondary gain).

Figure 136

Worktable, mahogany

126 Dressing Glass Label of Anthony Quervelle Philadelphia, Circa 1825-1835

Height 30",
Width 23",
Depth 17"

Collection of Munson-Williams-Proctor Arts Institute, Museum of Art, Utica, New York. 83.15.

The work area consists of a lift-top storage area with a concave arched veneered mahogany drawer. Below this is a leafage-carved "spouting fountain" pedestal which rests on a concave arched four-cornered platform that is supported by lion claw feet. The inside of the worktable bears a 126 dressing glass Quervelle label. Note that the leafage above the feet is spiraled. Please compare to figure 135a which has horizontal leafage not associated with Quervelle's shop.

Figure 137
Worktable, mahogany, band of rosewood inlay

Delmes Label of Anthony Quervelle
Philadelphia, Circa 1825-1835

Height 30",
Width 23",
Depth 17"

Private Collection

Photograph by Douglas Armsden, by courtesy of Richard Mills, through *The Magazine Antiques*.

figure 137a
Rare Label of Anthony G. Quervelle, engraved by Delmes

Photograph by Douglas Armsden, by courtesy of Richard Mills, through *The Magazine Antiques*.

This worktable was illustrated in "The furniture of Anthony G. Quervelle Part III: The worktables," by Robert C. Smith, *The Magazine Antiques*, August 1973, figure 2, p. 262. Typical of Quervelle's work is the band of rosewood veneer in the top and case with recessed semi circular front with gadrooning below. The pedestal is carved with foliage in a "spouting fountain" manner, beneath which are concentric disks. Below this is a rectangular platform which supports the feet. The spiral foliage above the lion claw feet is found on several labeled Quervelle pieces in this volume (See figures 57, 82 and 136).

Figure 138

Lyre-support Worktable, mahogany and mahogany veneer

Workshop of Anthony G. Quervelle (1789-1856)
Two Stenciled Labels, one pictured
Philadelphia, Circa 1825-1835

Secondary woods: pine and poplar, original finish.

Height 30",
Width 24",
Depth 18"

Private Collection

Image and Description Courtesy of Didier, Inc., New Orleans

"The shaped, masked veneered top with a banded veneered edge flips to reveal a looking glass underneath and tray having fitted compartments, four retaining the original leather covered mirrors. The removable original tray has been restored to its original color. As in other worktables by Quervelle, the case has curved front corners and shaped facing of the fake drawer. The front of the working one is in the form of a semicircle, recessed beneath an overhanging arch with veneered lower front edge. A shaped trestle-like platform with a banded edge connects the lyre supports topped at the bottom with mahogany caps, joined at the top with an ebonized turning and decorated on each side of the scroll with mahogany buttons. The whole rests on scroll feet and original brass casters."

Figure 138b
Lyre Worktable with top opened to reveal mirror and work compartment.

Figure 138a
Stencil of Anthony Quervelle

A calling card (illustrated) attached
to the interior of the top section identifies this as the work of Charles and
John White, who worked together from
1828 until 1851. The table has the original wooden knobs carved to imitate
glass. A somewhat unusual feature is
the gadrooned edge of the lift top. The
vase form of the pedestal is decorated
with acanthus leafage that radiates
upward and outward. This reverses the
usual downward flowing "spouting
fountain" effect foliage, which is
more common, especially with
Quervelle. The development of the
pedestal motif is virtually identical
to that of the David Fleetwood card
table, illustrated in figure 90 of this
volume. This suggests the possibility
that Charles White could have been
supplying furniture for David Fleetwood. The two makers' shops were
in close proximity on the same street
(David Fleetwood at 95 and Charles
White at 109 Walnut Street).

Figure 139a
The Charles H. and John F. White calling card attached to the inside of the work table.

Figure 140

Pineapple Support Worktable,
mahogany

Label of Charles H. White Cabinet and
Chair Manufacture/109/ #109/Walnut
Street/ Philadelphia, Circa 1825

Woods: baywood, with mahogany
and elm burl veneer, white
pine, poplar and twentieth century
brass pulls.

Height 28 1/2",
Width 20",
Depth 15"

Philadelphia Museum of Art:
Purchased: Thomas Skelton
Harrison Fund, 1973

Photo by Will Brown, 1977

The rectangular case with inset corners has two drawers with raised panel fronts. A pineapple pedestal below is well carved. Lion claw feet support the concave arched rectangular platform. The form of the pedestal and base is derived from a design for a music stool in Nicholson's Cabinet Maker.[5]

5 Philadelphia Museum of Art, *Philadelphia: Three Centuries of American Art*, 1976: 264.

Extension leaves are placed on either side of the case and can be raised to provide more workspace. This is a feature much more common on New England work tables of the period. The front surface of all four scroll supports is decorated with acanthus carving that terminates in disks above and below. A shelf at the base has lion's claw front feet with turned feet in the rear. Worktables of this form with four supporting corner columns and shelf below were also manufactured in New York City. The overall form relates to figure 142, which was a style favored in New York City.

Figure 141
Worktable, mahogany

Philadelphia or Possibly New York, Circa 1820-1825

Height 32",
Width 21",
Depth 17"

Collection of
Mr. F.J. Carey III

Figure 142

Worktable with Four Pineapple Supports, mahogany and satinwood

"Probably Philadelphia, Possibly New York City", Circa 1810-1825

Secondary woods: drawer sides, bottom, and back are poplar, inside of carcass is white pine.

Height 30 1/4",
Width 22 3/4",
Depth 16 1/2"

Private Collection

The rectangular case has two drawers with satinwood fronts and original mahogany pulls, supported by four pineapple carved columns with shelf below. Inset Gothic arches flank the drawers. This rectangular worktable form with column supports on the corners and shelf is also common in New York. A similar form worktable with the label of *Haines (New York City)* is illustrated as Plate 7, page 129 of the May 2005 issue of the magazine *Antiques*. The use of contrasting satinwood drawer fronts is more common with Philadelphia furniture than New York and might suggest this worktable is of Philadelphia origin influenced by New York design.

This piece has two swell front drawers with original mahogany knobs. The front of the case extends outward, lateral to the drawers. This feature is more common on New York worktables. The pedestal is decorated with a foliage-carved urn form with gadrooning at the base. Four lion claw feet support the rectangular concave platform in a typical Philadelphia manner. The somewhat crude two-dimension carving of the pedestal and feet suggest this worktable may have been made by a rural cabinetmaker.

Figure 143
Mahogany Worktable
South Eastern Pennsylvania, New Jersey, or New York, Circa 1825-1835

Secondary Woods:
drawers are poplar,
inside of case is white pine.

Height 32",
Width 19 3/4",
Depth 16 3/4"

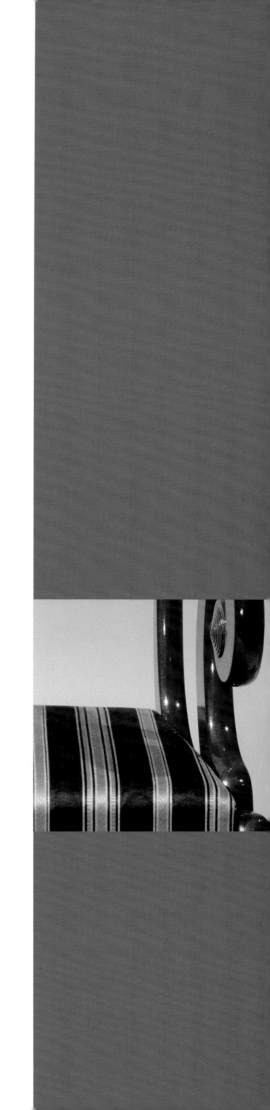

CHAPTER 10
CHAIRS

CHAIRS

Numerous chair styles developed in the Empire period. These included the klismos, "Grecian", or "scroll back" side chairs, square-back chairs, cabriole or "Drawing-Room Chair," fancy chairs and armchairs. The klismos chair was based on fifth-century B.C. Greek chairs seen on vases recovered at Pompeii and Herculaneum.[1] Percier and Fontaine favored the klismos chair form, followed by Thomas Hope. The backs of chairs were painted, gilded, carved and inlaid with woods or brass ornamentation.

Philadelphia chairs exhibit both English and French influence. Inlaid brass ornament found on some Philadelphia klismos chairs may have been taken from English designs, while the strong rectilinear quality and curve of the rear stiles straight down into the rear legs (marking a separateness from the horizontal seat rails) seems more French.[2] A box-like wooden slip seat frame is often associated with Philadelphia chairs and seems to have been derived from French sources originally.

Philadelphia chairs are distinct from chairs made in other parts of the country in that they often had a rolled lip on the crest rail, similar to those on Philadelphia sofas.[3] On the back splats of side chairs there might be cornucopia, lyre, leaf designs or inlaid brass in a star design. The Philadelphia price list of 1828 listed extras on plain chairs as being "Brass or wood line in top rail round the panel" and "scroll or knee to front leg."[4] Legs of chairs were often saber-shaped, curved, straight, turned Roman style or tapered toward the bottom, ending in spade feet.

Chairs with padded backs were widely used in parlors and became increasingly popular. A variant of this type included the scroll-back side chair, usually highly ornamented with carving, gilding, and lion's paw feet. This was found more in New York than in Philadelphia.

The term "fancy chair" applies to chairs that have an elaborate use of paint, inlay, caning, carving or fabric. Fancy chairs were often found in the parlor of the house as impressive counterparts to other parlor furniture including pier, center and card tables.

Certain aspects of chair types have been specifically attributed to certain makers, such as reeded front legs and bulb-shaped terminals at the bottom of legs being attributed to Ephraim Haines, but many Philadelphia cabinetmakers evidently used similar designs since apparently there was a lot of borrowing of ideas. Chairs with turned spade feet have often been attributed to Henry Connelly on the basis of his using the same leg on other forms, such as sideboards, but once again it is entirely possible many other makers used this design as well. Thomas Whitecar is believed to have designed the highly recognizable amebic oval design found on the back splats of side and armchairs in Philadelphia.

[1] Fitzgerald 114
[2] Cooper 112
[3] Fitzgerald 115
[4] Otto 54

This shield back form is derived from antique Greco-Roman military shields. The five elements of the splat are decorated with foliage above and merge into a sun burst pattern at the base. The front rail is serpentine. The legs taper and are thumb molded. The side seat rails are mortised through the rear legs. This is typically Philadelphia, as are the internal glue blocks, which are two-part vertically oriented. Compared to New York or New England examples of shield back chairs, Philadelphia examples tend to have a somewhat larger shield with greater overall mass than those of other American regions.

Figure 144
Mahogany Shield Back Chair
Philadelphia, Circa 1790-1810

Height 38 1/2",
Width 20 1/2",
Diameter 19 1/2"

Figure 145
Arm Chair, mahogany
Philadelphia, Circa 1790-1800

Height 37",
Width 24",
Depth 22"

Private Collection

This form illustrates classical motifs based loosely on classical architectural elements. The crest rail of the rectangular back is decorated with reeding and floral rosettes. A square back has three uncarved vertical support banisters. The legs are tapered with thumb moldings.

The chair has four banisters, which are reeded and carved with foliage. The front legs are tapered, terminating in a bulb shaped foot below the reeding. Chair makers such as Ephraim Haines are known to have used this bulbous terminal foot design (see figures 148 and 150). A similar chair shares the same square back and reeded banisters and legs, illustrated in Charles Montgomery's *Federal Furniture*, figure 94, page 146. The "bell shaped seat" is a name given for this type of stuffed seat in the *London Chair-Makers' and Carvers Book of Prices for Workmanship* in the 1802 edition.[5]

[5] Montgomery 146

Figure 146
Side Chair, mahogany
Philadelphia, Circa 1800-1820

Height 35",
Width 15",
Depth 17 3/4"

Collection of
Mr. F.J. Carey III

Figure 147
Arm Chair, mahogany

Attributed to Henry Connelly
Philadelphia, Circa 1800-1820

Secondary woods: front and side
rails are cherry, back rail is ash.

Overall Height 34",
Seating Height 17",
Depth 18 1/2"

Private Collection

This chair has a rectangular back with carved and reeded spindles with turned and reeded arm supports. The Philadelphia Book of Prices for 1795 suggests the Philadelphia name of the arms as being "French elbows ...the elbows motis'd on the stump of the front foot 13-6."[6] A similar chair is pictured in *Federal Furniture*, by Charles Montgomery, figure 91, page 142. The Figure 91 armchair shares the same "sweep side rails", turned and reeded arm supports, and reeded legs which end in turned spade feet. The design of the spindles on the back is nearly identical to the figure 91 armchair. The rather unusual feature of the rear legs being a simplified version of the front legs (rather than being square legs) is repeated in this chair as well. The conical "ice cream cone" spade foot has often been attributed to Connelly based on similar turned spade feet used on a sideboard labeled by Connelly.[7] This chair is attributed to Connelly due to the overall form and the use of spade feet, which Connelly frequently employed. The feet were sometimes designed according to the customer's preference and thus the designation of all spade feet as relating to Connelly is arbitrary.

[6] Montgomery 142

[7] Montgomery 142

This side chair, one of a set of ten, was part of a large suite of furniture ordered by Girard from Ephraim Haines in 1807, including a pair of Sheraton-style pier tables, a pair of Sheraton armchairs, and a Sheraton-style Settee.[8] Girard apparently developed a taste for furniture made *en suite* which was a poplar practice in France. One documented example of furniture made *en suite* was by Anthony G.

Quervelle, a French émigré cabinet-maker, who made a set of three center tables and four pier tables *en suite* for the East Room of the White House in 1829. Haines, who began his work as a cabinetmaker and later became a merchant of exotic woods, was knowledgeable in the use of ebony for decorative effect and produced both these chairs and the settee in the finest taste.

[8] Robert D. Schwarz, *The Stephen Girard Collection, A Selective Catalogue* (Philadelphia: Girard College, 1980) Figures 24, 25, 26, 27.

Figure 148
Side Chair, ebony

Made by Ephraim Haines
Bill of Sale, Philadelphia November 21, 1807: Ten ebony chairs…$250

Secondary Woods: leg blocks are eastern white pine and seat rails are ash.

Height 35 3/4",
Width 20 7/8",
Depth 18"

Courtesy of the Stephen Girard Collection, Girard College, Philadelphia, PA

This chair is similar in design to the armchair from the set of ebony seating furniture made by Ephraim Haines in 1807 for Stephen Girard and to an armchair pictured in Charles Montgomery's *Federal Furniture* (Bonanza Books, NY, 1978), page 142, figure 91. The rectangular back features carved and reeded banisters (which have small bulbs toward the bottom with carved foliage), reeded arms, and turned and reeded arm supports; this differs from Winterthur Museum's only in that the arms are plain instead of reeded. Winterthur's and the present chair share a similar sharply carved "slash bud" floral motif on either side of the front seat rail, below which there is carved foliage that rests above the reeded front legs. Both have turned spade feet, while the chair made by Haines features a tapered bulb foot. The rear legs of Winterthur's and the present chair are simplified versions of the front legs.

"The high style elements of this suite with its airy half-spindle backs, carved legs and sleek arms are a watermark in American furniture design."[9] The carved legs with slightly bulbous and tapered feet are somewhat characteristic of Haines and are similar to the legs in figure 148.

[9] Schwarz , Description of Figure 27

Figure 150
Settee, ebony

Made by Ephraim Haines
Bill of Sale, Philadelphia November 27, 1807: one sofa...115

Secondary woods: seat frame is ash and leg blocks are yellow poplar.

Height 36",
Width 72",
Depth 25 1/2"

Courtesy of the Stephen Girard Collection, Girard College, Philadelphia, PA

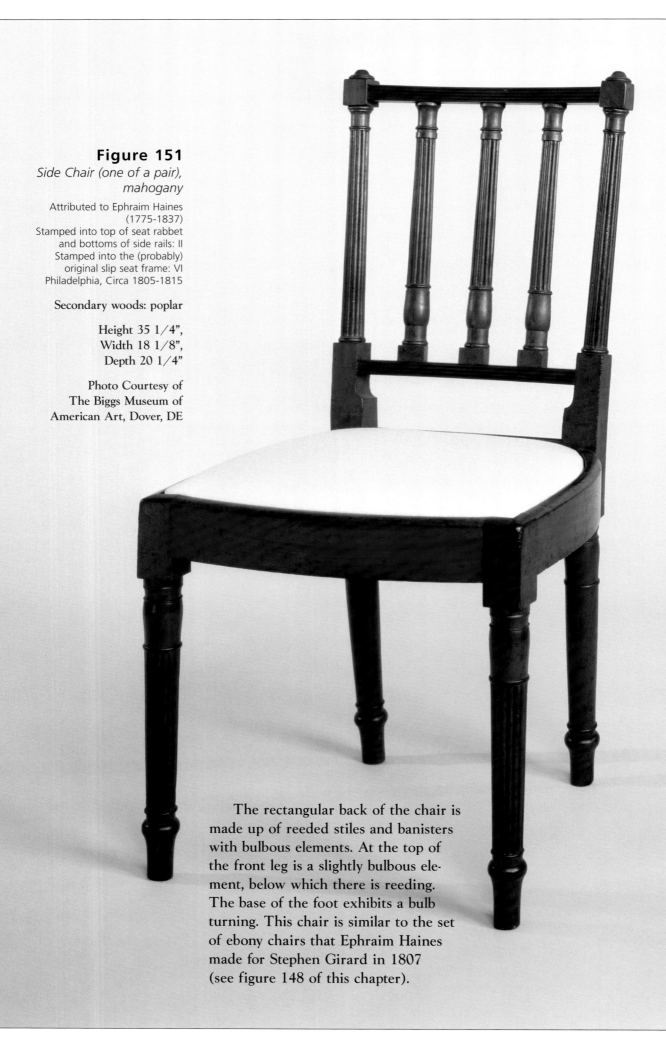

Figure 151
*Side Chair (one of a pair),
mahogany*

Attributed to Ephraim Haines
(1775-1837)
Stamped into top of seat rabbet
and bottoms of side rails: II
Stamped into the (probably)
original slip seat frame: VI
Philadelphia, Circa 1805-1815

Secondary woods: poplar

Height 35 1/4",
Width 18 1/8",
Depth 20 1/4"

Photo Courtesy of
The Biggs Museum of
American Art, Dover, DE

The rectangular back of the chair is
made up of reeded stiles and banisters
with bulbous elements. At the top of
the front leg is a slightly bulbous element, below which there is reeding.
The base of the foot exhibits a bulb
turning. This chair is similar to the set
of ebony chairs that Ephraim Haines
made for Stephen Girard in 1807
(see figure 148 of this chapter).

The Egyptian influence seen on this side chair is discussed in Donald L. Fennimore's, "Egyptian Influence in Early nineteenth-century American Furniture," *The Magazine Antiques* (May 1990) p. 1194-1195. The design of the back may have been derived from George Smith's *Collection of Designs for Household Furniture and Interior Design*, which was based on an ornamental back plate for wall lamps in a design for the Egyptian Room that Thomas Hope published in *Household Furniture and Interior Decoration* in 1807.[10] The reeded front feet end in limp lion paws in a manner frequently associated with Joseph Barry.

[10] Donald L. Fennimore, "Egyptian Influence in Early Nineteenth-Century American Furniture," *The Magazine Antiques* May 1990: 1195.

Figure 152
Side Chair (one of a pair), mahogany, mahogany veneer

Attributed to Joseph Barry
Philadelphia, Circa 1810-1815

Secondary woods: cherry, ash, and Atlantic white cedar

Height 35 5/8",
Width 19 1/4",
Depth 20 1/4"

Photo Courtesy of
The Biggs Museum of
American Art, Dover, DE

Figure 153

Side Chair (from a set of 6),
mahogany,

Attributed to Joseph Barry
Philadelphia, Circa 1800-1820

Secondary woods: rails are ash,
glue blocks are poplar.

Overall Height 35 1/2",
Seat Height 18 1/2",
Depth 16"

Private Collection

The back is nicely furnished with a reeded rectangular section filled with upholstery, above which there is a crest rail with fleur de lis. The lower edge of the crest rail is carved with scrolls. This pattern is seen on certain sofas and other items attributed to Joseph Barry (see figure 210 of this text for a sofa decorated with an identical scroll and fleur de lis design). The front legs are reeded and have concave, ring turned drums at the tops, the legs terminate in a variation of the bulb foot.

Figure 154a
Side Chair

These chairs are related to the sofa attributed to Barry, illustrated in figure 210. The lower edge of the crest rail on the chairs is shaped like the cutout on the crest rail of the sofa with opposing scrolls; the arms and arm supports on the sofa and armchair are similar; and the legs on the chairs and the sofa are the same, including the reeding and terminal bulbs. "The chairs originally belonged to the Weightman family, important manufacturing chemists in Philadelphia in the early nineteenth century. The lower edge of the crest rail rises to a pointed arch in "the rich Egyptian ...Style", Barry advertised."[11]

[11] Fennimore and Trump 1223

Figure 154 and 154a
Armchair and Side chair (from a set of twelve chairs), mahogany

Attributed to Joseph Barry
Philadelphia, Circa 1810

Secondary woods: poplar

Height (of side chair) 34 1/2",
Width 22 1/4",
Depth 19 1/2"

Height (of armchair) 34 3/4",
Width 23",
Depth 20 1/4"

Private Collection

Figure 155a

**Figure 155
(opposite page)**

Armchair, mahogany, partially gilt, painted and bronzed with gilt-brass castors

Made by Joseph Barry & Co. Philadelphia, Circa 1829-1833

Secondary woods: tulip poplar

Height 45 1/2", Width 25", Depth 28" (overall)

Photo and Description Courtesy of Hirschl & Adler Galleries, New York

"This chair is one of a set of armchairs of undetermined number made by Joseph Barry & Co. for Isaac Minis, a prominent Jewish Savannah citizen, successful financier, and land owner. In a general way, American easy chairs are extremely rare. This very unusual example follows the general form and ample scale of a pair of armchairs with open arms from the Preble family of Portland, Maine, which are of Boston or possibly Portland origin, but few other American chairs of this type have been recorded. The crest rail with ornamented scrolls and anthemia is reminiscent of that on a unique Barry fauteuil of smaller scale (private collection, formerly collection of Hirschl & Adler Galleries, FAPG 1551D.02; see Trump & Fennimore, p. 1220 pl.X), but in the present example, the carved ornament of the crest rail is enriched with *verde antique* painting, gilding, and bronzing, which has survived largely intact. The beautifully carved leafy scrolls that support the arms are also painted, gilded,

and bronzed like the crest rail, and the flutes of the legs, some of the ring turnings around the legs, as well as the molding at the tops of the front, back, and side rails and are enriched with gilding, which again survives largely in fine condition. Related more to French than English prototypes, the design for this set of armchairs was presumably derived from French imperial models, including those conceived by Percier and Fontaine about 1800-02 for Malmaison and modified and published by Pierre de la Mèsangere in his serial publication, *Meubles et Objets de Gôut* (1796-1830). Specifically, the crest rail in the present example relates to an armchair included in the design scheme for the Music Room at Malmaison, Napoleon and Josephine's château that Percier and Fontaine redesigned and redecorated between 1800 and 1802 (see Francois Baudot, *Empire Style* [London, Thames & Hudson, 1999], pp.24-5 illus. in color)."

Figure 156
Scroll Armchair, Mahogany
Philadelphia, Circa 1815-1830

Height 37",
Width 25 1/2",
Depth 30"

Photo Courtesy of the Museum of
Arts and Sciences of Daytona
Beach, Florida

Mahogany veneer decorates the scroll crest rail. The stiles sweep backward in a scroll manner and are ornamented with concentric disks. Concentric disks were often used as accents in Philadelphia empire furniture of this period. The arms are swept under in dramatic scrolls that also end in disks. The front and side rails are mahogany veneered. The front feet are decorated with leafage carving above and terminate below in bulbs, which have vertical reeding.

This chair was part of a large suite of furniture ordered by Lydia Poultney from Thomas Whitecar in 1809. The invoice still exists. The front legs and stiles are reeded and the crest rail and splat are cut out with the amebic central oval pattern characteristic of Thomas Whitecar.

Figure 157
Sidechair, Mahogany

Made by Thomas Whitecar
Philadelphia, 1809

Height 35 1/16",
Width 18 1/8"

Photo Courtesy of the
Philadelphia Museum of Art

Figure 158

Arm Chair, mahogany

Attributed to Thomas Whitecar
Philadelphia, Circa 1810-1820

Secondary woods: frame is poplar,
glue blocks are pine.

Overall Height 34",
Seat Height 18 1/2",
Depth 18"

Private Collection

The crest rail and splat are decorated with the amebic central oval pattern attributed to Thomas Whitecar. Both arms are curved and reeded and rest upon turned and reeded bulbous arm supports. Below the supports, the front legs are reeded and tapered, ending in bulb feet. Reeded front legs, which terminate in bulb-shaped feet, have often been attributed to Ephraim Haines in the past on the basis of the ebony furniture he made for Stephen Girard in 1807 (see figures 148 and 150 of this text).[12] Today, it is understood that other Philadelphia cabinetmakers shared similar designs. The back legs are swept back and plain.

[12] Montgomery 146

An amebic oval design typical of Thomas Whitecar decorates the crest rail. The back splat is constructed of interlocking concentric circles. On the armchair the stiles are reeded and end at the arm supports, which are scrolled and reeded. The front legs of both chairs are reeded with leafage carving above and terminate in a variant of bulb feet.

Figure 159
Mahogany Armchair and Side Chair (of a set of 12)

Attributed to Thomas Whitecar
Philadelphia, Circa 1810-1820

Height 35",
Seat Height 17",
Width 19",
Depth 16"

Courtesy of Philip Bradley
Antiques, Downingtown, PA

Figure 160

Side Chair, Mahogany

Attributed to Thomas Whitecar
Philadelphia, Circa 1810-1820

Height 35 1/4",
Seat Height 18",
Width 19 1/2",
Depth 16 1/4"

Private Collection

This chair has the amebic oval design typical of Whitecar on the crest rail and splat. There is reeding on both stiles. The front legs are bulbous at the top with leafage carving and reeded below, ending in a variant of bulb feet. The back legs are swept back.

The back splats feature the amebic oval design commonly associated with Thomas Whitecar. The way the seat is upholstered (rising above the frame, rather than being built into it) is typical of Philadelphia practice in the period. The legs are reeded in the front and terminate in small turned bulbs.

Figure 161
Child's Chair, mahogany
Philadelphia, Circa 1815

Height 38",
Width 19"

Collection of
Mr. F.J. Carey III

Figure 162

Curly Maple Side Chairs

Philadelphia, Circa 1830-1835

Overall Height 32",
Seat Height 17",
Depth 16"

Collection of the Andalusia
Foundation

Reeding and other turnings decorate the front feet. The rear leg, stiles and crest rail are one harmonious swept unit that is very successful. This form became popular in the Victorian Era as the balloon back stile.[13] The turned stretchers are seen frequently on earlier Pennsylvania ladderback chairs but are somewhat unusual in this period. The splat is richly carved with foliage-decorated scrolls.

[13] R.W. Symonds and B. B. Whineray, *Victorian Furniture* (London: Studio Additions, 1962) 146.

Figure 163
Child's Lolling Chair, mahogany
Philadelphia, Circa 1800-1820

Height 38",
Width 19",
Depth 18"

Collection of
Mr. F.J. Carey III

Figure 164

Easy Chair, mahogany

Philadelphia, Circa 1805-1820

Secondary woods: poplar, Atlantic white cedar, and chestnut

Height 49",
Width 27",
Depth 30"

Photo Courtesy of
The Biggs Museum of American
Art, Dover, DE

The serpentine lines of the armrests, back and wings suggest that this easy chair may have been patterned from a French bergere prototype. The bergere was popular in France and England but less common in the United States. Since there were French craftsmen living in Philadelphia and many pattern books featuring both French and English interpretations of French designs were available, there was a proliferation of French inspired furniture in Philadelphia, including recamiers, bergeres and French secretaries (secretaire a abattant). There are clearly American adaptations on this chair, including the design of the front legs which have a series of concentric disks at the top, followed by reeding that terminates in slightly swelled bulbous tapered feet (all four feet once had casters, the front feet are replacements from the bottom of the reeding, and the rear legs are extended about 3 3/4"[15]).

[15] Zimmerman and Goldsborough 37

This chair is called "French" by Quervelle in his 1835 invoice to D. Turnbull of Rosedown Plantation. It is significant because it is one of the few chairs that is a proven product of his shop. The klismos form features a back splat of opposing cornucopias. A crest rail above is paneled.

Figure 165
Side Chair, mahogany

Made by Anthony G. Quervelle
Philadelphia, August 1835

Height 33 1/2",
Width 18 1/2",
Depth 16"

Photo Courtesy of Rosedown
Plantation State Historical Site,
Louisiana Office of State Parks

Figure 166

*Upholstered Klismos Side Chairs
with Flame Walnut Crest Rails
(Set of eight)*

Attributed to Richard Parkin
Philadelphia, Circa 1830-1840

Height 33",
Seat Height 17"

Photo and Description Courtesy of
Carswell Rush Berlin,
New York City

"An assembled set, each with a broad, curved crest rail, semi-upholstered seats and carved anthemion back rests, on carved tapering legs. Two chairs, evidently from a different set, were originally made to accommodate slip seats. Minor differences in carving and dimensions distinguish these from the other six chairs. Restoration to two legs and one crest rail. These stylish, transitional chairs combine highly Classical klismos-style crest rails and back rests with front legs in the Gothic taste. They are identical to a pair of chairs in the Landis Valley Museum in Lancaster, PA bearing the label:

Richard Parkin/Cabinetmaker/Egyptian Hall/
134 South Second Street/Philadelphia.

The style of these chairs relates to Parlour Chair patterns illustrated on pages 15 and 16 in Thomas King's *Modern Style of Cabinet Work Exemplified*, 1829, reprinted by Dover Publications (New York, 1995), a design book known to have been in Philadelphia, and influencing cabinetmakers in the period. These were made after the brief period, 1820-1825, when Parkin was in partnership with cabinetmaker Thomas Cook. This partnership produced an important sideboard now in the Baltimore Museum of Art which draws heavily on Plate XI of Thomas Hope *Household Furniture and Interior Decoration*, 1807, another influential English pattern book. Cook remained active in Philadelphia until 1837."

The front legs have a scroll-like curve and are decorated with a molding with reeding at the top. Both stiles have similar edge molding and the back splat and crest rail are decorated with foliage.

Figure 167
Side Chair, mahogany
Philadelphia, Circa 1820-1830

Height 33 1/8",
Width 17 3/4",
Depth 21 1/2"

Philadelphia Museum of Art: Gift of Andrew Jones and Jorge Celio, 1996

Photo by Graydon Wood

Figure 168

Klismos Side Chair, mahogany and mahogany veneer

Philadelphia, Circa 1820-1830

Secondary wood:
slip seat is poplar

Overall Height 33 1/2",
Width 17 1/2",
Depth 21"

The Metropolitan Museum of Art,
New York City, Friends of the
American Wing Fund, 1984.
(1984.126)

The crest rail is carved at the top with scrolls, which seem to form a shell at the center. The stiles have thumb moldings that terminate at the top in carved scrolls. The skirt features a carved flower in the center with scrolls at each side. The front legs are also carved with scrolls. The crest rail is contained within the stiles, which is a construction method more common in New York, but was also used by Philadelphia makers.

Side chairs of this type were made in sets by many chair makers in Philadelphia during the first few decades of the nineteenth century. Most had a carved back splat under the crest rail. This chair is unusual because its splat is not only carved, but stenciled as well. Furthermore, the stenciling is atypical in that it is gold with red detailing rather than black detailing. A crest rail is paneled with brass line inlay. Chairs closely related to these are pictured in Robert C. Smith, "The furniture of Anthony G. Quervelle Part V," *Antiques Magazine*, March 1974, 517, figure 8 and page 519, figure 11.

Figure 169
Side Chair, mahogany, maple and poplar
Philadelphia, Circa 1815-1830

Height 33 5/8",
Width 19",
Depth 21 1/2"

Collection of
Mr. Charles V. Swain

Figure 170
Two Sets of Pairs of Side Chairs,
mahogany
Philadelphia, Circa 1820-1835

Height 31 1/2",
Width 18",
Depth 20"

Photo Courtesy of Freemans
Auction Gallery, Philadelphia

The saber legs of both pairs are
swept into curved stiles with paneled
crest rails. The back splat of one pair
is divided into three horizontal
elements while the other pair has
carved central slats.

The crest rail is ornamented with horizontally spreading leaves. Below this is an intricately carved splat in a twisted floral and leaf design. The portion of the stiles adjacent to the splat is also carved. The saber legs are in a modified klismos style. A chair of similar design is pictured in *Federal Philadelphia The Athens of The Western World*, by Beatrice Garvan, page 71 (Philadelphia Museum of Art 1987).

Figure 171
Side Chair, mahogany
Philadelphia, Circa 1815-1825

Secondary woods: white pine

Height 33",
Width 18",
Depth 17 1/2"

Collection of
Mr. F.J. Carey III

Figure 172

Side Chair, mahogany

Philadelphia, Circa 1815-1825

Height 33",
Width 19 1/2",
Depth 17 3/4"

Collection of
Mr. F. J. Carey

This chair has saber legs that sweep into curved stiles. The lower splat is decorated with an open central area containing three ornamental balls. The crest rail is outlined with reeding.

Figure 173

Side Chair (one from a set of 8), mahogany

Philadelphia or New York,
Circa 1815-1825

Length 32",
Width 17"

Private Collection

The back splat contains a richly carved shell with scrolls on either side and boasts richly carved leafage with volutes on each side. The saber legs are in a klismos style.

The source of inspiration for this side chair is the Greek klismos chair, designs for which were found on classical artifacts. An inset panel of mahogany veneer decorates the crest rail. The back splat features a rectangular panel with mahogany veneer, which is connected to the stiles by lyre-shaped elements with acanthus carving on either side. The front legs are saber and the back legs have an outward sweeping curve.

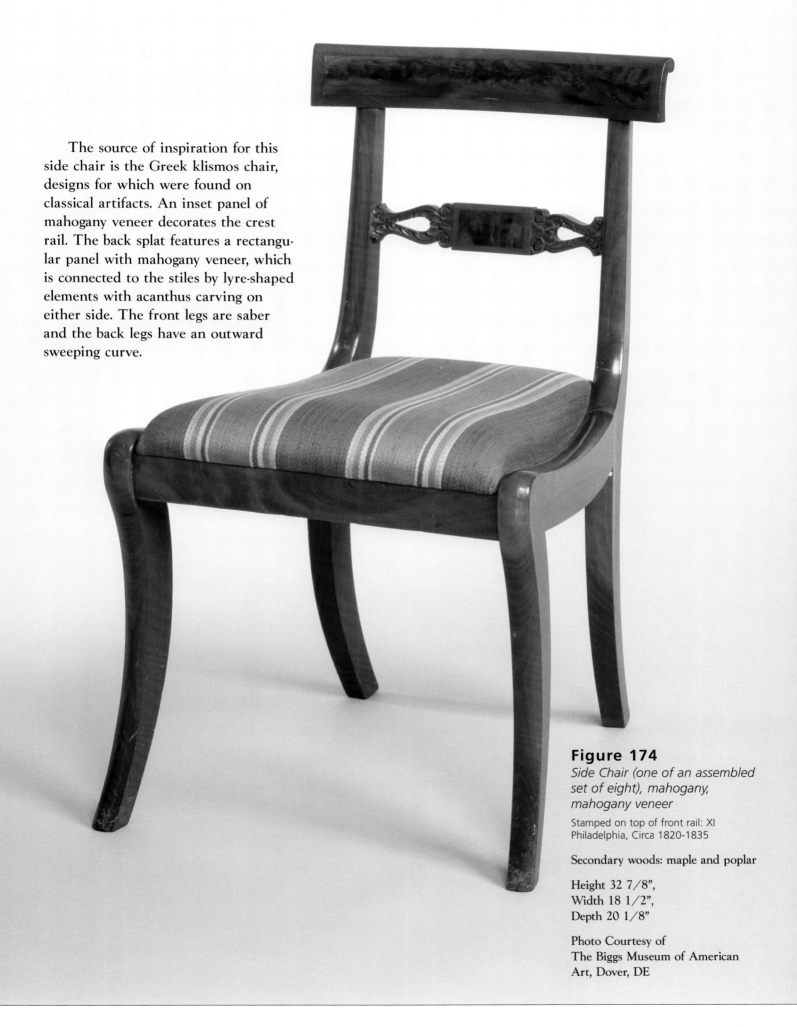

Figure 174
Side Chair (one of an assembled set of eight), mahogany, mahogany veneer

Stamped on top of front rail: XI
Philadelphia, Circa 1820-1835

Secondary woods: maple and poplar

Height 32 7/8",
Width 18 1/2",
Depth 20 1/8"

Photo Courtesy of
The Biggs Museum of American
Art, Dover, DE

Figure 175

*Pair of Klismos-Form Armchairs,
mahogany and mahogany
veneer, with ebony inlay*

Philadelphia, Circa 1820

Secondary woods: oak

Height 35 1/2",
Width 20 3/4",
Depth 23 3/8"

Photo Courtesy of Hirschl & Adler
Galleries, New York

Inscribed (one the top of the front
seat rail of one): I; (the other): II

The rectilinear design of these
chairs was popular after 1800; the
design most likely originated from
English and French classical styles
from publications such as Rudolph
Ackermann's *Repository of Arts*,

Thomas Hope's *Household Furniture
and Interior Decoration* (1807), **and**
George Smith's *Collection of Designs
for Household Furniture and Interior
Decoration* (1808).[16] The saber legs
imitate the Greek klismos design.

[16] Garvan 69-71

This chair displays saber legs with a thumb molding that is swept through the top of the side rail up to the crest rail in an elegant and successful manner. The chair is executed in curly maple which appears to have been a favored wood of Nicholas Biddle, based on the many surviving examples of this wood type at Andalusia. Both corners of the crest rail and the back splat below are richly carved with foliage and scrolls.

Figure 176
*Curly Maple Side Chair
(one of set of six)*
Philadelphia, Circa 1820-1830

Height 33 1/2",
Seat Height 17",
Depth 21"

Collection of the
Andalusia Foundation

Figure 177
Chair, mahogany veneer, rosewood graining, painted and gilt decoration
Philadelphia, 1820-1835

Secondary woods: ash

Height 32 1/4"

Philadelphia Museum of Art: Gift of Mrs. Van Horn Ely, 1965

Both legs are curved in a klismos manner. The stiles swing back in a manner reminiscent of bergere chairs of the period. Stenciled floral and line decoration adorn the crest rail, front seat rail and front legs.

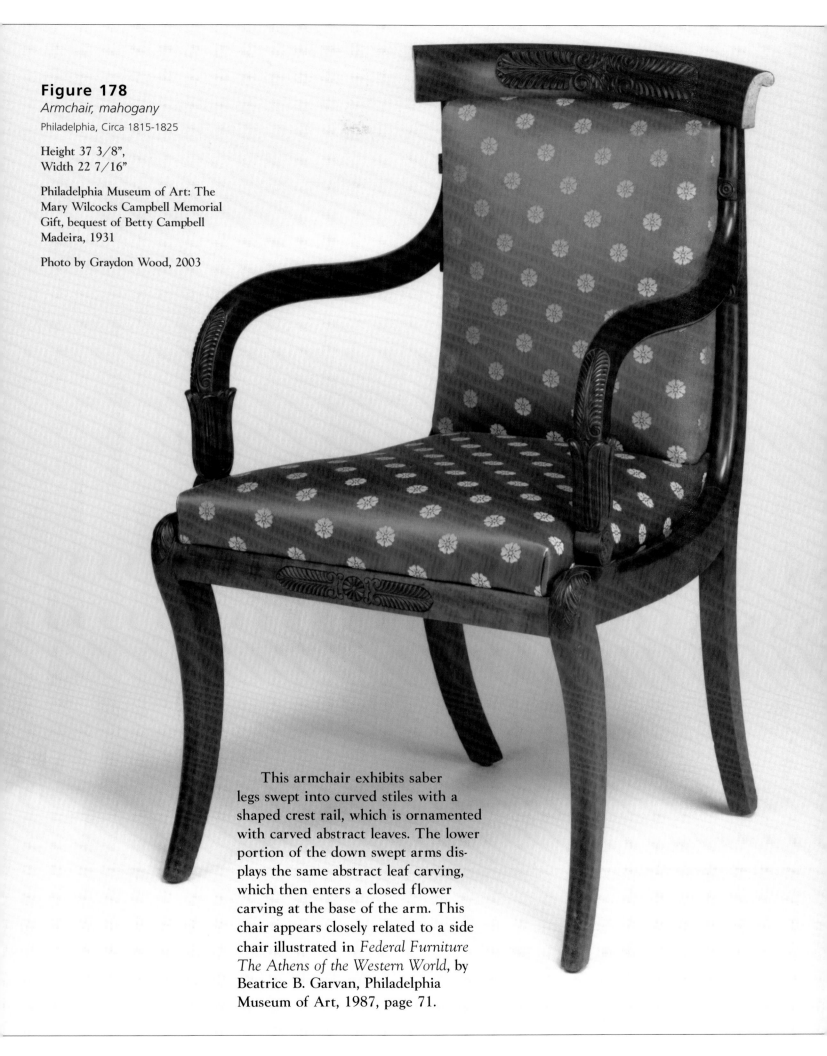

Figure 178

Armchair, mahogany

Philadelphia, Circa 1815-1825

Height 37 3/8",
Width 22 7/16"

Philadelphia Museum of Art: The
Mary Wilcocks Campbell Memorial
Gift, bequest of Betty Campbell
Madeira, 1931

Photo by Graydon Wood, 2003

This armchair exhibits saber
legs swept into curved stiles with a
shaped crest rail, which is ornamented
with carved abstract leaves. The lower
portion of the down swept arms displays the same abstract leaf carving,
which then enters a closed flower
carving at the base of the arm. This
chair appears closely related to a side
chair illustrated in *Federal Furniture
The Athens of the Western World*, by
Beatrice B. Garvan, Philadelphia
Museum of Art, 1987, page 71.

Figure 179

Klismos Side Chair (one of a pair), mahogany, mahogany veneer, rosewood inset in back and front rail, brass inlay

Philadelphia, Circa 1805-1815

Secondary woods: white ash, slip seat is eastern white pine.

Height 31 1/2",
Width 17 3/4",
Depth 23"

Philadelphia Museum of Art: Purchased: Thomas S. Harrison Fund, 1974

This chair has a wide, rectangular curved crest rail that extends beyond the stiles, which is representative of Philadelphia work. Geometric brass inlay and floral motifs are set with rosewood inserts. The feet are in a saber klismos manner. See figure 180 for a further discussion of a chair from the same set.

This chair is in the klismos form, with tapered legs that curve outward. The curved tablet crest rail has rectangular stringing of brass inlay that curls at the ends in scrolls, inside which there is a palmette between two inlaid brass stars. The stiles are inlaid on either side with two brass circles with stars inside. Above each front leg there is an inlaid brass flower encased by a circle. On the center of the front seat rail is an inlaid brass leaf design. This chair appears to be from the same set as the chair in figure 179.

Figure 180
Side Chair, mahogany, rosewood, brass, (from a set of eight)
Philadelphia, Circa 1805-1815

Secondary woods: white pine and ash

Height 31 3/4",
Width 18 9/10",
Depth 25 3/4"

Courtesy, Winterthur Museum

Figure 181

Pair of Side Chairs, mahogany

Philadelphia, Circa 1805-1815

Secondary wood: poplar

Height 31 3/4",
Width 19",
Depth 23 3/4"

Private Collection

The klismos chair originated in ancient Greece and never completely disappeared from western furniture design. However, it rose to great popularity in America during the early nineteenth century. This particular interpretation is the most historically accurate and is unique to Philadelphia. Variants were made with brass inlay, ebony veneer, intaglio carving and, as seen here, molded decoration. A full discussion of chairs of this form is available in David B. Warren, *et al, American Decorative Arts and Paintings in the Bayou Bend Collection*, page 124, entry F199. The high box-like upholstery seat frame is typical of Philadelphia. This seat frame is derived from French design sources.

This particular interpretation of the ancient Greek klismos chair is unique to Philadelphia and the most archaeologically correct made in America. Other examples closely related to this chair are illustrated in the Philadelphia Museum of Art's exhibition catalogue, *Philadelphia Three Centuries of American Art*, page 266, figure 222a and page 276, figure 222b. See also Donald L. Fennimore, *et al, Eye for Excellence*, page 70. Note that the crest rail extends laterally beyond the stiles in a typical Philadelphia manner.

Figure 182
Klismos Chair, mahogany, ebony
Philadelphia, Circa 1805-1815

Secondary wood: ash

Height 31 3/4",
Width 19",
Depth 23 1/2"

Private Collection

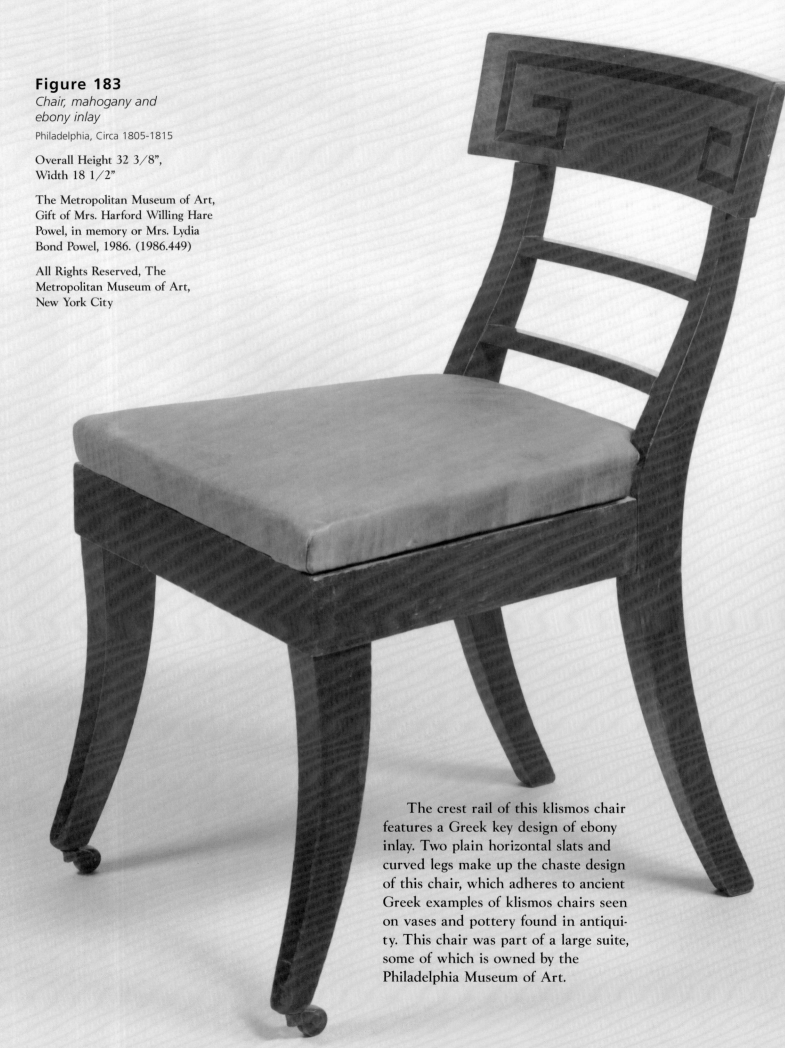

Figure 183
Chair, mahogany and ebony inlay
Philadelphia, Circa 1805-1815

Overall Height 32 3/8",
Width 18 1/2"

The Metropolitan Museum of Art,
Gift of Mrs. Harford Willing Hare
Powel, in memory or Mrs. Lydia
Bond Powel, 1986. (1986.449)

The crest rail of this klismos chair
features a Greek key design of ebony
inlay. Two plain horizontal slats and
curved legs make up the chaste design
of this chair, which adheres to ancient
Greek examples of klismos chairs seen
on vases and pottery found in antiquity. This chair was part of a large suite,
some of which is owned by the
Philadelphia Museum of Art.

This side chair in the klismos form has a curved rectangular tablet crest rail which extends beyond the stiles in a manner favored by Philadelphia chair makers. The tablet features intaglio-carved and ebonized rosettes, stringing and anthemia in a panel pattern.

The stiles on the back are curved with two narrow slats across the mid-back. Below the box frame trapezoidal-shape slip seat, on the front seat rail, are intaglio-carved and ebonized rosettes, which rest above each saber leg.

Figure 184

Klismos Side Chair, mahogany

Philadelphia, Circa 1805-1815

Height 32",
Width 18 7/10",
Depth 23 1/2"

Courtesy,
Winterthur Museum

Figure 185

Side Chair (one of a set)

Philadelphia, Circa 1810-1825

Secondary wood: ash, pine, and oak

Overall Height 32 1/2",
Seat Height 18",
Width 18 1/4",
Depth 22"

The Metropolitan Museum of Art,
Anonymous Gift, 1963 (63.143)

The crest rail is upholstered and rests on two stiles. This chair is another variation of the klismos chair that deviates from the norm of curved front legs, replacing them instead with turned and reeded legs. All exposed wood surfaces of the chair are painted and then decorated with gilt geometric and floral designs. The large size of the upholstered box frame seat is typical of this type of Philadelphia side chair. This chair is from the same set as figures 186 and 187.

Figure 186

Side Chair (one of a set)

Philadelphia, Circa 1810-1825

Secondary woods:
ash, pine, and oak

Overall Height 32 1/2",
Seat Height 18",
Width 18 1/4",
Depth 22"

The Art Institute of Chicago

Gift of James Biddle, 1970.436 3/4

Photograph by Bob Hashimoto

The two front legs of this klismos-style chair are straight and tapered, which deviates from the classical designs of klismos chairs found in antiquity, in which all four legs are saber. Dramatic Greek motif stencil decoration elevates the visual impact of the chair. This chair is from the same set as figures 185 and 187.

This klismos-style side chair is one of a set. The other chairs are at the Metropolitan Museum of Art (figure 185), the Art Institute of Chicago (figure 186), and at Winterthur Museum. These chairs share turned and reeded front legs, an identical design on the skirt and sides and upholstered seats and backs. The back legs on all chairs are saber. The chairs were originally located at a home in Bristol, Pennsylvania, and then moved to Andalusia. They were painted by J.P. Fondé. Further discussion of this paint decoration can be found on page 87 of chapter 4, part IV of this text.

Figure 187
Side Chair (one of a set)
Philadelphia, Circa 1810-1825

Secondary woods:
ash, pine, and oak

Overall Height 32 1/2",
Seat Height 18",
Width 18 1/4",
Depth 22"

Collection of the
Andalusia Foundation

Figure 188
*Side Chair, maple,
gold leaf and gesso*

Benjamin Henry Latrobe (1764-1820)
Philadelphia, Circa 1808

Secondary woods: poplar,
oak, and white pine

Overall Height 34 1/2",
Width 19 3/4",
Depth 19 1/2"

The Metropolitan Museum of Art,
Purchase, Mrs. Paul Moore Gift, by
exchange, 1994. (1994.189)

The crest rail, skirt, stiles and front legs are painted with gilt decoration. This klismos chair has outward curved legs and exhibits caning, which was usually reserved for the most fashionable furniture during the mid-seventeenth century. Replaced by upholstery in the late seventeenth century, it reemerged in late eighteenth century seating furniture and was purchased in woven sheets in different patterns.[17] The combination of the design and decorative elements of this chair make it a formal variation of a plain klismos prototype. See figure 189.

[17] Garvan 71

Both chairs are painted and then decorated with classical gilt designs. Note that while similar, the crest rail decoration varies between the two. The back and seat of the chairs are caned, which was considered fashionable. The chair on the right appears to be from the same set as figure 188.

Figure 189

Klismos Chairs; painted and gilded yellow poplar, gilded gesso, original and replacement cane, and reproduction silk upholstery fabric, cord and tassels

Designed by Benjamin Henry Latrobe, American (born England) 1764-1820
Possibly Made by Thomas Wetherill, American, died 1824
Possibly Painted by George Bridport, American (born England) 1794-1819
Philadelphia, 1808

Secondary woods: white oak and white pine

Overall Height 34 1/4",
Width 20",
Depth 19 1/2"

The Saint Louis Art Museum. Funds given by the Decorative Arts Society in honor of Charles E. Buckley

Figure 190a
Detail of the expertly carved arm support

Figure 190
Lyre Arm Chair, mahogany
Philadelphia, Circa 1810-1825

Private Collection

The crest rail is carved with a wreath and leafage. A heavily carved lyre decorates the splat. Both arm supports are expertly carved dolphins. Heavy reeding with a central slashed bud medallion adorns the front seat rail. The front saber legs are reeded and surmounted by scrolls, the sides of which are decorated with concentric disks.

This form closely follows the "X" stretcher design of antique Roman stools. "X" frames are discussed in more detail in John Morley's *The History of Furniture*, Boston, Bulfinch Press, 1999, pages 55-56, 60-61, 105-106, 204; Morley states on page 105, "The X-frame chair hardly needed revival; it had never disappeared. It retained its regality, although its details varied." The colorful curly maple graining effect, the turned stretchers and the shape of the rounded scroll feet are a Philadelphia chair maker's interpretation of this classical form.

Figure 191
Curly Maple Stool
Philadelphia, Circa 1820-1830

Height 24 1/4",
Width 24 1/4",
Depth 17 1/2"

Collection of the
Andalusia Foundation

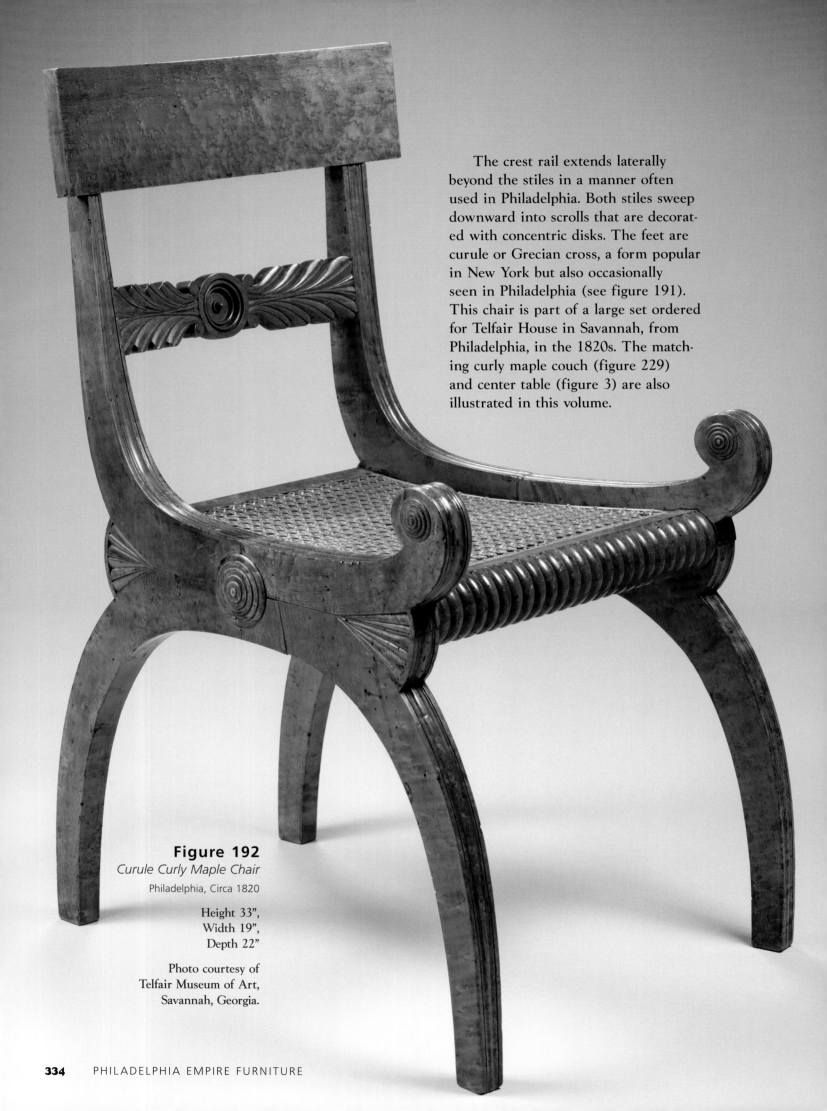

The crest rail extends laterally beyond the stiles in a manner often used in Philadelphia. Both stiles sweep downward into scrolls that are decorated with concentric disks. The feet are curule or Grecian cross, a form popular in New York but also occasionally seen in Philadelphia (see figure 191). This chair is part of a large set ordered for Telfair House in Savannah, from Philadelphia, in the 1820s. The matching curly maple couch (figure 229) and center table (figure 3) are also illustrated in this volume.

Figure 192
Curule Curly Maple Chair
Philadelphia, Circa 1820

Height 33",
Width 19",
Depth 22"

Photo courtesy of
Telfair Museum of Art,
Savannah, Georgia.

Figure 193
*Dolphin-Cornucopia Side Chair,
mahogany*
Philadelphia, Circa 1815-1825

Secondary wood: oak

Height 34 1/4",
Width 19",
Depth 15 3/4"

Philadelphia Museum of Art:
Thomas Skelton Harrison Fund and
funds contributed by W.B. Dixon
Stroud, 1992

Photo by Graydon Wood, 1992

The central splat is formed by two opposing dolphins whose tails rise up to merge with the cornucopias of the crest rail above. Both reeded stiles rise into the crest rail with a central panel and cornucopias at the corners. The front seat rail is heavily carved with foliage. The front surface of the back feet is also foliage carved. Both saber front feet are decorated with acanthus carving that terminates in carved dolphins. This chair shares many similarities with figure 194 and may well be the work of the same currently unidentified shop.

"These chairs are from a set of twenty-four owned by President James Monroe. Six are in the collection of the Monroe home at Ashlawn/Highlands in Charlottesville and two are in the collection of the James Monroe Museum and Memorial Library in Fredericksburg. They were at least used at his home in Oak Hill in Loudon Co., and may have been used at the White House during his presidency."

Author's Note: This chair appears to be from the same maker as the dolphin cornucopia side chair from the Philadelphia Museum of Art, illustrated in this section as figure 193. The main difference is the use of a cornucopia motif, as opposed to dolphins, on the back splat.

Figure 194
Side Chair (one from set of six), mahogany
Philadelphia, Circa 1815-1825

Secondary wood: ash and birch

Height 34 1/2", Width 20 1/4", Depth 21 1/2"

Photo and Description Courtesy of J. M. Flanigan American Antiques, Baltimore, Maryland

Painted chairs were considered to be in the highest taste during the Empire period. "The possibility of John Mitchell being the maker of these chairs is based on the fact that John Mitchell supplied Stephen Girard with Chairs *black and gold* (1809), Chairs *rush seats* (1810) and *painted and gilded chairs* (1816)."[18] From the estate of Stephen Girard.

[18] Schwarz, Description of Figure 40

Figure 195
Painted Side Chair
(one of a pair)

Probably by John Mitchell
Philadelphia, Circa 1815

Secondary woods: poplar, soft maple, and redgum

Height 32",
Width 17",
Depth 15 1/2"

Courtesy of the Stephen Girard Collection, Girard College, Philadelphia, PA

Figure 196

Pair of Painted, Stenciled and Gilt-Decorated Fancy Chairs

Philadelphia, Baltimore, or New Jersey
Circa 1820-1840

Overall Height 32 3/4"

Photo and Description Courtesy of
Christie's Auction Gallery,
New York City
© Christie's Images Limited 2006

"Each with a ring-turned crest centering clasped rosette set within back scrolling stiles centering a gilded anthemion-shaped splat above a trapezoidal rush seat fronted by a ring-turned rail, on ring and column-turned tapering legs headed by gilt stenciled leaves joined by a flat front stretcher centering a gilded rosette, all on a blue-green ground with gilded detailing. The decorative features including the structural design and ornament (on the large anthemion splat, front legs, ring turned front rail and front stretcher) indicate a Pennsylvania or New Jersey origin."

This chair, which bears the Biddle family crest, is derived from a design of Ackermann's which was reproduced in *Regency Furniture and Interiors*, London, page 94, plate 67. (See images 43 and 44 of this volume). The form is a modification of klismos with swept rear legs and rectangular straight tapered front legs. The splat boasts extensive foliage carving.

Figure 197
Mahogany Hall Chair (one of a pair)
Philadelphia, Circa 1830

Height 16 1/2",
Overall Height 33 1/2",
Depth 19 1/2"

Collection of the
Andalusia Foundation

Figure 198

Chaise Gondole Form Chair, rosewood

Philadelphia, Circa 1830-1840

Secondary wood: poplar

Height 32 3/4",
Width 18 3/4",
Depth 21"

Photograph and Description
Courtesy of the
Winterthur Museum

"This type of chair was rarely made of rosewood. It seems to have been infrequently made in Philadelphia, although numerous examples in mahogany survive that have been attributed to New York. Rudolph Ackerman noted in his *Repository of the Arts*...(May 1810, page 327) that chairs of this type "derive from Roman chairs [and were] often placed in a saloon [living room], or as extra chairs in a drawing-room or boudoir." He also noted that "the form of the back produces a very agreeable support to the person seated" (October 1824, page 244). This chair and its mates are said to have descended through the family of Mildred Benson Packard of Philadelphia."

This chair contains a large tin tub which was designed to be filled with water for relief of rectal pain, probably secondary to hemorrhoids. At that time, this painful condition had no surgical cure, and the sitz bath was used as a remedy. The bottom of the front feet are a variant of typical Pennsylvania bulb forms. Please note the brass drainage spigot of the tub, seen immediately below the front seat rail.

Figure 199
Sitz Bath, mahogany
Philadelphia, Circa 1810-1825

Seating Height 18",
Width 27",
Depth 31"

Collection of the
Andalusia Foundation

Figure 200
Maple Bergere Chair,
(one of a pair)
Philadelphia, Circa 1825-1835

Height 34 1/2",
Width 22 1/2"

Collection of the
Andalusia Foundation

The low and arched upholstered back has a shape reminiscent of French bergere chairs of the period. The back, arm supports and seat are upholstered to give the impression of a gondola-like form. Both broad tapered feet and front rail are maple. This Philadelphia interpretation of the bergere chair is relatively rare.

This unusual armchair is gilded and carved with shells and foliage. The legs rest on brass casters. This type of chair would have been considered one of the most fashionable of its type when it was made. "The vogue for painted and gilt furniture was probably heightened by the popularity of French furniture among United States leaders, including Jefferson, Monroe and John Adams."[19] This form is a Philadelphia interpretation of French classicism combined with earlier forms from the French royal court.

[19] Montgomery 145

Figure 201
Gilded Armchair
Philadelphia, Circa 1830-1840

Secondary wood: poplar

Height 40",
Width 26",
Depth 23 1/2"

Collection of
Mr. F.J. Carey III

Figure 202
Easy Chair
Philadelphia, Circa 1800-1820

Dimensions unrecorded

Private Collection

The rolled curve of the armrests and wings above follow the lines of earlier eighteenth century Philadelphia wing chairs. Turned legs display the influence of classicism on early Philadelphia design.

The circular "barrelback" curve of the chair is derived from classical stone monumental architecture and shows the influence of classicism on the earlier Philadelphia easy chair form. Several related examples of this chair are currently at Winterthur.[20] An elliptical front rail contributes to the circular design of the frame. The front feet are reeded in a classical manner. The back legs flair out sharply, which is a common Philadelphia feature.

[20] Montgomery 116

Figure 203
Circular (barrelback) Easy Chair
Philadelphia, Circa 1800-1820

Height 48",
Seating Height 19",
Depth 27"

Private Collection

Chairs Outside Philadelphia

Figures 204
Pair of Black Fancy Chairs with Gold Stenciling
Baltimore, Circa 1815-1825

Height 32 1/2",
Seating Height 17 1/2",
Depth 18 1/2"

Private Collection

Figure 204a
Detail of the opposing swan splat

A rectangular gilt design decorates the crest rail and stiles. The splat is adorned with opposing swans. The turned front legs and front stretcher are decorated with gilt foliage. This Grecian chair form is boldly decorated with ornamental stenciled gilt. The stretcher between the front legs has a central medallion with gilt foliage.

The double swan motif is a design taken from Plate XXI, Thomas Hope, Household Furniture and Interior Decoration, 1807. Please refer to the magazine *Antiques* May 2006 article of Nancy Goyne Evans for further information on this form.

This form of fancy chair has elaborate medallion and foliage stenciling with winged griffins decorating the lower splat. The crest rail displays a Greek key design. This type of chair was made in Maryland, Pennsylvania, New Jersey and New York, especially in the Hudson Valley. For additional information on these chairs see Anna Tobin D' Ambrosio, *Masterpieces of American Furniture* from the Munson-Williams-Proctor Institute (Utica, New York, 1999) 54-55.

Figure 205
Pair of Fancy Side Chairs; soft maple, yellow poplar, hickory, rush, paint
Probably Baltimore, Circa 1820-1840

Height 32 7/8",
Width 18",
Depth 19 1/4"

Collection of Munson-Williams-Proctor Arts Institute, Museum of Art, Utica, New York.

Museum Purchase 59.126.1-2

Photo by John Bigelow Taylor, N.Y.C. 1996

Figure 206

*Black Painted Armchair
(one of a pair)*

New York or Philadelphia,
Circa 1810-1825

Height 32",
Seat Height 16",
Depth 18 1/2"

Collection of the
Andalusia Foundation

This pair of chairs was originally painted green and was later repainted black. The pair is closely related to a red painted, stenciled armchair at Wintherthur, illustrated in *American Painted Furniture 1660-1880*, by Dean A. Fales, Jr., Bonanza Books, New York, 1986, page 144, illustration 235. The French legs descend and taper outward. The scroll arm supports lend grace to this form.

Figure 207a
Detail of the distinctive palmetto palm carving of the splat.

Figure 207
Sidechair, maple, white pine, southern yellow pine

Probably South Carolina, Circa 1830-1835

Overall Height 33 1/4", Seat Height 15 1/2", Width 17 3/4", Depth 14 1/4"

Private Collection

The chair is constructed of maple, except for the splat, which consists of white pine or southern yellow pine. The tapered rectangular feet and scrolled crest rail are consistent with late classical design. The construction of the chair appears somewhat primitive. The splat is decorated with what appears to be a palmetto palm. The palmetto palm is the state symbol for South Carolina. The chair was original-ly painted a white cream color and is now largely stripped. Although fancy chairs were imported into the south from northern states, the primitive con-struction of the chair and especially the pimento splat suggests this was the work of a local joiner. It was possibly slave made on a South Carolina planta-tion. Southern manufactured fancy chairs, especially those with a palmetto palm motif, are extremely rare.

CHAPTER 11
SOFAS AND COUCHES

SOFAS AND COUCHES

Early nineteenth century sofas and couches were commonly found in elegant parlors and drawing rooms. Sofas had ends of equal height, while couches had ends of different heights. The sofa provided comfort and lent a distinguished air to the room when guests visited the home. Many different forms of sofas existed, the cheapest and most common being the "plain sofa," based on the Roman sofa called a fulcra, which had identically scrolled ends and a long, wooden crest rail.[1] The plain sofa was one of solid proportion with identical ends in the form of scrolls that curved into the seat rail. More expensive versions of this type incorporated carving at the center of the crest rail's tablet and extensive reeding, carving and veneering. Features of Philadelphia sofas of this type often include carved lion's paw feet (with the back legs being uncarved patterns of the front), heavy florid carving, and a massive overall form in comparison to New York and New England sofas.

The second type of sofa is known as the square-ended, or "box sofa," which became popular in the 1820s. Box sofas were formed by vertical boxes at the ends of the sofa, which rested on large, turned Roman feet.[2] This proved to be a popular form that was often embellished with carving on the back rail and box elements, and was monumental in size. Noticeable differences exist between Philadelphia and New York box sofas, one being that the backs of Philadelphia sofas are much larger in size than those of New York. Feet on Philadelphia box sofas tend to be carved in the front with simplified, flat surface outlined versions of the front ones in the back without carved decoration.[3] Shell motifs were often placed on the upper portion of the box unit.

The third type, the "Grecian couch" or "Double scroll sofa," contains complex scrolls on the back and was often made in pairs.[4] This most expensive form is modeled after Greek examples and is made for reclining more than sitting. It became known as the recamier after a French portrait of Madame Jeanne Julie Adelaide Recamier reclining on a couch of this form, painted by Jacques-Louis David in 1800. The form is similar to the plain sofa, but the scrolled headboard is asymmetrical and the back is formed from two double scrolls. The main feature of the Grecian couch is that the back does not extend over the entire back of the sofa, but leaves a part of it exposed. This was meant to indicate its use as a piece of furniture used to relax and recline on, rather than sit. The other distinguishing feature is that one arm is large and the other usually forms a smaller scroll at the foot (sometimes the arm may be absent altogether). Later the Grecian sofa became known as a Lounge.

Henry Holland, an English cabinetmaker who employed French craftsmen and designs, designed a Grecian sofa ending in a scroll or lyre, with klismos, turned or animal legs, which became popular in the early nineteenth century.[5] Sheraton also published examples of this type of couch called a "Grecian squab" in 1802.[6] In 1803, Sheraton defines Grecian in an essay in his *Cabinet Dictionary* as, "used adjectively to signify any thing executed or shaped in the imitation of the taste of the Greeks."[7] Sheraton attempted to explain in this essay, the use of the Grecian sofa by describing a scene of ancient Romans reclining on this

[1] Fitzgerald 117

[2] Fitzgerald 118

[3] Robert Smith, "The Furniture of Anthony Quervelle-Part V: Sofas, Chairs and Beds," *The Magazine Antiques* Mar. 1974: 513.

[4] Fitzgerald 118

[5] John Morley 228

[6] Morley 228

[7] Montgomery 293

type of sofa while dining. Sheraton maintained that:

> The old Romans sat at meat as we do, till the Grecian luxury and soft-ness corrupted them; and then they lolled, or reclined at dinner, after the Grecian manner...The Manner of lying at meat amongst the Romans, Greeks, and more modern Jews, was the same in all respects. The table was placed in the middle, round which stood three beds covered with cloth or tapestry, according to the quality of the master of the house. Upon these the guests lay inclining the superior part of their bodies upon their left arms, the lower part being stretched out at full length, or a little bent.[8]

The Grecian sofa was never used for dining in America as far as it has been documented.

Sofa designs drawn from sources of antique Greek, Roman, and Egyptian styles were popularized by English designers, who introduced them to American cabinetmakers. The turned Roman leg was revived and applied to many furniture forms including couches, where it became fashionable to incorporate the exaggerated rounded or concave/convex turning to the legs. From the Grecian sofa evolved other furniture forms that were newly intro-duced such as the bench, a type of sofa without armrests that was usually placed by windows, and the sofa-bed, which began to replace the traditional bed in later years. The Ottoman sofas, heavily cushioned and very large in size, was also shown in designs of the time, but were not overly popular. The Grecian sofa was popular for many years beyond the Empire period, and can still be seen in modern designs today, although without the extravagant carving.

[8] Montgomery 293

Figure 209

Sofa, mahogany

Made by Thomas Whitecar
Philadelphia, 1809

Height 37",
Width 75 9/16",
Depth 27 9/16"

Photo Courtesy of the
Philadelphia Museum of Art

The crest rail is figured mahogany. Both arm supports sweep downward to bulbous reeded columns below, which are floral medallions. The feet have horizontal and vertical reeding and end below with bulbs. This sofa was part of a large furniture order from Lydia Poultney placed in 1809. The invoice for this still exists at the Philadelphia Museum of Art.

Figure 208

Sofa, mahogany

Philadelphia, Circa 1800-1820

Height 36",
Width 76",
Depth 22"

Private Collection

The crest rail is carved with cornucopias that face each other. Both arms turn downward in small scrolls with carving in a leaf design below. The legs are reeded ending in bulbs.

A full discussion of this sofa can be found in Donald L. Fennimore and Robert T. Trump, "Joseph B. Barry, Philadelphia cabinetmaker," *The Magazine Antiques*, May 1989, pages 1212-1225. The fleur de lis pattern and complex scrolling are seen on other Barry attributed items including several chairs illustrated in the chapter of this volume (see figures 153 and 154). Bulbous reeded arm supports are also often featured on Philadelphia arm chairs (see figures 147 and 149). The front legs are reeded and terminate in bulbs.

Figure 210
Sofa, mahogany

Attributed to Joseph B. Barry
Philadelphia, Circa 1810-1820

Secondary wood: poplar

Height 37 1/2",
Width 76",
Depth 28 1/2"

Private Collection

Figure 211 and 211a

Sofa, mahogany

Attributed to Joseph B. Barry
Philadelphia, Circa 1800-1820

Height 33 1/4",
Width 80",
Depth 23"

Private Collection

A version of the "plain sofa," this classical sofa may have been based on one of Sheraton's published designs. The raised portion of the back rail is joined by two long curves that blend into the scrolled arms. Two cornucopias from which flow foliage decorate the central portion of the crest rail. There are rectangular panels on the front rail above the feet, which exhibit a leaf pattern with a slashed bud in the center. The bulbous feet, known as a Roman feet, are reeded and ebonized and rest on large brass casters. Carved foliage and slashed bud panels are characteristic of Joseph Barry's specialist carvers. This sofa, with exception of the feet, is identical to the Jonathan Thomas family sofa illustrated as plate 7 in "Joseph B. Barry, Cabinetmaker," *The Magazine Antiques*, by Donald Fennimore and Robert Trump, May 1989, page 1220. The Thomas family sofa has saber legs instead of Roman.

Figure 211a

Detail of the crest rail illustrating the cornucopia without flowing leafage.

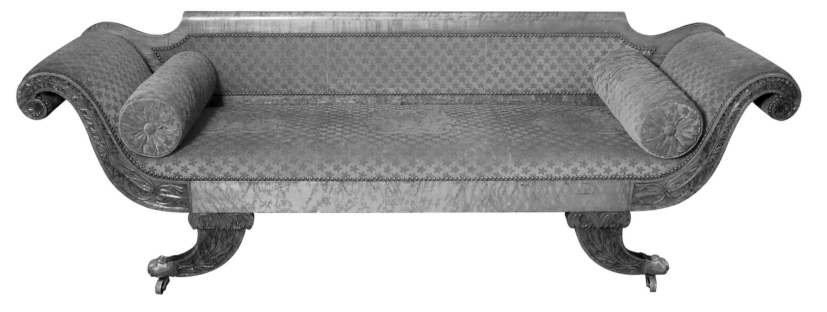

This sofa has foliate-carved scroll ends end in floral disks. Both scroll ends have more lateral tilt and length than average, which lend a pleasant effect to the overall proportions. The front and crest rails are curly maple and the maple foliage-carved saber feet exhibit the same excellent carving as the scrolls.

Figure 212
Carved Curly Maple Sofa
Philadelphia, Circa 1815-1830

Height 28 1/2",
Width 82 1/2",
Depth 22 1/2"

Collection of the
Andalusia Foundation

Figure 213 and 213a

Sofa, mahogany

Attributed to Charles White
Philadelphia, March 1827

Dimensions unrecorded

Private collection

This "plain sofa," simple in carving and form, is believed to be part of a large set of furniture made for the Newbold family by Charles White. The set of furniture, documented in a letter by White, was sent as a wedding gift to the family by steamboat (figure 36a illustrates this letter). There are rectangular panels containing a leaf design on the outer edge of the seat rail, directly above the legs, and foliage carving on the scrolls of the legs. The curve of the arms and turned feet can be traced back to designs by Sheraton, who published similar designs in his "Cabinet Dictionary", that were derived from ancient Greek and Roman sources. With its gentle, flowing scrolls including the feet, this piece represents a chaste example of the most popular type of sofa in the period.

Figure 213a
detail of the carving of the scroll foot

Classic Empire mahogany carved sofa attributed to Charles White, based on the same letter written by White that is illustrated in figure 36a. At the top of the back is a rounded rail, with a carved scroll at each end that turns downward. This is sometimes called a "bracket." A similar feature is sometimes seen on headboards of Empire beds.[9] The scroll end rod or "bracket" is a feature common on New York sofas and headboards that is occasionally found in Philadelphia and Baltimore work.[10] The pronounced tapered scrolls of the arm rests are typically Philadelphia in design. Intricate carving of the winged lion's-paw feet gives this piece a heavier, more impressive aura, characteristic of Philadelphia sofas.

[9] Edgar G. Miller Jr., *American Antique Furniture, Volume 1* (New York: Dover Publications, 1966) 333.

[10] Gregory R. Weidman, *Furniture in Maryland 1740-1940* (Baltimore: Schneidereith and Sons, 1984) 167.

Figure 214
Sofa, mahogany

Attributed to Charles White
Philadelphia, March 1827

Height 35",
Width 56 1/2",
Depth 23"

Private collection

Figure 215
Mahogany Sofa

Attributed to Anthony g. Quervelle
Philadelphia, Circa 1825

Dimensions-
Length- 89",
Height- 34 1/2",
Depth- 22"

Mahogany veneer decorates the crest rail. Both arm supports have a long vertical rise which scrolls abruptly outward ending in disks. Above the lion claw feet there is an abrupt horizontal division, above which are curling anthemion pedals. The form of the scroll arms and feet relate this to a number of Quervelle attributed sofas as discussed by Robert C. Smith in his Quervelle article in *The Magazine Antiques*, **March 1974.**

Both Robinson and Forst signed their names, the word "Philadelphia" and date "January 12, 1838" in pencil on the outside back. They appear to have both been journeymen working under someone else's employment, since they are not listed as being in business for themselves in the Philadelphia city directories. The crest rail is decorated at both ends with eagles' heads. The feet are well carved saber forms with foliage.

Figure 216
Sofa, mahogany

Made by Joseph D. Robinson
Originally upholstered by Frederick Forst
Philadelphia, 1838

Secondary woods:
poplar and white pine

Height 36",
Width 89 1/2",
Depth 24 1/2"

Private Collection

Figure 217 and 217a

Mahogany Sofa

Philadelphia, Circa 1820-1830

Height 33 3/4",
Width 88",
Depth 22 3/4"

Collection of the
Andalusia Foundation

This sofa exhibits extremely well-carved foliate decoration to the scroll arms which terminate in floral buds enclosed within disks. The crest rail has a panel of mahogany veneers.

Both ends of the front seat rail have double disk squares separated by a medallion consisting of a bud and leaf design. The feet begin as lions claws, merging above into eagles.

Figure 217a
Detail of the lion paw eagle foot.

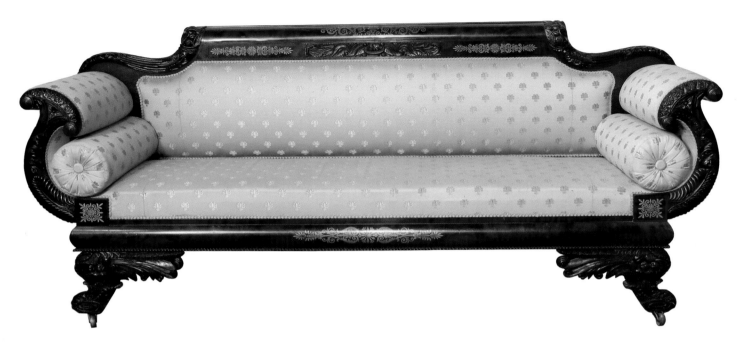

This "cornucopia" form sofa has its arms in the general shape of the symbol of prosperity and abundance, a popular design from 1810 to 1830.[11] The apex of the carved cornucopia arms has a leaf and floral design. A central portion of the seat rail is stenciled, as is the top rail. Gadrooning lines the bottom of the seat rail. The outward and inward curving of the arms allows for a small circular space below, in which a pillow (then known as a squab) would be placed. Both front feet are a stylistic rendition of a lion foot with decorative foliage elements.

[11] Miller 336

Figure 218 and 218a
Sofa, mahogany with stenciling
Philadelphia, Circa 1830

Height 27",
Width 86",
Depth 23"

Collection of
Mr. F.J. Carey III

Figure 218a
detail of the fine quality carving and stenciling of the arm support.

Figure 219 and 219a
Cornucopia and Dolphin Sofa,
mahogany
Philadelphia, Circa 1825-1830

Height 34",
Width 84",
Depth 25"

Collection of Joseph Sorger

This sofa is known as a "cornucopia" sofa because its arm supports are bouquets of fruit. These symbolize prosperity and abundance and were a very popular design from 1810-1830.[12] Both cornucopias arise from large foliage-decorated disks that are positioned above the legs.

The sofa rests on carved, turned dolphins with twisted tails in the front. The back legs are uncarved profiles of the front legs in a typical Philadelphia manner.

[12] Miller 336

Figure 219a
detail of the cornucopia and dolphin foot

The ornament at the top of the crest rail is expertly carved. At the raised portion there are cornucopias on either side from which fruits and vegetables flow to meet in the center of the crest. Below this there is a rectangular panel of mahogany veneer outlined in curly maple veneer. This theme of cornucopias is repeated at the top of the lion claw feet. The scrolled arms and other portions of the crest rail are heavily carved with foliage. A paper receipt for the sale of the sofa from Horace Pippitt was found in the original webbing of the sofa.

Figure 220, 220a, and 220b

Elaborately Carved Sofa, mahogany

Invoice of Horace Pippitt cabinetmaker Philadelphia, Circa 1820-1833

Height 35",
Width 86",
Depth 24"

Collection of Joseph Sorger

Figure 220a
Detail of central crest rail

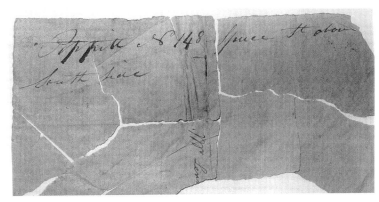

Figure 220b
Horace Pippitt receipt

Figure 221
Couch, mahogany and mahogany veneer
Philadelphia, Circa 1825-1830

Height 40 1/4",
Width 94 1/2",
Depth 27 1/2"

Philadelphia Museum of Art: Gift of
Shelby W. Thayer, her son Russell
Thayer, and her daughter Shelby
Thayer Bullitt, 1974

Photo by Graydon Wood, 2003

The crest rail is scrolled and heavily carved with foliage with a central large tablet. This tablet is divided into an upper portion of two opposed cornucopias and a lower portion of mahogany veneer. The scroll arms are asymmetric with the lower scroll arm being fully carved with foliage and the higher scroll arm exhibiting foliage carving only to the upper portion. Reeding and large disks decorate the front rail, below which are dolphin foot supports.

The crest rail is curved with serpents running along and ending at the scrolls. A central panel is a carved American Indian princess holding an American flag. The basis of this design may be the *Diplomatic Medal* ordered by George Washington and executed by Augustin Dupré in France in 1790.[13] This monumental form exhibits heavily scrolled, reeded arms. The front rail is divided at both ends by double disks. Well-carved dolphins adorn the feet.

[13] Philadelphia Museum of Art, *Philadelphia Three Centuries of American Art* 278.

Figure 222
Mahogany Carved Sofa With Indian Princess Scene
Philadelphia, Circa 1820-1825

Secondary woods: pine and poplar.

Height 40",
Width 102",
Depth 25.5"

Photo Courtesy of
Mr. Joseph Sorger

Figure 223
Carved Mahogany Sofa
Philadelphia, Circa 1820-1840

Height 45 1/4",
Width 90",
Depth 22 3/4"

Photo and Description Courtesy of
Christie's Auction Gallery,
New York City
© Christie's Images Limited 2006

"The central tablet headed by carved foliage design flanked by gadrooned shaped crest rail terminating in dolphin heads, above a formerly upholstered back and seat with scrolled arms with foliate carving over a veneered seatrail with rounded carved details, on paw feet with feathered eagle returns, fitted with castors."

"Currently without any meaningful provenance, this sofa possesses a strongly architectonic character that ties it, albeit loosely, to a design published by Thomas Hope in his influential *Household Furniture and Interior Decoration* (London: 1807; reprint by Dover Publications, NY, 1971, page 55, plate XVIII no. 5), where the profile of the arms and the parade of rosettes along the seat rail provide a starting point for a local interpretation. A review of the pages in Anthony G. Quervelle's sketchbook reveal various details that are incorporated in this sofa, most especially the large and brilliantly carved shell at the center of the crest rail that is found as the dominant decorative device on the arms of two sofas each of which is captioned "Box Sofa." Various pieces have also appeared that bear some kind of relationship to this piece, including a pair of recamier sofas formerly in the collection of Andy Warhol (see catalogue, sale 6000, Sotheby's, April 29-39, 1988, no. 3211 illus.), in which a large shell of the same type crowns each of the asymmetrical arms of the sofa."

Figure 224
Monumental Sofa in the Neo-Classical Taste, mahogany

Possibly Anthony G. Quervelle
Philadelphia, Circa 1825-1830

Secondary woods: mahogany, pine and tulip poplar, caned seat with upholstered slip seat, and gilt-brass castors.

Height 35 3/8",
Length 96 1/4",
Depth 23 7/8"

Photo and Description Courtesy of Hirschl & Adler Galleries, New York

Figure 225
Painted Sofa
Philadelphia, Circa 1825-1835

Height 42",
Seat Height 17",
Width 24"

Collection of the
Andalusia Foundation

This unusual sofa, grain painted to simulate curly maple, incorporates disks, decorative leafage, wings and other painting for effect. The treatment of the feet is especially notable. A winged element of the foot is painted in the same flat plane with the arm supports and seat rail, while the claw feet project from behind this.

This curly maple sofa, or day bed as it is sometimes called, has a wide front rail with scroll supports at the ends above and scroll carved feet below. The gentle scrolled arm supports provide a simplistic, yet elegant feel to the piece.

Figure 226
Grecian Sofa or Day Bed (one of a pair), curly maple
Philadelphia, Circa 1825-1835

Seat Height 16",
Width 82",
Depth 23"

Collection of the
Andalusia Foundation

Figure 227

*Grecian Couch (Recamier),
painted maple (one of a pair)*

Philadelphia, Circa 1810-1825

Height 31",
Width 79",
Depth 23"

Collection of
Mr. F.J. Carey III

A scrolled back support terminates midway. The seat rail is painted. One end of the rail curves outward, while the other curves inward. Decorative stenciling and painting work on the front, sides, and back adds depth and elegance to the form. The feet are a scroll-saber variant, similar to many of Sheraton's designs for recamiers.

A double scroll crest rail is decorated with foliage carving and reeding, as is the front rail which ends in heavily carved scrolls. The feet are lion claw with cornucopias.

Figure 228

"Grecian Couch" or Double Scroll Sofa, mahogany

Philadelphia, Circa 1825

Dimensions unrecorded

Joan Bogart Antiques, Rockville Centre, NY

Figure 229
*Couch
(one of mirror image pair),
curly maple*
Philadelphia, Circa 1820-1830

Secondary wood:
maple with caning

Height 33",
Width 66",
Depth 20"

Photo Courtesy of Telfair Museum
of Art, Savannah, Georgia

The back rail and end rails are scrolled and terminate in concentric disks (see figure 192, Curule chair from the same suite). Vertically segmented convex reeding decorates the front rail. All scroll feet end in concentric disks. This couch is part of a suite of maple furniture purchased by the Telfair family of Savannah during the 1820s in Philadelphia.

Figure 231
Mirror image Quervelle lounge

This pair of lounges illustrates the movement to Restoration style with flat surface abstraction of classical form. The "volute calyx" foot and overall form relate to designs in John Taylor's *Upholsterer's and Cabinet Making Pocket Assistant* (Gordon, 1825).[14] One of the pair bears a Delmes engraved Quervelle label.

[14] Thomas Gordon Smith, "Quervelle Furniture at Rosedown, in Louisiana," *The Magazine Antiques* May 2001: 779.

Figure 230 and 231
*Lounge, mahogany
(mirror image pair)*

Delmes Label of Anthony G. Quervelle Philadelphia, August 1835

Height 32",
Width 72",
Depth 23 1/2" (both lounges)

Photo Courtesy of the Rosedown Plantation State Historical Site, Louisiana Office of State Parks

Figure 232
Mahogany Sofa

Made by Anthony G. Quervelle
Philadelphia, August 1835

Height 35",
Width 84",
Depth 22 1/2"

Photo Courtesy of the Rosedown
Plantation State Historical Site,
Louisiana Office of State Parks

This sofa features the same volute calyx feet and linear abstract use of veneer over flat surface as the pair of Quervelle lounges at Rosedown (figures 230 and 231). This is a trademark of the Restoration style that ended Philadelphia Empire classicism.

The upper crest has small scrolls that meet at the back of the large arm-rests. Both arm supports have a carved anthemion or Roman shell design. Gadrooning lines the lower rail and the Roman bulbous feet are carved with a leaf design. This sofa closely relates to one published in Robert Trump's arti-cle, figure 2, "Part V: Sofas, chairs and beds," *The Magazine Antiques*, March 1974, page 513; which has similar feet, crest with gadrooning and anthemia. The inside of the arm of the sofa contains the following inscription: G.W. Pickering, Maker September 5, 1833 Barry.

Figure 233, 233a, and 233b

Box Sofa, mahogany

Made by G.W. Pickering, shop of Joseph Barry Philadelphia, September 5th 1833

Overall Height 35 3/4",
Seat Height 16 1/2",
Width 90",
Depth 25 1/2"

Private Collection

Figure 233b
Pencil inscription of Joseph Barry.

Figure 233a
Detail of the box end illustrating carving of the shell and foot.

Figure 234, 234a, and 234b

Box Sofa, mahogany

Stencil of Cook & Parkin
Philadelphia 1820-1825

Height 35",
Width 89",
Depth 24 1/2"

Photo Courtesy of McAdams' Ltd.
Antiques, Columbia, Missouri

This box sofa has arm rests that are finely carved with naturalistic shells reminiscent of Philadelphia rococo carving. The Roman front feet are constructed in two parts with the upper disks being applied over a circular extension of the foot in a donut-like manner so that the disks are actually somewhat mobile. These disks can actually be rotated independent of the foot below. The crest rail is veneered with carving to both ends.

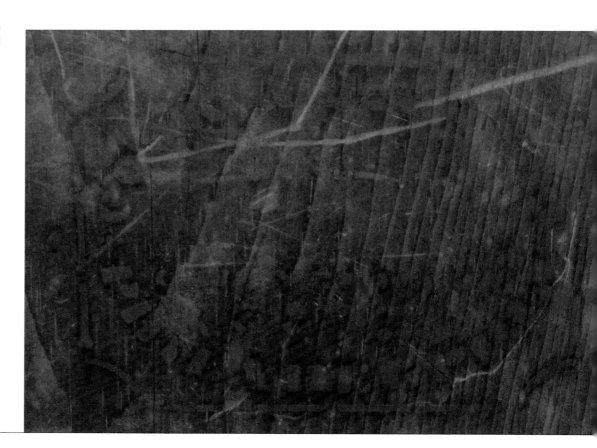

Figure 234b
Cook and Parkin Stencil

Figure 234a
Detail showing double shell at the top of the box end. The top of the Roman foot has a separate donut-like applied element that can be rotated independently of the rest of the foot.

Figure 235 and 235a

Mahogany Box Sofa

Attributed to Cook & Parkin
Philadelphia, Circa 1820-1825

Secondary wood: white pine

Overall Height 33",
Width 78",
Depth 25 1/4"

Private Collection

The monumental nature of this piece is unmistakably a sofa by Cook and Parkin. This sofa has the two piece Roman foot discussed in figure 234a. It also exhibits a superior complex double shell carving similar to that seen in the best Philadelphia highboys of fifty years earlier (1750-1775). Clearly, the Philadelphia carving community passed their tradition to future generations.

Figure 235a
Construction details

The Joseph Barry sofa on the left uses a box end that is removable with screws. A Cook and Parkin box end on the right is mortised to the frame and cannot be removed. Note the upper disc element of the Cook and Parkin foot is donut-shaped and applied separately over the rest of the foot and can be rotated independently.

Figure 236 and 236a

Box Sofa, mahogany

Stencil of Charles and John White
Philadelphia, Circa 1825-1835

Dimensions unrecorded

Photo Courtesy of
Mr. Joseph Sorger

This marked Charles and John White sofa displays an unusual un-carved, semi-circular and concave foot, above which the armrests contain Gothic arches decorated above with a simple outline molding with disks at the ends. The crest rail is paneled with carving only at the ends. The front rail is veneered and has gadrooning.

Figure 236a
Stencil of Charles and John White

The sofa appears to be almost identical to the marked Charles and John White sofa illustrated in figure 236. It has the same Gothic arches, scrolling and gadrooning and varies by having foliage carved Roman feet. This sofa was found in the same home with the marked White Bros. sofa, with the history that they had always been together.

Figure 237
Box Sofa, mahogany
Attribution to Charles and John White
Philadelphia, Circa 1825-1835

Height 25 1/2",
Width 89",
Depth 30"

Photo Courtesy of
Mr. Joseph Sorger

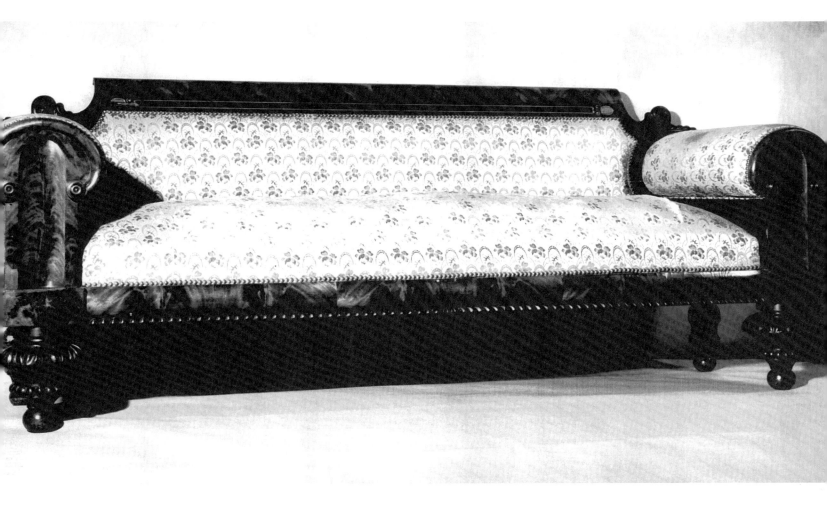

Figure 238
Box Sofa, mahogany

Label of David Fleetwood
Philadelphia, Circa 1825-1835

Height 35",
Width 85",
Depth 25"

Photo Courtesy of
J. Michael Flanigan,
American Antiques

The upper crest rail has an inlay of brass and ebonized wood with small scrolls at the ends as seen on other Philadelphia box sofas. The arm supports exhibit large, well-carved shells. The lower rail is mahogany veneered and gadrooned. The bulbous feet exhibit leafage carving. The calling card of David Fleetwood that was attached to the rear of this sofa is illustrated as image 24 of chapter 4 of this text.

The back support is surmounted by a mahogany rail with circular ends. This style of back support suggests the sofa was created toward the end of the Empire period. The oval-shaped arm supports relate somewhat to those of box sofas, but are larger. These are carved with an eagle and foliage design. Ogee moldings decorate the seat and side rails. The front foot is a lion paw gripping a large ball with foliage above. The back feet are uncarved patterns of the front, which is typical of Philadelphia cabinetwork.

Figure 239
Eagle Sofa, Mahogany

Philadelphia, Circa 1825-1840

Height 39",
Width 92 1/2",
Depth 29 1/4"

Photographs Courtesy of Smithsonian Institution National Portrait Gallery

Figure 239a
close up of the box end illustrating the eagle and leafage carving and unusual ball and claw foot.

Sofas and Couches Outside Philadelphia

Figure 240

Pompeii Red Painted Sofa

Baltimore, Circa 1815-1825

Overall Height 37",
Seat Height 17 1/2",
Width 97",
Depth 24 3/4"

Private collection

A complex shape of the crest relates to a "cupids bow" design found on a Baltimore painted sofa now located at the Maryland historical society.[15] The bottom rail curves up into scroll supports, all of which are decorated with a variety of fruits that end in a floral motif at the scroll tips. Both the saber feet and crest rail are painted Pompeii red with gilt floral, scroll and anthemion decoration. Baltimore sofas of this type are extremely rare, especially in Pompeii red. The contrast of the black rail and scrolls with the red crest rail and feet has a dramatic effect.

[15] Weidman 168

This couch exhibits reeding and circular disks to adorn the classic Greek form. The reeding, especially of the feet, appears similar to a sofa at the Wye house, which is attributed to Edward Priestley of Baltimore (active 1801-1837) (See *Chipstone American Furniture*, 2002, page 34, figure 56 by Alexandra Kirtley)

Figure 241
Grecian Couch

Possible Attribution to Edward Priestley
Baltimore, Circa 1815-1830

Overall Height 32",
Width 89",
Depth 26"

Collection of the
Andalusia Foundation

CHAPTER 12
SIDEBOARDS

SIDEBOARDS

During the Empire period, sideboards were one of the most expensive and impressive pieces of furniture one could own. Sideboards were designed for the dining room and replaced side tables that were often used when entertaining guests. The sideboard provided plenty of storage space for dishware, wine bottles and glasses, and was a much more convenient way of organizing all the necessary items needed for fancy dining at home. As the early nineteenth century progressed, sideboards

became larger in size and the space below the top that was previously empty became cupboards. Heavy columns, plain or carved with leaves, and either lion's paw or round and tapering feet characterize sideboards of the Empire period. Brass ornaments were used by some makers such as Joseph Barry, but usually only for the handles of the drawers and the feet. More elaborate brass inlaid Philadelphia sideboards do exist. These sideboards incorporate extensive inlay and boulle work, such as the Gratz sideboard illustrated in figure 246. Barry is the only known craftsman to advertise in Philadelphia that he made "boulle work" or brass inlay.[1]

Philadelphia sideboards are distinguished by a marble-topped dropped center section surmounted by a mirror which is flanked by carved or plain back elements; New York or Boston pieces were often made with a broad, flat top.[2] The backs of the sideboards are often intricately carved with classical detail of foliate ornament and cornucopias spilling with fruits. Cornucopias made a perfect design for the sideboard since they represent prosperity and abundance, both of which are appropriate to a dining room.[3] Philadelphia sideboards usually rest on short turned legs (sometimes which rest on brass casters) or carved lion's paw feet. Matching knife boxes and/or a cellarette

resting atop the sideboard increases its dynamic effect in a room.

In the Philadelphia price list of 1828, sideboards were advertised as being available in the following forms: "Plain Sideboard with cases and marble top, Pedestal End Sideboard with open center and four solid columns, Egyptian Sideboard, Pedestal End Sideboards with a sunk center and glass mirror in back, and the Round Pedestal Sideboard with one solid swept door."[4] The four classical columns that projected from a finely veneered facade were sometimes relieved by stenciling or brass fittings.[5] The columns of the Egyptian sideboards were sometimes made of figures, such as the one illustrated in figure 264.

The 1830s saw the gradual onset of the new Restoration fashion which reduced classical elements such as columns and feet to flat linear forms known as pillar and scroll, which were devoid of carving. This transformation simplified classical carved decorative elements into a series of flowing highly veneered flat surfaces, which utilized the beauty of the veneers rather than carving for effect. This modification of classical decorative forms, while progressive and novel, nevertheless reduced the visual impact. The new pillar and scroll sideboards and other furniture forms lacked the ornamentation that had characterized the best classical furniture; i.e. carving, stenciling, brass ornamentation, etc.

[1] Fairbanks and Bates 268

[2] Fitzgerald 124

[3] Fitzgerald 124

[4] Celia Jackson Otto 70

[5] Fitzgerald 124

The general form including the slashed bud insets above the columns and the brass lion feet closely relate to the Joseph Barry sideboard illustrated in figure 243. The cupboard doors exhibit Gothic arch panels favored by Joseph Barry. The columns end in limp lion paw feet which have also been seen with other Barry-attributed pieces. This type of brass lion paw foot was probably imported and examples can be found on New York and New England furniture as well.

Figure 242
Sideboard in the Neoclassical Taste, mahogany with gilt brass lion-head pulls and lion's paw feet
Attributed to Joseph Barry (1760-1838)
Philadelphia, Circa 1813-1818

Height 51 1/4",
Width 95 3/4"

Purchased with funds from the Marriner S. Eccles Foundation for the Marriner S. Eccles Masterwork Collection

Utah Museum of Fine Arts, University of Utah, Salt Lake City Utah

Museum #1993.026.001

Figure 243
Sideboard, mahogany, brass mounts
Signature of Joseph Barry
Philadelphia, 1813

Secondary woods:
poplar and white pine

Height 52",
Width 82 1/4",
Depth 25"

Private Collection

Barry signed his name and the date "1813" in pencil on the underside of the bottle carousel located in the right pedestal. A full discussion of this sideboard and its maker is in Donald L. Fennimore and Robert T. Trump, "Joseph B. Barry, Philadelphia cabinet-maker," *Antiques Magazine*, May 1989, pages 1212-1225. This sideboard employs Gothic arches, beehive feet, slash-bud carving, and cupboard columns with limp lion claw feet, all of which were used by Barry as well as other Philadelphia cabinetmakers.

"The rectangular broken front surmounted by an arched splashboard above a conforming case fitted with one long drawer above a pair of paneled cupboard doors flanked by upswept square plinth above a short drawer flanked by lotus-carved reserves above a paneled long door flanked by reeded and tapering Corinthian columns with vase shaped foliate carved legs, on hairy-paw feet. A closely related sideboard which is signed J.B. Barry and dated 1813 is illustrated in *The Magazine Antiques* (May 1989), volume CXXXV, no. 5, page 1214."

Figure 244
Classical Carved Mahogany Sideboard
Attributed to Joseph Barry (1810-1822)
Philadelphia, Circa 1810-1815

Height 55 1/2",
Width 76 3/4",
Depth 24 1/2"

Photo and Description Courtesy of
Christie's Auction Gallery,
New York City
© Christie's Images Limited 2006

Authors note: This style of
sideboard may also have been
made in Baltimore.

Figure 245
Sideboard, mahogany, ebony, brass
School of Joseph B. Barry
Philadelphia, Circa 1808-1815

Height 50 9/10",
Width 87 3/5",
Depth 25 3/4"

Tradition of ownership by Rachel Gratz (1783-1823) who married Solomon Moses or by her sister Rebecca Gratz (1781-1869), whose descendants owned it until 1973.

Courtesy,
Winterthur Museum

The large central space is open. There are two large cupboards on either side that have arched Gothic panels flanked by columns, which appear to be ebonized. The columns of the sideboard are reeded and tapered and at the top of each there is a capital with acanthus carving. Each column terminates in three-toed limp hairy lion's paws. Above the cupboards and central space there are five drawers with brass pulls, beside each there is

rectangular carved patera (these rectangular sections appear to be ebonized). On each side of the top there is a low sided, concave plinth, above which is a pediment over a sided plinth. Atop each plinth there is a matching knife case. A full discussion of this sideboard is in Donald L. Fennimore, *"Searching for Roots: The Genealogy of a Philadelphia Sideboard"* (Cleveland, Ohio: Western Reserve Antiques show Catalogue, 1990, 14-15).

This sideboard relates closely to the Joseph Barry attributed secretary desk, shown in figure 290, which also descended in the Gratz family. The sideboard and matching knife boxes boast buhl work on an ebonized background with extensive use of linear, geometric, and floral buhl work to decorate the predominately rectangular surfaces. The sides of the gallery are brass and the splashboard is elaborately carved with floral leafage and a lion-like figure. The brass columns are most unusual.

Figure 246
Sideboard and Knife Boxes; mahogany, brass inlay with polished lacquer
Philadelphia, Circa 1810-1820

Height 44 4/5",
Width 100 1/2"

Philadelphia Museum of Art: Bequest of Miss Elizabeth Gratz

Photo by Graydon Wood, 1995

Figure 247and 247a

Pedestal-End Sideboard, mahogany veneers

Attributed to the shop of Anthony Quervelle
Philadelphia, Circa 1826-1830

Secondary woods: poplar and pine

Height 58",
Width 73",
Depth 24"

Private Collection

Photo and Description Courtesy of Didier, Inc., New Orleans

Figure 247a

detail of the cornucopia carving

"The original looking glass is surrounded by veneered panels and columns on either side with an ionic capital carved with acanthus and curled acanthus, flanked on either side by brackets carved in a graceful composition of cornucopia, fruit and leaf. It rests on pedestal ends with extending canvas covered slides over convex drawers retaining period glass floral pulls. A recessed white marble top rests on a middle convex drawer with glass floral pulls gadrooned on the bottom over carved brackets in an elongated feather and scroll which connects a carved feather, rosette, scroll and bud in leaf. Recessed panel doors on each end have a convex, figured mahogany veneered triangular motif carved on top and bottom with a pineapple flanked by columns having an ionic carved capital on a turned base resting on a projecting platform over paw feet carved with acanthus and sawtooth. The back legs are turned. The "VALENTINE" family provenance on backboard of beveled mirror."

"Having a stepped rectangular top with a central gray and white marble surface, backed by an architectural mirrored panel with Doric columns flanked by scrolling acanthus-carved corbels, the case having a central section with a pull-out green baize slide over a slightly bowed frieze drawer with faceted glass pulls and two inset-panel doors with gadroon drawer divides enclosing shelf, flanked by two pedestals, each having a convex drawer flanked by anthemion plinths over a recessed ebonized wood line-inlaid inset-panel door with Doric column stiles enclosing one shelf, one with a bottle lazy-susan, over a protruding shaped base and raised on four acanthus-capped animal paw feet."

Figure 248 and 248a
Mahogany Sideboard
126 Dressing Glass Label of
Anthony G. Quervelle
Philadelphia, Circa 1825

Height 59 1/4",
Width 71 1/2",
Depth 26"

Photo and Description Courtesy of
Weschler's Auction Gallery,
Washinton D.C.

Figure 248a
*126 Dressing Glass Label of
Anthony Quervelle*

Center drawer with paper label printed:

*Anthony G. Quervelle's
Cabinet and Sofa Manufactory
South Second Str***
Below Dock, Philadelphia*

Figure 249 and 249a
Mahogany Sideboard
Attributed to Anthony G. Quervelle
Philadelphia, Circa 1825

Height 43 1/2",
Width 72 3/4"',
Depth 23 1/2"

Private Collection

Both outer cupboard doors are curved in a vertical cylindrical manner. The inner cupboard doors are decorated with a diamond motif that is closely associated with Quervelle's work. Above and below the inside cupboard doors is gadrooning which is finished in the center with a "micro-carved" sunburst (see makers chapter 4 image 32 Anthony Quervelle, regarding micro-carving). The columns have Corinthian capitals. Both carved back splats are cornucopias. The mirror is supported by columns with Corinthian capitals. Acanthus carving decorates the crest of the lion claw feet with detailed hair carving on the sides. The back turned feet, as illustrated, appear identical to the Quervelle attributed sideboard in figure 251b. However, it should be noted that the turnings of a foot alone can not be used as the sole basis for making attributions, as some joiners may have specialized in supplying turned or carved feet, as well as other items, to shops for assembly. The carved cornucopia back splats, columns flanking the mirror and other features are very similar to the labeled Quervelle sideboard in figure 248.

Figure 249a
Back foot
Bulbous rear foot turnings that are identical to figure 251b

The center section is sunken with a white marble top, the back of the center section is a rectangular mirror outlined with veneered mahogany. On either side of the mirror, there is carved cornucopia overflowing with fruits, leaves, clusters of grapes and scrolls. Beside the cornucopia is a volute from which emerges a drooping flower. Below the marble top there are drawers flanked by columns with carved capitals accented with black shellac. The two large cupboard doors have vertical cylinder fronts. Two smaller drawers above the cupboard doors and the long drawer below the marble top section have swelled fronts and molded glass knobs. The front feet are lion's paws with acanthus leaves above, while the back are ball and inverted vase turned feet. Attribution is based on a signed example in a private collection.

Figure 250
Sideboard, mahogany, glass, marble
Possibly shop of Anthony Quervelle
Philadelphia, Circa 1837-1844

Height 55 3/5",
Width 67 1/2",
Depth 23 1/10"

Courtesy, Winterthur Museum

Museum Purchase

Figure 251, 251a, and 251b

Sideboard, mahogany

Strong Attribution to Anthony G. Quervelle Philadelphia, Circa 1820-1830

Height 59",
Width 72",
Depth 24 1/2"

Private Collection

This sideboard is what was called in the Philadelphia Price List of 1828, "Pedestal End Sideboard with a sunk center and glass mirror in back." The back has carved cornucopias on either side, met in the center by a mirror with carved scroll supports. The top drawers and center cupboard have glass knobs. Below the long center drawers is a line of gadrooning. The four columns have Corinthian capitals. On the center door of the cupboard is a convex fan design that is often seen in pieces by Anthony Quervelle.

This piece is attributed to Quervelle based on the high quality carving of the back and the feet, and the combination of stylistic elements including the fan, gadrooning, columns and proportions of the piece. The overall form appears to be closely related to the Quervelle attributed sideboard at Winterthur illustrated as plate I in Robert Smith's article Part IV, with identical carving on the sides of the mirror. This carving includes a droopy flower emerging from a volute

(which is present on the bases of the three Quervelle pedestal tables in the White House), as well as identical cornucopias. This piece has additional decorative elements not found on the Winterthur sideboard. These include a fan motif in the lift up central door, a circular curve to the mirror and supports that are intricately decorated with delicate acanthus leaf carving. Of special interest is a small shell motif carved at the point of origin of the sunburst, which is also seen on a worktable attributed to Quervelle, illustrated in figure 134a and image 30, and a Quervelle-attributed wine cellarette, illustrated in figure 360 (see makers chapter 4, Anthony Quervelle, regarding micro-carving). The design balancing horizontal and vertical cylindrical surfaces is one of the achievements that elevate Philadelphia furniture of this period from that of its contemporaries in New York or Boston. This sideboard exemplifies a masterpiece by design and execution.

Figure 251a

Detail of carved scroll support, decorative cornucopia carving and droopy flower emerging from a volute.

Figure 251b

Detail of the turned rear foot, the back foot appears identical to figure 249a.

Figure 252
Sideboard, mahogany, gilt stencil
Philadelphia, Circa 1825

Height 67",
Width 69",
Depth 22 1/2"

Photo and Description Courtesy
of Aileen Minor

"Classically carved and gilt stencil decorated sideboard, with raised centered mirror with original mirror plate, stepped cornice and flanking columns, over centered King of Prussia marble serving slab, with four silver drawers over four cupboard doors with carved fluted fans in each corner, divided by full columns with carved capital with carved acorns, resting on turned feet with egg and dart carving, on casters. (Original gilt stylized classical stencil decoration)."

The mirror is decorated with stenciling and columns. Both cornucopia back splats are painted and gilded. All columns have Corinthian capitals. Above the columns there is leafage carving. This sideboard is unusual in that all three tops surfaces are marble rather than the usual marble drop center section. The small size is also unusual.

Figure 253
Sideboard, mahogany
Philadelphia, Circa 1825

Height 58",
Width 54",
Depth 21 1/2"

Private Collection

Figure 254

Gilt-Stenciled Inlaid and Carved Mahogany Marble-Top Sideboard

Attributed to Anthony G. Quervelle
Philadelphia, Circa 1830-1840

Height 69 1/2",
Width 81 3/4",
Depth 23 1/4"

Photo and Description Courtesy of
Christie's Auction Gallery,
New York City
© Christie's Images Limited 2006

"The rectangular green marble top above a bolection-molded drawer and gadrooned edge over an arched stencil-decorated apron over a recessed interior with mirrored back and medial shelf, all surmounted by a rectangular mirror enclosed in a gilt-stenciled surround, the whole flanked by a rectangular pedestal each centering a bolection-molded short drawer above a recessed gilt-stenciled cupboard door, each flanked by bird's eye maple colonettes, on animal paw feet. The boldly carved lion's paw feet with gadrooned knees and ring-turned back legs on this example are similar to two pier tables illustrated in Robert C. Smith, "The Furniture of Anthony G. Quervelle," *The Magazine Antiques* (May, volume CIII, no.5, 1973), page 989, plate II and page 991, figure 10."

The design of this sideboard closely follows sketch 13 in the Anthony Quervelle Sketchbook, illustrated in chapter five. A complex carved pattern consisting of a fruit basket with radiating scrolled leafage adorns the backsplash. Both large cylinder ends of the case contain cupboards. Between these rests a large slightly dropped center section, decorated with a star and surmounted with drawers above. The sideboard rests on unusual lion paw feet that are decorated above with double cornucopia. This sideboard is among the original furnishings ordered by President Andrew Jackson for his home, the Hermitage.

Figure 255
Basile End Sideboard, Mahogany
Attributed to Anthony Quervelle
Philadelphia, Circa 1825-1835

Secondary woods: white pine, mahogany, and poplar.

Height at Center 44 1/2", Width 97"

Photograph Courtesy of The Hermitage, Nashville, TN

Figure 256 and 256a

Sideboard, mahogany
Attributed to Charles White
Philadelphia, March 1827

Height 55 1/4",
Width 65 1/2",
Depth 22"

Private Collection

The backsplash has an array of floral embellishment with a basket of fruits in the center. An arrangement on either side includes an anthemion design combined with gentle scrolls. All three top drawers have wooden knobs. The doors of the cupboards have arched panels with carving at the top of each. Each column is intricately carved with an acanthus design. The feet are carved lion's paw combined with an overhanging leaf motif, which is frequently seen on Philadelphia as well as other American pieces. This sideboard is believed to be part of a large set of furniture made for the Newbold family by Charles White (see figure 36a of this text). The set of furniture, documented in a letter by White, was sent as a wedding gift to the family by steamboat and has remained in the same family for years.

Figure 256a
Detail of cornucopia-carved backsplash

Use of a straight top with end brackets was more common on Baltimore or New York sideboards than Philadelphia. A straight-fronted sideboard design with full carved backsplash was available from Philadelphia cabinetmakers, but was less popular with local patrons than the drop-center sideboard (a similar straight-front sideboard design by Cook and Parkin is illustrated as image 21 in chapter three

of this volume). The upper half of the backsplash is carved with multiple motifs including a shell, cornucopias and floral buds and is closely related to the carving of a headboard of the bedstead in figure 331. An invoice identified this sideboard as being made by Isaac Jones. The brasses are replacements and should originally have been glass knobs.

Figure 257 and 257a
Sideboard, mahogany, tulip poplar, pine and chestnut
Made by Isaac Jones
Philadelphia, Circa 1831

Height 56 3/8",
Width 66 5/8",
Depth 24 5/8"

Courtesy, The Winterthur Library: Decorative Arts Photographic Collection

Figure 257a
Detail of the backsplash with a central shell motif with flanking cornucopia and circular floral-decorated disks. Compare to the headboard of Mahogany Bed (figure 331a).

Figure 258
Straight Front Sideboard,
mahogany
Stenciled label of Michel Bouvier
Philadelphia, Circa 1825

Dimensions unrecorded

Photograph courtesy of Pook and
Pook Auctions, Downingtown, PA

The straight flat top surface has, at present, no backsplash. Each column is decorated with spiral foliage. A middle cupboard area has a slight concave curve. The front lion claw feet are unusually elongated with short leafage above. One of the few labeled Bouvier pieces known.

Figure 258a
Stencil of Michel Bouvier

This sideboard is decorated with a geometric design that incorporates ovals on the panels of the cupboard doors. The corner columns have Corinthian capitals, above which is a line of horizontal gadrooning. Stenciling is utilized to outline the various geometric shapes. The backsplash is decorated with finials and a central pediment with a diamond design. There are lion's paw feet in the front.

Figure 259
Sideboard, mahogany, mahogany veneer
Philadelphia, Circa 1825-1830

Secondary wood: white pine

Height 45",
Width 56",
Depth 22"

Collection of
Mr. F.J. Carey III

Figure 260

Sideboard, mahogany with mahogany veneer, poplar, and eastern white pine
Philadelphia or Baltimore,
Circa 1825-1835

Height 49",
Width 73 3/8",
Depth 23 3/4"

The Art Institute of Chicago

Mrs. Alfred S. Burdick, Alfred T. Carton, Hibbard Family heirs, Mrs. Paul B. Magnuson, and Decorative Arts Purchase Fund, 1974.8

This sideboard has been illustrated in Donald L. Fennimore's, "Egyptian influence in early nineteenth-century American furniture," *The Magazine Antiques* (May 1990) page 1200, figure 12. Fennimore notes, "The sideboard has paired pylons under deep overhanging cove moldings— a concept identical to the formal pylon entrances to Egyptian temples..." The increasing popularity of Egyptian motifs resulted from what George Smith, in 1808, called "a more close investigation and imitation of the beautiful remains of

ancient sculpture and painting, which have been studied by enlightened travelers, and also been laid before the public in various books of great cost and elegance."[6] Among those books was Benoit de Maillet's *Descriptions de l'Egypte* (Paris, 1735), Piranesi's *Diverse maniere* and Frederik Ludvig Norden's *Travels in Egypt and Nubia* (published in English language edition in London, 1757).[7]

6 Fennimore, Egyptian influence 1196

7 Fennimore 1196

This sideboard is similar in design to the sideboard currently on exhibit at the Art Institute of Chicago, illustrated in figure 260. Its features differ in that there is a recessed marble inset above the center drawer, two smaller drawers on both sides and lack of gadrooning at the base. The feet of the two sideboards are also different; in the present sideboard the feet are in a vase form with carved leaves at the top. The feet of the sideboard at the Art Institute of Chicago sideboard are similar, but below the leaves there is turned reeding. This sideboard was made in the Egyptian style, with paired pylons under overhanging cove moldings. The recessed marble inset was a popular decorative feature on Philadelphia sideboards, but this sideboard may have been made in Baltimore.

Figure 261
Sideboard, mahogany, glass and marble
Philadelphia or Baltimore,
Circa 1825-1835

Secondary woods:
poplar and white pine

Height 43 15/16",
Width 75 7/8",
Depth 26 5/8"

The Saint Louis Art Museum.
Decorative Arts Society Funds and
Eliza McMillan Fund

Figure 262
Sideboard, rosewood with marble top
Philadelphia, Circa 1830-1840

Secondary woods: pine, poplar, and cherry

Height 41", Width 60"

Philadelphia Museum of Art: Gift of Mr. and Mrs. C. Jared Ingersoll, 1976

This sideboard appears to have been made in the latter part of the Philadelphia classical period, with the two corners supported by scrolls, each of which is supported by a rectangular and trapezoidal foot. The gilt floral and foliage decorations are stenciled and the carving is minimal. Large mirrors decorate the cupboard doors and add depth. The overall form, especially the use of mirrors and the lower shelf, suggests the possible alternative function of this piece as a pier table.

Large uncarved scrolls and hidden drawer handles with no hardware are hallmarks of the "Pillar and Scroll" Restoration style, which marked the end of Philadelphia Empire as the 1830s progressed. Hidden handgrips below the drawer bottoms function as handles. A lack of carving or hardware is in keeping with the new Restoration fashion. The Rosedown invoice from Quervelle documents that this was one of the most costly pieces ordered for the Louisiana plantation. Sideboards were one of the most expensive items for household furnishing at this time.

Figure 263 and 263a
Sideboard, mahogany
Made by Anthony G. Quervelle
Philadelphia, August 1835

Height 43",
Width 60",
Depth 24"

Photos Courtesy of Rosedown Plantation State Historic Site, Louisiana Office of State Parks

Figure 263a
Rosedown invoice signed by Anthony Quervelle in August, 1835

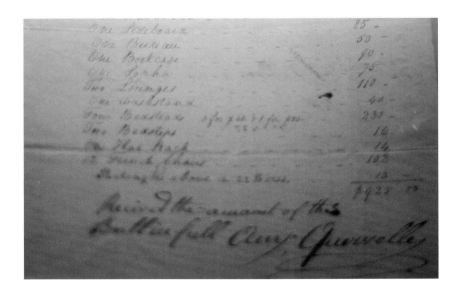

Figure 264
*Sideboard; mahogany,
Egyptian marble top*
Made by Joseph B. Barry
and Lewis Krickbaum
Philadelphia, Circa 1835-1837

Secondary woods:
white pine and poplar

Height 42",
Width 72",
Depth 24" (with marble),

Height 39 1/2",
Width 72",
Depth 21" (without marble)

Philadelphia Museum of Art: Gift of
Mr. & Mrs. Charles J. McManus, Jr.

Photo by Graydon Wood

This sideboard employs a bottom apron of egg-and-dart molding above which each side has a mahogany veneered shelf, which supports two female caryatids. Above the caryatids there is a wide ogee molded apron and a marble slab.

Sideboards Outside of Philadelphia

A provenance identifies the maker of this sideboard as Andrew Snowberger, one of the founders of the Snowhill Cloister, located near Greencastle, Pennsylvania, The cloister was a branch of the Ephrata Cloister, a celibate order which assisted General Washington in the treatment of Americans wounded after the Battle of Brandywine in 1777. This piece is identified as being a gift from Andrew Snowberger to the dining area of the Snowhill Cloister nunnery where Snowberger's two daughters served as members. The design of this piece has a dropped central section with a fan veneered central cupboard below. The front columns are slightly larger than is common and they have well carved capitals. Above each column is a panel decorated with a Gothic cross design. A sunburst fan on the center cupboard

magnifies the impressive radiance of the wood. All feet are carved and appear to be lion's paws, but could just as well be eagle's talons. This sideboard combines sophisticated Philadelphia design elements, including a central sunburst fan, full columns, and Gothic inset crosses, to create a spectacular architectural and visual effect. The time, effort and expense in constructing such a piece, especially the making and the coordination of the tiger maple veneers, probably accounts for the rarity of this form in tiger maple. The sideboard also exhibits unusual rectangular glass knobs backed in ebony. The mirror also has an ebony outline. A masterpiece in design and execution made more important by its maker Andrew Snowberger and its association with the Snowhill Cloister.

Figure 265
Sideboard, bird's eye maple and bird's eye maple veneer
Andrew Snowberger
Snowhill Cloister,
Greencastle, Pennsylvania
Circa 1820-1825

Secondary woods: drawer sides and back are cherry, bottom and glue blocks are poplar. Rectangular glass knobs set on ebonized wood blocks, and the toes of the eagle feet and mirror border are also ebonized.

Height 49",
Width 86 1/4",
Depth 25 1/8"

Private Collection

Figure 266
Sideboard, mahogany
School of William Camp or Joseph Barry
Baltimore or Philadelphia,
Circa 1810-1820

Secondary woods: drawer sides are
mahogany, bottom and back are
poplar, front is mahogany. Interior is
white pine and poplar.

Height 46",
Width 73",
Depth 25"

Private Collection

The top is decorated with a mahogany backsplash with scrolled end brackets. A backsplash ending in scrolls is more frequently seen with Baltimore sideboards, but was also used by other American cabinetmakers. On the doors of the cupboards are arched Gothic panels which are repeated above the columns, a design feature often used by Joseph Barry or William Camp. All four reeded Corinthian columns are met by acanthus carving at the tops. The feet are turned and reeded in a "beehive" manner, often associated with Joseph Barry of Philadelphia or William Camp of Baltimore. A gallery ending in scrolls is seen more frequently with Baltimore sideboards, but was also used by other American makers.

Figural heads of the front columns of this sideboard closely match those of a "frame for marble slab" made by Priestley for Edward Lloyd Jr. at Wye Heights.[8] Male caryatids "atlantes" were derived from Atlas, who held the world on his shoulders.[9] The effect of human figure columns is dramatic, giving great vertical lift to this form. The drawers and other rectangular surfaces are outlined in brass and ebony inlay.

8 Alexandra A. Kirtley, "Survival of the Fittest: The Lloyd Family's Furniture Legacy," *American Furniture 2002* (Milwaukee, WI: Chipstone Foundation, 2002) figure 65, page 38.

9 Morley 41

Figure 267 and 267a
Sideboard with Carved Figure Heads, Mahogany with ebony and brass inlay
Attributed to Edward Priestly, Baltimore, Circa 1825-1835

Height 40",
Width 82 1/2",
Depth 24"

Collection of the
Andalusia Foundation

Figure 267a
Detail of Figural Column illustrating "atlantes"

Figure 268
Sideboard, mahogany
Stencil of Journeyman Cabinet Makers
Baltimore, Circa 1835-1840

Height 49",
Width 73",
Depth 22"

Photo & Description (in quotes)
Courtesy of Flomaton Antique
Auction, Flomaton, Alabama

Solid and mottled mahogany sideboard with deep ogee skirt with three drawers over triple serpentine front with Gothic arched inlaid panel doors, ebonized diamond escutcheons. The four scrolled columns and flaring scrolled feet are indicative of the "Pillar and Scroll" style. There is a 6" panel inlaid back with brass gallery. Stenciled in drawer: "Journeyman Cabinet Makers, Baltimore." Please note that exposed hardware is avoided to prevent disruption of the flowing appearance of the matched veneers (see figure 263). This sideboard illustrates the movement of classicism into flat, linear curving surfaces that decorate through the use of contrasting veneers rather than carving or ornamentation. This is a hallmark of the Restoration movement that ended the neoclassical period in America.

Three drawers at the top, and square doors that open outward at the bottom make this sideboard an interesting variation. The top drawers have circular brass hardware decorated with stars. The large sunburst and spiral reeded columns make this a fancier and more expensive piece. The feet are bulbs that rest on small brass casters. The overall form, especially the hardware, is suggestive of the work of John Meads and William Alvord. The back feet are rectangular uncarved forms, typical of New York.

Figure 269
Sideboard, Mahogany
Attribution to Meads and Alvord
Albany, New York,
Circa 1820-1830

Secondary woods: drawer sides and bottom are poplar, front is white pine, interior frame is white pine.

Height 46 3/4",
Width 50 1/2",
Depth 22 1/2"

Private Collection

CHAPTER 13

DESKS, SECRETARY BOOKCASES (DESK AND BOOKCASE), FALL FRONT DESKS (SECRETAIRES A ABATTANT) AND CYLINDER DESKS

DESKS, SECRETARY BOOKCASES (DESK AND BOOKCASE), FALL FRONT DESKS (SECRETAIRES A ABATTANT), AND CYLINDER DESKS

In the early nineteenth century, the lower portion of the secretary bookcase was used as a desk for writing and the upper portion for organizing books by the man of the household; it was as unique a piece to him as the worktable was for a woman. Ladies' secretaries developed in the eighteenth century. They were smaller in size, but often made with equally excellent craftsmanship. There are three types of secretaries made in Philadelphia during the Empire period, the first listed in the

Philadelphia Book of Prices of 1828 as a "French Secretary." It was also known as the fall-front secretary, or secretaire a abattant. Developed in France during the second half of the eighteenth century, this was widely popular in France and in German speaking countries. The simplest type had veneered columns extending the height of the secretary with a pair of "flat panel doors" beneath the fall front writing area, and four "turned stump feet."[1] Michel Bouvier may have designed secretaries of this form. Designs for the fall-front secretary were believed to have come to Philadelphia by German and French craftsmen, since the English did not favor this type of desk.

The second type of desk popular in the Empire period was the desk-and-bookcase or "cabinet book case and secretary." It differed in that it had veneered columns or pilasters in the lower and upper sections. George Smith designed one that Quervelle adopted. Both the fall-front and desk-and-bookcase secretaries were made of mahogany and

mahogany veneer, with a fall front writing compartment with inside drawers often made with bird's eye maple curly maple, or other woods to achieve a surprisingly attractive effect. The outside of the piece is restrained in form, but when opened the refinement of the Philadelphia workmanship is revealed. The importance of the restrained form may have been derived from French sources that emphasized the unity of design and classical proportions between the elements (the columns, capitals, bases and arches).[2]

The Philadelphia desk (secretary) and bookcase consisted of a lower part for a man to use for writing and the upper part contained shelves for books and was referred to as the "head work" in the Philadelphia Book of Prices of 1828.[3] Different arrangements of drawers in the head work existed, but usually an open space existed in the middle as a compartment to file away letters and important documents. The amount of exterior decoration and the interior arrangement of the head work depended on how much

[1] Robert C. Smith, "The Furniture of Anthony G. Quervelle, Part IV: Some case pieces." *The Magazine Antiques* (January 1974, Volume 105) 180.

[2] Charles L. Venable, American Furniture in the Bybee Collection, (Auston: U of T Press, 1989) 100.

[3] Smith 181

the patron was willing to spend. For example, for an additional labor charge of fifteen cents the center space could be ornamented with a "plain veneered arch".[4]

All secretaries incorporated geometric designs that employed rectangular shapes, which frequently had Roman columns rising from the base. The drawers and Doric columns on secretaries divide the piece into a distinct architectural design. Secretary drawers were neatly compacted inside and would lend to the impressive feel of the piece when opened. The upper bookcase portion of the desk was often enclosed with glass-paneled doors, which could remain plain or covered with fabric to hide the contents. Lion's paw feet were commonly used as the front feet, while the back feet were usually turned. Turned vase shaped front feet were also used in less expensive pieces. Many different styles were employed for Philadelphia secretaries including different types of lift-up lids and several types of arrangements for the inside drawers. Ornamentation included sunbursts, gilding, gadrooning, inset veneered woods (sometimes curly maple, burl ash or ebony), and painting.

The French are believed to have been the original designers of the secretary and many Philadelphia makers seemed to have taken their designs from French architects. Thomas Sheraton borrowed the French designs as well, and published them in, "The Cabinetmaker and Upholsterer's Drawing Book," in 1802, including specific instructions on how to execute the piece geometrically. He also provided different designs for ornamentation and form. George Smith included secretary designs in his "Collection of Designs for Household Furniture and Interior Decoration," published in 1808 and 1826. Although English furniture makers included designs for the secretaries, it is believed that secretaries made in Philadelphia follow French design sources more keenly because they were a more popular form in France than in England. This is especially true of the secretaries a abattant.

[4] Smith 181

Figure 270

Secretary Desk, mahogany veneer, stainwood inlay

Philadelphia, Circa 1795-1805

Secondary wood: white pine, yellow pine, poplar and cedar

Height 106 1/2", Width 85 1/2"

The Metropolitan Museum of Art, Purchase, Joseph Pulitzer Bequest, 1967. (67.203a-h)

A triangular, rounded pediment is decorated with sea shell inlay. The apron of the pediment is decorated with swag floral inlay, set on satinwood. All cabinet drawers and doors are decorated with circular floral motifs in the corners and have large oval mahogany panels. This form shows several elements of early classicism, including the use of flat surfaces to mimic the influence of antique stone artifacts.[5] The use of garlands is derived from classical Greek and Roman life, where they were used to decorate ancient houses and palaces; they were worn decoratively and were required by the etiquette attached to dining.[6] The sea shells are also classically derived. This form traditionally would be consistent with Hepplewhite's designs, but really represents the early penetration of classical form into Philadelphia decorative arts.

[5] Morley 219

[6] Morley 40

Although clearly not in the Empire style of the period, this bookcase features ovals on the panel doors, which are veneered in mahogany surrounded by satinwood. The use of different woods for veneering was important to many makers of the period and was especially evident in the interiors of secretaries. This piece is illustrated to show how geometric designs were applied to bookcases derived from classical sources. It has been documented that German and French cabinetmakers who immigrated to Philadelphia during the period contributed to this type of design which rejects earlier rococo styles in favor of flat, geometric forms derived from ancient Greek and Roman sources. The form of this "Hepplewhite" secretary is thus derived from antique monumental architecture and represents an early expression of Philadelphia classicism.

Figure 272 and 272a

Cylinder Desk, mahogany

School of Joseph Barry
Philadelphia, Circa 1800-1815

Secondary woods:
white pine and cedar

Height 56 1/2",
Width 44",
Depth 23"

Collection of
Mr. F.J. Carey III

Figure 272a

*Cylinder desk open to
illustrate writing surface*

The cylindrical cover of the writing surface and large rectangular drawers above appear similar to French and German designs. There is a unique spatial arrangement within. The cylindrical cover of the writing surface opens by sliding up inside the piece from which a writing surface folds out. Inside are nine small drawers in the upper portion that are veneered with bird's eye maple. Above the drawers are spaces designed to store letters. Below there are six drawers with brass handles and a central divided storage space. Turned and reeded bee-hive feet support the case. The fronts of the lower cabinet drawers are veneered with a large Gothic arch in a manner made popular in Philadelphia by Joseph Barry. Similar style desks were also produced in Baltimore.

Figure 273

*Desk, possibly lower section of
secretary bookcase, mahogany
with mahogany, burl, maple,
and rosewood veneers*

Stencil of Charles H. White and
John F. White
Philadelphia, Circa 1828-1835

Secondary woods:
yellow poplar, white pine,
red cedar, maple

Height 47",
Width 55 1/8",
Depth 24 3/4"

The upper section consists of a fold down writing surface flanked by concave gothic arches that are very similar to the arches on the ends of the stenciled Charles and John White sofa illustrated in this text as figure 236. The lower doors are flanked by Corinthian columns, with the central area decorated with a sunburst. The interior of the desk illustrated as figure 273a features gothic arches that are similar to those seen on the labeled Quervelle secretary desk featured as figure 281 in this text. The double curved pigeon holed moldings appear to have been directly copied from Quervelle's sketch number 2, illustrated in chapter 5 of this text. It is clear from these observations that the Whites admired and used Quervelle design elements in their furniture. The feet are all replacements and the front feet have only three toes rather than the correct four seen on period lion paw feet. It appears probable that this desk is the lower fragment of a secretary bookcase which has lost its upper section. This is currently being investigated by the Philadelphia Museum of Art staff.

Figure 273a
Charles H. and John F. White stencil.

Figure 273b
Desk interior

Figure 274
Secretary,
mahogany
School of Joseph Barry
Philadelphia, Circa
1800-1820

Height 89",
Width 60",
Depth 22"

Secretary section a
period replacement.

Photo Courtesy
of Freeman's
Auction House

This secretary features a prominent use of multiple Gothic arches introduced by Barry, as noted in Barry's advertisement in the Philadelphia Aurora General Advertiser on January 19, 1810. The beehive feet are also closely associated with Barry. This form uses multiple flat surfaces derived from monumental architecture.

Figure 275
Breakfront Bookcase, mahogany

Label of Joseph B. Barry & Son
Philadelphia, Circa 1810-1818

Dimensions unrecorded

Private Collection

Photo Courtesy of
The Magazine Antiques

"This handsome Sheraton piece, owned by Robert Mackay of Savannah, is still in that city, in the possession of a direct descendant. Barry was in that city in 1798. *Charles F. Mills.*" The beehive feet are characteristic of Barry; the design of the arched glass panels of the bookshelf appears to have Gothic elements. Barry advertised on January 19, 1810 in the Philadelphia Aurora General Advertiser the new partnership with his son: "The business will in Future be conducted under the firm of JOSEPH B. BARRY & SON...They have now in their ware-rooms a variety of the newest and most fashionable Cabinet Furniture, finished in the rich Egyptian and Gothic style..."[7] The design of the muntins is in the new Gothic style, which Barry expounded.

[7] Robert T. Trump, "Joseph B. Barry, Philadelphia cabinetmaker," *The Magazine Antiques* Jan. 1975: 162.

This secretary bookcase has a gilt scroll stencil on the apron of the pediment. The upper columns have no capitals and the lower columns are carved with Corinthian capitals. Both bottom cabinet drawers are decorated with a large semi-circular book matched mahogany veneer. The bookcase has mirrors instead of panes of glass. This was not a very common practice on Empire bookcases because it was fashionable to have textiles placed behind glass doors. The feet are well carved lion's paw.

Figure 276
Secretary Bookcase, mahogany
Philadelphia, Circa 1825-1835

Height 80 1/2",
Width 40 1/2",
Depth 25"

Collection of
Mr. F.J. Carey III

Figure 277 *Secretary Bookcase, mahogany*
Philadelphia, Circa 1820-1830

Dimensions unrecorded

Private Collection

Corinthian capitals decorate the upper pilasters and lower columns. The lower columns support the fall-front writing area. Both cabinet doors and fall-front writing surface are paneled out in an ancient Etruscan manner. The muntins have probably been removed from the upper bookcase doors. Carved lion paws decorate the front feet, while the back feet are turned.

Figure 277a
The opened fall-front desk reveals curly maple drawers and dividers.

Lewis Redner signed his name in pencil on the underside of the cornice. Thomas Loud's stencil is located on the center of the board, just behind the writing surface. This case originally housed a giraffe piano with a wood frame. As was normal for wood framed upright pianos, the great string tension eventually warped and split the frame, which rendered the works unusable within about forty years. They were removed and the carcass converted to a desk and bookcase with a highly finished bird's eye maple interior.

Figure 278

Desk and Bookcase (Giraffe Piano), rosewood

Philadelphia, Circa 1828-1835
Made by Lewis Redner, Sold by Thomas Loud and Brothers

Secondary woods:
ebony, maple, tulip poplar, ash and white pine.

Height 75 1/4,
Width 51",
Depth 29 3/4"

Private Collection

Figure 279 and 279a

Desk and Bookcase, carved and veneered mahogany

Philadelphia, Circa 1820-1830

Secondary woods: interior wood of back upper section is poplar, interior of tiger maple drawers is Spanish cedar, framework of drawers' is poplar, lower cabinet interior case: back is poplar, bottom is pine, and side panels are mahogany. Frame is constructed with white pine.

Height 103",
Writing Height 33",
Width 48",
Depth 24"

Private Collection

The upper columns have Corinthian capitals and the lower columns are modified Ionic. A "paneled out" construction in the manner of ancient Etruscan decorated walls adorns the front surface of the fall front desk and cabinet doors.[8] The door muntins arch at the top with an angle that corresponds to that of the acanthus decorated corner acroterion. Between these, the triangular central pediment is veneered mahogany. The overall effect is directly derived from pediments frequently seen surmounting Greek temples and other monuments. All glass knobs are original.

[8] Morley 218

Figure 279a
Interior showing figured maple drawers.

Figure 280 and 280a

Secretary Bookcase, carved and veneered mahogany

Strong Attribution to Anthony Quervelle
Philadelphia, Circa 1825-1830

Secondary woods: frame is poplar and pine, rear feet are made of maple.

Height 102 1/4",
Width 49 1/4,
Depth 24"

Photo courtesy of Joseph Sorger

Although unlabeled, this piece almost certainly was made in Quervelle's shop. The upper portion appears elongated by using reverse tapering columns in the form of arrows with the quiver above and the arrowhead ending in gilded vases of poplar. This decoration replaces the columns and round plinths of the labeled Quervelle desk and bookcase (figure 282 in this text) that won a silver medal at the exhibition of the Franklin Institute in 1827 (featured in Robert C. Smith's article, "Part IV: Some case pieces," *The Magazine Antiques*, figure 4, page 183.)[9] The design of the muntins of the glass doors are in the form of an attenuated pointed arcade overlaid with elongated lozenges, which may have been derived from a pattern for bookcase doors by Thomas Sheraton.[10] Below the bookcase doors the convex drawers of the writing area create an impressive transition to the lower part of the form. The sunburst, placed between two Doric columns with brass capitals, has the outer edge veneered with lunette inserts of stained ash, above which are carved wreaths of oak leaves. Anthemion carvings flank the two corners above. The rails of the secretary bookcase are gadrooned. The front lion paw feet are surmounted with the same compact acanthus foliage as the attributed Quervelle French secretary in figure 286.

[9] Smith 190

[10] Smith 188

Figure 280a

Interior with curly maple drawers and Gothic arch letter partitions. The configuration of the interior is identical to figure 281, which is labeled by Quervelle.

Figure 281

Secretary Bookcase, mahogany

126 Dressing Glass Label of Anthony Quervelle (1789-1856)
Philadelphia, Circa 1825-1835

Secondary woods: eastern white pine, basswood, yellow poplar, bird's eye maple and glass, brass, gilded gesso.

Height 102 1/4",
Width 50 3/4",
Depth 23 5/8"

Collection of Munson-Williams-Proctor Arts Institute, Museum of Art, Utica, New York

Museum Purchase (60.257)

Photo by John Bigelow Taylor, N.Y.C

The cornice has vertically oriented foliage carving and is supported by two large tapering columns, just as the secretary illustrated in figure 280. Small lateral drawers below the book case section are curved inward. The fall-front section of the lower case opens to reveal a series of curly maple veneered small drawers, separated by Gothic arched spaces above the felt covered writing space. Below this, two large doors are decorated with a typical Quervelle sunburst with lunette stained burl ash at the end of each ray. This sunburst has a garland of carved foliage marking its edge and the typical Quervelle anthemion carvings in the upper two corners. The feet below have gadrooning to their crests, which is carried across the base as well. The effect is that of vertical lift and motion, adding a sense of energy to the form.

The lower case boasts a typical Quervelle sunburst with stained ash lunettes at the ends. This sunburst is surrounded by a garland of oak leaves and the upper corners above this are decorated with anthemion petals. A fall-front area and corners above are decorated with a typical Quervelle lozenge and raised ovals. The upper portion is flanked by Doric columns with brass capitals, below which there are carved fruit baskets. The muntins are in a crisscrossed pattern below, with Gothic arches above and an oval at the center. Vertically oriented leafage adorns the cornice. The lion paw front feet are surmounted by gadrooning, which also runs across the bottom rail. This secretary won the Silver Medal at the Franklin Institute exhibit for best cabinet bookcase and secretary in 1827.[11]

[11] *Philadelphia Three Centuries of American Art*, Philadelphia Museum of Art, 276.

Figure 282
Secretary Bookcase, mahogany and mahogany veneer

126 Dressing Glass Label of
Anthony G. Quervelle
Philadelphia, 1827

Height 109 1/2",
Width 66 1/2",
Depth 25 1/2"

Philadelphia Museum of Art: Given by Mr. and Mrs. Edward C. Page in memory of Robert E. Griffith, 1960

Photo by Graydon Wood, 1997

Figure 283

Secretary Bookcase, mahogany

Delmes Printed Quervelle Label
Philadelphia, August 1835

Height 90 1/2",
Width 41 1/2",
Depth 23"

Photo Courtesy of Rosedown
Plantation State Historic Site,
Louisiana Office of State Parks

A full Delmes Quervelle label is located in the interior writing area. The design is heavily influenced by the Pillar and Scroll movement towards flat, uncarved surfaces. The overall effect is a large flat surface that lacks much of the energy of the earlier Quervelle secretaries. Scroll columns with carved lion paw feet at the base represent the only carved surface of this secretary desk.

Figure 284

Secretary Bookcase; mahogany, rosewood veneer, silvered glass and gilt decoration

Made by Isaac Jones
Philadelphia, 1837

Secondary woods:
pine and poplar

Height 72",
Width 48"

Philadelphia Museum of Art: Gift of
Miss Pauline Townsend Pease, 1979

Photo by Graydon Wood, 2003

This piece combines carving, gilding, stenciling and contrasting rosewood veneer to produce a lively and monumental form. A dramatic egg-and-dart molding embellishes the cornice. All ionic columns have gilt capitals. The central eagle and corner resting lion pediments are unusual and give a dramatic effect to the form. This desk is the only labeled piece in a large suite of furniture made for Elijah Van Syckel in 1837 (see figures 318 and 330 for the wardrobe and bedstead from this suite).

Figure 285

Neo-Classical Secretary Bookcase, mahogany with bird's eye maple and rosewood interior Philadelphia, Circa 1825-1830

Secondary woods: maple, poplar, pine and mahogany, glass, ivory knobs, and baize and tooled leather writing surface.

Height 101 11/16",
Width 64 7/8" (overall),
Depth 25 1/4" (overall)

Photo & Description Courtesy
of Hirschl & Adler Galleries, New York

"Clearly within the Philadelphia and presumably Quervelle aesthetic, this piece shares not only the scale of a secretary bookcase made and labeled by Quervelle, about 1825-27 (see Robert C. Smith, "The furniture of Anthony G. Quervelle Part IV: Some case pieces," *The Magazine Antiques*, [January 1974] p. 183, fig. 4 and *Classical America* 1815-1845, exhib. Cat [The Newark Museum, New Jersey, 1963], pp. 62 no.56 illus., 79 fig. 56) and submitted by him to the exhibition at the Franklin Institute, Philadelphia, in 1827 (where it won a silver medal), but also such details as the lozenge-shape appliques to the two drawers that flank the central "drawer" that opens to form a writing compartment. The large scale of this piece stands as testimony to the huge townhouses that began to proliferate in major East Coast cities in the second quarter of the nineteenth century. The lock on the glass door to the right above bears a maker's mark as follows:

LEWIS.McKEE & CO. /
TERRYSVILLE, CONN.

Lewis McKee & Co., lock makers, were in business in Terrysville, Connecticut from 1833-41. Eli Terry, the well known clockmaker, was the original owner."

Figure 286 and 286a
"French Secretary," mahogany

Strong attribution to Anthony Quervelle
Philadelphia, Circa 1825-1830

Secondary woods: lower drawers: sides, front, and back are mahogany, bottom of drawers are red cedar, interior of drawers are poplar. Frame is white pine with poplar panels. Front and sides of upper drawers are mahogany, back of drawers are poplar, bottom of drawers are red cedar. Frame of upper drawer mahogany. Front columns are burl maple.

Height 69",
Height (writing surface) 28 1/2",
Width 42",
Depth 24"

Private Collection

This "French secretary" or secretaire a abattant is illustrated in Robert C. Smith's article, "The furniture of Anthony Quervelle; Part IV: Some case pieces," plate II (*The Magazine Antiques*, January 1974, pages 180-193). Although unlabeled, this piece is almost certainly the work of Quervelle's shop. Robert C. Smith identifies this secretary as extremely similar to a labeled Quervelle French secretary in a private collection in Philadelphia, which he was unable to picture. The piece contains many unusual and specific stylistic elements which appear unique to Quervelle's shop. The detail of the moldings above the interior drawer spaces are identical to those of a desk design of Anthony Quervelle (illustrated as sketch 2, Anthony Quervelle sketchbook, chapter 5 of this text).

(continued on next page)

Figure 286a
Secretary with fall front opened to reveal interior

This same interior space divider molding is noted on figure 8 in the same Smith article, which illustrates the interior of a secretary bookcase that closely relates to the labeled, prizewinning secretary bookcase of Quervelle's at the Philadelphia Museum of Art. The feet of the secretaire a abattant exhibit unusually compact acanthus foliage above the claw feet, which appear virtually identical to the foot arrangement of the Joseph Sorger secretary bookcase (figure 280) that shares many stylistic elements with both the labeled secretaries at the Philadelphia Museum of Art and those at the Munson-Williams-Proctor Institute of Quervelle's. Multiple other features of the piece can also be related to Quervelle's, including the use of veneered stained burl maple columns, the use of a semicircular panel in the upper rectangular element of the pediment of the secretary, and the use of gilt stenciling, which is often seen on Quervelle's pier and center tables.[12] The general construction of this piece is a rectangular box base with a sloping, cone shaped section above which is surmounted a smaller rectangular element containing a drawer. This represents a pattern which appears to be distinctive to a small number of Philadelphia made fall-front secretaries of this period.

[12] For a further discussion of the Quervelle Attribution please see Fitzgerald 129

mounted by ball finials and brass mounts above an upswept pediment over a paneled and burl inlaid fall-front desk opening to reveal an elaborately bird's-eye maple veneered interior with an arched central reserve flanked by two valanced pigeon holes above four short drawers flanked by columnar pilasters before a baize-lined writing surface all flanked by brass over a baize-lined mounted columnar supports over paneled burl veneered cupboard doors opening to reveal four short drawers, on carved feet. With its architectonic appearance, use of contrasting veneers, and construction techniques, this fall front secretary is one of six related examples made in Philadelphia. Linked to an as yet unidentified Philadelphia cabinet shop, the maker of this secretary was consistent in his overall design and use of materials. This piece, along with an example in the collection of the Dallas Museum of Art, is illustrated and discussed in Charles L. Venable's *American Furniture in the Bybee Collection* (Austin, 1989), pages 100-103."

Figure 287 and 287a

Classical Inlaid Mahogany and Brass Mounted Secretaire a Abattant

Philadelphia, Circa 1815-1830

Height 62 1/2",
Width 36",
Depth 21 1/4"

A brass mount on the triangular pediment depicts a woman watering flowers. The fall-front writing surface is flanked by two mahogany columns with brass Doric capitals, above which are two swell-front drawers.

All interior drawer fronts are bird's eye maple veneer. Pilaster supports decorated with gilt brass figural medallions flank the lower cabinet doors. The front feet are lion claw and the back turned in the usual Philadelphia manner.

Figure 288 and 288a

Secretaire a Abattant With Triangular Architectural Pediment, mahogany, bird's eye maple with ormolu mounts

Philadelphia, Circa 1815-1830
Height 76.5", Width 38", Depth 23"

Courtesy of the Stanley Weiss Collection, Providence, Rhode Island

Figure 289
Secrétaire à Abattant, rosewood,
partially ebonized
Attributed to Joseph B. Barry
Signed and inscribed (with incised stamp,
on brass lock on fall-front):
[crown]/J.BRAMAH/ [crown]/ PATENT
Philadelphia, Circa 1820

Secondary woods:
mahogany, pine, and poplar, with
die-stamped brass inlay inset with
ebony, brass locks and hinges and
leather writing surface, partially
tooled in gold.

Height 65 1/2",
Width 42 3/4",
Depth 21 3/4", 42 1/2"
(Depth with fall-front open)

Photo & Description Courtesy
of Hirschl & Adler Galleries,
New York

"One of the most elaborate pieces of American Neo-Classical furniture to have appeared, this secrétaire à abattant is closely related to an unique suite of furniture that includes a three-part winged secrétaire à abattant (Beatrice Garvin, *Federal Philadelphia 1785-1825, The Athens of the Ancient World*, exhib. cat. [Philadelphia Museum of Art, Philadelphia, 1987], p. 75 illus.), a sideboard and knife boxes (Jonathan L. Fairbanks & Elizabeth Bidwell Bates, *American Furniture 1620 to the Present* [Richard Marek Publishers, New York, 1981], p. 268 illus.), and a companion cellarette (Philadelphia Museum of Art, *Philadelphia—Three Centuries of American Art*, exhib. Cat. [Philadelphia Museum of Art, Philadelphia, 1976], pp.265-66 no. 221 illus.), all of which were made for the Simon Gratz family of Philadelphia about 1820 and are now in the collection of the Philadelphia Museum of Art. Distinguished by a lavish use of brass and ebony marquetry, or "Boulle," panels that represent the highest development of ornamental inlay found on Philadelphia pieces of the Neo-Classical period, this group of furniture has been attributed to Joseph B. Barry."

This fall-front secretary desk exhibits the same complex brass buhl work as figure 289. Multiple classically derived brass foliage motifs are offset by an ebony backround. Circular brass chain ornamentation and brass feet add luster. The use of ebony is seen at times in French furniture and is unusual in Philadelphia furniture. This piece relates closely to the attributed Barry sideboard that also descended through the Gratz family, which is illustrated in this volume as figure 246. The attribution to Joseph Barry is conjectural and is based on his advertisements, which mentioned "buhl work." Barry is the only Philadelphia cabinetmaker known to have advertised "buhl work" as an optional feature. See figures 246 and 289, which are closely related.

Figure 290

Fall-Front Secretary Desk, mahogany, mahogany veneer, ebony, brass

Attributed Joseph Barry
Philadelphia, Circa 1825

Secondary woods:
white pine and poplar

Height 65 3/4",
Width 76",
Depth 21"

Philadelphia Museum of Art:
Gift of Simon Gratz in Memory
of Caroline S. Gratz

Photo by Will Brown, 1987

CHAPTER 14
CHESTS OF DRAWERS, WARDROBES AND DRESSING TABLES

CHESTS OF DRAWERS, WARDROBES AND DRESSING TABLES

At the beginning of the nineteenth century, the chest-on-chests of the Federal era (baroque and early classical) were out of style and were replaced by dressing chests of drawers and large wardrobes. Usually bedroom furniture, chests often had four drawers and were sometimes surmounted by a mirror, which was known as a dressing glass. For a fancier chest of drawers, brass knobs, at times in the form of lion's heads, and turned, reeded columns replaced fluted quarter columns found on eighteenth century chests of drawers. Philadelphia chests often were made with bulbous ring turned "beehive" feet or lion's paw feet. Chests incorporated multiple elements including full columns, convex and concave surfaces, lion's paw feet, foliage and other carvings directly from antiquity. Prototypes were taken from English pattern books (based on French models). The main stylistic impetus was from ancient Greek and Roman ornament and architecture. Glass and mahogany knobs became more common as the first quarter of the century progressed. A variant of the traditional chest, five drawer chests (two small drawers on either side of the top and three drawers of equal size below) appeared during this period quite often.

The wardrobe was a large case piece divided by two doors. One side stored hanging clothes and the other side contained drawers. The wardrobe rested on a few types of feet, including ball, turned vase forms or lion's paw. Fancier wardrobes might have two columns on either side and carving or reeding. Both Thomas Sheraton in 1793 and George Smith in 1808 illustrate a wardrobe of the same basic design. Smith, in his Collection of Designs for Household Furniture, describes wardrobes as, "very useful appendages to the dressing room and bed chamber..."[1] The wardrobe, which was popular in the sixteenth and seventeenth centuries, became known as the linen press as clothing styles became less bulky and more items could be folded away.[2] By the nineteenth century, wardrobes had expanded to make room for more drawers and compartments to store clothes.

[1] Fitzgerald 128
[2] Fitzgerald 126

The top is a thick mahogany veneer built upon a pine frame. All four graduated drawers bow outward and have the original brass oval hardware. The front sides of the case are decorated with vertical reeding and the feet are tapered turnings that end with bulbs. This form was popular in Philadelphia and fairly large numbers of this bureau form have survived.

Figure 291
Bow front Chest of Drawers, mahogany
Philadelphia, Circa 1800-1820

Height 39 1/4",
Width 42 5/8",
Diameter 25"

Private Collection

Figure 292

Chest of Drawers, mahogany
School of Joseph Barry
Philadelphia, Circa 1800-1820

Secondary woods: sides, back, and
bottom of drawers are poplar.
Drawer fronts are white pine, drawer sides are mahogany. Back board
is poplar. Top and bottom of frame
are white pine.

Height 41 1/2",
Width 43 1/4",
Depth 23 3/4"

Private Collection

The lower drawers are flanked by
two reeded columns that are capped
by acanthus foliage. Expertly matched
mahogany veneers radiate vertically
through the drawers. The lower three
drawers are elliptical and related to
plate 15 of Sheraton's 1802 Drawing
Book. All feet are turned and reeded in
a beehive design that is often seen on
sideboards and secretaries associated
with Joseph Barry.

Leafage carving on the front bulb feet relates closely in design and execution to those on the signed Joseph B. Barry sideboard pictured in Wendy A. Cooper, Classical Taste in America 1800-1840, page 132, figure 92. The capitals of the reeded columns are cast in brass and screwed in place. They are singular, since all other known Philadelphia examples exhibit carved wood capitals.

Figure 293

Chest of Drawers, mahogany

School of Joseph Barry
Philadelphia, Circa 1815-1835

Secondary woods:
poplar and white pine

Height 43",
Width 47 1/2",
Depth 24"

Private Collection

Figure 294

Chest of Drawers, mahogany, mahogany veneer
School of Joseph B. Barry
Philadelphia, Circa 1810-1820

Secondary wood:
poplar and white pine

Height 40 3/8",
Width 46 1/2",
Depth 26 1/4"

Photo Courtesy of The Biggs
Museum of American Art,
Dover, DE

The four-drawer chest has carved and reeded columns that terminate in limp lions paws. This relates to what Joseph Barry advertised as being an elliptic bureau with columns. The front feet are carved with acanthus leaves and the back feet are simpler versions of the front without carving. The treatment of the columns with limp hairy paw feet at the base closely relates to the signed Joseph Barry sideboard in figure 243. Brass lion's masks on all the pulls were often seen on chests made by Barry and heighten the beauty of this fashionable chest.

The elliptical top has conforming elliptical graduated drawers below. Reeded columns are decorated with acanthus leafage capitals. The base of the column is supported by limp lion claw feet in a manner often associated with the school of Joseph Barry. The feet are turned.

Figure 295
Chest of Drawers, Mahogany and Mahogany Veneer

School of Joseph B. Barry
Philadelphia, Circa 1810-1820

Height 39",
Width 46",
Depth is 26"

Photo Courtesy of
Mr. F.J. Carey III

Figure 296

Chest of Drawers, mahogany,
mahogany veneer
School of Joseph Barry and Son
Philadelphia, Circa 1810-1820

Height 42 1/8",
Width 46 3/8",
Depth 23 1/2"

Photo Courtesy of
J. Michael Flanigan,
American Antiques,
Baltimore, Maryland

The mahogany top has an elliptical front edge. Four graduated drawers below this are also elliptical. The columns that flank the drawers are in the form of standing Egyptian figures. Particularly striking are the caryatid capitals decorating the trapezoidal columns. The feet are typical beehive feet, a foot form loosely associated with Barry.

This bureau is an example of what Barry described in advertisements for Egyptian style furniture. The elliptical front drawers, trapezoidal columns with Egyptian figures, and beehive feet are signature motifs found on Barry's bureaus during the early Empire period. The columns boast caryatid capitals closely associated Barry's work in general, as well as the beehive feet and the elliptical contour of the drawers.

Figure 297
Elliptic Bureau With Columns and Egyptian Figures
Attributed to Joseph Barry and Son Philadelphia, Circa 1815

Height 42",
Width 47 3/4",
Depth 23 1/2"

Private Collection

Photo Courtesy of Hirschl & Alder Galleries, New York

Figure 298

Chest of Drawers, mahogany
Attributed to Joseph Barry
Philadelphia, Circa 1812-1820

Dimensions unrecorded

Photo Courtesy of
Doyle Auction Galleries,
New York City

This chest of drawers, with carved figures surmounting each column, is in the Egyptian style that Barry advertised in 1812. This style was popularized in England by Thomas Hope and George Smith, among others. Barry is recognized as being among the first, if not the first, cabinetmakers to make Egyptian style furniture (including elliptical chests of drawers) in Philadelphia during the Empire period.

The Egyptian figures (also called Persians or mummy heads), beehive feet, and brass handles on the drawers are hallmarks of Barry's work. Several similar chests have been attributed to him on this basis, such as plate IV in Donald Fennimore's article, "Egyptian influence in early nineteenth-century American Furniture," *The Magazine Antiques* (May 1990), page 1198.

The lion's head brass handles, as seen on this piece, were often used by Barry and other Philadelphia cabinet-makers, including Quervelle. The columns are reeded and have acanthus carved capitals. The feet are turned vases that rest on small balls. This piece is both functional and well ornamented.

Figure 299
Chest of Drawers, mahogany
Philadelphia, Circa 1810-1830

Height 41 1/2",
Width 44 1/4",
Depth 22 1/2"

Private Collection

Figure 300
Pennsylvania Butler's Desk, tiger maple and mahogany
Possibly Philadelphia, Circa 1825-1835

Collection of
Mr. Joseph Sorger

Dimensions Unrecorded

The top drawer pulls down to reveal a writing surface. Inside are several compartments and small drawers. The bird's eye maple veneer is superbly crafted. This piece rests on a contrasting mahogany frame and feet. The front feet are lion's paw and the back feet a simple turned vase form. An interesting inset tombstone veneer design is found on either side of the top drawer.

This elegant chest of drawers with a four-drawer configuration has two columns that rise from the base up to the top of the piece. All drawers are elliptical. The lion's paw front feet are well executed. Note the original turned wood knobs.

Figure 301

Chest of Drawers, mahogany

Philadelphia, Circa 1825-1830

Height 45 5/8",
Width 46 3/4",
Depth 27"

Collection of
Mr. Joseph Sorger

Figure 302

Chest of Drawers, mahogany

Philadelphia, Circa 1825-1830

Height 46 1/2",
Width 42 1/4",
Depth 24 1/4"

Collection of
Mr. Joseph Sorger

This unusual five-drawer chest reverses the standard Empire arrangement of a top overhanging drawer with three recessed drawers below. The columns flank the top drawers and rest on a ledge above the long bottom drawer, dividing the piece in a rather novel manner. An unusual treatment of the acanthus carving obscures the fronts of the lions paw feet.

Expertly book matched mahogany veneers embellish the front drawers. The columns are bird's eye maple with brass Doric capitals and nearly identical to those used by Quervelle on his prize-winning secretary desk, which is illustrated in figure 282. All pressed glass knobs are original.

Figure 303

Chest of Drawers, mahogany and bird's eye maple

School of Anthony Quervelle Philadelphia, Circa 1825-1830

Secondary woods: pine and poplar

Height 42 1/4", Width 44 1/2", Depth 22 1/2"

Private Collection

Figure 304
Twin Chests of Drawers,
mahogany
Made by Charles White
Philadelphia, March 1827

Secondary wood: white pine

Height 47",
Width 45 1/2",
Depth 24"

Private Collection

This identical pair of chests is attributed to Charles White. The attribution is based on a letter that details a list of furniture, including two chests of drawers, given to the Newbold family by Charles White (This correspondence is illustrated in figure 36a of this text). All feet have a somewhat unusual turned vase form.

This chest has the typical Empire drawer configuration, with two upper swelled front drawers above three straight fronted drawers. Brilliant figured maple enhances the appearance. The carving of the capitals and the treatment of the turned feet are very similar to that of the capitals and back feet of the secretary desk illustrated in figure 279. Both pieces may be the work of the same currently unknown Philadelphia cabinet shop.

Figure 305
Chest of Drawers and Mirror, bird's eye maple
Philadelphia, Circa 1825-1830

Secondary wood: poplar

Height 42 1/2",
Width 43",
Depth 22 1/2"

Collection of the
Andalusia Foundation

Figure 306

Dressing Bureau with Mirror; maple, marble, brass, glass, iron, stencil

Made by Walter Pennery
(Apprentice, Shop of John Jamison)
Philadelphia, Circa 1830

Secondary wood: poplar

Height 87 2/5",
Width 43 2/5",
Depth 24 1/2"

Courtesy of
Winterthur Museum

Museum Purchase with funds provided by Special Funds for Collection Objects

This impressive dressing bureau has a recessed center section with marble, below which are drawers with gilt scrolled leaf stenciling. Below these, supporting the sides, are verde antique scroll columns supported by stenciled trapezoidal plinths. The feet are verde antique lion's paws. A movable mirror in a coved black frame with a gilt stenciled anthemion border is held in place by a vertical board support surmounted by a large verde antique and gilt scallop shell. Inscribed in pencil on the underside of drawer in second row, center is, "The year of our lord one thousand eight hundred/and thirty/Philadelphia June 11th 1830/Walter Pennery." This dressing bureau from the shop of John Jamison was awarded a silver medal in 1830 for excellence at the Franklin Institute's annual exhibition for the promotion of the mechanic arts in Philadelphia.

Figure 307
Dressing Bureau with Mirror, rosewood and marble

Made by Isaac Jones
Philadelphia, 1837

Height 90",
Width 40 1/2",
Depth 21 3/4"

Courtesy of
Winterthur Museum

This four-drawer dressing bureau rests on carved verde antiqued lion's paw feet in the front and turned feet in the back. The lower three drawers are graduated with flat fronts and wooden knobs and are flanked by two columns with carved gilt and verde antiqued Corinthian capitals that support the overhanging drawer above. This overhanging drawer has a torus molded front with a gilt and verde antiqued gadrooned border. On the top of the chest are two stenciled rectangular plinths that support gilt and verde decorated Corithian columns. These support the mirror and are connected above by a cornice which is decorated with stenciling and egg-and-dart molding. The looking-glass plate is surrounded by gilt borders and gilt-stenciled foliated ornaments. This dressing bureau is a part of a bedroom suite made for Elijah Van Syckel, a Philadelphia wine and liquor merchant.

Figure 308

Bureau with Mirror, mahogany

Possibly School of David Fleetwood
Philadelphia, Circa 1820-1830

Secondary wood: poplar

Height 78",
Depth 40"

Collection of the
Andalusia Foundation

Bureaus of this form may have
been associated with the shop of David
Fleetwood or others. The standard
Empire overhung top drawer is enhanced
by the use of convex swell front drawer
surfaces on all drawers instead of just
the uppermost as is usual. Both columns
supporting the mirror are topped with
gilt urns carved with gadrooning and
foliage in a typical Philadelphia manner.
An ebonized and gilt mirror frame with
columns adds contrast. The feet are a
series of ring turnings above which is a

concave art shelf. This shelf supports
columns which have an unusual elongated variant of Corinthian capitals. Above
this rests a case work with four drawers
and a sunken center section. The upper
mirror support columns are surmounted
by an open triangular pediment with
foliage decorated corner acroterion.
Several Philadelphia makers, including
David Fleetwood, have tradionally been
associated with this form of dressing
table.

Figure 309
*Dressing Table, mahogany
with maple, walnut and
mahogany inlay*
Philadelphia, Circa 1825-1830

Height 84",
Width 35 1/2",
Depth 20"

The Art Institute
of Chicago

Restricted gift of
Mrs. Henry C. Woods, 1970.38

The front columns of the
dressing table feature a carved
acanthus and scroll design at
the tops, which is repeated
above on the tops of the
columns that surround the
mirror. The feet are a series
of concentric disks that terminate in brass casters. Several
Philadelphia makers, including
David Fleetwood, have been
traditionally associated with
this form of dressing table.

Figure 310
Dressing Table, Mahogany
Philadelphia, Circa 1825

Height 71",
Width 39",
Depth 20"

Photo Courtesy of the Owens
Thomas House of
the Telfair Museum,
Savannah, Georgia

This mirror is supported by columns with modified Corinthian capitals, above which is a triangular pediment decorated with urn finials. The case has five drawers with a drop central section that probably originally contained a white central slab. Below the drawers is a gadrooned molding that features a "micro-carved" central shell. Micro-carving is discussed in chapter 4 and is a Philadelphia feature with some association to Quervelle's shop. The supporting columns below have Corinthian capitals.

The mirror frame with semi-circular columns has bulls-eye circular corner squares. Two supporting columns for the mirror are connected by a triangular pediment. The work area features a drop center section with white marble reminiscent of Philadelphia sideboards of the Empire period. All columns supporting the case and turned feet below are uncarved.

Figure 311
Dressing Table, mahogany and white marble

Label of Charles White
Philadelphia, Circa 1825-1830

Height 90",
Width 36 1/2",
Depth 20 1/2"

Collection of
Mr. F.J. Carey III

Figure 312

Bureau with Mirror, mahogany
Made by Anthony G. Quervelle
Philadelphia, August 1835

Height 74 3/4",
Width 42",
Depth 17"

Photo Courtesy of Rosedown
Plantation State Historic Site,
Louisiana Office of State Parks

This bureau shows Restoration influence with loss of columns, carving and
other classical elements. The urn finials
relate closely to that on the Quervelle
hat/coat rack, also at Rosedown (see
figure 368 of this text).

Figure 313
Wardrobe

Philadelphia, Circa 1810
Attributed to Joseph Barry

Secondary Woods:
base is white pine, sides
are mahogany, backboards
are poplar.

Height 78",
Width 46 1/2",
Depth 19"

Private Collection

This wardrobe has two large flame book matched mahogany doors. Above is an inset panel that is surmounted by a triangular cornice decorated with a central pineapple finial and bulls-eye panels. The feet are limp hairy lion claws with a bulbous beehive pattern above. This unusual type of foot is closely associated with the feet seen on the signed Joseph Barry sideboard illustrated in figure 243. The triangular pediment relates to pediments also seen on the back gallery of Barry Sideboards. The unusual small size is relatively rare and desirable.

Figure 314

Painted Armoire, pine, painted and gilded

Philadelphia, Circa 1820-1830

Height 88",
Width 54",
Depth 20"

Collection of the
Andalusia Foundation

This armoire uses paint and gilt decoration to transform a flat surfaced utilitarian form into an object of classical beauty. The front feet consist of square blocks that are painted with an anthemion design. The stenciled gilt design seen on the panels of the doors and the pediment is derived from ancient classical prototypes.

The left side has room to hang clothes, while the right side is made up of many drawers. On either side of the columns are small closets that open outward, providing even more space, perhaps for shoes and smaller items. The columns are reeded and terminate at the top with modified Ionic columns. The feet have a variant beehive shape. This wardrobe exhibits strong French influence as seen from wardrobes made in New Orleans.

Figure 315
Wardrobe or Linen Press, mahogany
Philadelphia, Circa 1800-1820

Secondary wood:
poplar and white pine

Height 85",
Width 76",
Depth 25"

Private Collection

Figure 316

Wardrobe, Mahogany with Stencil and Ebonized Decoration

Strong attribution to Anthony Quervelle Philadelphia, Circa 1825-1830

Height 89 1/4",
Width 72 3/4",
Diameter 19 3/4"

Photo Courtesy of
the Museum of Arts and Sciences,
Daytona Beach, Florida

The concave stenciled cornice is supported by four columns that are foliage carved, ebonized and stenciled. Between each pair of columns is a carved ebonized urn. Below each urn is an inset Gothic arch. Both paneled doors have multiple carved elements, including anthemion, stars and scroll-ing. The doors and other front surfaces are additionally decorated with medallions interlocking leafage and line stenciling. Both front feet are double dolphins. The design is virtually identical to sketch number 19 of the Quervelle sketchbook, illustrated in chapter five of this volume.

The cornice flairs outward as it rises. A concave arch decorates the molding below. The large door and Corinthian column on each side are constructed as one unit and is hinged to move together. The modified ogee feet show French inspired Restoration influence. An inside drawer has Quervelle's later period Delmes label that illustrates a dressing table with mirror.

Figure 317
Wardrobe, mahogany
Delmes Label of Anthony G. Quervelle
Philadelphia, August 1835

Height 98",
Width 62",
Depth 28"

Photo Courtesy of Rosedown Plantation State Historic Site, Louisiana Office of State Parks

Figure 318

*Wardrobe, rosewood
(one of a pair)*

Made by Isaac Jones
Philadelphia, 1837

Height 91 1/2",
Width 60",
Depth 31"

Courtesy,
Winterthur Museum

This massive wardrobe has gilt and verde antiqued paw feet in the front and square tapered verde antiqued feet in the back. The two double-paneled hinged doors have borders of gilt stringing and are flanked by two large columns with Corinthian capitals.

Above the hinged doors are two drawers with carved gilt echinus ornament under a flat overhang. This piece was originally owned by Elijah Van Syckel, a wealthy Philadelphia wine and liquor merchant.

Chests of Drawers, Wardrobes and Dressing Tables Outside Philadelphia

Both mirror supports are trapezoidal columns with Persians capitals connected by a triangular pediment rail. The front supports for the drawers are delicate scrolls with acanthus carving at the upper knee portions.

Figure 319
Dressing Table, mahogany

Baltimore or possibly Philadelphia, Circa 1800-1820

Height 58",
Width 43",
Depth 19 1/2"

Collection of
Mr. F.J. Carey III

Figure 320

Dressing Table, Mahogany
Boston, Circa 1810-1825

Height 66 1/2",
Width 37",
Depth 20 1/2"

Photo courtesy of
the Museum of Arts
and Sciences of Daytona
Beach, Florida

The rectangular and arched mahogany veneered mirror is supported by two cylindrical columns decorated with gilded ball finials. The mahogany case below contains a single drawer with brass gilded hardware. This is supported by four cylindrical columns decorated with gilded brass mounts. The double concave shelf below these columns is supported by ebonized ball feet. This table illustrates the conservative Boston fashion, which closely followed French furniture prototypes based on monumental stone classical architecture. In contrast, the Philadelphia empire style of the time made greater use of carving, stenciling and local stylistic modification of classical forms.

Figure 321
Clothes Press, mahogany

Attributed to Henry Banta
Bergen County, New Jersey,
Circa 1820-1830

Secondary woods: inside of doors and back are poplar, top is white pine, case shelves are white pine. Interior of upper section and back are poplar, top is white pine, sides are mahogany. Lower drawer sides, back, and bottom are poplar, front is white pine.

Height 93",
Width 47 3/4",
Depth 21 1/4"

Private Collection

This clothes press is closely related to a New York wardrobe attributed to Michael Allison, now in the Winterthur Collection.[3] The pediment (including the brass rosettes), the cornice molding, paneled doors of the upper section, overall proportions, fire-gilded finials and hardware are similar to the Winterthur piece. This piece is believed to be the work of Henry Banta, who trained under Michael Allison and then worked in Bergen County, NJ. The columns exhibit acanthus carving in the lower portion with pineapple motifs carved above. Front feet are lion's paw with overhanging leaves. The execution of the carving is of the highest quality and skill.

3 Montgomery, Item 452, p.443

Figure 322
Dresser with Ogee Mirror,
mahogany
American, Circa 1830-1840

Height 76",
Width 44",
Depth 22"

Photo and Description Courtesy of
Flomaton Antique Auction,
Flomaton, Alabama

"This four-drawer dresser features a banded inlaid top with a depressed center section with ogee columns on either side. There are inlaid panels on the sides of the dresser. Above the drawers there are large "S" scrolled mirror arms and an ogee mirror."

This bureau demonstrates the use of flat veneered surfaces and "S" and other scrolling typical of the late classical transition to the "Pillar & Scroll" Restoration style.

Authors note: Carving is eliminated in favor of flowing surfaces of matched veneers. Notice that even the round mirror supports convert into sheets of flat veneer.

CHAPTER 15
BEDSTEADS

BEDSTEADS

Styles of bedsteads in France during the first half of the nineteenth century included the traditional high post, the French bedstead, and the lit de repos, or sofa-bed. The term French bedstead or "lit a la turque", was a bed that featured a scrolled headboard and footboard of equal height. The French bed, or sofa-bed, produced a dramatic change in the design of bedrooms and began to replace the traditional bed. The absence of pillars, a headboard, a footboard and drapery made the design of the sofa-bed a

very simple piece in comparison to traditional beds, but apparently the design was favored in the royal courts. The bedroom of Queen Louise of Prussia at Charlottenburg features this type of bed, surmounted by white drapery hanging on the walls in chaste folds.[1] The English borrowed these styles, and also designed a "field bed," which was similar to a high post with elaborate drapery. George Smith illustrated a design for a field bed in *A Collection of Designs for Household Furniture*, 1808. A version of the French sofa-bed is depicted in Ackermann's *Regency Furniture & Interiors*, which is a more elaborate type with draperies thrown over a scepter-rod that comes out from the wall (plate 83). A different version of the sofa bed is shown by Sheraton in *The Cabinet-maker an Upholsterer's Drawing Book*, 1802, which features a square head and footboard accompanied by a board that encloses the back, meant to rest against the wall. Above the bed is a canopy or crown, from which draperies hang from either side and down the back. Sheraton's design for the English State bed shows an ornamental high post bed with elaborate drapery and carving on the posts, headboard, feet and top canopy.

In Philadelphia during the Empire period, two types of beds were popular. Both were of large size and great mass.

The first was the French or "lit a la turque," with scrolled head and footboards of equal height. This was later known as a "sleigh bed". This bed was listed in the Philadelphia price list of 1828 as having a size of six feet by four feet, with extras for glued blocks on the front to receive columns when the bed was placed sideways against the wall.[2] On some examples the feet were carved lion's paws. The second type is the conventional high post form with a high carved headboard and occasional canopy on top, which was advertised as being an "English bedstead." The term "bedstead" refers to the bed frame, while the word "bed" was used to describe the mattress.[3] The degree of richness of any type depended on personal taste and how much money a person was willing to spend. There were various types of woods used for beds, the most popular being mahogany, but maple, curly maple and cherry were sometimes used. Empire high post beds have carved posts, headboard and feet. Philadelphia headboards are often carved with a combination of classical motifs such as scrolls, cornucopias, anthemion and other leaf designs. Plain headboards often featured panels that were similar to those on cupboard doors of sideboards and on bureaus. The bed posts often featured large spiral reeding. Low post beds, or field beds, also existed but were considered for servants or children.

[1] Morley 230
[2] Otto 50
[3] Miller 574

"Four matching, turned and carved posts; chunky baluster leg with donut at ankle; rectangular element with lamb's tongue at shoulders above which is baluster with carved floral (rosette) swags and bell flower pendant surmounted by urn-shaped element with acanthus carved decoration; reeded shaft with acanthus carved capitals above which is unornamented, turned throat tapering slightly towards top; top capped with brass fitting and pin; rails have turned rope knobs; headboard with two plain set-in panels is flat across top and slight cyma curve at shoulder with straight sides; brass plates contoured to concave portion of shoulder and on bottom edge where headboard joins posts."

Figure 323
High Post Bed, mahogany and brass

Invoice of Joseph Barry
Philadelphia, Circa 1807-1810

Height 95 1/4",
Width 61 3/4",
Depth 81"

Photo and Description Courtesy of the Hagley Museum & Library Collections

Photo by Laszlo Bodo

Figure 324
Bed, mahogany, cherry, and tulip poplar
Attributed to Joseph B. Barry
Philadelphia, Circa 1810-1820

Height 89 1/4",
Width 63 1/2",
Depth 82"

Private Collection

This bed, with all four posts fully carved, is reputed to have been originally owned by Joseph Bonaparte (1786-1844) and used by him when he slept in his house at 260 South Ninth Street in Philadelphia. A documented Joseph Barry bedstead is pictured in Donald L. Fennimore and Robert T. Trump, "Joseph B. Barry, Philadelphia cabinet-maker," Antiques Magazine, May 1989, page 1215, plate IV. This same bedstead is also pictured as figure 323 in this chapter.

Figure 325 and 325a
High Post Mahogany Bed
Philadelphia, Circa 1800-1820

Dimensions unrecorded

Private Collection

Figure 325a
Detail of the urn portion of the foot post

The headboard is paneled with a triangular pediment. The head posts are uncarved outlines of the foot posts. Both foot posts are reeded with acanthus carving above and below. The middle portion of the posts are decorated urns with floral and swag carving. Below a squared section are turned feet.

Figure 326
*High Post
Mahogany Bed*
Philadelphia, Circa 1810-1820

Height 94 1/2",
Length 82 1/4",
Width 67 1/2"

Private Collection

The headboard is paneled with an arched triangular pediment, a common configuration in the Empire period. Both foot posts are reeded with acanthus carving above and below. The lower middle portion of the posts is squared and decorated with slash-bud panels at the top and bottom. Bed bolt covers consist of applied lower slash bud square panels. The feet are tapered with a bulbous turning. This style foot was popular on Pennsylvania furniture of the period. Both head posts are uncarved outlines of the foot posts. The head posts would have been covered with drapery.

Figure 327 and 327a
High Post Mahogany Bed

School of Joseph Barry
Philadelphia, Circa 1810-1820

Secondary wood: rails are maple

Height 93",
Length 84 1/2",
Width 61 3/4"

Private Collection

Figure 327a
Detail of the carving of the foot post

This bed exhibits a paneled, triangular pedimented headboard with small Gothic arches at the corners. The design of the carved posts is complex. They begin at the top with acanthus carving descending to reeding, which then incorporates further acanthus carving interrupted by a short segment of horizontal disc turning to give the impression of a band around a portion of the leafage. There are then spiral turnings which are both aligned to the reeding above and rotated in opposite directions. This then becomes a square slashed bud motif below from which olive branches descend to the bulb turned feet. The rails are maple veneered in mahogany. The slashed bud motif and Gothic arches are forms commonly associated with Joseph Barry and other Philadelphia cabinet shops. All four posts are fully carved.

Figure 328
High Post Maple Bed
Philadelphia, Circa 1820-1830

Dimensions unrecorded

Private Collection

Two scrolls decorate the ends of the crest of the headboard. The design of the posts feature a series of bulbous and elaborate cylindrical turnings that are outlines of carved turnings found on the best Philadelphia beds of this period (see figure 329 for comparison). Acanthus leaf carving, gadrooning and other carved designs have been omitted, probably as a matter of economy. The bulls-eye disks are the main decorative element.

Figure 329 and 329a
High Post Bed, cherry

Possible Attribution to
Anthony Quervelle
Philadelphia, Circa 1820-1830

Height 92",
Width 64",
Depth 82"

Private Collection

This "English bedstead" design, as Quervelle referred to it, is closely related to Figure 14 of Robert Smith's article, "Part V: Sofas, chairs and beds," The Magazine Antiques, March 1974, page 521. The entire bed is skillfully carved with foliate and gadroon carved posts, which relate to the forms on labeled Quervelle card tables. Square blocks with enclosed circular turnings are also seen on the Indian princess paneled sofa, illustrated in figure 222. The headboard carving is complex, with cornucopias and leaf volutes that are especially associated with Quervelle's work. This bed represents one of the apexes of Philadelphia bedstead design during the latter half of the Philadelphia Empire period. The use of cherry wood by Quervelle is documented in the Robert Smith's article, Part V (cited above).

Figure 329a
Detail of headboard and head posts

Figure 330

Bedstead, rosewood
Made by Isaac Jones
Philadelphia, 1837

Dimensions unrecorded

Height 112", Width 76", Depth 89"

Courtesy, Winterthur Museum

This bedstead with the matching wardrobe shown in the backround was made as part of a suite of furniture for the wealthy Philadelphia wine merchant Eliajah Van Syckel by cabinetmaker Isaac Jones. The cornice is decorated with a gilt egg-and-dart carved molding. The columns have gilt capitals and are stenciled below, as is the headboard. All feet are in the form of gilt decorated pylons.

Figure 331
High Post Bed, Mahogany

Possibly made by Isaac Jones
Philadelphia, Circa 1820-1830

Height 87",
Width 62",
Depth 75"

Private Collection

Figure 331b
Detail of the carving of the foot post.

There is elaborate carving on the posts and headboard. All four posts boast carved spiral twist turnings. Under the spiral twist is a carved tobacco leaf design followed by a ringed portion below that is a bale of wheat supporting spiraled tobacco leaves. The top of the headboard contains a design that incorporates gentle scrolls, leaves, cornucopias and a central sea shell.

This particular arrangement, featuring a central shell, is similar to one carved on the back gallery of a sideboard by Isaac Jones (DAPC at Winterthur), illustrated in figure 257. The headboard is paneled below the carved crest. The legs are bulbous and tapered, ending in bulbous, tapered and turned feet with a brass cylindrical cap.

Figure 331a
Detail of the shell and cornucopia carved head board.

Figure 332

Bedstead, mahogany

Made by Anthony G. Quervelle
Philadelphia, 1835

Height 108",
Width 64",
Depth 81"

Photo Courtesy of Rosedown
Plantation State Historic Site,
Louisiana Office of State Parks

This bedstead is one of three remaining at the Rosedown Plantation of the original four ordered from Quervelle by Douglas Turnbull in 1835. It has leaf carving limited to the top of the head board. The form is a flat uncarved version of beds such as the cherry Quervelle attributed bed illustrated in figure 329.

One of the three beds at Rosedown proven to be made by Quervelle, this bed illustrates the loss of carving typical of the end of classicism, as influenced by the Restoration style. The carving is limited to grapes and grape leafage that spiral into disks at the ends of the headboard.

Figure 333
Bedstead, mahogany

Made by Anthony G. Quervelle
Philadelphia, 1835

Height 108",
Depth 81",
Width 64"

Photo Courtesy of Rosedown
Plantation State Historic Site,
Louisiana Office of State Parks

Figure 334
Bedstead, mahogany

Made by Anthony G. Quervelle
Philadelphia, 1835

Height 110",
Width 66 1/2",
Depth 82 1/2"

Photo Courtesy of Rosedown
Plantation State Historic Site,
Louisiana Office of State Parks

This bedstead has heavily turned columns which are uncarved profiles of earlier, more elaborate Quervelle bed posts. The crest of the headboard has acanthus carving which spirals into disks at either end.

This day bed form, not often seen in the North, was used for napping during the extreme heat of southern afternoons. The main bedsteads were typically made up by slaves with Spanish moss each morning and were not used until night. The posts are well-carved and the crests end in disks, a motif favored by Quervelle and other Philadelphia makers. Bulbous carved feet have been seen on Philadelphia chests, especially those attributed to Joseph Barry.

Figure 335
Day Bed, mahogany
Probably Philadelphia, Circa 1820-1830

Height 34 1/4",
Width 75 1/2",
Depth 30 1/4"

Photo Courtesy of Rosedown Plantation State Historic Site, Louisiana Office of State Parks

Figure 336
Day Bed, mahogany
Probably Philadelphia, Circa 1820-1830

Height 34 1/2",
Width 75 1/2",
Depth 30 1/4"

Photo Courtesy of Rosedown
Plantation State Historic Site,
Louisiana Office of State Parks

This day bed was one of two that remained in active use at the Rosedown Plantation until its closure after the Civil War. The form has equal height head and foot posts. These are elaborately decorated with carving, as are the foliage carved bulbous feet, which end in small brass balls.

The headboard, footboard and feet are scrolled. Both rails have cut-out scrolls on the lower edges. The combination of these decorative elements relates this bed to the "Pillar & Scroll" style of the 1830s, which followed the demise of the Empire style. This type of bed, with head and foot-boards of equal height, was referred to as a "French bed."

Figure 337
Sleigh Bed, mahogany
Probably Philadelphia, Circa 1830-1845

Height 45 3/4",
Width 61 1/4",
Depth 97 3/8"

Photo Courtesy of Flomaton Antique Auction, Flomaton, Alabama

Figure 338
Empire Sleigh Bed,
rosewood
Philadelphia, Circa 1830-1840

Dimensions unrecorded

Private Collection

This bed has S-scroll ends with a carved shell at the terminus. The form combines the classical feature of carved shells with the restoration feature of scroll feet.

Bedsteads Outside of Philadelphia

Figure 339
High Post Bed, cherry
Pennsylvania, Circa 1825-1830

Height 103",
Width 62",
Depth 83"

Private Collection

The design of the carved posts is a complex series of foliage carved turnings, gadrooned edged urns and spiral acanthus leafage. A central basket of fruit, flanked by cornucopias, adorns the headboard. The tapered feet are decorated with spiral foliage.

Figure 339a
Detail of carved headboard and head posts

Figure 340 and 340a
High Post Bed, mahogany

Probably Virginia,
Circa 1825-1830

Height 94",
Width 59",
Depth 81"

Photo Courtesy of Phillip Bradley
Antiques, Downingtown, PA

All posts have turned foliage columns with gadrooned and foliated urns and vases. The headboard is decorated with scroll carving on the sides and central carved fruit basket. Hooks attach the headboard to the head post, a typical feature of Southern bedsteads. During hot summer nights, the headboard was removed to allow increased circulation. The form closely follows Philadelphia styling, not surprising as there was much social and commercial interaction between Philadelphia and the South.

Figure 340a
Detail of removable headboard showing the hook connections between the head-board and the head posts.

CHAPTER 16
LOOKING GLASSES

Looking Glasses

The looking glass was a fashionable and functional addition to any room in the house. Looking glasses were placed above mantelpieces, in hallways and on or above chests in bedrooms. The minimally carved frames of the Federal period were replaced by heavily gilded frames with turned balusters. Looking glass frames of varying styles and shapes were available, from plain mahogany to highly ornamented gilded and gessoed pieces.

Certain types, such as the girandole, are decorated with candle sconces, thus providing an important extra source of lighting by reflecting candlelight off of the mirror. Girandoles were circular with a convex mirror often surrounded by decorative elements including small circular balls and other forms of ornamentation. A convex glass surface creates distortion in the mirror, allowing a panoramic viewing field. During social gatherings, a lady might obtain a birds-eye view of the social milieu. Regardless of the presence or absence of candle sconces, these mirrors are loosely referred to as Girandoles.

Rectangular looking glasses with reverse painted glass panels above a mercury or silvered plate were also popular during the period. A wide range of Empire motifs appeared on looking glass frames, such as cornucopias, floral and leaf designs, lyres, dolphins and fruit. The size of looking glasses increased as room size and height grew larger during the Empire period.

This looking glass descended in the Rush family and belonged to Benjamin Rush (1746-1813), the famous Philadelphia physician who served with Washington in the Revolution and tended to the sick during the great yellow fever epidemic of 1793. The vertical orientation of the eagle's wings is echoed by the vertical rising leafage at the bottom of the mirror. The overall form has great balance and energy. This looking glass was acquired from the Rush homestead in Paoli at the Charles Whittaker sale of the estate of Deborah Norris Rush Estate on April 21, 1991.

Figure 341
Girandole Looking Glass, gilded and gessoed, white pine
Probably Philadelphia, Circa 1790-1810

Overall Height 51",
Width 29 1/2"

Private Collection

Figure 342

Pair of Girandole Looking Glasses, gilded and gessoed, white pine

Possibly Philadelphia,
Circa 1810-1820

Overall Height 42",
Width 18"

Private Collection

The circular convex looking glass with conforming frame is decorated with a series of twenty-nine circular balls. Below the frame is leafage carving with a central teardrop-like leafage motif. Above the circular frame is a platform with leafage radiating from its base with a spread-wing eagle above. The appearance of the eagle and arrangement of the leafage is quite similar to the Edward Shippin girandole illustrated as plate 440 in William Macpherson Horner's *Blue Book Philadelphia Furniture* (1935).

The two cornucopias are connected above by an arch decorated with leafage on which a rampant eagle rests. The cornucopia features apples, grapes, pears and other fruits in accurate, three-dimensional detail. One of the greatest of the cornucopia form mirrors of this period.

Figure 343
Cornucopia and Eagle Looking Glass, gesso and gilded wood
Probably Philadelphia, Circa 1820-1830

Height 52 1/2",
Width 37 3/4"

Photo courtesy of the Museum of Arts and Sciences of Daytona Beach, Florida

Figure 344
Cheval Looking Glass
Attributed to Anthony Quervelle
Philadelphia, Circa 1825

Height 71",
Width 40",
Depth 29"

Private Collection

A trestle base is supported by four well-carved lion claw feet with spiral-carved foliage. The base of each column has a decorative scroll bracket support. Both supporting columns are capped with Corinthian capitals surmounted with urn finials. The mirror frame is painted black and decorated with sten-ciled leafage. Quervelle related design features include the use of stenciling combined with carving. The urn finials appear identical to those on the Quervelle chest of drawers (figure 312) and coat rack (figure 368) at Rosedown Plantation.

Figure 345

Looking Glass, mahoganized
cherry, white pine

Sold by David Pidgeon
Philadelphia, Circa 1825-1828

Secondary wood: white pine

Height 29 3/4",
Width 16 1/4",
Depth 3 1/4"

Private Collection

David Pidgeon's printed paper label is glued to the back board. It notes that he ran a hardware and fancy goods store at 286 South Second Street in Philadelphia. Pidgeon did not remain at that address; the 1828 Philadelphia city directory records him at 126 North Third Street.

Figure 346

Looking Glass, gilded and gessoed tulip poplar

Sold by Caleb P. Wayne
Philadelphia, Circa 1823-1843

Secondary woods:
white pine and poplar

Height 31 1/2",
Width 21 1/2",
Depth 3"

Private Collection

Wayne's printed label is glued to the back board. It notes that he was a looking glass, fancy hardware and cutlery merchant at the south west corner of Fourth and Market Street in Philadelphia. The label also lists an extensive variety of household goods. The turned gesso and gilt balusters display floral and foliage designs, which are typical decorative motifs of the Empire era.

The rectangular frame is decorated with gilt columns. Upon each column is an elaborate floral bouquet. These floral bouquets are identical to those found on the Caleb Paul Wayne mirror illustrated as figure 346. Along the edge of the mirror is a grape leaf border.

Figure 347
Gilt Looking Glass
Attributed to Caleb B. Wayne
Philadelphia, Circa 1823-1843

Secondary woods:
white pine, poplar

Height 28",
Width 39",
Depth 3"

Private Collection

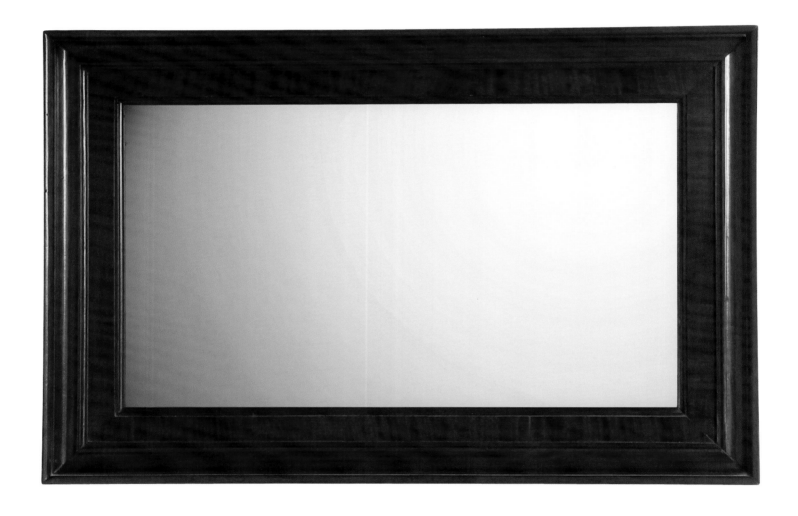

Figure 348 *Looking Glass,*
mahogany
Sold by James Borbidge
Philadelphia, Circa 1816-1818

Secondary wood: white pine

Height 21 1/2",
Width 32 1/2",
Depth 2 1/2"

Private Collection

Borbidge's printed paper label is glued to the back board. It states that he owned a looking glass store at 48 North Third Street in Philadelphia, also recorded in the Philadelphia city directory for 1816. He relocated the next year, for the number 48 is crossed out and penned in its place is the number 17. James Borbidge was probably related to Thomas Borbidge, the only other person with that surname in Philadelphia at the time, who was a forwarding and commercial merchant.

Looking Glasses Outside Philadelphia

Figure 349

Figure 350

This type of looking glass is often referred to as a girandole (round gilt frame with convex glass). The eagle at the top of the piece was a commonly used motif in both American and English examples. There are two eagle heads at the bottom that are drawn together in the center with a bow. Four suspended candle arms placed near the glass allowed for the favorable refection of candlelight when in use. The appearance of the eagle and especially the rock pile below closely relate to a New York mirror currently at Boscobel.[1] The use of acorns (intermixed here with balls) is a feature seen on American mirrors, especially from New York. Flame torches representing liberty are an American theme. Outward facing eagle heads were used in other classical New York furniture, such as lyre chairs attributed to Lannuier.

[1] Berry B. Tracy, Federal Furniture and Decorative Arts at Boscobel (New York: Harry N. Abrams Inc.,1981) 114, Figure 79.

Figure 349 and 350

Pair of Looking Glasses, gold leaf over gesso over white pine

Probably Albany, New York, Circa 1800-1820

Overall Height 41"

Private Collection

Figure 351 *Girandole Looking Glass, gilded and gessoed, white pine*
American or English, Circa 1800-1830

Overall Height 43",
Overall Width 36"

Private Collection

The central convex mirror has a circular frame decorated with a gessoed floral motif with surrounding gilded balls. Below the frame is a naturalistically carved shell flanked by leafage issuing spiraled candle holders. Above is an eagle surmounting a rock pile with leafage flanking both sides. The mirror was found in a home in West Philadelphia in the 1970s.

The looking glass frame is supported by two turned, slightly-tapering mahogany columns which rest on arched carved feet. Brass candle supports are attached to the fronts of the columns. The finials of this type are seen in Philadelphia and New York. This looking glass was designed to be viewed from the front and back, and placed in the center of the room.

Figure 352
Cheval Looking Glass, mahogany
Philadelphia, New Jersey or New York, Circa 1830-1840

Dimensions unrecorded

Philip Bradley Antiques, Downingtown, PA

Figure 353
Looking Glass, mahogany
Stencil of Miller, 84 Mark Street,
New York City, Circa 1825-1835

Height 43 1/2",
Width 19 1/2"

Private Collection

The frame is decorated with two spiral and acanthus carved columns with a molded cornice above. The four corners are decorated with fire gilded brass medallions. The upper panel contains an oil painting on board depicting a schooner sailing past a lighthouse. The octagonal shape of the lighthouse suggests the Sandy Hook lighthouse built in 1764. The use of oil painting as opposed to reverse painting on glass is unusual and suggests that this was a more expensive mirror when purchased. The top of the frame contains a partial stencil which reads "_____ Miller, looking glass maker, 84 Mark street, New York."

Figure 354

Looking Glass, mahogany

Possibly Newport, Rhode Island,
Circa 1810-1820

Height 55",
Width 26 1/2"

Private Collection

This looking glass exhibits unusual double columns flanking the mirror and is decorated with bulls-eye disks, extensive reeding and applied carving to the crest. Decoration of the columns, disk motifs and reeding all relate to Philadelphia looking glasses of the classical period. Recent research suggests that despite these similarities, this looking glass is the product of a Newport, Rhode Island cabinetmaker.

Figure 355

Looking Glass, mahogany and mahogany veneer

American, Circa 1830-1840

Dimensions unrecorded

Private Collection

The columns surmounting the mirror are not carved and exhibit S-curves in a pillar and scroll manner. The panel and cornice above also lack carving as is typical of restoration style. This form of mirror marks the end of classicism with its elements being reduced to flowing linear surfaces.

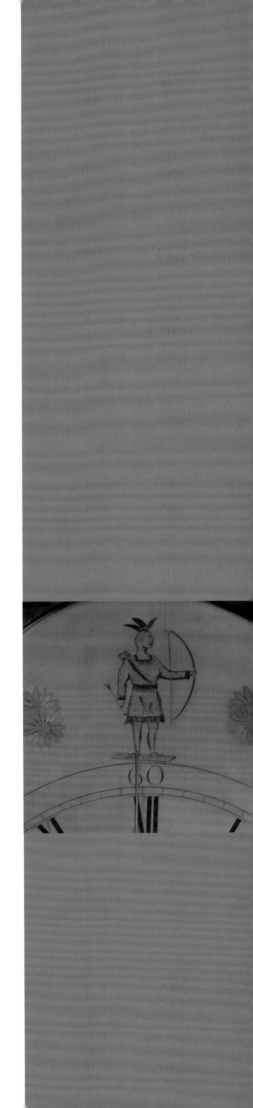

CHAPTER 17

CLOCKS AND OTHER DECORATIVE ELEMENTS

Clocks and Other Decorative Elements

From the time of its founding, Philadelphia was a clock-making center. As the first quarter of the nineteenth century progressed, tall clock cases became somewhat wider. Earlier quarter columns of the case were replaced by full, free standing columns. Ogee bracket and French feet gave way to circular turnings and lion paw feet. Simultaneously, the mass production of Connecticut shelf clocks provided a cheaper and more reliable alternative for time keeping. This resulted in the complete demise of the tall clock by 1840. Architectural elements, derived from classical antique sources, dominated early American shelf clock design (see figure 382).

Other items included in this chapter are unusual decorative pieces that illustrate other aspects of an early nineteenth century home. A few of the decorative pieces shown are rare examples, such as the rotating dumb waiter, which may be one of the last surviving examples of its type. It is important to include these items to understand nineteenth century Empire furnishings in their varying shapes and forms. Unfortunately, the inventory of decorative arts of the Empire period is not comprehensive due to the fact that many forms did not survive or now exist only in inaccessible collections.

Figure 356

Tall Case Clock, mahogany

Signed by Joseph B. Barry
(inside the hood)
Philadelphia, Circa 1815

Secondary woods:
white pine and poplar

Height 97",
Width 23 5/8",
Depth 11 1/4"

Philadelphia Museum of Art:
Purchased with funds contributed
by Mr. and Mrs. E. Newbold Smith
in honor of the 125th Anniversary
of the Museum, 2001

Photo by Graydon Wood, 2001

The mahogany case with quarter columns to the waist has four free-standing quarter columns with carved caryatid heads. A broken arch pediment is divided by a carved eagle standing on a foliage carved plinth. The base panel is chamfered and reeded with very anthropomorphic ball and claw feet in the front and turned rear feet in the back. Additional information is in Donald L. Fennimore and Robert T. Trump, "Joseph B. Barry, Philadelphia Cabinetmaker", *The Magazine Antiques*, May 1989, pages 1212-1213, plate 1.

Figure 357 and 357a

Tall Case Clock, mahogany

Label of William D. Rapp,
Race Street, Philadelphia, Circa 1830

Dimensions unrecorded

Private Collection

The mahogany case has a broken arch hood with four free-standing columns. Chamfered edges decorate the waist section. The base is decorated with a rectangular molding and rests on bun feet. The relatively wide waist and turned feet are typical of Philadelphia tall clocks during their final late period. A label is attached to the inside of the backboard and reads, "WM. D. RAPP, WATCHMAKER, JEWELLER and dealer in Yankee Clocks, NO.250 RACE STREET, PHILADELPHIA."

Figure 356a

Detail of William D. Rap label, attached to the inside of the back board.

This cellarette has a stepped, reed-ed rectangular base which supports two heavily carved lions upon which rests on a sarcophagus form cellarette with front and side panels. The front panel is decorated with a large grape carving and is surrounded by a border of grape leaves with grape clusters. The top has a concave molding.

Figure 358
Cellarette, mahogany

Possibly School of Joseph B. Barry
Philadelphia, Circa 1800-1820

Height 29",
Width 29",
Depth 23"

Philadelphia Museum of Art: Given in memory of Caroline S. Gratz, by Simon Gratz, 1925

Figure 359

Cellarette, mahogany
Philadelphia, Circa 1820-1825

Secondary woods: pine throughout
except for tulip poplar inside the
lions, gilt-brass hardware and
zinc lining.

Height 20 3/4",
Width 27",
Depth 21 3/8"

Private Collection

Photo and Description Courtesy of
Hirschl & Adler Galleries, Inc.,
New York City

"This unusual cellarette is closely related to a cellarette in the collection of the Philadelphia Museum of Art, Pennsylvania, which, as part of an impressive suite of Philadelphia furniture, is thought to have been made for Simon Gratz, member of a distinguished family of Sephardic Jews who had lived in Philadelphia since 1759 (Philadelphia Museum of Art, *loc. cit* pp. 265-266 no. 221 illus.) Both

cellarettes appear to have been based on elements in plates 94 and 98 of George Smith's *A Collection of Designs for Household Furniture and Interior Decoration*, published in London in 1808. Although the cellarette in the Philadelphia Museum, as well as the accompanying pieces, have been attributed to the shop of Joseph Barry, no documentary evidence has been found to confirm definitively this attribution."

This cellarette bears a host of Quervelle's favorite design motifs including a mahogany sunburst with crescent edges of burl ash flanked by two applied ornaments of multiple anthemion petals. These ornaments are nearly identical to those seen on the panels of the bases of several labeled Quervelle secretary desks, including the secretary belonging to the Munson-Williams-Proctor Institute and the secretary from the Philadelphia Museum of Art, illustrated in figure 281 and 282, respectively. The gadrooning below reverses in the center, where there is

small leafage "micro-carving" that relates to similar carving seen on a Quervelle attributed worktable in figure 134a (image 30 of maker's chapter 4) and two Quervelle attributed sideboards, in figures 249 (image 32) and 251 (image 31). The top has a raised lozenge, embellished at the base with leafage carving that is interrupted in the center with shell motifs.

Provenance: acquired from the Rush Homestead in Paoli at the Charles Whittaker sale of the estate of Deborah Norris Rush on April 21, 1991. Descended into the Rush-Biddle Family.

Figure 360
Wine Cellarette, mahogany
Strongly Attributed to Anthony G. Quervelle
Philadelphia, Circa 1825

Height 19",
Width 27 1/8",
Depth 15 3/8"

Private Collection

Figure 361

Wine Cooler, mahogany, mahogany veneer
Philadelphia or Baltimore, Circa 1810-1830

Secondary woods: poplar

Height 34 5/8",
Width 14",
Depth 14"

Photo Courtesy of The Biggs Museum of American Art, Dover, DE
Photo Courtesy of the Philadelphia Museum of Art

Few examples of wine coolers of this type exist. The attribution to Philadelphia is largely based on the use of tulip poplar in the mahogany veneered base.[1] Strips of mahogany conform to a basket shape, which is topped with a "drop" or finial, sometimes seen below the tops of card tables or on the pediments of clocks. The pedestal below is a combination of concentric disks and reeding. A triangular base rests on three carved lion's paw feet. The broadly reeded cylinder pedestal is commonly used by Baltimore craftsmen in this period.

[1] Zimmerman and Goldsborough 132

Figure 362

Figure 362a
Detail of the bottom of the tea caddy
showing Richard Jordan's initials

This caddy was made by Richard Jordan of Newton, Gloster County N.J. for the Vaux family of Philadelphia. The maker's initials, R.J., are stamped on the bottom. In addition to cabinet-making, Jordan was a prominent Quaker minister. Upon his death, a Staffordshire plate illustrating Jordan's home was designed for members of the Quaker community.[2] A letter from the Vaux family, which accompanies the caddy, notes that Jordan used elm wood from the "Treaty Elm" in the Kensington section of Philadelphia under which William Penn signed the Great Treaty of Friendship with the Lenape Indians in 1682.[3] The tree blew down in a storm in 1810 and wood from the tree was gathered to make commemorative pieces, several of which are currently at Winterthur Museum. It was purchased from the Vaux family at the Freeman Fine Arts Sale of April 15, 1999.

[2] Elouise Baker Sarson, *American Historical Views on Staffordshire China* (New York: Doubleday Doran and Co., 1939) 174.

[3] Mary Maples Dunn and Richard S. Dunn, "The Founding," *Philadelphia A 300-Year History*, Ed. Russell F. Weigly (New York: W.W. Norton & Company 1982) 5.

Figure 362 and 362a
Tea Caddy, Elmwood derived from the Penn "Treaty Elm" in Kensington

Made by Richard Jordan
Philadelphia, Circa 1810

Secondary woods:
elm with white pine bottom

Height 4 1/2",
Depth 3 15/16",
Length 5 5/16"

Private Collection

Figure 363

Wash Basin, Mahogany
Made by Thomas Whitecar,
Philadelphia 1809

Photo Courtesy of the
Philadelphia Museum of Art

The rectangular stand has a cut-out top for holding the basin. A mahogany drawer is located in the upper portion of the case. The base of the four rectangular feet are supported with an X-shaped bracket. Part of the original suite of furniture that Whitecar supplied to Lydia Poultney of Philadelphia in 1809.

David Sackriter may have specialized in making only knife boxes, as such specialized work was a tradition that began in England. A cylindrical body of mahogany is hollowed out and the convex flutes are carved from the solid.[4] The lion claw winged feet and pineapple finial are shallowly but well carved.

[4] *Philadelphia Three Centuries of American Art*, Philadelphia Museum of Art, page 231, Item 189.

Figure 364

Pair of Knife Boxes, mahogany, mahogany veneer

Signature of David Sackriter in pencil on bottom of one box, January 12, 1814 Philadelphia, 1814

Secondary wood: pine

Height 28 1/2",
Width 12 1/2",
Depth 12 1/2"

Dallas Museum of Art,
The Faith P. and Charles L. Bybee
Collection, gift of Faith P. Bybee

Figure 365

Ham/Mint Julep Table, flame mahogany, white marble top
Probably Philadelphia, Circa 1830

Height 17",
Width 35"

Photo and Description Courtesy of Flomaton Antique Auction, Flomaton, Alabama

"This julep table, as it was referred to, features an ogee skirt with panel and leafy carvings, a narrow waist with unusual tapered classical columns which flank the mirror, a side door compartment and an ogee base with scroll carved apron and feet." It is close- ly related to another example labeled by Quervelle pictured in Robert C. Smith, "The furniture of Anthony G. Quervelle Part IV: some case pieces," *The Magazine Antiques*, January 1974, page 189, figure 11.

Figure 366
*Curly Maple Pedestal Torcheres
(one of a pair)*
Philadelphia, Circa 1820-1830

Height 43",
Diameter of Marble Top 14"

Collection of the
Andalusia Foundation

These pedestal supports were found
in a Bristol home on the Delaware,
close to Andalusia and other great
summer retreats built to escape the
heat and disease of Philadelphia
summers. This set of torcheres was
acquired from the same home as the
window seat in figure 377. Torcheres
are a rare form in American furniture.

Figure 367
Pedestal Table, mahogany, rosewood, gilding paint

Philadelphia, Circa 1825-1835

Secondary woods: poplar

Height 41 1/4",
Width 16 1/2",
Depth 14 3/8"

Photo by John Bigelow Taylor, N.Y.C.

Collection of Munson-Williams-Proctor Arts Institute, Museum of Art, Utica, New York

The rectangular rosewood-veneered stencil-decorated base supports an elaborate antique foliage verde decorated pedestal top. Detailed information is in Anna Tobin D'Ambrosio, editor, Masterpieces of American Furniture from the Munson-Williams-Proctor Institute, Utica, New York, 1999, pages 56-57.

Figure 368
Hat Stand, mahogany
Made by Anthony G. Quervelle
Philadelphia, August 1835

Height 79 1/2"

Photo Courtesy of Rosedown
Plantation State Historic Site,
Louisiana Office of State Parks

All supporting arms are a series of
scrolls in a Restoration manner. The
surmounting urn has a typical
Philadelphia shape. The base contains a
rectangular tin pan to catch water from
wet clothing or umbrellas.

Figure 369

Coat Rack, mahogany

Probably Philadelphia, Circa 1800-1820

Height 69 1/4",
Width of Feet 19 1/2"

Private Collection

Coat racks were apparently a very common item in Philadelphia homes of the early nineteenth century, as documented in Moreau de Saint-Mery's description of his journey to America in 1798.[5] The post contains a series of ring turnings with an acorn motif at the top. This coat rack was found in a colonial era home in Philadelphia in the 1950s. Despite its common usage in early nineteenth century, coat racks from this era relatively rare.

[5] Montgomery 435

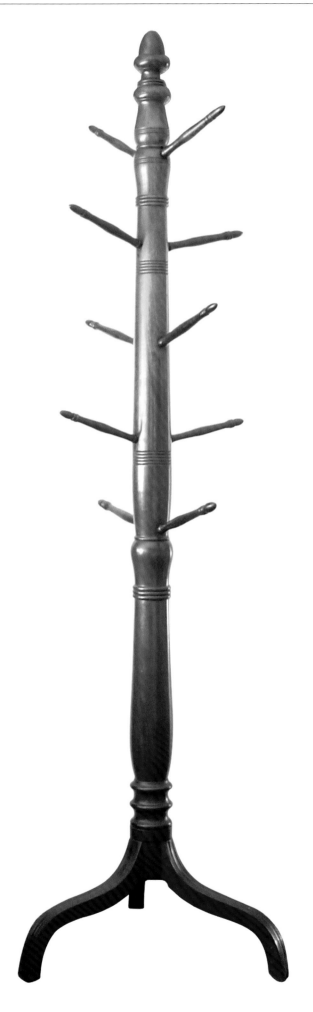

Figure 370

Figure 371

Both chandeliers are in the taste of the time period. Figure 370 has a wreath of angels that encircles the top, immediately below the ceiling. Figure 371 has classical female figures in the center of the piece and the heads of other figures at its apex. Cornelius was one of the most famous metal workers in Philadelphia during the first half of the nineteenth century and was renowned for his impressive, fanciful designs.

Figures 370 and 371
Two Chandeliers by Cornelius and Co., gilded brass

Philadelphia, Circa 1830-1850

Dimensions unrecorded

Private Collection

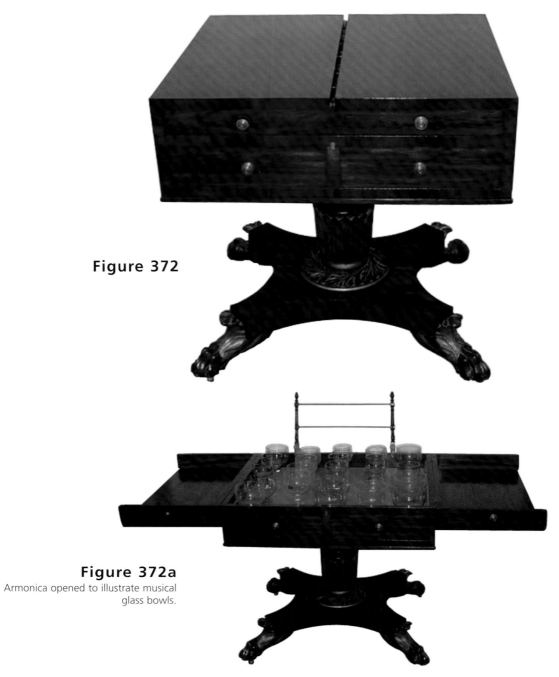

Figure 372

Figure 372a
Armonica opened to illustrate musical glass bowls.

Figure 372 and 372a

Grand Harmonicon Table,
mahogany

Philadelphia, Circa 1820-1830

Height 32",
Width 30",
Depth 26"

Courtesy of the Cumberland
County Historical Society,
Carlisle, PA

Benjamin Franklin, after a trip to Europe, noted that glass bowls of varying size and thickness could produce a desired pitch if rubbed properly by wet fingers. This discovery yielded the armonica, a compact musical instrument which utilized glass bowls to produce harmonic tones. This piece represents a simplistic, later variation of Franklin's actual armonic instrument and is known as the harmonicon. Originally developed, patented, and marketed in America by Francis Hopkinson Smith of Baltimore, the instrument saw

popularity in 1825-1833[6]. The upper cabinet top and apron opens from the middle to reveal a series of harmonically tuned leaded glasses, which represent the musical instrumentation of the piece. The supporting column and its base are carved with verde antique surfaces. A four cornered concave arched platform is supported by four lion paw feet. Individual glass units are played by rubbing the hand against the upper edge. The sound is haunting, but seductive and pleasant.

[6] Weidman 152

This extremely rare piece is in fact the only one of its form known. A three-tiered stand, or dumb waiter, is illustrated in Charles Montgomery's *American Furniture The Federal Period*, 1978, figure 390, page 394. At the time of print, this illustrated stand and one other (a drinking stand) are the only pieces of American furniture that resemble a dumb waiter. Montgomery states, "For some reason, dumb-waiters appear not to have been a popular furniture form in the United States and are not listed in the cabinetmaker's price books." This and No. 390 are the only pieces of American furniture known to the writer, which seem to approach the character of English dumb-waiters. Both are quite different from the common English form, which normally has three or more trays of diminishing size fitted to an upright pillar supported on a tripod base. Sheraton noted in his Cabinet Dictionary (pg. 203):

> The Dumb-waiter, amongst cabinet-makers, is a useful piece of furniture, to serve in some respects the place of a waiter, whence it is so named. There are different kinds of these waiters, but they are all made of mahogany, and are intended for the use of the dining parlour, on which to place glasses of wine, and plates, both clean and such as have been used."[7]

The dumb waiter illustrated here may have been based on English designs, modified with trays not of diminishing size, but instead equal size. The possibility that Quervelle may have been the maker of this dumb waiter is based on the careful avoidance of repetition in any of the five columns that rise through each section. The individual attention to the design and carving of these columns is characteristic of Quervelle, who has often given special attention to minor differences in order to avoid repetition in his work. An example of this is discussed in the article, "The furniture of Anthony G. Quervelle Part II: The pedestal tables," by Robert C. Smith, *The Magazine Antiques*, July 1973, pages 93-94. Smith points out in this article that there seems to be no two identical pieces of Quervelle furniture except for those made as a pair or as part of a set, additionally Quervelle ventured so far as to change the direction of gadrooning from one table to the next, which demonstrates the lengths he would go to ensure his mark on every piece of furniture he produced. Without having another dumb waiter to compare, it is hard to be completely sure who made this table; although the time and consideration of the maker for the design of this piece is a clue that it was a talented craftsman.

[7] Charles Montgomery 394

Figure 373
*Rotating Dumb Waiter,
mahogany*
Possibly School of Anthony Quervelle
Philadelphia, Circa 1820-1830

Height 60 1/2",
Diameter 17 1/2"
(of the trays)

Collection of
Mr. F.J. Carey III

Figure 374
Canterbury, mahogany
Philadelphia, Circa 1810-1820

Height 22",
Width 18",
Depth 14 1/2"

Photo Courtesy of
Mr. F.J. Carey III

This form, which appeared initially in the late eighteenth century, was for use in storing musical books and sheets. A rectangular upper section has three internal dividers, with the center divider modified as a hand grip.

All four corner columns are decorated with ring turnings and surmounted by small urn finials. The case contains a single drawer. Below are bulbous beehive feet of a type associated with the school of Joseph Barry.

This wash stand, similar in form to a pier table, has carved verde antiqued paw feet in the front and square tapered feet in the rear. Large scrolls decorated with gilt foliate stencils support the front drawer with gilt borders and stencil, above which there is a white overhanging marble top.

The bottom rectangular shelf is inset in the front and is also decorated with gilt foliate stencils. It is part of a bedroom suite made for Elijah Van Syckel, a Philadelphia wine and liquor merchant. See figures 284, 318 and 330 for other items from this suite.

Figure 375
Wash Stand, rosewood, marble, gilt, stencil
Made by Isaac Jones
Philadelphia, Circa 1825-1840

Height 30 1/2",
Width 32 1/4",
Depth 20"

Courtesy, Winterthur Museum

Figure 376 *Restoration Paint and Gilt Stencil Decorated Wash Stand*
Philadelphia, Circa 1830-1840

Height 29 3/4",
Width 29",
Depth 18"

Photo Courtesy of Mr. Carswell Rush
Berlin, New York City

This washstand is closely related in form and decoration to a washstand made by Isaac Jones in the collection of Winterthur Museum (illustrated in figure 375). The washstand by Jones is en-suite with two armoires, bedstead, bed steps and dressing bureau.

This window seat is faux painted to simulate curly maple. The form, derived from a classical Greek prototype, uses a variation of a ring turned Roman foot. Often made in pairs, window seats were placed below adjacent windows for effect. This window seat was found in a Bristol home with klismos chairs (now at Andalusia and several museums), illustrated in the Chairs chapter of this volume (figures 185-187).

Figure 377
Window Seat or Bench, tulip poplar
Philadelphia, Circa 1820

Width 52",
Height 18 1/2"

Collection of the
Andalusia Foundation

Figure 378

Brass Medallion of
Benjamin Franklin
Made at the Philadelphia Mint, 1840

Diameter
(including walnut frame) 8"

Private Collection

Above the image of Franklin text reads, "EXECUTED BY THE GAL-VANIC PROCESS OF JACOBI BY FRANKLIN PEALE 1840." A letter now in the possession of the Smithsonian National Portrait Gallery, dated January 15, 1840, from Robert M. Patterson (Director of the U.S. Mint, 1835-1851) to Levi Woodbury (Secretary of the Treasury to Andrew Jackson) describes this medal. Two medals were struck at the U.S. Mint in Philadelphia and sent by Robert M. Patterson to Mr. Woodbury. One was a gift to Andrew Jackson and the other was apparently given to Mr. Woodbury. The letter indicates the hub was made by Mr. Peale utilizing a portrait lathe. The medallion descended in the Frazier family of Philadelphia.

Figure 379

Tall Case Clock, mahogany

Made by George Baldwin
West Chester, PA, Circa 1825

Secondary wood: poplar

Height 94 1/2",
Maximum Width 20 1/2",
Maximum Depth 10"

Private Collection

Other Decorative Elements Outside of Philadelphia

George Baldwin of Sadsbury Township, Chester County, initialed and numbered the front brass plate of the movement. The case is attributed to Thomas Ogden who worked in West Chester from 1814 to 1831.

Waist and base panels have chamfered sides and the front of the base panel is recessed. The ball feet are typical late classical forms. West Chester was a thriving agricultural community a short distance from Philadelphia.

Figure 380 and 380a

Jacob Custer Tall Clock, cherry, tiger maple

Norristown, PA, Circa 1832

Secondary wood: poplar

Height 89",
Depth 13 1/2",
Width 18 1/4"

Private Collection

Figure 380a

Detail of the engraved copper dial illustrating arrow head spandrels and an Indian warrior.

Jacob Detweiler Custer was a self taught mechanical genius who in addition to making clocks of various types was one of the first American watchmakers. He was employed by the Union during the Civil War making various items including minie balls.[8] He may also have been involved in the design of the rotating turret of the Union ship, *Monitor*. This clock has a cherry case with a typical Empire paneled base, a chamfered waist, and a tiger maple veneered upper door. The movement has wooden plates with brass gears typical of Custer's early work and is eight day time only.[9] The copper dial has engraved arrowhead spandrels and an Indian warrior with bow and arrow. Custer worked a short distance outside of Philadelphia in Norristown, PA.

[8] James W. Gibbs, *Pennsylvania Clocks and Watches* (PA: Pennsylvania University Press, 1984) 143.

[9] Gibbs 141

Figure 381

Tall Case Clock, mahogany

Maryland or Possibly Baltimore, Circa 1825-1830

Height 97",
Width 19 1/4",
Depth 10"

Private Collection

The hood has a broken arch decorated with egg-and-dart molding. Each column flanking the hood and the waist are divided into two turned elements. The top element is spiral, while the bottom element is checkered. Both front feet are small versions of a typical lion paw and leafage empire foot. The use of full free-standing columns in the waist portion is typical of American Empire clock cases. The upper portion of the painted dial contains the coat of arms of the state of Maryland.

Figure 382 and 382a

*Hollow Column Clock,
mahogany*

George Marsh & Co.
Bristol, Connecticut, 1832

Length 17 1/4",
Height 37 3/16",
Depth 5"

Private Collection

From 1820 to 1835 a host of Empire shelf clocks were mass manufactured. Bristol, Connecticut was one of the major clock manufacturing centers. The assembly line style of manufacturing undercut prices of hand-made tall clocks, resulting in the decline in their production during the period. Of the many forms of American Empire shelf clocks, the George Marsh hollow column clock shown here is considered the finest in overall design and style.[10] The square weights fall through the columns. The movement is an eight day strap brass time and strike. A highly successful arrangement of classical elements suspends the clock dial between two columns of an eagle decorated arch.

Authors note: a carved fruit basket is the more common splat seen on this model of George Marsh clock. The eagle splat variant of this clock is especially rare.

[10] Lester Dvoretsky and Robert Dickstein, *Horology Americana* (New York: Horology Americana Inc., 1972) 144.

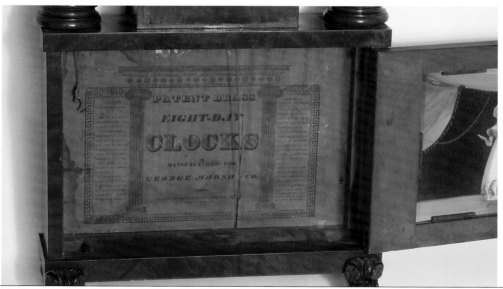

Figure 382a

Detail of George Marsh label. Note the square holes in the bottom corners to accept the falling weights.

Both front feet and columns are flat veneered scrolls typical of the transformation to pillar and scroll restoration style. The swell front overhung top drawer and circular disks represent earlier empire features. Miniature furniture samples of this type were never intended for sale and are uncommon.

Figure 383
Salesman Sample Chest of Drawers
Pennsylvania, Circa 1835-1840

Secondary wood:
poplar, white pine

Height 14",
Width 12 3/4",
Depth 10"

Private Collection

CHAPTER 18
QUALITATIVE EVALUATION OF PHILADELPHIA EMPIRE FURNITURE

QUALITATIVE EVALUATION OF PHILADELPHIA EMPIRE FURNITURE

I. JUDGING CLASSICAL EMPIRE FURNITURE

This section attempts to illustrate that classical furniture must be judged on its individual merits and not on that of attribution, etc. The authors have personally seen labeled pieces of Philadelphia furniture, including worktables labeled by Anthony Quervelle, which are unsuccessful, undecorated and unworthy of praise or recognition. This illustrates that all makers, including the most famous, also

made pedestrian furniture which was not meritorious and had little to offer. The same can be said of Duncan Phyfe pieces. The authors have seen labeled pieces of Phyfe's work which were awkward, unadorned, poorly proportioned and unworthy of any praise, despite the fact that the famous maker's label was attached. This illustrates that one must be able to judge any furniture form on its own merits and not by the label. There are sometimes great forms from unknown makers and unadorned and unsuccessful forms exist from important labeled makers. Those buying labeled pedestrian furniture should know the form itself has little to offer. The authors would, for example, much rather have a well-proportioned, well-carved, and unsigned Philadelphia card table than a poorly carved and signed example. This section will attempt to present different forms to illustrate successful

examples and to separate these from less successful examples of the forms, so the reader can better perform their own analysis on individual pieces to judge their merit.

II. OUT OF PERIOD FURNITURE (AFTER 1850)

Classical furniture continued to be manufactured in Philadelphia and other cities throughout the nineteenth and well into the twentieth century. The presence of band saw marks, modern pointed screws, round nails and machine made dovetails all suggest manufacture after 1850. It should be remembered that skills such as carving were retained in some shops and the quality of out of period empire furniture can, at times, be quite good. To help in identification, several pieces of out of period furniture are illustrated.

Example 1

Dolphin Card Table, mahogany
Philadelphia, Circa 1850-1890.

This table has excellent carving and detail. The screws are pointed and the bottoms of the feet are finished with a powered band saw. The presence of square nails date the piece prior to 1890.

Private Collection

Example 2

Swan Arm Loveseat or Sofa, mahogany
American, Circa 1890-1920

A well-carved piece of small size, typical of later manufacture. The back feet are fully carved, while period Philadelphia sofas usually leave the back feet as uncarved wood profiles. The back of the feet exhibit band saw cuts. All nails are circular.

Private Collection

III. Evaluation of the Relative Quality of Individual Pieces

The determination of relative quality for any individual piece of furniture is always somewhat subjective. Two different individuals looking at the same object may have varying opinions regarding the quality and value of the item. However, certain guidelines can be of benefit in judging the relative merit of an individual piece of furniture. The first of these is form. This relates to the relative grace, sense of balance and poise of the item. Also important is the quality of the materials from which an object is made; the quality of the mahogany wood used in construction, for example. The third element of analysis is quality of execution. The degree and skill of any carved or stenciled elements also contribute to the relative success or failure of an individual form.

The authors have created a ten-point rating system for evaluating various furniture forms for the purpose of providing a guideline for such qualitative assessments. Forms of the highest quality are allotted ten points. Average examples of various forms are assigned five points. Items of poor design, materials and execution are assigned one point. Intermediate ratings are assigned to items above or below one of these three categories. Using this system, the following pages will illustrate various forms with their numerical rating assigned.

EVALUATION OF BREAKFAST TABLES

Breakfast Table 1
RATING 3
Mahogany Breakfast Table
Philadelphia, Circa 1825

A straight cylindrical pedestal on this table seems somewhat monotonous and creates a narrow vertical appearance to the piece. The carving and wood quality are average.

Private Collection

EVALUATION OF BREAKFAST TABLES

Breakfast Table 2
RATING 7
Mahogany Breakfast Table
Philadelphia, Circa 1825

The pedestal is divided into an upper cylindrical and lower hexagonal form, which is attractive and successful. Both carving and wood quality are above average.

Private Collection

Evaluation of Breakfast Tables

Breakfast Table 3
Rating 10

Mahogany Breakfast Table
Philadelphia, Circa 1825

The pedestal exhibits a complex gadrooned carved urn. Leafage on the pedestal radiates outward in a "spouting fountain" manner. The quality of the mahogany, form and carving are all of the first order. Even without the Quervelle label attached to the drawer, this form would still be recognized for its excellence.

Private Collection

EVALUATION OF LYRE WORK TABLES

Lyre Work Table 1
RATING 2
Mahogany Falx Painted Lyre Work Table
Probably Lancaster County, Pennsylvania, Circa 1835

All feet are late scroll forms that support a convex rectangular platform. The Lyre is stylized as a single flat surface. The soft wood case is faux painted to imitate mahogany.

Private Collection

EVALUATION OF LYRE WORK TABLES

Lyre Work Table 2
RATING 7

Mahogany Lyre Based Work Table
Philadelphia, Circa 1810-1820

Wood quality, carving and overall form are very good. This table lacks brass ornamentation often seen with this form. The drawers would have benefited from the use of contrasting light wood, such as curly maple.

Private Collection

Evaluation of Lyre Work Tables

Lyre Work Table 3
Rating 10

Mahogany and Curly Maple Lyre Based Work Table
Philadelphia, Circa 1810-1820

The execution of this table represents the highest standard form of the Philadelphia lyre-based work table. Both drawers boast contrasting curly maple. The lyre and base are decorated with various forms of brass ornamentation. The turret decoration is well turned.

Collection of the Heritage Center Museum of Lancaster County

Evaluation of Lyre Work Tables

Lyre Work Table 4
Rating 10

Lyre and Dolphin Work Table
Philadelphia, Circa 1815-1825

Both drawer fronts and the front of the platform are curly maple for contrast. The platform is narrower in width at the front, which creates a sense of depth. The turret corners are white pine, which is then gessoed with leafage decoration and gilt. The lyre is also then decorated with gilt dolphins. The form, materials and carving are all excellent.

Private Collection

EVALUATION OF CARD TABLES

Card Table 1
RATING 7
Mahogany Card Table
Philadelphia, Circa 1820-1830

The mahogany is of fine quality. The pedestal is decorated with gadrooning and a sheath of acanthus leafage. The carving quality is very good. The overall style is typical of Philadelphia in the 1820s and is well-proportioned with carving to the front corners of the skirt.

Private Collection

EVALUATION OF CARD TABLES

Card Table 2
RATING 10
Mahogany Card Table
Philadelphia, Circa 1812

Wood quality is excellent. The leafage carving of the urn and knees are of top quality. The overall form is well-proportioned and benefits from applied brass ornamentation. This table exhibits fine balance and poise. The use of both carving and applied brass work further enhances the overall effect.

Private Collection

Evaluation of Card Tables

Card Table 3
Rating 10
Mahogany Card Table
Philadelphia, Circa 1810-1820

The quality of the mahogany is excellent. The top is veneered in rays of mahogany. The entire urn is decorated with extremely tight, brilliantly carved foliage. A platform below is also decorated with carving of equal quality. All sides of the saber feet are veneered with mahogany panels. The proportions are excellent, while the urn has been given full size so that the carving can be better appreciated. This represents one of the ultimate masterpieces of Philadelphia craftsmanship during the classical period.

Private Collection

EVALUATION OF BEDSTEADS

Bedstead 1
RATING 8
High Post Cherry Bed
Pennsylvania, Circa 1825-1830

The quality of the wood is very good. The carving is good, but rather rigid and lacks a flowing quality. The overall form is successful.

Private Collection

Detail of the headboard and head posts

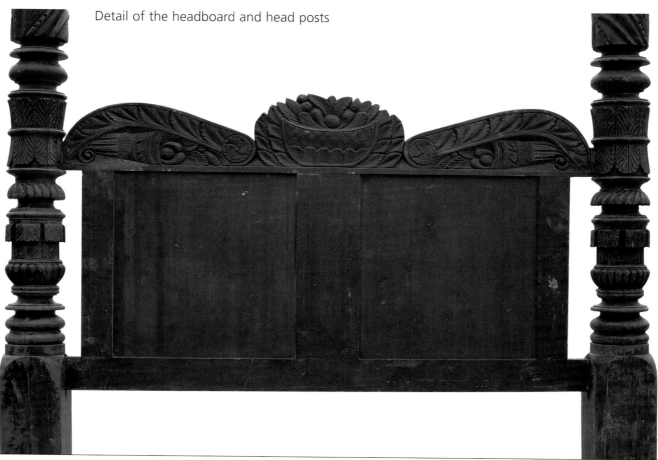

Evaluation of Bedsteads

Bedstead 2
Rating 10
High Post Cherry Bed
Philadelphia, Circa 1820-1830

Wood quality is excellent. The carving is flowing and vibrant. The overall form is excellent and is enhanced by the multiple bulls-eye disks placed on the lower corners.

Private Collection

Detail of the headboard and head posts

Evaluation of Scroll Arm Sofas

Sofa 1

Rating 8

Scroll Arm Sofa
Philadelphia, Circa 1820-1840

The carving quality is excellent. The mahogany is of first quality and the overall form successful. The central tablet is left uncarved.

Photo courtesy of Christies Auction Galleries, New York
© Christie's Images Limited 2006

EVALUATION OF SCROLL ARM SOFAS

Sofa 2
RATING 10
Scroll Arm Sofa
Philadelphia, Circa 1825

The carving is superlative, especially the carved Indian figure of the central tablet. The quality of the mahogany is excellent. The dolphin feet make the form especially successful.

Photo courtesy of Joseph Sorger

Evaluation of Box Sofas

Sofa 1
Rating 8

Box Sofa
Philadelphia, Circa 1825-1835

The mahogany is of excellent quality. The overall form is good. The carving, especially of the arm rest, is of the highest quality.

Private Collection

EVALUATION OF BOX SOFAS

Sofa 2
RATING 10

Box Sofa
Philadelphia, 1833

The quality of the mahogany is excellent. The form is correct and typical. Both the feet and arm rest are richly carved. The front rail is gadrooned.

Private Collection

EVALUATION OF SIDEBOARDS

Sideboard 1
RATING 8

Drop Center Mahogany Sideboard
Philadelphia, Circa 1825

The wood quality is excellent. The carving quality is excellent with extremely well-carved feet which exhibit extensive leafage above the lion claws. The proportions of this monumental form are also good. This sideboard is labeled from Quervelle's shop.

Courtesy of Weschler's Auction Gallery, Washinton D.C.

EVALUATION OF SIDEBOARDS

Sideboard 2
RATING 9

Drop Center Mahogany Sideboard
Philadelphia, Circa 1825

The quality of the mahogany is superb. The carving of the feet, columns and cornucopia side supports are excellent and extremely closely related to the prior example. The outer cupboard doors are formed as vertical cylinders to conform to the vertical lift of the columns. Both center doors are decorated with diamond lozenges.

Private Collection

EVALUATION OF SIDEBOARDS

Sideboard 3
RATING 10

Drop Center Mahogany Sideboard
Philadelphia, Circa 1825

The carving of the cornucopias with the droopy flower motif is of the first quality as is the carving of the feet and the gadrooning. The outer cupboard doors are vertical cylinders while the center cupboard door is a sunburst pattern. The proportions give this sideboard a monumental and dignified presence. Wood quality is excellent.

Private Collection

EVALUATION OF SIDEBOARDS

Sideboard 4
RATING 10

Drop Center Tiger Maple Sideboard
Snowhill Cloister, PA, Circa 1820-1825

The wood quality of the tiger maple veneers is virtually impeccable. The veneers of the cupboard and other drawers are carefully matched against each other in vertical and horizontal planes. Carving quality is excellent, especially of the eagle claw feet. The proportions of this sideboard are also excellent and the gothic inset crosses also add appeal.

Private Collection

Evaluation of Marble Top Center Tables

Table 1
Rating 6

Marble Top Center Table
Philadelphia, Circa 1835-1850

The quality of the mahogany and marble is excellent. The carving is well-executed. The form is a transition from late classicism with elements of Gothic revival including the pedestal and unusual scroll feet. The mixing of classical with other stylistic elements (in this case Gothic) is less desirable. This detracts from the success of a given form.

Courtesy of Christies Auction Galleries, New York City
© Christie's Images Limited 2006

Evaluation of Marble Top Center Tables

Table 2
Rating 10

Marble Top Center Table
Philadelphia, Circa 1825

The quality of the mahogany and mosaic top is the highest possible. The excellent carving of the pedestal and feet is further decorated with gilt. The overall form is also excellent and well-proportioned.

Courtesy of Destrahan Plantation, Destrahan, Louisiana

BIBLIOGRAPHY

Beck, Doreen. *Book of American Furniture.* England: The Hamlyn Publishing Group Limited, 1973.

Bjerkoe, Ethel Hall. *The Cabinetmakers of America.* New York: Bonanza Books, 1957.

Busch, Jason T. "Furniture Patronage in Antebellum Natchez." *The Magazine Antiques* May 2000.

Butler, Joseph T. *American Furniture From the First Colonies to World War I.* London: Triune Books, 1973.

Carson, Marian S. "Sheraton's Influence in Philadelphia." *Philadelphia Furniture and its Makers,* Ed. John J. Snyder. New York: Main Street Universe Books, 1975.

Collard, Frances. *Regency Furniture.* England: Antique Collectors' Club Ltd., 1985.

Cooper, Wendy A. *Classical Taste in America 1800-1840.* Baltimore Museum of Art, 1993.

Dallett, Francis J. "Michel Bouvier, Franco-American cabinetmaker." *The Magazine Antiques* Feb. 1962.

Ducoff-Barone, Deborah. "Philadelphia Furniture Makers 1816-1830." *The Magazine Antiques* May1994.

Dunn, Mary Maples, and Richard S. Dunn. "The Founding." *Philadelphia A 300-Year History.* New York: W.W. Norton & Company 1982.

Dvoretsky, Lester and Robert Dickstein. *Horology Americana.* New York: Horology Americana Inc.,1972.

Elder, William. American Furniture 1680-1880. Baltimore Museum of Art, 1987.

Fairbanks, Jonathan, and Elizabeth Bidwell Bates. *American Furniture 1620 to Present.* New York: Richard Marek Publishers, 1981.

Fennimore, Donald L. "A labeled card table by Michel Bouvier." *The Magazine Antiques.* Apr. 1973.

Fennimore, Donald L. "Egyptian Influence in Early Nineteenth-Century American Furniture." *The Magazine Antiques* May 1990.

Fennimore, Donald and Robert Trump. "Joseph B. Barry, Philadelphia Cabinetmaker." *The Magazine Antiques* May 1989.

Fitzgerald, Oscar P. *Three Centuries of American Furniture.* New Jersey: Prentice-Hall Inc., 1982.

Garvan, Beatrice. *Federal Philadelphia 1785-1825, the Athens of the Western World.* Philadelphia Museum of Art, 1987.

Gibbs, James W. *Pennsylvania Clocks and Watches.* PA: Pennsylvania University Press, 1984.

Grandjean, Serge. *Empire Furniture 1800-1825.* London: Faber and Faber, 1966.

Ketchum, William C., Jr. *Furniture 2: Neoclassic to the Present.* New York: Cooper-Hewitt Museum, 1981.

Ketchum, William C., Jr. *American Cabinetmakers Marked American Furniture 1640-1940.* New York: Crown Publishers Inc., 1995.

Kirtley, Alexandra A. "Survival of the Fittest: The Lloyd Family's Furniture Legacy." *American Furniture 2002.* Milwaukee, WI: Chipstone Foundation, 2002.

Maynard, W. Barksdale. *Architecture in the United States 1800-1850.* New Haven; London: Yale University Press, 2002.

Miller, Edgar G., Jr. *American Antique Furniture, Volume 1.* New York: Dover Publications, 1966.

Miller, Richard G. "The Federal City." *Philadelphia: A 300-Year History.* Ed Russell F. Weigly. New York: W.W. Norton & Co., 1982.

Montgomery, Charles F. *American Furniture The Federal Period.* New York: Bonanza Books, 1978.

Morley, John. *The History of Furniture: Twenty-five Centuries of Style and Design in the Western Tradition.* Boston: Bulfinch Press, 1999.

Musgrave, Clifford. *Regency Furniture 1800-1830.* London: Faber and Faber, 1961.

Naeve, Milo M. "Daniel Trotter and his ladder-back chairs." *Philadelphia Furniture and its Makers,* Ed. John Snyder. New York: Main Street Universe Books, 1975.

Nutting, Wallace. *Furniture Treasury.* New York: Macmillan Publishing Co. Inc., 1928.

Otto, Celia Jackson. *American Furniture of the Nineteenth Century.* New York: The Viking Press, 1965.

Petraglia, Patricia. *American Antique Furniture 1640-1840.* New York: Friedman/Fairfax Publishers, 1995.

Philadelphia Museum of Art. *Philadelphia: Three Centuries of American Art.* 1976.

Richardson, Edgar P. "The Athens of America 1800-1825." *Philadelphia: A 300-Year History.* Ed Russell F. Weigly. New York: W.W. Norton & Co., 1982.

Sarson, Elouise Baker. *American Historical Views on Staffordshire China.* New York: Doubleday Doran and Co., 1939.

Schwarz, Robert D. *The Stephen Girard Collection, A Selective Catalogue.* Philadelphia: Girard College.

Scribner Schaumann, Merri Lou. "Henry Connelly, Cabinetmaker..." *Cumberland Co. Historical Society Journal* 1996.

Singleton, Esther. *French and English Furniture.* New York: McClure, Philips & Co., 1903.

Smith, Robert C. "Late classical furniture in the United States, 1820-1850." *The Magazine Antiques* Dec. 1958.

Smith, Robert C. "The Furniture of Anthony G. Quervelle: Part I, The Pier Tables." *The Magazine Antiques* May 1973.

Smith, Robert C. "The Furniture of Anthony G. Quervelle: Part II, The Pedestal Tables." *The Magazine Antiques* July 1973.

Smith, Robert C. "The Furniture of Anthony G. Quervelle: Part III, The worktables." *The Magazine Antiques* Aug. 1973.

Smith, Robert C. "The Furniture of Anthony G. Quervelle: Part IV, Some Case Pieces." *The Magazine Antiques* Jan. 1974.

Smith, Robert C. "The Furniture of Anthony Quervelle: Part V, Sofas, Chairs and Beds." *The Magazine Antiques* Mar. 1974.

Smith, Robert C. "Philadelphia Empire furniture by Antoine Gabriel Quervelle." *The Magazine Antiques* Sept. 1964.

Smith, Thomas Gordon. "Quervelle Furniture at Rosedown, in Louisiana." *The Magazine Antiques* May 2001: 779.

Sutton, Robert K. *Americans Interpret the Parthenon*. Colorado: U P of Colorado, 1992.

Symonds, R.W., and B. B. Whineray. *Victorian Furniture*. London: Studio Additions 1962.

Tracy, Berry B. *Federal Furniture and Decorative Arts at Boscobel*. New York: Harry N. Abrams Inc., 1981.

Trump, Robert T. "Joseph B. Barry, Philadelphia Cabinetmaker." *The Magazine Antiques* Jan. 1975.

Venable, Charles L. *American Furniture in the Bybee Collection*. Auston: U of T Press, 1989.

Wainwright, Nicholas. "The Age of Nicholas Biddle 1825-1841." *Philadelphia: A 300-Year History*. Ed. Russell F. Weigly. New York: W. W. Norton & Co., 1982.

Weidman, Gregory R. *Furniture in Maryland 1740-1940*. Baltimore: Schneidereith and Sons, 1984.

Zimmerman, Philip D. "The American sofa table." *The Magazine Antiques* May 1999.

Zimmerman, Philip D. and Jennifer Faulds Goldsborough. *The Sewell C. Biggs Collection of American Art, A Catalogue*. Vol. 1. Iceland: Oddi Printing, 2002.

INDEX

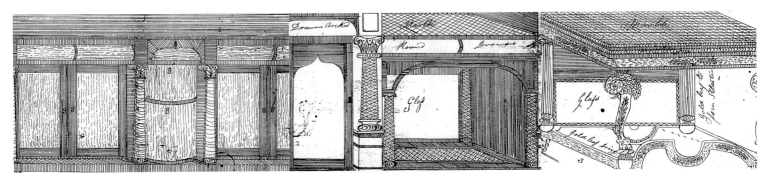

ACKNOWLEDGEMENTS

The authors would like to thank all those who have allowed their furniture to be photographed and to appear in these pages. Without the numerous images provided from private collections, this volume would not be able to illustrate many of the most interesting, beautiful and important pieces of Philadelphia Empire furniture.

We would also like to thank the following museums/institutions/dealers for providing us with images for this book:

The Andalusia Foundation, The Philadelphia Museum of Art, The Metropolitan Museum of Art, The Baltimore Museum of Art, The Dallas Museum of Art, The Telfair Museum of Art, Savannah, Winterthur Museum and Library, Destrahan Plantation, Destrahan, Louisiana, The James Buchanan Foundation, Lancaster, PA, Girard College, The Athenaeum of Philadelphia, Christie's Auction House, The Magazine Antiques, Flomaton Auction House, Mark McCarty, Elizabeth Jones, Ralph Leed, Ned Stenson, The St. Louis Art Museum, Weschler's, The White House Historical Society, The Westtown School, Rosedown Plantation State Historical Site, Dolphin County Historical Society, Cumberland County Historical Society, The Art Institute of Chicago, McAdams Ltd. Antiques, Columbia, Missouri, The Munson-Williams-Proctor Art Institute, Aileen Minor, J.M. Flanigan American Antiques, Baltimore, Freeman's Auction House, Utah Museum of Art, Hirschl & Adler Galleries, NY, Doyle, Hagley Museum, Heritage Museum of Lancaster, Pook and Pook Auctions, Downingtown, PA, The Smithsonian Institution, National Portrait Gallery, Biggs Museum, The Hermitage, Tennessee, Cumberland County Historical Society, Historical Society of Pennsylvania, Joan Bogart, Aileen Minor, Independence National Historical Park, River Road Historical Society, McAdams' Ltd. and Stanley Weiss.

The following people deserve thanks for their images, continued assistance and knowledge of this topic:

Ms. Ann Joyce, Mr. Don Fennimore, Mr. Carswell Rush Berlin, Mr. F.J. Carey III, Phillip Bradley Antiques, Downingtown, PA, Mr. Fred Peach, Mr. James Biddle, Mr. Robert Trump, Mr. Joseph Sorger, Elizabeth Feld, Mr. William McCarraher and Didier Inc., Mr. Vito Angelucci.

Notes

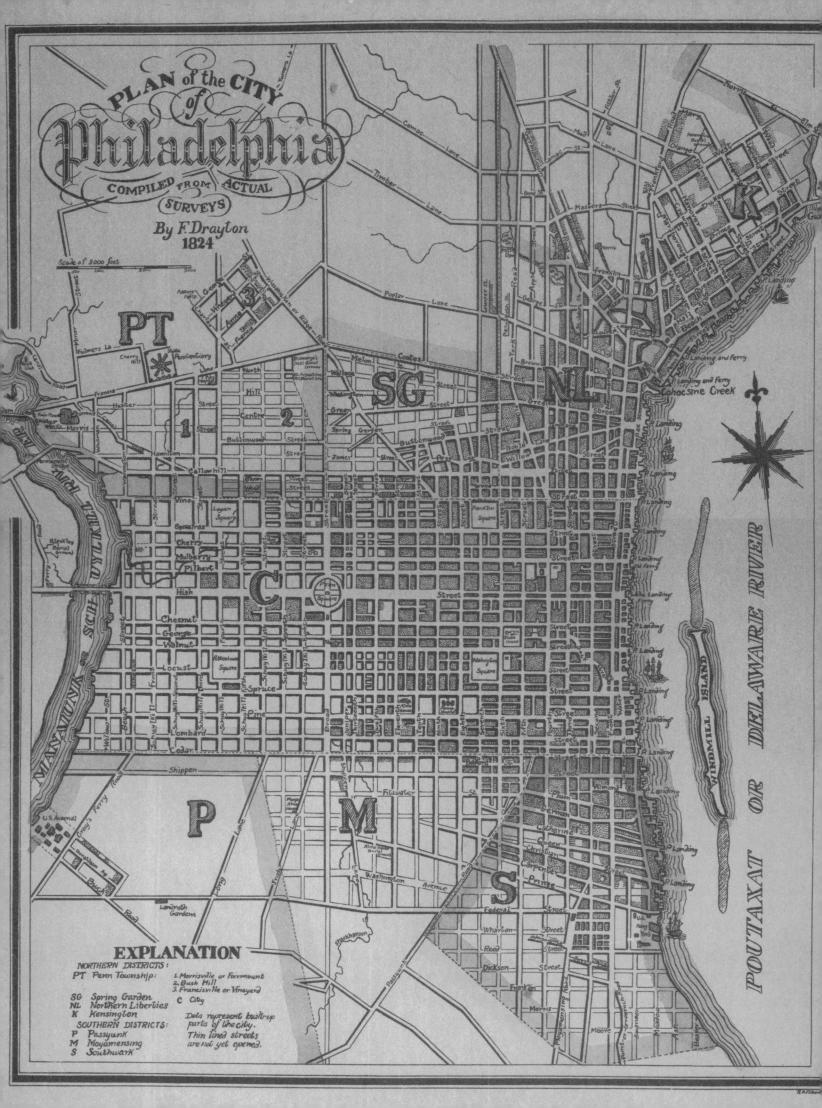

PLAN of the CITY of Philadelphia

COMPILED FROM ACTUAL SURVEYS

By F. Drayton 1824

Scale of 3000 feet

EXPLANATION

NORTHERN DISTRICTS:
PT Penn Township:
   1. Morrisville or Fairmount
   2. Bush Hill
   3. Francisville or Vineyard

SG Spring Garden
NL Northern Liberties   C City
K   Kensington
SOUTHERN DISTRICTS:
P   Passyunk   Dots represent built-up
M   Moyamensing   parts of the city.
S   Southwark   Thin lined streets
           are not yet opened.

POUTAXAT OR DELAWARE RIVER

WINDMILL ISLAND